The IDEOLOGIES of the DEVELOPING NATIONS

The IDEOLOGIES of the
DEVELOPING NATIONS

Revised Edition

Edited and with an Introduction by
PAUL E. SIGMUND

Foreword by
Reinhold Niebuhr

FREDERICK A. PRAEGER, *Publishers*
New York • Washington • London

FREDERICK A. PRAEGER, PUBLISHERS
111 Fourth Avenue, New York, N.Y. 10003, U.S.A.
5, Cromwell Place, London S.W.7, England

Published in the United States of America in 1967 by
Frederick A. Praeger, Inc., Publishers

This is a revised and enlarged edition of the book published in the United States of America in 1963 by
Frederick A. Praeger, Inc.

Second printing, 1968

Library of Congress Catalog Card Number: 66–14384

Printed in the United States of America

FOREWORD

Paul Sigmund has performed an invaluable service in providing for the students of current global politics an anthology of the political theories and ideologies of the leaders of the emerging nations of the world. These nations, located in such disparate regions and continents as Latin America, Africa, the Middle East, and Southeast Asia, are revealed in Mr. Sigmund's study to be animated by two similar passions, which they express in their dissimilar policies. They are interested in gaining or consolidating their integral nationhood against a background of previous subservience to a dominant power; and they are anxious to achieve technical competence and triumph over the poverty to which they were subjected in their either primitive or traditional economies.

It is important for the political observers of the Western world to note what attracts these nations to, and what repels them from, the democratic theories and practices of Western culture, and what affinities, if any, they have with the collectivism of the Communist world. The revelations of Mr. Sigmund's study about the differences among the conservative, moderate, and radical political leaders of these nations—differences that express themselves across the boundaries of their several regions—will be instructive to all students of the present contest between democracy and Communism.

It is important to know what motives prompt the general desire to remain neutral in the contest, why the new nations are more inclined to a one-party system than to a two-party or multiparty democracy as we know it in the West, why the leaders have invented various amendments to what we regard as pure democracy, and what promises and perils inhere in these adjustments. It is equally important to know how the principle of national federation—an issue in most of the emerging nations—may become, on the one hand, a safeguard against despotism and, on the other, a peril to national integrity.

v

In addition to its obvious usefulness, this study has the merit of being an extremely interesting display of the similarities and differences in the policies and moods of the leaders of the emerging nations. Their names appear daily in our public press. It is fascinating to learn how much an African leader may agree with one in Asia or Latin America, yet disagree with another leader in his own continent.

At a time when we are slowly—all too slowly—accustoming ourselves both to the extent of our power and responsibility in the world and to the undoubtedly long duration of our burdens, such a wise and perceptive analysis of the factors, forces, and personalities we encounter in the world will be invaluable to the American people.

—REINHOLD NIEBUHR

CONTENTS

ACKNOWLEDGMENTS

Permission to use copyrighted material has been acknowledged in footnotes at the beginning of each selection. My thanks are also due the following for providing me with relevant publications: The Embassy of the Republic of Tunisia, Washington, D.C.; The Supreme Council of Revolutionary Youth, Cairo, Egypt; *La Jeunesse du Rassemblement Démocratique Africain*, Conakry, Guinea; Chukumwa Azikiwe; The Delegation of Cuba to the United Nations; and Ramón Yllarramendy. My grateful appreciation also goes to Dr. Reinhold Niebuhr, for whose course at Harvard University many of these readings were collected; to Professor Rupert Emerson, for his constructive criticism of my Introduction; to my colleagues at Harvard, whose collective expertise supplied deficiencies in my own knowledge; to Mrs. Alfred G. Tottey, Jr., for her expert secretarial assistance; to Arnold Dolin, for his editorial work; and to the students and youth of the developing areas with whom I have been associated in various collective enterprises during the last decade—and to whom this book is dedicated.

For the second edition acknowledgment should be made to my students and colleagues who have made suggestions for additions and deletions. I also wish to thank my research assistants, Frank Upham, Sidney Stein, and Gerald Wetlaufer.

—P. E. S.

Princeton, N.J.
January, 1967

The IDEOLOGIES of the
DEVELOPING NATIONS

INTRODUCTION
TO THE FIRST EDITION *

The dictionary defines "ideology" as "a systematic scheme or co-ordinated body of ideas about human life or culture"—a definition that seems to equate ideology with philosophy or social theory. In common usage, however, the word has additional connotations —of commitment (both emotional and intellectual), of action-orientation (the maintenance of the *status quo*, which may be the goal of conservative ideologies, is itself an action), and even of conscious or unconscious distortion of the facts to fit a pre-established doctrine.[1] The period from the seventeenth century to the nineteenth century in Europe has been described as the "age of ideology," for it saw an extraordinary outpouring of theories about the nature of man in relation to the present or future state of society. It was also a period of political, economic, and social revolution, in which the traditional order of medieval Europe gave way to a modern industrial society and men became conscious of the variety of alternative paths open to them in their own personal lives, in their religious, philosophical, and political creeds, and in the ordering of society.

This crisis of modernization has now affected large areas of Asia, Africa, the Middle East, and Latin America. What is often described as the "anticolonial revolution" is more than an attempt to assert political autonomy and to end European domination. It is also a social and economic revolution brought about by the attempt of the members of a Westernized elite to bring their countries into the modern world, to create modern states and industrialized economies where traditional cultures and subsistence production had predominated.

The fact that, in addition to its anticolonial character, this is a revolution of modernization makes it possible to consider Latin

---

*A few minor revisions have been made to bring this introduction up to date.

[1] This is the sense in which it is used by Karl Mannheim when he defines ideologies as "more or less conscious disguises of the real nature of the situation." (*Ideology and Utopia* [New York: Harcourt, Brace & Co., 1954], p. 49.)

America, which has been politically independent for 130 years, in the same category as nations that have only recently received their independence. The leaders of the old nations of Latin America and of the new nations in other parts of the world are experiencing similar problems of economic development and social change, and are often developing similar solutions to them.

To explain to themselves and to others the nature and justification of the changes they wish to induce, the nationalist leaders have been compelled to give more specific content to the general goal of development to which they all subscribe. In doing this, they have been able to draw upon ideologies developed earlier in Europe. Especially in Latin America, the ideologies of the period of early industrialism in Europe have been adapted to fit an analogous situation in nations now experiencing the problems associated with modern development. Yet, if one takes a broader view of the developing areas as a whole, there is a notable absence of the conflict of ideologies that has characterized European political life during the last century. As recent debates in the United Nations have demonstrated, the leaders of the group of nations variously described as "new," "uncommitted," "emerging," or "developing" share many political, economic, and social ideas as to the type of society they are building. Although they may differ regarding the appropriate methods for reaching their goals, these leaders (with the exception of those in the most backward and tradition-bound areas) are united by a group of beliefs that give expression to common feelings about the past, present, and future.

These beliefs correspond to our definition of ideology in that they elicit an emotional commitment by the leadership and their followers and are directed toward action—the development of a new society in a certain direction, in conformity with certain goals. However, the doctrines of modernizing nationalism do not have the all-encompassing quality of the great ideological world-systems of Marxism, Christianity, or utilitarian liberalism, although they may coincide in some respects with one or another element in these ideologies. They are held by leaders with a wide variety of religious and philosophical outlooks, or with no particular metaphysical presuppositions. The particular problems of individual states also vary in accordance with their special situations. Yet, all the developing nations are undergoing the same general experience, and their reactions to it are similar in theoretical content and practical application. To determine whether these goals, aspirations, and doctrines—given their eclectic character and practical orientation—can be systematically organized in a way that would qualify them as an alternative ideology to current political creeds, it is necessary to give more detailed consideration to the specific content of the doctrines of modernizing nationalism.

National Independence and Freedom

A basic principle of the nationalist leaders has already been mentioned—the absolute primacy of the goal of national development. Since development takes place within the framework of the nation-state, whether it is in existence or in the process of being created, national independence is the first step on the road to development. As the inscription on Kwame Nkrumah's statue in Accra read, "Seek ye first the political kingdom and all other things shall be added unto it." It is as a prerequisite to development that the nationalist leaders demand freedom. However, this freedom refers to *national* rather than individual liberty. It is the assertion of the right of the nation to self-direction and independence of foreign domination. Freedom is demanded for "the people," not for the individual.[2]

It is sometimes difficult to determine exactly what constitutes the nation that ought to be free. In Africa, and to some extent in the Middle East, where movements for regional unification are strong, there has been some ambivalence about national boundaries as they were imposed by the Europeans. However, on the whole, the existing divisions seem to be accepted as the basis from which to work. Except where the alteration of the frontier involves the elimination of a colonial enclave, as in Goa or Dutch New Guinea, the existing boundaries are accepted, and it is felt that they may only be changed by the free consent of the governments involved.

The meaning of the term "the people" is also in need of clarification. Independence, freedom, and development are asserted as goals in the name of the people. It is the authority of the people that gives legitimacy to anticolonial revolutions and post-independence governments. Yet, there is always a certain amount of

[2] "We have chosen the freedom, the right, the power, the sovereignty of the people, and not of the individual. Before this people you should have no individual personality. Our personality becomes part of the personality of the nation." (Sékou Touré, quoted in *West Africa*, July 22, 1961, p. 799.)

elitism mixed with the "populism" of the nationalist leadership.[8] Before independence, it was assumed without any need of proof that the people desired to be liberated from colonialism. Yet, after independence, a massive political education program often must be carried on to assure that the popular will actually corresponds to the conception of it in the theory of the nationalist leadership.

The Creation of Modern Nationalism

There are difficulties in determining what constitutes "the nation" or "the people" because in many cases neither entity really exists. A sense of nationhood and loyalty to the people as a collective entity must first be created to replace or supplement other allegiances based on traditional or hierarchical status differentiations. In Max Weber's terms, the transition must be made from a "traditional" to a "rational-legal" order.[4]

Westerners are familiar with the organic process by which European society was transformed from a largely traditional and agrarian, even tribal, social organization into the modern, rationalized, and institutionalized nation-state. European economic development, new organizational and scientific techniques, and the new political ideas drawn from the classical and Christian heritage of the late Middle Ages resulted in the radical change of ways of living and ways of thinking about life associated with the emergence of modern industrial civilization. Powerful ideological justifications for status differentiation, hereditary privilege, and hierarchical social organization were developed in Europe between the twelfth and the nineteenth century, and enclaves of traditionalism still remain. However, the overwhelming power of the nationalist and equalitarian ideology has either overcome other loyalties in the West or, alternatively, achieved a kind of coexistence with them which has permitted the integration of diverse ethnic, religious, and social groupings within a pluralistic consensus in the modern

8 "He [the intellectual] looks up to the people and down on the masses." (Mary Matossian, "Ideologies of Delayed Industrialization," in John Kautsky [ed.], *Political Change in Underdeveloped Countries* [New York: John Wiley & Sons, 1962], p. 262.) On the "populism" of the nationalist leaders in relation to similar phenomena in Germany, Russia, and America, see the discussion by Edward Shils in the same collection (especially pp. 214-15).

4 David Apter has used these categories in his analysis of the creation of a new nation, in *The Gold Coast in Transition* (Princeton, N.J.: Princeton University Press, 1955).

nation-state. In most Western countries, the organic development of national unity over the centuries has created a sense of common purpose and civic responsibility, and led to a rationalization and legalization of the structure of authority.[5]

The creation of loyalty to the nation and the emergence of the nation as a functional community is now under way in many of the new states. Differences of caste, tribe, clan, or religion must be integrated into the political process, and it is precisely because they loom so large as an obstacle to the creation of the modern nation-state that the leaders place great emphasis on the primacy of "the nation" and the elimination of traditional status differentiations.[6] In nationalist thinking, there is a recognition of the need for the creation of a broader community on a regional and international level, but the first requirement is the implementation of the common ideal of universal participation in the nation. The recent experience of the Congo, India's continuing problem with communalism, earlier difficulties with Ashanti regionalism in Ghana, and differences between the various regions of Nigeria are all examples of the fissiparous tendencies against which the new nation-builders must work.

In dealing with the problem of the creation of a new society and a new center of loyalty and faith, the leaders of Asia, Africa, Latin America, and the Middle East have taken three different positions. First, there remain the traditionalists or conservatives like King Saud of Saudi Arabia, the tribal leaders of Africa, or dictators like Stroessner of Paraguay. Such leaders try to preserve the existing oligarchic order, and view the disruptive forces of modernization as a threat to their maintenance of power (as indeed they are). Yet, they cannot avoid being drawn into the world-wide

[5] The divisions, traditional-modern or traditional-rational-legal, are not absolute. There are no completely "modern" systems, and, conversely, modern elements can be perceived in many traditional political cultures. (Cf. discussion in Gabriel Almond and James S. Coleman, The Politics of the Developing Areas [Princeton, N.J.: Princeton University Press, 1960], p. 11.)

[6] "In three or four years, no one will remember the tribal, ethnic, and religious differences which have caused so much difficulty to the country and people in the recent past. . . . We are for a united people, a unitary state at the service of an indivisible nation." (Sékou Touré, La Lutte du Parti Démocratique de Guinée pour l'Emancipation Africaine [Conakry: Imprimerie Nationale, 1959], pp. 58, 149.) Cf. Thomas Hodgkin, "A Note on the Language of African Nationalism," African Affairs (Carbondale, Ill.), No. 1 (1961), pp. 22–40.

technological revolution, with all its subversive social and political consequences. In order to justify their positions, these leaders may appeal to religious beliefs, custom, or the requirements of order and stability but the attraction of modernization to the educated elite makes it difficult for their regimes to compete for support. The second category of leaders comprises those who wish to strike a balance between the maintenance of traditional structures and the radical transformation of society as a whole. One thinks of such diverse figures as Gandhi, Ayub Khan, Léopold Senghor, or Joseph Kasavubu as typical of the reforming elite who wish to integrate and utilize the traditional loyalties and hierarchical groupings in the formation of a new nation, creating a synthesis of the old and the new. Finally, there is the third group, which, while not necessarily aiming at the destruction of traditional groups, wishes to eliminate them from political influence and power as obstacles to the process of social and political transformation.[7] The radical modernizers see no rational basis for status differentiations not based on political or economic function, and they are willing to use persuasion, propaganda, monolithic political parties, and sometimes force as well to bring about the new community.

While the first does no more than pay occasional lip service to the ideals of modernization, the other two types of ruling elite accept them completely. Neither the reformers nor the radicals wish to wait for organic development to bring their societies into the modern world. However, the two groups differ significantly on methods. And this particular difference has already made its impact in Africa in the divisions in the Organization of African Unity; in Latin America in the profound division between Fidelist movements and reformist leaders like Frei, Figueres, and Haya de la Torre; and in Asia, where the Chinese revolution provides a Communist model of forced economic development that contrasts with the more gradual and democratic approach of India.

This is not to assert that there are not profound differences

---

[7] A similar but somewhat misleading distinction between "revolutionary" and "radical-reformist" Pan-Africanists is made by Colin Legum. in *Pan-Africanism* (rev. ed.; New York: Frederick A. Praeger, 1965), pp. 62–64. Cf. also David Apter's distinction between "mobilization" and "consociational" regimes, in *The Political Kingdom of Uganda* (Princeton, N.J.: Princeton University Press, 1961), pp. 4–5; and the division into neotraditional, transitional, and actively modernizing oligarchies, in Max F. Millikan and Donald L. M. Blackmer, *The Emerging Nations* (Boston: Little, Brown, 1961), pp. 79–88.

among the various representatives of both the radical and the reformist wings of the modernizing elite. To identify Sékou Touré's approach to social change with that of Fidel Castro, or Nehru's with that of Houphouet-Boigny or Haya de la Torre, is to ignore the diversity of national situations and of the solutions proposed. The division into traditionalists, reformers, and radicals is based on general similarities of attitude toward social, political, and economic change, within which there are considerable differences. However, it provides a more useful analytical tool than classifications reflecting European ideological categories or distinctions derived from the East-West conflict which are not related to the problems of modernization and development.

A National System of Education

Both the radicals and the reformers recognize the key role of education in nation-building. They criticize the unrealistic content and limited scope of the colonial educational systems, which reflected the standards and the needs of the metropoles and were often unrelated to local conditions and requirements. A system geared solely to the training of a few civil servants, teachers, and lawyers is not considered adequate for a nation undergoing an economic and social revolution. One of the first steps after independence, therefore, has been an increase in the number of primary and secondary schools and of universities and technical schools, as well as a reform of the content of education to meet the need for skilled and semiskilled personnel.

On a basic level, the problem of illiteracy is being attacked by massive programs of primary education, often with considerable political content. The literacy campaigns carried out by Fidel Castro in Cuba and by Sékou Touré in Guinea have demonstrated that an organized program can virtually eradicate this problem in a short time and can also be useful in building political loyalty. The illiterate masses who have had little or no relation to national politics are educated to read the party literature and to become aware of national and international problems from the party point of view.

It is not only the radical or revolutionary regimes that put a high priority on basic education and political indoctrination. All the modernizing nationalists recognize that the educational system can be used to develop loyalty to the nation—and to the party, often considered to be synonymous with the nation. The line between education for citizenship and political indoctrination is a thin one (as indeed it often is in the developed countries) but the modernizing nationalists universally accept the need for a high political content in education.

Because of both the political significance of education and its importance in developing the various levels of trained cadres required for economic development, the nationalist program usually calls for centrally planned control and development of the school system. Since education in many of the new nations had been carried out by missionary groups or under private auspices, there is a potential (and, in a few cases, actual) conflict between these groups and the nationalist leaders, who desire a "national" educational system. These tensions are aggravated by the accusation of radical nationalists (often themselves the products of mission schools) that missionary education is an instrument of colonial domination aimed at producing a subservient colonial mentality among the students. In some cases, this may lead to conflicts recalling the church-state struggles of Europe in the nineteenth and early twentieth centuries, while in others, a working adjustment may be worked out with a mutual recognition of the rights of private groups and the requirements of the new nations.

With national control of education, the curriculum is being altered to emphasize national history, culture, and politics. In Africa, where the Pan-African ideology is strong, there is also an increasing emphasis on the cultural heritage of the African peoples and their distinctive contributions to civilization (see discussion below of the "African personality").

Another aspect of the nationalist revolution as it affects education is the desire to develop a native teaching staff and reduce dependence on foreign teaching personnel. A number of African countries, for instance, are drawing up long-range programs of "Africanization" of education, but the expansion of education and the opening of other career opportunities for educated Africans make it likely that there will be a continued teacher shortage, despite the increase in teacher-training programs that has followed independence.

At the university level, a rapid development of educational facilities is also taking place, along with a shift of emphasis away from the humanistic bias of the colonial university and in the direction of technical subjects. The new University of Nsukka in Nigeria, sponsored by an American land-grant state university, is attempting to carry out this reorientation of the curriculum with emphasis on agriculture and technology rather than the classical subjects of the British university. In Guinea, a planned program for the development of technicians involves sending large numbers of students abroad to study technical subjects in both Eastern and Western countries. These efforts are aimed at producing native cadres who can carry out programs of national development, for education is a means to nation-building, not only in the sense of the creation of nationhood but also as a prerequisite of economic progress.

Economic Development Through "Socialist" Methods

When the nationalist leaders speak of the "development" of the nation, they are speaking primarily of *economic* development. The leadership and members of nationalist movements are acutely aware of the galling contrast between the poverty, illiteracy, and disease of their own countries and the affluence of the economically developed areas. For them, the crucial division in the world is not between the rival political faiths of Communism and liberal democracy, but between the rich and the poor, the economically developed and the underdeveloped, the technically competent and the technologically "backward" areas of the world. The key to the eradication of this difference in living standards lies in economic development, and more particularly in industrialization. With development and industrialization, it will be possible to achieve social equality, educational opportunity, and minimum standards of health and sanitation—in short, the modern welfare state. Without it, population growth and the "revolution of rising expectations" will bring about increasing suffering, political frustration, and social discontent.

Nationalist thinking has given less attention to the need for agricultural development than to the requirements of industrialization, although the present agricultural difficulties of the Soviet Union and China are an indication of the importance of the balanced development of the agricultural sector of the economy. A steel mill is a more dramatic symbol of economic development and national prestige than is a bag of fertilizer, and it seems to promise a much more immediate effect on economic growth. Moreover, agriculture is involved too closely with their former colonial status as a source of primary products to engender much enthusiasm among nationalist leaders.

In their drive toward industrialization, the modernizing nationalists are not prepared to follow the model of the United States, the European nations, or Japan, each of which achieved economic development under private auspices. The nationalist leaders, with the exception of some Latin Americans, are in agreement in rejecting the capitalist method of development as slow, inefficient, and unsuited to their conditions. It is their view that rapid economic growth can only be attained by "socialist" methods, although the precise meaning of this socialism is rarely defined in detail.

Capitalism is rejected and socialism preferred for moral as well as economic reasons. The socialism of the developing nations is said to be directed at the establishment of a society based on justice rather than profit, rational planning rather than the blind operation of the market, and forced economic growth and industrialization as opposed to the orientation of the economy to the production of raw materials for the profit of foreign enterprises. These goals are accepted by nearly all the leaders of Asia, Africa, Latin America, and the Middle East, although their implementation is not as commonly agreed upon or even understood.

Since the Soviet bloc describes itself as the "camp of socialism" or the "socialist countries,"[8] there is the appearance of similarity between Communist goals and methods and those of the emerging nations. Yet, while there is no denying the appeal of the Soviet example of economic development, to equate the two positions is to ignore a fundamental and recurring feature in the ideology of modernizing nationalism—its attempt to establish a separate identity in an intermediate position between East and West. The nationalist leaders insist that they are forging a new approach to economic development that avoids the errors of both capitalism and Communism. Whether it is the "communitarian society" of Frei, the "African socialism" of Senghor, "ujamaa" of Nyerere, the "communocracy" of Sékou Touré, or the "democratic, socialist, cooperative democracy" of Nasser, there is a common commitment to a new form of development that will allow planning and central control of the economy while continuing to permit some measure of private initiative. At the same time that these theories denounce a stereotyped capitalism for its excessive

[8] Even Julius Nyerere speaks of the Communist countries as the "socialist bloc" in "Nationalism and Pan-Africanism" (see below, p. 283).

individualism, its lack of concern with human and social values, and its fostering of the spirit of ruthless competition, they also criticize a stereotyped Communism for its excessive collectivism, its suppression of the individual, its materialism, and its narrow commitment to the national interest of a single country or group of countries.

Because of the intimate involvement of capitalism in the colonial enterprise, the criticisms of capitalism often seem considerably harsher than those of Communism. Even native capitalists are linked to the colonial rulers in nationalist theory. Capitalists are concerned only with profit, the argument goes, and they are willing to collaborate with those who have financial control—in the case of the colonial countries, with the foreign rulers. They are not concerned with the welfare of the people, with national independence, or with economic development—but only with the maximization of their profits (usually lodged in foreign banks).

This is an accurate description of the conduct of certain business leaders in the underdeveloped countries, but it ignores the contributions—financial, intellectual, and political—that others have made to the nationalist cause. In addition, even if the businessman is acting merely out of his own economic interest, independence may be more to his immediate benefit than foreign rule. It can give him a protected market, a government subsidy, and restrictions against foreign competition. Some of the strongest support for economic nationalism and "anti-imperialism" in Latin America, for instance, comes from the domestic business interests, and the Congress Party in India received heavy financial assistance from Indian business leaders throughout its long struggle with the British. In Africa as well, native businessmen have been deeply involved with nationalist parties.

Capitalism also suffers from its association with the evils of colonialism, described in the Leninist theory of imperialism. The theory of imperialism that has achieved the status of "conventional wisdom" among the nationalist leaders does not emphasize, as did Lenin, the importance of finance monopoly and finance capital in generating the need for overseas investment opportunities. The nationalists accept the more general Marxist theory that, because of increased production costs and their inability to dispose of consumption goods, the colonial countries seek a cheap source of raw materials and a market for their products.[9] It is the nature of capitalism to seek to maximize profits, the argument goes, and colonial domination assures the capitalists of a protected market from which all competition is excluded, and it maintains the colony in a permanent state of underdevelopment, so that wages will remain low and raw materials cheap.[10]

The part of the Leninist theory with the greatest appeal to nationalist thinking is Lenin's argument that the continued success of capitalism in advanced countries is based on capitalist bribes to the workers from the fruits of colonial exploitation. In nationalist thinking, Lenin's theory is transformed from an ideological justification of Marxist predictions into a burning indictment of the evils of colonial oppression. If the prosperity of the advanced nations is grounded on the exploitation of colonies, then foreign aid, for instance, is not an act of generosity or of mutual interest. It is either an attempt to maintain continued economic control or, alternatively, a meager effort to restore to Africa (or Latin America or the Middle East) the riches stolen during centuries of imperialist exploitation.[11] (The fact that countries such as Sweden have attained a high level of prosperity without colonies—demonstrating that the prosperity of the advanced nations depends on something more than colonies and cheap raw materials—is not considered, for the theory is not so much an argument as a rationalization or ideological justification for needed economic assistance from the West.)

The nationalists' suspicion of the economic influence of the

[9] The Senegalese nationalist leader Abdoulaye Ly attributes this theory to Rosa Luxemburg; quoted in Hodgkin, *op. cit.*, p. 32. However, the link between overproduction and the need for foreign markets is a commonplace of Marxist theory.

[10] "The economy of European nations consists fundamentally of selling manufactured products to underdeveloped countries at high prices and buying raw materials from them at the lowest possible cost." (Léopold Sédar Senghor, *African Socialism*; see below, p. 243.)

"Human greed . . . stimulated a search for territories from which raw materials could be obtained cheaply and plentifully. After the raw materials had been processed into manufactured goods, it became necessary again to look for markets which would be under their control, so that the manufactured goods could be sold at prices to suit them." (U Nu, *Toward a Socialist State* [Rangoon, 1958], p. 4.)

[11] "The states with a colonialist past are, more than others, compelled to offer to the nations aspiring to development part of the national wealth they sapped when that wealth was a booty for all looters." (Nasser, "Arab Socialism"; see below, p. 156.)

West is expressed in their theory of "neocolonialism." As developed by the radical nationalists, but also given wide credence among the more moderate group, this theory asserts that although political independence has been achieved, there are still links of economic dependence that vitiate the apparent autonomy of the new nations. The wealthy nations wish to exploit the proletarian nations in order to keep them poor and underdeveloped, as well as politically favorable to the policies of the "neocolonialist" powers. Proponents of the theory cite the powerful influence of the United States in Latin America, politically independent since the early nineteenth century, demonstrated by the unanimity with which (before the rise of Castro) the Latin American nations followed U.S. policy in the United Nations. They note that the new states of French-speaking Africa that are most dependent economically on France consistently supported the French position on the Algerian question in the United Nations, despite the unanimity of African support for the rebel nationalists. The division of Africa into two general groupings—and more particularly into many small and economically nonviable states (described as "Balkanization")—is seen as an effort both to maintain political influence and to assure economic domination and the maintenance of profits.[12] Above all, the events following the independence of the Congo, the secession of Katanga and the murder of Lumumba, have appeared to confirm the belief in the sinister machinations of international capitalist interests.

The extent to which these events are attributed exclusively to economic factors is a measure of the impact of Marxist theories of causation on the thinking of many of the leaders of emergent nationalism. To explain colonialism and the politics of the post-colonial era solely in terms of economic domination is simple and intellectually satisfying; moreover, it often seems to fit the facts. On this basis, colonial domination and imperialism are the result of capitalism, and the Western "capitalist" nations are necessarily imperialistic, while the Communist states, lacking an economic motive for imperialist expansion, are exempt from this criticism.[13]

[12] See, for example, the resolutions on neocolonialism adopted at the All-African Peoples' Conference, Cairo, March 23–31, 1961, in Legum, *op. cit.*, pp. 272–75.

[13] See, for example, Kofi Baako, "Nkrumaism," *The Party* (Accra), Nos. 4–7 (April–July, 1961). Baako states that "imperialism and its twin sister, capitalism, are by their very nature and content the main causes of wars."

Yet, many nationalist leaders recognize that the Leninist theory is inadequate. They perceive that colonial domination and post-colonial attempts to retain control and influence are the products of the rivalries of powerful nations, which will inevitably attempt to draw weak nations into their spheres of influence.[14] While the economic motive is a factor in the assessment of the conduct of the "capitalist" West, *all* powerful nations, whatever their economic system, are regarded as potentially imperialistic. This alternative theory of imperialism is quite compatible with the neutralist orientation of the nationalists. It applies to the Soviet Union as much as to the West—and, taking into account the lack of restraints on power in the U.S.S.R., with an even greater validity. Yet, those who give greater emphasis to power politics as an explanation of imperialism have experienced only Western imperialism and hence are likely to continue to direct their criticisms principally at the West. Imperialism usually means Western "capitalist" imperialism, and Soviet imperialism is only rarely criticized.[15]

In the stereotype of the nationalist ideology, both the domestic capitalists and the "international imperialists" are associated in their common desire to control the political process so as to assure that it does not interfere with their economic interests. The domestic capitalists are the "stooges" of the international exploiters. Together with the feudal aristocracy and traditional ruling classes, they form the controlling "oligarchy" whose power, supported by foreign interests, must be broken by the nationalist leaders.[16]

[14] Nyerere speaks of the two "power blocs" using the slogans of anti-Communism and anti-imperialism in a "second scramble for Africa." ("Nationalism and Pan-Africanism"; see below, p. 283.) Nasser also warns that both sides in the Cold War are trying to draw the U.A.R. into a "zone of influence." (*President Nasser's Speeches, 1959* [Cairo, 1960], pp. 469–70.) See also Reinhold Niebuhr, "The Relation of Strength to Weakness in the World Community," in Laurence W. Martin (ed.), *Neutralism and Nonalignment* (New York: Frederick A. Praeger, 1962), pp. 196–98.

[15] Archbishop Makarios of Cyprus was the only leader at the Belgrade Conference in September, 1961, to take a strong stand on Berlin and on the Soviet resumption of nuclear tests.

[16] Cf. Nasser, "Principles of Socialist, Cooperative Democracy," *Egyptian Economic and Political Review*, September–October, 1961, p. 23, in which he denounces "the inherited social system dominated by the imperialists and their stooges, feudalists, and capitalists." On the role of the "oligarchy" in Latin America, see Rómulo Betancourt, *Trayectoria Democrática de una Revolución* (Caracas: Imprenta Nacional, 1948). In Africa, the terms, "Uncle Tom" and "Quisling" are used to the same effect. (Cf. Hodgkin, *op. cit.*, p. 29.)

Here economic and political objectives join with the equalitarianism of nationalist social thought in the demand for the elimination of economic differences in the new "socialist" society being built. The prejudice against both domestic and foreign capitalism is not only based on the narrow concern of the capitalists with the maximization of profits and their supposed opposition to economic development in the emerging nations. It is also derived from a view of capitalist society as one that is essentially based on social and economic inequality. Contrasted with the passionate concern of the nationalist leaders to eliminate inequality and to develop economically, the wealthy nations are seen as conspiring with the wealthy classes in the poor nations to maintain poverty, illiteracy, and underdevelopment.

The "socialism" of the new nations is thus fed by antiforeign feelings, by a passion for social equality, and by a desire for rapid economic development. It is influenced by the Marxist analysis of capitalism and the Leninist description of imperialism, but it does not accept the entire Marxist-Leninist theory as the basis of action. It is a *nationalist* socialism, and therefore it rejects the Marxist-Leninist theory of the class struggle, at least as applied to internal economic relations. The working men (and, more important, the peasants) *do* have a country—despite Marx's assertion to the contrary—and the unity of the people in building the nation requires that the nationalist leader play down the special interests of any one class, including the proletariat. The African leaders who are most influenced by Marxism assert that Africa is *now* a classless society and therefore is not subject to the contradictions of the Marxist class struggle.[17]

In addition, it is a *humanist* socialism and therefore opposed to Marxist materialism. The nationalist leaders—whether Nasser, Nkrumah, or Senghor—insist that there is no opposition between their socialism and spiritual or religious values.[18] In fact, they

---

[17] "[The African] rejects the class struggle because of African social groups' identity of living conditions and lack of differentiation into antagonistic classes." (Sékou Touré, quoted in Legum, *op. cit.*, pp. 129–30.) Nasser, in his speech to the National Congress of Popular Forces, on May 21, 1962, specifically ruled out the class struggle as part of "Arab socialism" (see below, p. 151).

[18] "Islam in its early days was the first socialist state." (Nasser, "Principles of Socialist, Cooperative Democracy,". p. 27.)

"Today I am a nondenominational Christian and a Marxist socialist, and

assert that their socialism is more in accord with religious and moral norms than the *laissez-faire* capitalism they reject.

It is also a socialism *planned by an elite.* If socialism means participation by the worker in the process of economic planning, there seems to be little evidence of thinking in this direction in the writings or speeches of these nationalists. Although Nasser speaks of his socialism as "cooperative," and although there may be admiration and imitation of the Yugoslav system of workers' councils, there does not seem to be any real intention in the new nations (any more than there is in Yugoslavia) of allowing important economic decisions to be made democratically or as the result of any but the most superficial public discussion. Even in the developed countries, only the general lines of economic policy are decided on by popular consultation. Still more in the case of the developing nations, economists of a wide variety of political and economic beliefs accept the need for a rationalized development through expert planning.[19] When the Kennedy Administration reorganized the U.S. foreign-aid program in the Agency for International Development (AID) in 1961, it indicated that greater U.S. assistance would be forthcoming to those countries presenting an integrated program or plan of economic development. It recognized that in countries where the per capita income is under $100 a year (and this applies to areas containing 50 per cent of the world's population),[20] the transition from traditional and subsistence economies to an expanding and developing dynamic economic system must be made by government planning, whether it is described as socialism or not.

The socialism of the modernizing nationalists often involves

I have not found any contradiction between the two." (Nkrumah, *Ghana: The Autobiography of Kwame Nkrumah* [New York: Thomas Nelson and Sons, 1957], p. 13.)

"We stand for a middle course, for a *democratic socialism* which goes so far as to integrate spiritual values, a socialism which ties in with the old ethical current of the French socialists." (Senghor, *African Socialism;* see below, p. 244.)

[19] Latin American criticisms of development through state planning are the exception. (Summarized in Albert O. Hirschman, "Ideologies of Economic Development in Latin America," in Albert O. Hirschman [ed.], *Latin American Issues, Essays and Comments* [New York: The Twentieth Century Fund, 1961], pp. 23 ff.)

[20] See Millikan and Blackmer, *op. cit.,* pp. 149–59.

some measure of nationalization. The ideology of the nationalist leaders leads them to regard nationalization as a preferred means of assuring national control and direction of economic development. In addition—as was made clear in Nasser's speech of July 22, 1961, when he nationalized major industries and confiscated the holdings of the wealthiest Egyptians—nationalization is considered useful as a measure to bring about social equality and eliminate hostile foreign influences (the alliance of domestic capitalists with former colonial rulers or foreign capitalist interests). Problems may be created, however, if ideological preconceptions interfere with a realistic assessment of the best method to achieve the goal of maximum economic growth. Guinea, for instance, has been forced to dismantle its State Trading Commission, through which it attempted to nationalize all import and export activity and to control most of the distribution of goods. The Guineans learned that it was difficult, if not impossible, to centralize in a government bureau in Conakry all the countless decisions involved in distribution; while retaining a centralized development plan, they have now substantially decentralized decision-making in this area.

The difficulty with the nationalist ideology of economic development is that it does not distinguish between the new-style economically productive business innovators and the old-style nonproductive absentee landlords and moneylenders. There is still a lingering suspicion of the businessman's role as essentially exploitative and a hesitancy to recognize his contribution to national development.

Yet, recently, the doctrinaire espousal of nationalization has given way to a search for new forms of economic life, combining over-all government promotion and direction of economic development with a measure of individual initiative and private ownership. Nasser followed his large-scale nationalizations with measures to promote private ownership of land (up to 100 acres) and of small enterprises. Fourteen years of economic planning in India have also shown that nationalization is not always the appropriate way to economic development. Despite his espousal of socialism, Prime Minister Nehru was frank to admit that nationalization would not assure the rationalized development of the economy that India seeks. The Indian experience seems to demonstrate that as an economy expands, an entrepreneurial class of "innovators" emerges which can invest and utilize the new surpluses more efficiently than government planners.[21]

In Africa, there is little evidence of impending large-scale nationalization even among the more radical nations. Both the radicals and the more moderate governments agree that controls on private business are needed, and both recognize that it has a place in the national economy. However, the radicals tend to prefer a mixture that leans more heavily in the direction of state control.

The same pattern emerges in attitudes toward investment by foreign private capital. The moderate reformers are more eager to encourage private companies and investors to engage in economic development, but they are also aware of the need for appropriate government regulation to assure that this investment is directed toward the development of the country. The radicals, while eager to have foreign capital, often prefer to secure it through direct government-to-government relations, and the restrictions they place on foreign private investment may discourage the additional flow of such capital in their direction, particularly when there are other countries that can offer better terms.[22]

This does not mean, however, as the Marxist analysis would have it, that the individual nation (like the individual worker in the days before the advent of trade unionism) is always at the mercy of international monopoly capitalism because of its weak competitive bargaining position. Larger nations and federal group-

---

[21] See Nasser's speech "Arab Socialism" (below, pp. 154–55), delivered on May 21, 1962. Nehru discusses nationalization in "Indian Socialism" (below, pp. 129–30).   On the role of entrepreneurs in the economies of the developing nations, see Barbara Ward, *India and the West* (New York: W. W. Norton & Company, 1961), Chap. xv; Millikan and Blackmer, *op. cit.*, Chap. v; W. W. Rostow, *The Stages of Economic Growth* (New York: Cambridge University Press, 1960), pp. 50 ff.; Edward Shils, "The Concentration and Dispersion of Charisma," *World Politics*, XI, No. 1 (October, 1958), 1–19.

[22] Examples of the two approaches would include the moderate policies toward foreign and domestic capital adopted by Nigeria and Senegal, and the more stringent controls by the governments of Guinea, Ceylon, and Indonesia. Ghana under Nkrumah invited foreign investment, but its official position favored government loans as a preferable method of development. (Cf. Kofi Baako, "Nkrumaism," *The Party* [Accra], No. 6 [June, 1961]: "The Nkrumaist prefers loan capital to investment capital. . . . Loan capital allows the receiver . . . say, the government—to use its loan to set up any state enterprises within the framework of its socioeconomic plan.")

ings are often in a better position to assert control over economic activity by foreign investors (and this is one of the numerous reasons for the movements for a common market in Latin America, and for regional federation in Africa and the Middle East), but even the smaller nations, if they are politically independent, can gain certain advantages from the current competition by foreign investors for investment opportunities in developing countries. The increase in the percentage of profits allocated to Iran and other countries by an Italian oil company from the standard 50–50 arrangement to a 75–25 division is an example of the possibilities to be derived from such competition.

That similar advantages can also come from competition among the governmental sources of capital is clear to all the leaders of the developing nations. The reformists and radicals among the modernizing elite agree on the virtues of "aid without strings" from both East and West. The examples of Nasser's success in playing off the rival blocs in the Cold War and of the construction of steel mills in India by rival teams from the Soviet Union and West Germany have not been lost on other nationalist leaders. It should not be surprising, therefore, that increasing numbers of nations in Asia, Africa, Latin America, and the Middle East turn to the Soviet Union, Eastern Europe, and China for economic assistance, since this policy conforms both to their own urgent need for additional foreign capital and to their ideological position of neutralism or nonalignment in international affairs.

If the developing nations are internally strong, if by maintaining economic links with the West as well as the East they avoid becoming dependent on the Soviet bloc, and if they are themselves committed to democratic methods, aid from the East may strengthen democracy and weaken internal pressures for the more drastic methods of totalitarian control. This is the case already in India, where aid from the Soviet bloc has helped the Congress Party in its struggle to develop the country in the face of both the external example of China and the internal threat of the Indian Communist Party.[23]

When it is a question of *military* aid from the Soviet Union, the situation becomes more complicated. Nasser does not seem to

[23] See Paul Sigmund, "The Uses of Neutralism," *Commonweal*, LXXIII, No. 21 (February 17, 1961), 523–26. Reprinted in David K. Marvin, *Emerging Africa* (San Francisco: Chandler Publishing Company, 1965), pp. 223–31.

have compromised his independent policy by accepting Soviet and Czech weapons, but it would appear that, if only because of the need for ammunition and replacement parts, a certain dependence may result. In addition, the military advisers who accompany this aid may also influence government policy. In apparent recognition of the difference between the two types of aid, the nations of the uncommitted world have so far been much less eager to secure military assistance than economic aid from the Soviet bloc, although India, Indonesia, Guinea, and Mali, in addition to Egypt, have received such military assistance.

Strong Government Under a Single or Dominant Party

All the nationalist leaders see the need for a strong government to achieve the goals of modernization and development. To carry out a social and economic revolution in addition to a political transfer of power requires a government that can act vigorously to educate the people in the new nationalism and to initiate a program of forced economic development. Development requires foreign assistance, whether private or governmental, and a strong government is also considered necessary to direct and control the use of this capital in accordance with national objectives.

The failure of parliamentary regimes to provide this type of effective leadership has meant that a reforming military elite has taken control in a number of the new states. Unlike the old military oligarchies of Latin America and the Iberian peninsula, these new military rulers are committed to the goals of modernization and development. They reject as inapplicable and even fraudulent the party systems borrowed from European parliamentary practice. However, they may retain, in an altered form, the representative assembly and periodic elections by universal suffrage, which are needed to demonstrate that political power comes from the people, the sole source of legitimacy in the modern state.[24]

The modernizing military oligarchies usually justify their authoritarianism as temporary in character, preparing for the introduction of democracy when economic and social progress permit. In the past, the model for this type of transitional authoritarianism

---

[24] Nasser is currently attempting to establish a modified parliamentarism in the United Arab Republic. For a defense of army rule without deference to democratic forms, see Abdul Karim Kassem, The Principles of the July 14th Revolution (Baghdad, 1959).

has been the modernizing rule of Kemal Atatürk in Turkey, which prepared the way for what appeared to be an orderly transition to democracy (although recent events in Turkey have called into question the success of that transition).

A similar transitional role may be played by the popular leader with quasi-charismatic qualities derived from his part in the nationalist effort to gain independence. This is frequently the case in Africa, as well as in countries like India, where the tradition of subordination of the military to the civilian authority is strong. The nationalist leaders have developed an effective instrument of modernization in the single or dominant nationalist party reaching down into every level of national life. Military reformers like Nasser have recognized its effectiveness and have attempted to develop their own nationalist parties to organize the people, to control and to respond to public opinion, and to give legitimacy to the government.

Both the moderate and radical wings of the nationalist elite favor the single or dominant national party, and such parties exist in many of the new nations of Africa, in several countries in Asia, and, in the case of Mexico, in Latin America as well.[25] However, the structure of a dominant moderate or reformist party is usually different from that of a radical one. Where the radicals create an entirely new structure from the basic unit (or "cell") to the leadership, the reformists often make use of existing groups and traditional loyalties to build their parties. In the latter instance, the dynamic of social change is considerably diminished since groups with an interest in the present arrangement of society often form an important segment of the party.[26]

Similarly, the more moderate parties are less eager to mobilize and control the various voluntary groups in the society as auxiliaries of the party. The radical leaders argue that the task of nation-building requires that student, youth, labor, and women's groups

[25] Senghor has defended the existence of an opposition party (see below, pp. 247 f.), but Senegal now has, in effect, a one-party system. Nigeria, because of its federal structure, is an exception to the one-party rule in Africa.

[26] This distinction based on attitudes toward other groups in the society differs from the mass-party, elite-party dichotomy based on internal structure, which is utilized by Thomas Hodgkins, in *African Political Parties* (Baltimore, Md.: Penguin Books, 1961), pp. 68–75, and by Ruth Schachter, in "Single Party Systems in West Africa," *American Political Science Review*, LV, No. 2 (June, 1961), 294–307. Houphouet-Boigny's PDCI, for example, is a mass party with a moderate reformist program.

be organized and directed toward national goals by the party, rather than being left to their own parochial concerns. In the more extreme versions of this theory, every such group organized in the colonial period is viewed as an instrument of colonialist and imperialist attempts to influence the thinking of the colonized peoples. Whether it is the Boy Scouts or the Young Men's Christian Association, or international affiliation with groups like the World Assembly of Youth or the International Confederation of Free Trade Unions, all are suspect as organizations that either divert the energies of the interest group in question from the task of nation-building or are actively used by an external enemy to subvert national independence. (In Africa, some of the more moderate regimes have also borrowed the radicals' techniques and decreed the dissolution of student, youth, and labor groups or their integration into the party, particularly when they are opposed to the government.)

The nationalist leaders admit to a degree of elitism in their views on the relation of party and government to the people. Whether in the "guided democracy" of Sukarno, the "basic democracy" of Ayub Khan, or the "democratic dictatorship" of Sékou Touré, the popular will from which a government or ruling party must derive its legitimacy in a democratic age seems to consist as much in what the people *should* desire as in what they *do* desire. That there should be some confusion on this point is not surprising since democratic theory has always been ambiguous in this respect. The classical democratic assumption of the automatic coincidence of the subjective will of the majority and the objective standard of natural law or the greatest good of the greatest number has not always been realized in fact. Rousseau himself admitted that a "legislator" was required to prepare the people to exercise their responsibilities as participants in the general will.[27] In a sense, the nationalist leaders see themselves as the "lawgivers" of the new dispensation, involving the entire population, and imposing modernization, economic development, and "democracy."

As in the case of the reformist military regimes, the single party is defended as a transitional stage necessary to establish the essential preconditions of liberal democracy. The new nations are

[27] Jean Jacques Rousseau, *The Social Contract*, Chap. vii. The "legislator" also appears in Greek thought and in Machiavelli's *Discourses*.

said to lack a minimum national unity and consensus on basic
values, the economic basis for a middle class to give stability to
the system, a sufficiently high literacy rate to make political discussion and choice meaningful, and a tradition of self-restraint
on the part of both majority and minority necessary for the give
and take between those in power and the loyal opposition that is
characteristic of a democratic system.[28] Yet, despite the admitted
authoritarian elements, the single party is said to be democratic
in structure and purpose. It is a mass organization open to all the
citizenry—and this is an important difference from the Leninist
conception of the party as an elite group.[29] It is the energizing
force that carries out the program of development, but it is also
in touch with the people and communicates their feelings to the
leadership. In some defenses of the single party by leaders of
Africa, Asia, and the Middle East (and by Cuba's Castro as well),
it is even argued that a new and superior form of democracy is
being developed in the single party.

The single or dominant party system is said to be more democratic than a system of two or more parties, since the Western
parties usually represent narrow class, religious, or ethnic interests
rather than the nation as a whole. Even in the two-party system,
rule is exercised by a majority that may be as small as 50 per cent
plus one, instead of by the whole people.[30] Those most influenced
by the Marxist analysis argue that in the case of the United
States, for instance, both parties are under the control of the same
oligarchy of wealthy business interests. To an even greater extent,
the multiparty systems of the colonial or semicolonial period are
viewed as a facade for control by foreign or capitalist interests.
Outside influences use the divisions and rivalries of the multiparty system and play upon the selfishness of petty politicians
who are concerned only with playing the parliamentary game,

[28] For a typical expression of the view that under present conditions there
is no alternative to one-party rule in Africa, see Immanuel Wallerstein, *Africa,
The Politics of Independence* (New York: Random House, 1961), p. 163. An
opposing view, which denounces the Western paternalism implied in this
attitude, appears in Obafemi Awolowo's autobiography, *Awo* (Cambridge
and New York: Cambridge University Press, 1960), pp. 300–305.

[29] Fidel Castro has now adopted a Leninist conception of the party as an
elite "vanguard of the proletariat." (See below, p. 327.)

[30] Sukarno criticizes "free-fight liberalism, where half plus one is always
right" (see below, p. 96). Cf. Julius Nyerere, "Democracy and the Party
System" (below, pp. 294–302).

rather than working for reform and development. In a new nation where, except for "the agents of imperialism," there is no sharp differentiation of economic interest, the single party is more appropriate to the economic and social development of society, and more necessary in order to resist outside pressures and pursue the interest of the nation as a whole.[31] The requirements of democracy are observed, say the defenders of the single-party system, *within* the parties rather than between them. There is no need for more than one party if there is freedom of discussion, democratic election of party leaders, and responsiveness of those in power to a mass membership that is broadly representative of the whole population. Multipartyism encourages disunity and factionalism, even subversion, at a time when there is the greatest need for national unity.

If this argument sounds suspiciously like the Soviet defense of "democratic centralism," this is no accident. Sékou Touré, the leading apologist for the single party, is frank to acknowledge the influence of the Leninist theory. However, while not ignoring Lenin's insistence on rigid party discipline, Touré emphasizes the importance of the maintenance of democratic procedures within the party and sees it as a mass movement rather than a conspiratorial elite.[32] Not only the Marxists defend the single party for nations undergoing the revolution of modernization. Leaders as diverse as Nyerere of Tanganyika and former President Sukarno of Indonesia assert that it is in keeping with the traditional methods of decision-making in their societies, which tend to operate on the basis of consensus rather than dialectical opposition. Democracy is "talking until you agree," says Nyerere, not opposition for opposition's sake.[33]

The analogy in the one-party theory is more with Rousseau than with Lenin. The single party is "democratic" not because it is a vanguard that has an insight into the real meaning of economics and history, but because all participate and there is a continual

[31] See Sékou Touré on Africa as a classless society (p. 17, n. 17); Nasser's defense of the National Union Party (see *President Nasser's Speeches, 1959*); and Castro's description of the bourgeois party as "a gang of politicians, a conglomeration of individuals who defend class interests" (below, p. 327).

[32] Below, pp. 224 ff. Use of the term "democratic centralism" to describe the party structure is characteristic of the radical wing of African nationalism, but it is not used by other nationalist parties.

[33] "Democracy and the Party System" (below, pp. 294–302).

dialogue among leader, leading party, and the masses. The ambiguity in Rousseau's "general will" and its potential for tyranny, whether by the leader or by the majority, is shared by the theory of the single party, which often tends to minimize the possibility of a conflict between the individual and the group, party, or nation.

Yet, in his classic defense of the single party, Madeira Keita, now Minister of Justice of the Republic of Mali, recognizes that there are real dangers in this system. Keita emphasizes the great demands that the absence of an organized opposition places upon the leadership of the single party. (Keita also notes that he prefers the term "unified party," emphasizing the variety of tendencies within the movement.) Perhaps in anticipation of subsequent developments, the French-speaking African intellectual Cheikh Anta Diop, commenting on Keita's speech, expressed the fear that unless the African territories formed a larger federation, the single-party systems in each country would become the instrumentalities of "petty ephemeral dictatorships" of the Latin American type.[34]

In the absence of institutional safeguards for the expression of dissenting opinions, there is a danger that the charismatic leader, convinced of his mission to reform society, may suppress even legitimate criticism of those in power. Some observers see in the auxiliary organizations of youths, students, labor, etc., the means of institutional expression of criticism, but Roberto Michels' "iron law of oligarchy," a sociological generalization from the experience of the concentration of power at the top of any institutional hierarchy, suggests that this might not often take place.[35] Particularly when nationalist leaders are enjoying the perquisites of power after a revolt against existing laws, it may be difficult to develop respect for the sharing of power in accordance with legal and institutional norms.

The danger is all the more real, since the single-party ideology, while allowing and encouraging mass affiliation and freedom of

[34] See Madeira Keita, "The Single Party in Africa" (below, pp. 233, 237).

[35] Michels, *Political Parties, A Sociological Study of Oligarchical Tendencies of Modern Democracy* (Glencoe, Ill.: The Free Press, 1958). The argument concerning auxiliary organizations is made by Clement Moore, in "The National Party: A Tentative Model," in C. J. Friedrich and Seymour Harris (eds.), *Public Policy*, X (1960), 262 ff. See also Douglas Ashford, "Labor Politics in a New Nation," *Western Political Quarterly*, XIII, No. 2 (June, 1960), 312–31.

discussion for differing points of view, is often unwilling to accord these rights to the representatives of the traditional order, the "feudal classes," or to those who are considered to be or to have been collaborators with foreigners. Loose charges of "reactionary feudalist" or "imperialist stooge" can be used to stifle legitimate dissent, and the prisons can contain both loyal and disloyal oppositionists. The theory of the single party can result in the revolutionary transformation of society by means of persuasion and democratic discussion, or it can be used to justify the imposition of the will of an oligarchic elite by coercion, propaganda, and Rousseauan mysticism about the will of the people.

An optimistic view is that once the single party has initiated economic development and succeeded in replacing local, tribal, caste, and religious loyalties with a sense of involvement in the nation, it will develop a healthy pluralism of parties or interest groups. Within the national consensus, there will thus be an institutionalized opportunity for the expression of differences as to the method or pace of social change, or even simply of the opposition of the "outs" to the "ins."[36] The Congress Party of India, for instance, once contained within its ranks the leaders of the present Communist and Praja Socialist parties, and recently the supporters of the right-wing Swatantra (Freedom) Party have split off from it.

On the other hand, a more pessimistic critic might doubt whether those who hold power are not more likely to label legitimate economic and social grievances as the product of foreign intrigue and domestic reaction, and thus to step up the pace of repressive measures as the opposition becomes less able to pose a threat to those in control.

Regional Cooperation or Federation

As the example of Nigeria seems to indicate, there is also the possibility that movements toward federation may promote politi-

---

[36] Tom Mboya has said that opposition parties will develop "in ten or more years . . . as a normal and natural process of the individual freedom of speech and freedom to criticize the government." (Quoted in Legum, *op. cit.*, p. 124.) Characteristically, Sékou Touré links the existence of the opposition party to the state of economic development. In developed countries, he says, political opposition "by its presence and action, increases the dynamism of the party in power." (Quoted in Immanuel Wallerstein, "Political Theory in an African Context," paper presented to the African Studies Association, September, 1960, p. 13.)

cal pluralism. States of differing political persuasion in geographical proximity may hesitate to suppress political groups in a position to retaliate in a neighboring state of the same federal grouping. Yet, thus far, the two unsuccessful examples of such federation—the union of Syria, and Egypt in the United Arab Republic, and that of Senegal and the Sudan (now the Mali Republic) in the Federation of Mali—seem to indicate that organic federation between states of differing ideologies and social systems is very difficult.

The movement toward regional federation or confederation is not an important one in Asia (although the Bandung Conference of 1955 gave a symbolic expression to the solidarity of Asians and Africans). But in Africa, the Middle East, and Latin America, the desire to create regional structures is strong enough to be a major factor in the ideological appeal of certain nationalist leaders, such as Nasser and Nkrumah, both within and outside their own territorial limits. Nasser has used Pan-Arab feeling to increase Egyptian influence elsewhere in the Middle East; and at one point after the Suez crisis, he seemed close to realizing the dream of Arab unity. In Africa, the movement toward closer cooperation on a Pan-African level receives the support of all groups, but there is disagreement as to the methods and rate by which the goal of a united African continent is to be attained. The radicals call for political union and measures such as the establishment of an African Military High Command, while the moderates support the establishment of functional links (customs, a common currency, etc.) that can form the basis of closer cooperation in the future. The moderates accuse the radicals of fomenting subversion and attempting to alter existing national boundaries, while the radicals view the moderates as tools of "neocolonialism."[37] Yet, both groups agree on the danger of the balkanization of the continent, and both urge a Pan-African regional grouping. Despite the schism in Africa, the appeal of the Pan-African ideal is so great that the present divisions may only be temporary, and a broader form of Pan-African cooperation may be developed in the future.

---

[37] In the first edition of this book, the radicals and the moderates were described, respectively, as the "Casablanca" and the "Monrovia" powers. With the formation of the Organization of African Unity, this terminology became outmoded, but the differences described above still persist.

In Latin America and the Middle East, efforts at regional co-operation have had little success. The mystique of regional cooperation or unification is not enough, it seems, to overcome personal antagonisms and nationalistic rivalries. Territorial expansion by a strong power is one classic way in which unification has taken place, but the new nations thus far lack the military power to engage in this form of unification, and the great powers, their relationship delicately stabilized in a balance of mutual terror, seem reluctant to involve themselves in a major way in the rivalries of the new nations.

Another possible means to union is a joint effort against a common enemy. The African threat of a crusade to liberate Angola and the Republic of South Africa may someday result in the realization of the projected African army repeatedly discussed during the Congo crisis.[38] Fidel Castro has attempted to use hostility to "Yankee imperialism" in a similar way in Latin America, and the Suez crisis was one of the few occasions in which the Arab world was united.

The remaining alternative, that of a gradual evolution of regional cooperation, is not an appealing one to the impatient nationalists, but it is possible that closer ties will come about through the development of further economic and cultural links rather than by political means. The United Nations Economic Commission for Latin America (ECLA), with headquarters in Santiago de Chile, has already influenced Latin American economic thinking along regional lines, and preliminary efforts have been made to create common organs of regional economic cooperation in Latin America. The Economic Commission for Africa is also exerting a similar influence, and the obvious mutual interdependence of many of the African states has already led to the lowering of some of the economic barriers raised at the time of national independence. The African states continue to meet together, and the tentative gropings of youth, student, and trade-union organizations in Latin America and Africa for regional cooperation either within or out-

[38] An African army was proposed by President Nkrumah in his speech to the United Nations on September 23, 1960, and by Julius Nyerere speaking to the Pan-African Seminar of the World Assembly of Youth (WAY) at Dar-es-Salaam on August 6, 1961. The Organization of African Unity has established a Liberation Committee with headquarters in Dar-es-Salaam but it has no armed forces at its disposal.

side existing international organizations are a further reassertion of the federalist ideal.[39]

The Revival of Traditional Culture

Part of the impetus to regional cooperation comes from the awareness of a common heritage of values. Again, this is not true of Asia as a whole, although the consciousness of an underlying unity among the diverse cultures of India is an important element in Indian nationalism. However, the common background of Islamic culture and Arab language in the Middle East, Latin America's belief in a community of values derived from the Iberian peninsula but given a different content by its fusion with Indian and Negro elements, and (especially) the rediscovery or creation of an African culture symbolized by Senghor's Negritude and Nkrumah's "African personality"—all serve in varying degrees to strengthen the common bonds in their respective regions.

Despite their desire for modernization, the nationalist leaders feel a need to maintain elements of their traditional cultures and the moral values they represent. Nehru has alluded to the "spiritual loneliness" of the Westernized elite, which both needs and rejects the values of traditional civilization. The description in Nasser's *Philosophy of the Revolution* of an Egyptian family in

[39] The relation of the voluntary organizations of students, youth, labor unions, etc., to the movements for regional federation lies outside the scope of this book. Relevant regional groups include the All-African Trade Union Federation formed in Casablanca in May, 1961, the African Trade Union Conference established in Lagos in 1962, the Pan-African Youth Movement (MJP), the Latin American Student Congress, the Organización Regional Interamericana de Trabajadores (ORIT), and the African Regional Organization (AFRO). Only ORIT and AFRO are associated with an international organization, the International Confederation of Free Trade Unions. In recent years, both the Communist front organizations (e.g., the World Federation of Democratic Youth, the International Union of Students, the World Federation of Trade Unions, and the International Federation of Teachers' Unions) and the non-Communist groupings (e.g., the International Student Conference, the World Assembly of Youth, the International Confederation of Free Trade Unions, and the World Confederation of Organizations of the Teaching Profession) have greatly increased their regional programing in Asia, Africa, the Middle East, and Latin America. For examples on the Communist side, see Robert H. Bass, "Communist Fronts," *Problems of Communism*, IX, No. 5 (September–October, 1960), 8–17. A detailed account of the political struggle over the establishment of the All-African Trade Union Federation appears in Legum, *op. cit.*, pp. 81–92.

which one son is English-educated, a daughter French-educated, the father comes from an Egyptian peasant family, and the mother has a Turkish background is typical of the cultural confusion produced by the disorganizing impact of the West.

The reassertion of certain features of traditional culture is psychologically necessary to balance the overwhelming technical, economic, and military superiority of the West. Characteristically, the nationalist leaders stress the moral, religious, or spiritual superiority of their culture in contrast to the materialism, utilitarianism, and technocracy of the West (and not only of the West, since these qualities can be attributed with even greater validity to the Communist world).[40] They hail the distinctive contributions of native music, literature, art, and poetry, and warn against the "mental colonialism" that has separated the intellectuals from their cultural heritage and subjected them to the alien values of the dominant European civilization.[41] The cultural renaissance in the developing nations is thus a partial rejection of the Western culture, which was held up previously as a model. It is an effort to establish national pride and self-respect—integral factors in the building of new nations.

Indian nationalism had a rich culture to draw on, but the interest in African culture and history that now forms an important part of the ideology of African nationalism stemmed from the work of English anthropologists and French-speaking African in-

[40] "Among Indian and African civilizations, which are essentially spiritualistic, the idea of economic utility is appreciated otherwise than in the old or young materialistic civilizations, or civilizations issuing from formative processes where, in spite of spiritual factors, the materialistic element dominates." (Mamadou Dia, The African Nations and World Solidarity [New York: Frederick A. Praeger, 1961], pp. 89–90.)

"The tendency of Indian civilization is to elevate the moral being, that of the Western civilization is to propagate immorality." (Gandhi, Indian Home Rule; see below, p. 105).

"Between the ideology of Communism and the materialist conceptions of the West, Islam is the only point of view that can prevent the spirit of humanity from being destroyed." (Ayub Khan, "Islam in Pakistan"; see below, p. 136.)

"A third revolution is taking place, as a reaction against capitalistic and Communistic materialism—one that will integrate moral, if not religious, values with the political and economic contributions of the two great revolutions [French and Russian]." (Senghor, African Socialism; see below, p. 246.)

[41] The term "mental colonialism" is used by Haya de la Torre (see below, p. 345). See also Sékou Touré's discussion of the French attempt to "depersonalize and Westernize" the African intellectual elite (below, p. 213).

tellectuals in Paris. The very names Ghana and Mali are a conscious attempt to recall the glories of the medieval empires under
those names, and the governments of Senegal, Mali, Guinea, and
Ghana have subsidized and popularized the work of African and
European scholars on these subjects. To the charge that there is
a racist element in the glorification of the past accomplishment
of the African, Léopold Senghor replies that a period of self-assertion of African values is necessary to correct the distortions of
African culture and history produced by the inevitable bias of
European historians. In righting the balance to emphasize the
positive achievements and values of the "African personality," a
dialogue between the two views will be created that can contribute to universal culture. A national and regional cultural revival
thus precedes a higher and truer internationalism that will include
African culture and civilization on an equal basis with that of
other parts of the world.[42]

Nonalignment in International Affairs

With some exceptions dictated by special circumstances, most of
the new nations in Asia, Africa, and the Middle East (but not in
Latin America) have adopted a policy of nonalignment with either
East or West in the Cold War. While remaining outside alliances
and power groupings, they have not hesitated to pass judgment on
the actions of the great powers, seeing themselves as specially fitted
for this role because of their nonaligned position. Since each of
the new nations has a vote in the U.N. General Assembly, they
have an international forum in which, particularly in recent years,
they exert a voting strength far out of proportion to their power
in international affairs. They are thus encouraged, if not compelled, to take positions on a wide range of problems and to pursue an active international policy.

Since the General Assembly is dominated by their votes, the
representatives of the developing nations view it as an instrument
to defend the small and weak nations against the large and powerful. Conscious of their own weakness in physical power, they have
resisted attempts to dilute the effectiveness of the U.N., since it

---

[42] Senghor, "What Is 'Negritude'?" (see below, pp. 248–51). See also the in-
terview with Ayo Ogunshaye in Melvin Lasky, "Africa for Beginners," *Encounter*, XVII, No. 1 (July, 1961), 44–46.

remains the best forum for the exercise of moral pressure by them upon the great powers.

To Western critics, the nationalist leaders seem to overemphasize the virtues of moral suasion and to underestimate the importance of a military balance in maintaining the present uneasy peace—and even in maintaining their own national independence. Yet, the nonaligned nations are not willing to leave to the stronger nations the problems of international war and peace because their entire effort to develop would be destroyed by a war between the great powers.

At the same time, they also insist that they be left to regulate their internal and regional affairs among themselves. As the example of the Congo demonstrates, the major powers may not be willing to comply with this demand, particularly when it is put forward by countries with ambitions of their own in the area. Moreover, the nationalists' principle of nonintervention is not an absolute. The Latin Americans condemn the United States for not taking action against authoritarian dictatorships in Central and South America, and the Africans have pressed us to take drastic action against our allies who still hold colonial territories. Nonintervention is a doctrine to be applied to legitimate regimes, but not to colonial or reactionary governments.

The claim of the uncommitted nations to represent the "unbiased conscience of humanity,"[43] is somewhat tarnished by what appears to Western eyes to be a greater readiness to condemn Western misdeeds than those of the Soviet Union, as well as by the neutrals' support of the use of violence in the case of Goa. Examples like India's attitude on Kashmir or Morocco's claim to Mauritania indicate that on questions affecting what are considered to be their vital interests, the uncommitted nations are no more likely to defer to international morality and opinion than do the more powerful nations whom they upbraid for their immoral behavior. Yet, despite the fact that no nation is ready to abjure the use or threat of violence, the very military weakness of the new nations which leads them to adopt a moralistic attitude also makes armed conflict among them less likely, provided the great powers

[43] Statement by Premier Saeb Salaan of Lebanon to the United Nations General Assembly; quoted by Ernest W. Lefever, in "Nehru, Nasser, and Nkrumah on Neutralism," in Martin, op. cit., p. 103.

restrain themselves or are restrained from becoming deeply involved in their rivalries.

In addition to their role as the moral conscience of humanity, the uncommitted nations also view themselves as a balance or intermediary between the two power blocs. Nationalist thinking has added the theory of the "third area" countries to the older bipolar view of world politics. Like the bipolar theory, this view of international relations overlooks the pluralistic elements in the West and (especially since the recent Sino-Soviet ideological division) in the East as well, but it serves the purpose of establishing a separate identity and special role in international affairs for the new nations. Yet, the two roles—that of the independent moral conscience exercising an unbiased judgment on each case, and that of the balance wheel located precisely midway between the positions of East and West—need not lead to the same conclusions. The conception of themselves as the mean between the extremes, typical of the thinking of emergent nationalists, leads to an automatic assumption of a middle ground on East-West questions, with quite different results from the attempt to make an independent assessment of the moral worth of the claims of the two antagonists.[44]

However, one might question whether the third area can also be described as a third bloc. Many of the speakers at the Belgrade Conference denied that it was their intention to act as a bloc, and the divisions among the nations of Asia, Africa, and Latin America are such that the probability is slight that they will be able to act together on any regular basis. Moreover, with the exception of Cuba, Latin America has so far not been considered a member of the uncommitted group. However, a common concern with development, a similar suspicion of strong and wealthy nations, and parallel problems of social and economic reform make it likely that closer links will be developed among the developing nations,

[44] "Neither side has won us and we are determined that neither side will." (Statement by an African diplomat at the United Nations; quoted by Henry Kissinger, in *The Necessity for Choice* [New York: Harper & Brothers, 1961], p. 330.) This should be compared with Modibo Keita's statement: "[Nonalignment] must not be compared with *équilibrisme*, with a balancing act which takes up no fundamental position and which aligns itself now with one, now with the other, of the two blocs." (Quoted in Legum, *op. cit.*, pp. 113–14.) Neutralism is criticized by Chief Awolowo (*op. cit.*, pp. 309–11) and (in certain forms) by Mamadou Dia (*op. cit.*, pp. 84–85).

particularly on issues such as colonialism and underdevelopment, on which there is a large measure of agreement.[45]

The most powerful motivating force determining the policy of the uncommitted nations is neither neutralism nor the urge to sit in judgment upon their fellows, but nationalism and the desire for national independence and prestige. A neutral or nonaligned position, meetings of the uncommitted nations, and a moralistic attitude toward world politics help to create an international climate in which the weak nations can better defend and develop themselves economically and politically. The East-West question and the ideological conflict surrounding it, while they may indirectly benefit the new nations, are more often viewed as obstacles to the goal of national independence, economic development, and social change. To divide the new nations into pro-Western and pro-Eastern is to be ignorant of this primary concern and of the frequently expressed disinterest of the new nations in becoming involved in the ideological struggles of the great powers.

Modernizing Nationalism and Communism

If, as the preceding discussion seems to indicate, there is a belief system that can be classified as the ideology of modernizing nationalism, if what the French call the *Tiers-Monde* has a world view of its own, then a terminology of international politics derived from the Cold War is inadequate. Different questions must be asked and a different classification utilized. At the outset, the question was posed as to whether the common ideas of modernizing nationalism could be described as an ideology, similar to but different from the ideological systems of Europe. This review of the ideas of the nationalist leaders has suggested that, if we omit the leaders of traditional and conservative oligarchies, the two other general types of nationalist leaders, the radicals and the reformers, share a body of political and economic theory, distinct from both Western liberalism and Soviet collectivism. It is a suffi-

---

[45] The denials by Nasser, Nkrumah, and others at the Belgrade Conference are quoted in Legum, *op. cit.*, p. 115. A typical expression of the three-bloc conception appears in Sukarno's "Lecture to the Students of Hasanuddin University": "These three groupings I regard as a phenomenon of the twentieth century: the group of Thomas Jefferson, the group adhering to the Communist Manifesto, and the group of Asian and African nationalism." (See below, pp. 91–92.) Note that Sukarno appears to consider Latin America part of the Western group.

ciently coherent body of ideas to be called an ideology—the ideology of modernizing nationalism. The goal of national development elicits an emotional response and commitment on the part of the members of the nationalist movement. It is accompanied by a set of doctrines about the proper methods to attain economic progress, the nature of world politics, and the special contribution of the new nations to world culture and world peace. The ideology has a function—to carry the nation through the period of modernization of traditional society and to justify the ensuing sacrifices and dislocations. For its content, it draws upon the political ideas of both East and West.

This is not to ignore the real dangers in the appeals of Communism to the developing nations. The examples of China, of Cuba since late 1959, or even of Russia itself demonstrate that the ideology of Marxism-Leninism has a particular appeal for a nation undergoing the upheavals and dislocations associated with modernization and development.[46] It is only to assert that Marxism-Leninism is not the only ideology appropriate to this process, and that, in fact, the modernizing nationalists have developed an alternative set of ideological assumptions and propositions that shares some elements of the Marxist-Leninist model, but differs significantly from it in other respects. Moreover, this ideology is in many ways superior to Marxism-Leninism, since it is more pragmatic and more related to the problem of modernization than are the simplistic dogmas derived from the experience of nineteenth- and early twentieth-century Europe which comprise the Marxist-Leninist solution.[47]

From the Marxist analysis, the modernizing nationalists have accepted certain elements and rejected others. While recognizing the central importance of economic motivation, they do not accept

[46] Cf. Adam B. Ulam, "The Historical Role of Marxism and the Soviet System," *World Politics*, VIII, No. 1 (October, 1955), 20–45.

[47] The inapplicability of classical Marxism to the problems of an agrarian society was recognized by Mao Tse-tung in his *On New Democracy* (see below, pp. 70–76), which describes "the joint dictatorship of several revolutionary classes," including the peasants and intelligentsia. The European derivation of Marxism-Leninism is also the basis of the criticism of Communism by Haya de la Torre of Peru (see below, p. 346), and by a group of African Marxists who, at the Second Conference of Negro Writers and Artists in Rome, March 25–April 1, 1959, adopted a resolution calling for a revision of Marxism to make it less Western and more universal in its application. (The resolution is printed in Legum, *op. cit.*, p. 238.)

Marxist economic determinism. In nationalist thinking, political forces are capable of subduing and controlling economic forces, and the state is not destined to wither away. Moreover, Marxist materialism is specifically rejected in favor of the recognition of the importance of the spiritual aspects of life. Marxist class analysis is also regarded as inadequate. History involves more than the struggle of the proletariat and bourgeoisie. Other groups in society are also significant, among them the rural elements, the intellectuals, and perhaps the military men as well. The nation as a whole is the primary unit of loyalty, not the class, and in the case of the African nationalists, it is denied that class divisions even exist in the new nations.[48]

In the case of Lenin's additions to Marxist theory, there is the same pattern of partial incorporation and partial rejection. On the one hand, the Leninist theory of imperialism is widely accepted, but on the other, the Leninist association of Western capitalism with imperialism does not prevent the developing nations from inviting Western investment and accepting Western aid. In addition, there remains a healthy suspicion of Soviet intentions which, while perhaps not as strong as the suspicion of the West, demonstrates the nationalists' assumption that tendencies toward domination are not a capitalist monopoly. The Leninist conception of the role of the party and auxiliary organizations in mobilizing the society has been accepted by the radical wing of modernizing nationalism, but thus far even the radical parties have been more open and less rigidly authoritarian in character than was Lenin's elite "vanguard of the proletariat." The same regimes also use Leninist vocabulary—"democratic centralism," "Young Pioneers," "Politbureau," etc.—but this does not necessarily mean that the centralized totalitarianism of the Soviet Party is reproduced wherever the same terms are used.

Undoubtedly, there are strong authoritarian tendencies in the desire of the nationalist leaders to remold their societies by government action, but thus far there is little evidence of the characteristic totalitarian attempts at thought control, absolute unanimity, and the establishment of the infallibility of leader and party. The

---

[48] Soviet writers have criticized African leaders for their refusal to apply the Marxist class analysis to the West African scene. See David L. Morison, "Communism in Africa: Moscow's First Steps," *Problems of Communism*, X, No. 6 (November–December, 1961), 8–15.

emphasis is on persuasion, negotiation, and conciliation, while the threat or use of violence that has typically accompanied the totalitarian attempts to transform society is largely absent.[49] Moreover, with the exception perhaps of Nkrumah's version of Pan-Africanism, the ideology itself is limited in its goals to national independence and development and does not have the universality or inherent expansionism of the totalitarian doctrines.

Marxism-Leninism also provides a model of forced economic development by state action—a goal that the modernizing nationalists share. However, the lack of success of the Soviet and Chinese regimes in developing the agricultural sector of the economy should be a warning that their method is not without failings. The nationalists are not willing, thus far, to carry out a ruthless program of collectivization of rural producers, although the establishment of rural cooperatives is often part of their program. Similarly, except in Cuba, Algeria, and the U.A.R., there has been little actual large-scale nationalization or confiscation of private business and native industry, as called for by Marxist-Leninist dogma.

With the exception of Cuba, even the nationalists most heavily influenced by Marxism have criticized Soviet policy and taken measures against domestic Communist subversion. Sékou Touré, who has borrowed Soviet organizational techniques and accepted considerable amounts of Soviet aid, has twice publicly indicated his opposition to Soviet interference in the affairs of other countries—in his 1960 speech to the United Nations and during the "teachers' plot" in 1961, which led to the departure of the Soviet Ambassador from Guinea. While they are willing to use the Soviet Union for their own purposes, as Nasser did in 1955 in order to reduce his dependence on the West for military and economic aid, the nationalist leaders have no desire to substitute one form of domination for another, or to adopt what is to them an alien ideology.

The modernizing regimes need an ideology because they are engaged in a social and economic revolution and they must dramatize the changes they wish to bring about. But it is an ideology resembling that of Atatürk more than that of Marx—an ideology of development and industrialization based in national culture

---

[49] The lack of violence in African politics is emphasized in Herbert J. Spiro, *Politics in Africa, Prospects South of the Sahara* (Englewood Cliffs, N.J.: Prentice-Hall, 1962).

and tradition and related to local conditions.[50] As the Cuban example demonstrates, it is necessary to have an organization as well as a specific program; if not, the local Communist Party's superior organizational techniques and tactical skill may enable it to take over the social and economic revolution that the nationalist leader is attempting to bring about. But with a strong party organization, a popular leader, and some progress in meeting the desire for modernization and development, a nation can pursue its own course without resort to Communist ideology or affiliation with the Soviet bloc.

These are the goals of modernizing nationalism: national independence; rapid economic development; the creation of a nation-state governed by a regime based on a populist identification of leader, party, and people; regional federation; and nonalignment in international affairs. There is no mention of liberal pluralistic democracy in the Western sense, because—except for countries like Nigeria and India, where the leadership, experience, and internal balance of forces favor political development along Western lines—the theory and practice of constitutional democracy as it is known in Europe or North America is not much in evidence. What has emerged in the developing nations is a reasonably coherent set of ideas about society and government which constitutes the ideology of modernizing nationalism. It is in the hope of achieving a better understanding of these ideas that the selections from the speeches and writings of a wide range of nationalist leaders are presented in this volume.

[50] For an earlier version of modernizing nationalism, see the program of "Kemalism," published by Atatürk's party in 1935. (Printed as Appendix E to Donald E. Webster, *The Turkey of Atatürk* [Philadelphia: The American Academy of Political and Social Science, 1939], pp. 307–18; note particularly the economic and cultural sections.) The Turkish example poses the question of the capacity of modernizing nationalism to maintain its dynamism when it is in power for an extended period.

INTRODUCTION
TO THE REVISED EDITION

The gratifying response to the first edition of this collection and the new writings by leaders and intellectuals in the developing nations have made it desirable to prepare a revised and expanded version. Changes have been made in this edition on the basis of my own judgment as to what theories and ideas are either of intrinsic importance or widely influential today in Asia, Africa, and Latin America. I have been assisted by many helpful suggestions by specialists in the areas concerned, but the ultimate decisions have necessarily been my own.

The introduction to the first edition has been retained, with a few minor changes to bring it up to date. While there have been important political developments in the four years since the first edition was published, it continues to be a reasonably accurate summary of the main themes in the thinking of the nationalist leaders. The significant developments since the first edition have been three. First, a number of important new statements of ideological principles have been published, some of which have been included in this edition. Second, the course of national and international politics, especially in Africa, has served to test some of the ideas and programs contained in the ideologies set forth in the earlier edition. Finally, there is now a considerable literature outside the developing areas which is devoted to a critical analysis of the theory and practice of the policy-makers in the developing nations. This new introduction will attempt to review these developments and to relate them to the themes discussed in the previous section.

Ideology and Modernization

The tentative definition of ideology given in the first introduction seems still valid, although there is no doubt that the term is an exceedingly difficult one to define with precision. Most recent discussions of ideology have emphasized function rather than content —the importance of an action-oriented belief system in explaining

41

the world, justifying action, limiting policy choices, and creating social solidarity. The origins of the term have been traced to the French philosopher Destutt de Tracy, who at the end of the eighteenth century attempted to establish an empirically based science of ideas—an attempt which provoked the opposition of Napoleon to the "ideologues" who were subverting morality and religion.[1] It was with Marx, however, in such works as *The German Ideology*, that the term received its present-day connotation of distortion, the attempt to conceal one's real motives behind a cloak of ideational rationalizations. But whereas for Marx ideology was based on the relations of the forces of production, for later writers it has meant any attempt to justify or rationalize a situation or a needed change through a systematic body of value-laden ideas.

Ideology, then, can be used in two principal senses—as a body of ideas that serves as a guide and impulse to action, and as a systematic distortion, exaggeration, or simplification which has other bases besides the attempt to understand and evaluate the world of experience and action. In the case of the political leader, this implies a difference between a sincere attempt to translate values into a systematic guide to action, and the devious and manipulative use of rational and emotional symbols to attain or retain power or to further some other interest. This is not to say that one can make this kind of assessment in every individual case, but only to indicate that the term can be used either descriptively or pejoratively. The discussion in this book tends to the first interpretation, although, as the earlier introduction has indicated, the need to persuade the people to participate in modernization and nation-building is an inducement to the development of ideological justifications which are inevitably somewhat exaggerated and simplified.

Nationalism has been criticized as a contentless ideology that merely defines the political frame of reference and goes no

---

[1] For recent discussions of ideology, see David Apter (ed.), *Ideology and Discontent* (New York: Free Press of Glencoe, 1964), especially the introduction and Chaps. I and V; Daniel Bell, *The End of Ideology* (rev. ed.; New York: Free Press of Glencoe, 1965), especially the epilogue; Robert E. Lane, *Political Ideology* (New York: Free Press of Glencoe, 1962); Judith N. Shklar (ed.), *Political Theory and Ideology* (New York: Macmillan, 1966); and I. William Zartman, "National Interest and Ideology," in Vernon McKay (ed.), *African Diplomacy* (New York: Frederick A. Praeger, 1966), pp. 25–54.

further.[2] Yet nationalists in the developing countries are concerned with more than simple geographic boundaries. It is a *modernizing* nationalism that is being analyzed here—and the adjective helps to explain the goals, if not the methods.

The literature on modernization and development has expanded considerably since the first edition of this book was published. It is generally agreed that *political* modernization describes the phenomena of centralization, integration, rationalization, and specialization of function which modern states exhibit. There remains a lively controversy as to whether democratization is also a characteristic of the modern politically developed state.[3] In *economic* terms, industrialization and self-sustained growth are two indices of development, while the size of per capita income and gross national product measure the relative position of various nations.[4] *Psychologically*, the development of an open and flexible attitude to change and to human relations is said to mark the citizen of the modern state. *Socially*, the breakdown of traditional and ascriptive distinctions and their replacement by standards based on universalistic norms and achievement are characteristic of modern social life.[5]

[2] Nationalism is "inherently a subjective sentiment from which nothing further may be logically derived." Leonard Binder, "The Ideological Foundations of Egyptian Arab Nationalism," in Apter, *Ideology and Discontent*, p. 129.

[3] On political development, see A. F. K. Organski, *The Stages of Political Development* (New York: Alfred A. Knopf, 1965); Samuel Huntington, "Political Development and Political Decay," in *World Politics*, XVII, No. 3 (April, 1965), 386–430 (an article which attempts to differentiate between political development and modernization); J. Roland Pennock, "Political Development, Political Systems, and Political Goods," *World Politics*, XVIII, No. 3 (April, 1966), 415–34, and the literature cited therein; Lucian Pye, "The Concept of Political Development," *Annals of the American Academy of Political and Social Science*, CCCLVIII (March, 1965), 1–11, and *Aspects of Political Development* (Boston: Little, Brown, 1965); Ann R. Willner, "The Underdeveloped Study of Political Development," *World Politics*, XVI, No. 3 (April, 1964), 468–82; and, especially, Cyril E. Black, *The Dynamics of Modernization* (New York: Harper & Row, 1966).

[4] Cf. W. W. Rostow, *The Stages of Economic Growth* (Cambridge and New York: Cambridge University Press, 1960); and Max F. Millikan and Donald L. M. Blackmer (eds.), *The Emerging Nations* (Boston: Little, Brown, 1961).

[5] Cf. Daniel Lerner, *The Passing of Traditional Society* (Glencoe, Ill.: The Free Press, 1958); and Lucian Pye, *Politics, Personality, and Nation-Building* (New Haven, Conn.: Yale University Press, 1962).

But modernization is a highly general goal, and the argument of the preceding section has been that there is also a very large consensus on means among the leaders of Africa, Asia, and the Middle East, if not of Latin America. It may be useful, therefore, to re-examine some of these means as well as the goals at which they are directed, both to determine whether there is, in fact, such a consensus and to evaluate the attempt to achieve those goals.

National Independence

In their attitude toward the question of national independence, the nationalist leaders and intellectuals continue to be divided along the radical and reformist lines sketched out earlier. The most radical position has now been taken by the Chinese, who urge that less developed countries achieve their independence by waging guerrilla war against the developed powers of the world. Despite differences on other matters, the Chinese and the Cubans are in fundamental agreement on this point—although Castro makes exceptions for certain countries in Latin America where an evolutionary development may be permitted.[6] The Algerians, due to their own history, also tend to endorse revolutionary violence as the way to achieve political independence, and one writer influenced by their experience has even praised violence for its liberating and elevating effects. The African leaders, most of whom came to power without violence, are less certain of its utility, although when they look to the situation in the southern part of their continent it is difficult for them to see any other solution.[7] The influence of Christianity and of Mahatma Gandhi, and their own fear of endorsing the use of violence against themselves, however, work in favor of a preference for nonviolent methods of achieving power.

A second area of differentiation between radicals and reformists

[6] See Lin Piao, "The Victory of the People's War," and Fidel Castro, "The Road to Revolution in Latin America" (below, pp. 83–89, and 330–35).

[7] See Frantz Fanon, "Concerning Violence," in *The Wretched of the Earth* (New York: Grove Press; London: McGibbon and Kee, 1965), pp. 27–84, and the extract below, pp. 187–98. See also Kwame Nkrumah, *Conscienism* (London: Heinemann Educational Books; New York: Monthly Review Press, 1964), p. 74 (on reform and revolution in Africa); and Tom Mboya, *Freedom and After* (Boston: Little, Brown, 1963), where he states, "Even those who accept Gandhi's philosophy find there are limitations to its use in Africa" (p. 52).

is that of neocolonialism. While both groups are opposed in principle to the continuation of colonial control through other means, the radicals' definition of the term is much broader, including almost any relationship with an economically or politically stronger developed country, particularly if that country is the former colonial power.[8] The moderates are less likely to use the term and less reluctant to make defense or economic agreements with the former metropole. Yet even in these cases there is an inevitable tendency to loosen the ties established in the colonial period and to develop alternative economic and political relationships.

An exploitative relationship is not the only one possible between a newly independent country and its former colonial master. A reverse exploitation is also possible when a former colonial power pays an artificially high price for the tropical products of its ex-colonies. The developing countries wish to extend this arrangement still further, arguing that because of the inequities of the world market it is necessary for the developed countries to subsidize the products of the less developed. This argument, which has been put forward in Latin America for a number of years, has now been extended to all the developing countries through the medium of the United Nations Conference on Trade and Development.[9]

In the view of the radical left and the Communists of the Fidelist or Maoist variety, revolutionary violence is the only solution to the continuation of neocolonialism. Nothing has really been changed by the transfer of political power, it is said, and only by a radical and violent transformation of social and economic structures can the society be modernized and developed. In a political universe which has seen examples of sham democracy, the falsification of electoral procedures, and the corruption of parties, the argument against a more moderate policy has great appeal. Yet when the former revolutionary is in power he is com-

---

[8] See the lengthy list of "manifestations" and "agents" of neocolonialism (defined as "the survival of the colonial system in spite of the formal recognition of political independence") in the resolution adopted at the Third All-African Peoples' Conference in Cairo in March, 1961, printed in Colin Legum, *Pan-Africanism* (rev. ed.; New York: Frederick A. Praeger, 1965), pp. 272–75. Kwame Nkrumah defines neocolonialism as "any oblique attempt of a foreign power to thwart, balk, corrupt, or otherwise pervert the true independence of a sovereign people" (below, p. 260).

[9] See the report by Raúl Prebisch, its Secretary General (below, pp. 379 ff.).

pelled to recognize that it is no easy matter to transform an entire society and culture. He may lay the blame on the machinations of imperialists and neocolonialists, but he soon discovers that his real enemies are underdevelopment, ignorance, apathy, and corruption.

Revival of Traditional Culture

One of the ways for a nation to assert its independence is to turn to its traditional culture for inspiration. This is also a means of re-establishing links between the new leaders and the majority of the population which has not been uprooted, modernized, and secularized. Examples of this have occurred in the Middle East, where leaders such as Bourguiba and Nasser struggle to demonstrate that their reforms are in keeping with the spirit, if not the letter, of the Koran.[10] The political vitality of traditional religion has also been demonstrated in Turkey, where the secularizing efforts of Ataturk have not prevented religious appeals by politicians in recent elections. Islamic elements were also principal supporters of the bloody Indonesian reaction against the Communist Party in the fall of 1965.

It is not always the case that traditional elements will block modernization. They sometimes serve as the basis for more typically modern interest groups or political parties, as is the case with the caste associations in India and the Northern Peoples Congress in Nigeria, which until the military coup of January, 1966, was using traditional lines of authority and association to create a modern political party.[11] In other cases, however, such as the communal parties of India, the insistence that a religious or ethnic group be given preference undermines the equality and unity which is required for the creation of a modern state.

Of the modernized versions of traditional culture in Africa, Senghor's notion of "Negritude" continues to be a source of dis-

[10] See Bourguiba, "The Fast of Ramadan" (below, pp. 173–78); and Kamil al-Shinnawi, "Against Ramadan Reform," in Benjamin Rivlin and Joseph Szyliowicz (eds.), *The Contemporary Middle East* (New York: Random House, 1965), pp. 174–78. The Islamic element in the Algerian revolution has become more evident since the overthrow of Ben Bella in June, 1965.

[11] See Lloyd I. Rudolph, "The Modernity of Tradition: the Democratic Incarnation of Caste in India," *American Political Science Review*, LIX, No. 4 (December, 1965), 975–89.

agreement, especially between English-speaking and French-speaking Africans. The controversy was given renewed emphasis in the spring of 1966 at the Festival of Negro Arts, sponsored by the Government of Senegal, at which Negritude was attacked by some as a form of reverse racism.[12] Regardless of the evaluation of the underlying philosophic conception which inspired it, the festival demonstrated that African independence has stimulated wide interest in native art, literature, music, and sculpture.

In Latin America, in addition to Haya de la Torre's theory of "Indo-America," mention should be made of the Mexican Government's effort to glorify the accomplishments of the pre-Columbian Indian civilizations, and to integrate the Indian and the mestizo into the national culture and life. This search for native cultural roots is less common among Latin American leaders, however, most of whom give little attention to the cultural contribution of the Indian.

Rapid Economic Development through "Socialist" Methods

Once national independence has been established, how is economic development to be achieved and neocolonialist dependence avoided? A majority of the leaders of Africa, the Middle East, and Asia (but not of Latin America) would reply, "through socialism." (The exceptions would include Haile Selassie of Ethiopia, the leaders of the Philippines, Turkey, Lebanon, Jordan, and Saudi Arabia, the new military rulers of Ghana and Nigeria, and, perhaps, Felix Houphouet-Boigny of the Ivory Coast.) This surprising agreement on the rejection of a stereotyped capitalism and acceptance of an undefined socialism was noted in the earlier edition, but a critical examination of this unanimity has revealed that the use of the term does not necessarily imply the adoption of the same measures, or even a common understanding of its meaning. Thus the excerpts in this book reveal an important difference of emphasis among the various versions of African socialism put for-

[12] Newell Flather, "Impressions of the Dakar Festival," *Africa Report*, XI, No. 5 (May, 1966), 57–60; and Ellen Kennedy and Paulette J. Trout, "The Roots of African Negritude," *Africa Report*, XI, No. 5 (May, 1966), 61–62. Not discussed in the latter article are "The French Influences of Léopold Senghor's Theory of Negritude, 1928–1948," the title of a paper given at the African Studies Association meeting in October, 1965, by Jacques Louis Hymans, who is preparing a book on Senghor's thought.

ward by Nkrumah, Sékou Touré, Senghor, Nyerere, and the Kenya cabinet, as well as the different types of socialism in other areas represented by the Destourian socialism of Bourguiba, the Ba'thist Party in Syria, the Arab socialism of Nasser, and Sukarno's now discredited Indonesian socialism. On the theoretical level, the emphasis may be on a Marxist-influenced state control and central direction (Nkrumah and Touré's writings), on a type of humanism and social concern (Senghor and Nyerere), or on increased economic equality and freedom from exploitation (Nasser). On the practical level there is also great diversity. Nkrumah had put so little of his theory into practice that it was relatively easy for the military regime which succeeded him to dismantle the state enterprises he had set up. Touré has been careful not to touch his greatest source of foreign exchange, the foreign-owned Fria bauxite plant, and has returned trade and distribution to private enterprise. The Kenya Government Sessional Paper's discussion of nationalization makes it clear that this will only be a last resort in that country, while Algeria and the United Arab Republic now have nationalized large sections of their industry, although not their agriculture. When we look to the former French colonies in West and Central Africa, other than Guinea and Mali, we find that their theoretical preference for socialism has meant in practice a limited amount of government planning and a small number of welfare programs which are often beyond their economic means to support.[13] Thus to say that many of the leaders of the

[13] On the meaning of African socialism, see the special issue of *Africa Report* of May, 1963; A. Fenner Brockway, *African Socialism* (London: Bodley Head; Chester, Springs, Pa.: Dufour Editions, 1963); and William H. Friedland and Carl G. Rosberg, Jr. (eds.), *African Socialism* (Stanford, Calif.: Stanford University Press, 1964). The latter has an article comparing the thought of Touré and Senghor by Charles F. Andrain, who has also written similar analyses in Apter, *Ideology and Discontent*, Chap. v (under the title "Democracy and Socialism: Ideologies of African Leaders"), and in *African Forum*, I, No. 3 (Winter, 1966), 41–60 (entitled "Patterns of African Socialist Thought"). Another useful source of African views is contained in the proceedings of the Colloquium on African Socialism held at Dakar in December, 1962, and published by Présence Africaine in Paris in 1963 under the title *Colloque sur les Politiques de Développement et les Diverses Voies Africaines vers le Socialisme*. For the genesis of Nasser's Arab Socialism, see Leonard Binder, "Nasserism: The Protest Movement in the Middle East," in Morton A. Kaplan (ed.), *The Revolution in World Politics* (New York: John Wiley, 1962), pp. 152–74, as well as Binder's *The Ideological Revolution in the Middle East* (New York: John Wiley, 1964).

Third World are socialists is not to reveal much about their ideas or their policies. It is also to ignore the numerous exceptions to this generalization, as well as the whole of Latin America, where comparatively few leaders are avowed socialists even when they pursue policies similar to those described as socialist elsewhere.[14]

Yet there are some common themes in the discussion of socialism in the developing countries. There is a belief in the necessity of government action to stimulate economic development and a corresponding rejection of laissez-faire liberalism. There is an endorsement of controls on foreign investment, combined with an undoctrinaire readiness to invite such investment to help to develop the country.[15] There is a denunciation of selfishness, exploitation, and class conflict, and a hope that by government appeals and political education the people can be persuaded to cooperate for the good of the nation. There is, most important, a belief that rational planning can result in the elimination of waste, inefficiency, and selfishness, both domestically and in international economic relations.

A general preference for the interests of society over those of the individual and for government over private action may be said to characterize governments which call themselves socialist, but these preferences will be implemented in a variety of ways. In Guinea the government tries to harness idle manpower through *investissement humain*. In Senegal, it is *animation rural*. In Tanzania it is self-help, "villagization," and the substitution of leaseholding for freehold titles. A number of these programs have been de-emphasized in recent years or replaced with more direct appeals to self-interest, but, if they have not had the hoped-for economic results, they have probably contributed to the political mobilization of the population.[16]

[14] This argument is put forward in greater detail in "Socialism and the Role of the State in Socio-Economic Change," Chap. IV of Charles W. Anderson, Fred R. Von der Mehden, and Crawford Young, *Issues of Political Development* (Englewood Cliffs, N.J.: Prentice-Hall, 1967). It is accompanied by a useful typology of the varieties of socialism in the developing areas.

[15] See, for example, the two-page advertisement in *The New York Times* of July 24, 1966, inviting foreign investment in the United Arab Republic. Between 1962 and 1964, Ghana, Guinea, and Mali, among the more radical African states, all drew up elaborate investment codes to induce foreign capital to help to develop their countries.

[16] For a pessimistic evaluation of the Guinean and Senegalese programs, see

Little criticism has been leveled at the various doctrines of socialism in the developing areas. It has been observed that the term itself is vague, and that those who appeal to it in theory do not always apply it in practice.[17] At least one American economist, however, has written a scathing attack on African socialism as "the wrong ideology in the wrong place at the wrong time," arguing that the lack of trained bureaucrats and the existence of a largely agricultural and subsistence economy make socialism in the sense of government-directed and controlled economic development unworkable in Africa at the present time.[18] He cites the failure of the state trading corporations and other centralized economic measures in Guinea. Experiences in Ghana, Nigeria, and Indonesia could also be cited to prove that the removal of competition does not eliminate, and may even encourage, waste, corruption, and inefficiency. It may even produce exploitation, the cardinal sin of capitalism, when the profits of the government-controlled sector of the economy are used to purchase luxurious homes, cars, and yachts for the new ruling class of politicians.

A further problem which has emerged in the discussion of socialism in the developing areas has been the relation between agriculture and industry. Much of the writing on socialism in African, Asian, and Latin American countries has emphasized the need

---

David Hapgood, *Africa: From Independence to Tomorrow* (New York: Atheneum, 1965). On those in Tanzania, see Fred G. Burke, "Tanganyika: The Search for Ujamaa," in Friedland and Rosberg, *op. cit.*, pp. 194–219.

[17] After his term as Vice Chancellor of the University of Ghana, Conor Cruise O'Brien spoke critically of the Ghanaian politicians under Nkrumah with "socialist slogans in their mouths and contractors' money in their pockets." The revelation after his overthrow of Nkrumah's use of his position to develop a large personal fortune did much to discredit his version of African socialism. Jeanne Mintz says of Indonesian socialism, "Although its slogans lay great stress on socialist doctrines, although its supporters reiterate its militant anti-capitalism and its unqualified rejection of political and economic liberalism, it can hardly be called a socialist system" (*Mohammed, Marx, and Marhaen: The Roots of Indonesian Socialism* [New York: Frederick A. Praeger, 1965], p. 224).

[18] Elliott J. Berg, "Socialism and Economic Development in Tropical Africa," *The Quarterly Journal of Economics*, LXXVIII, No. 4 (November, 1964), 571. It should be noted that Berg was careful to say that his analysis applied only to present-day Africa and not to a future situation in which the economy was more developed and there was a larger supply of administrators and bureaucrats. In his view it is socialism, not capitalism, which is "too complicated a system for a newly independent nation." (See Kwame Nkrumah, "Background to Independence," below, p. 255.)

for industrialization as the way to economic growth. Yet recent criticism has demonstrated that the first requirement is to feed the people and to develop exports so that they can earn sufficient revenue to purchase capital goods and build a domestic industry. Here the primary emphasis should be placed on getting farmers out of subsistence agriculture and into producing for the market, and on research and assistance in better farming techniques and the improved use of fertilizers. The problem has been underscored by recent indications that the United States stock of surplus food, which has been supplying food deficits in many parts of the world under Public Law 480, is rapidly dwindling, and that methods must be found to enable the developing countries to feed themselves.[19]

One method, by no means a solution but a step in dealing with the food problem, is the extension of birth control services and information. A considerable increase in public discussion of this problem, and, in Latin America, a possible modification of the opposition of the Roman Catholic Church, has meant that this particular kind of government action to promote economic development or at least prevent economic decline is likely to become more prominent in the writings and speeches of leaders of the developing areas in the future.[20]

Agricultural problems are different in different parts of the developing areas. In many Latin American countries and parts of Asia, the problem is one of inefficient farming methods and the concentration of landholdings in the hands of the few. In Africa, except for Kenya, land ownership is widespread and the problem is to get the small farmer to produce more. The partisans of African socialism often see cooperative farming as both an application of their ideology and a remedy for problems of food production, but so far, with the exception of the Gezira scheme in the Sudan, the cooperative schemes have not been notably successful. Even less successful have been the state farms in Ghana and Cuba.[21]

[19] On the food problem in developing countries see the breezily written but pessimistic *Hungry Nations*, by William and Paul Paddock (Boston: Little, Brown, 1964). The failure of West African leaders to deal adequately with the food problem is discussed in Hapgood, *op. cit.*, pp. 90 ff.

[20] For a discussion of the necessity of birth control, see the selection below by Bourguiba, pp. 182–83.

[21] On Cuba, see Jacques Chonchol, "Análisis Crítico de la Reforma Agraria Cubana," *El Trimestre Económico*, XXX, No. 1 (January–March, 1963), 69–143.

Much of the socialism versus capitalism debate deals with stereotypes rather than real systems of economics and politics. All governments today engage in planning, are concerned about the welfare of their citizens, and have placed some limits on private economic activity. And all, except for Communist governments, allow private investment, small business, and private landholding and agriculture. There are important differences in practice, but they are often differences of emphasis; on the other hand, two governments may be remarkably similar in practice while they describe what they are doing in very different ways.[22]

There is a difference, however, in value-preferences, terminology, and choices in a marginal situation. Given a choice, an American will opt for freedom of economic activity while the African or Asian may call for controls. In the event of a failure in economic development, the American is likely to blame the government while the African will place the blame on foreign capitalism, imperialism, or the structure of international trade. The American will describe his system as capitalist when his government controls 20 per cent of the gross national product, while the African or Asian will call his government socialist when far less is under government ownership or control.

There is still discussion of imperialist exploitation in the Leninist sense, but a new ideology of exploitation on the international level recently has been propagated in the developing areas. As a result of the Conference on Trade and Development held in Geneva from March to June, 1964, the focus has shifted to the exploitation which results from the terms of trade—the declining prices paid for raw materials and primary products in the international market as compared with the long-run rise in the price of manufactured goods. The conclusion drawn by many of the leaders of Asia, Africa, and Latin America, even those who do not call themselves socialists, is that there must be some kind of intergovernmental control mechanism to maintain raw material prices through commodity price agreements, and that until the less developed countries are able to build up their own industry, the developed countries should give a preference to the primary products of less developed countries and do away with their present tariff barriers and protection of domestic producers. The developed

[22] See Ralph K. White, " 'Socialism' and 'Capitalism', an International Misunderstanding," *Foreign Affairs*, XLIV, No. 2 (January, 1966), 216–28.

countries, especially the United States, have been reluctant to participate in what they see as an international cartel agreement which encourages inefficiency and taxes the consumer as a disguised form of foreign aid. Yet it can be argued that in nearly every developed country a program of farm price supports has been in effect that cushions the farmer from the same problems in the domestic market that the developing countries are experiencing internationally. The difference, of course, is that the domestic producers of primary products have elected representatives and pressure groups to defend their interests, while the developing countries have no such constituency.[23]

The Single or Dominant Nationalist Party

One of the most striking characteristics of the recent thinking of the leaders and intellectuals in the developing areas has been their disillusionment with the one-party political system. The first edition of this book included critical remarks by one Nigerian leader (who subsequently changed his mind). We now have adverse comments by writers of a variety of political perspectives as well as the experience of a series of military coups directed at corrupt and exploitative one-party governments in a number of African countries.[24]

Radicals criticize the single party because it enables conservatives and opportunists to repress those who wish to improve the lot of the people and end dependency on the metropole.[25] Libertarians argue that the single party leads to repression and stifles initiative, criticism, and free expression.[26] An intermediate position is taken by one writer who believes that while the single party is

[23] See selections below by Raúl Prebisch (pp. 368–82), as well as the discussions in Albert O. Hirschman (ed.), *Latin American Issues: Essays and Comments* (New York: The Twentieth Century Fund, 1961); and John Powelson, *Latin America: Today's Economic and Social Revolution* (New York: McGraw-Hill, 1964).

[24] Single-party governments were overthrown in 1965 and 1966 in Algeria, Dahomey, the Central African Republic, Upper Volta, and Ghana. The Nigerian revolt of January, 1966, was also directed at what were essentially single-party governments in the Western and Northern Regions.

[25] See the selection below by Frantz Fanon (pp. 187–98).

[26] See the selection below by Munif al-Razzaz (pp. 168–72), and William McCord, *The Springtime of Freedom* (London and New York: Oxford University Press, 1965), Part III.

necessary during the first years of independence it becomes increasingly reactionary and oppressive with the passage of time.[27] The supposed advantages of the one-party system in terms of stability, mobilization of talent for economic development, overcoming ethnic and other divisions, and its suitability to a communal society have also been challenged on both theoretical and factual grounds.[28]

The most telling criticism has been the actual conduct of many of the single-party regimes. Lacking a critical opposition, they have been able to engage in large-scale corruption and high living that make a mockery of the doctrines they profess. The golden bed purchased by the wife of one of Kwame Nkrumah's ministers was something of a symbol of this until Nkrumah's overthrow revealed that the minister was only following the example of his president.

It should be noted that this problem is by no means restricted to the more radical regimes. Moderate leaders have often been just as lavish in their spending, without receiving as much publicity. The temptations of unchecked power are great, and it demands the self-denial and devotion of a saint to resist the impulse to self-enrichment, although certain regimes (usually the more radical, e.g., Guinea, Mali, and Tanzania) have been notable for the puritanism and self-sacrifice of their elites.

The single-party system has assumed many different forms and it is difficult to evaluate it as a single phenomenon. In some cases, it has remained relatively open, and internal criticism has induced policy changes by the leadership. In others, the party itself seems largely to have disappeared after coming to power as its leaders take positions with the government, and a "no-party state" domi-

[27] See the article below by Bechir Ben Yahmed (pp. 184–86), and the debate on the single party from which it is drawn in the issues of *Jeune Afrique*, between November, 1963, and January, 1964. Earlier (October 7–13, 1961), its predecessor, *Afrique Action*, had published an article entitled "Pouvoir Personnel" (Personal Power), which was one of the first attacks on the charismatic leader and the single party.

[28] See the lectures by the West Indian economist Arthur Lewis, *Politics in West Africa* (London and New York: Oxford University Press, 1965), who proposes coalition government as the solution for African ethnic pluralism; Edward Shils, "The Role of the Opposition in the New States of Africa and Asia," *Government and Opposition*, I, No. 2 (January, 1966), 175–204; and Igor Kopytoff, "Socialism and Traditional Societies," in Friedland and Rosberg, *op. cit.*, pp. 53–62.

nated by politicians and bureaucrats replaces the one-party state.[29] An interesting experiment in providing a real choice and opportunity for criticism to the voter has been successfully carried out in Tanzania, where the party nominated two candidates for nearly every office in the September, 1965, elections (the presidency was a significant exception)—a direct result of Nyerere's thinking on "Democracy and the Party System" (excerpted below). What does not seem to have happened is the development of quasi-totalitarian "mobilization regimes" of the type feared not too long ago by Western observers. Whether because of institutional and personnel difficulties or internal beliefs and inhibitions, it is difficult to find a state among the developing nations (with the exception of Cuba) which approaches the totalitarian model in propaganda, thought control, and police repression. Some of the writings and speeches of the more radical leaders may make it appear that this will or should be the case, but investigation reveals that they are a long way from the German, Soviet, or Chinese models of totalitarianism.[30]

It is also an error to believe that all the states of Africa, the Middle East, and Asia which are not under military control have

[29] On the no-party state, see James S. Coleman and Carl G. Rosberg, Jr. (eds.), *Political Parties and National Integration in Tropical Africa* (Berkeley, Calif.: University of California Press, 1964), pp. 676–78; and Eduard Bustin, "The Quest for Political Stability in the Congo," in Herbert J. Spiro (ed.), *Africa: The Primacy of Politics* (New York: Random House, 1966), p. 41. The Coleman and Rosberg volume and Gwendolyn Carter (ed.), *African One-Party States* (Ithaca, N.Y.: Cornell University Press, 1962), provide useful insights into the various forms taken by the one-party state in Africa. An analysis of the specifics of the operation of the Tunisian single party may be found in Charles A. Micaud, Leon Carl Brown, and Clement H. Moore, *Tunisia: The Politics of Modernization* (New York: Frederick A. Praeger, 1964); and Clement H. Moore, *Dynamics of One-Party Government* (Berkeley, Calif.: University of California Press, 1965), and "Politics in a Tunisian Village," *Middle East Journal* (Autumn, 1963), pp. 527–40.

[30] See the discussion on this point in Clement H. Moore, "Mass Party Regimes in Africa," Spiro, *op. cit.*, pp. 85–115. Moore's criticisms are especially directed at Robert C. Tucker's article "Toward a Comparative Politics of Movement-Regimes," *American Political Science Review*, LV, No. 2 (June, 1961), 281–89. Tucker has since changed his views on the matter. For another interesting shift of position (more hostile to the single party), compare Martin Kilson's "Authoritarian and Single Party Tendencies in African Politics," *World Politics*, XV, No. 2 (January, 1963), 262–95, with his recent "Politics of African Socialism," *African Forum*, I, No. 3 (Winter, 1966), 17–26.

adopted the single-party form.[31] Kenya has specifically decided against legalizing the one-party state and has recently seen the left wing break off from the dominant national party and elect several representatives to the Parliament. Sierra Leone is studying the one-party option but has not yet adopted it. Sudan is governed by a party coalition and India, although largely under the control of one party, has allowed complete freedom to other parties—in some state governments it has entered into coalitions, and in one it was excluded from participation. Other countries with several active parties include Gambia, Morocco, Lebanon, Turkey, Israel, Malaysia, Ceylon, Indonesia, and the Philippines.

Yet the most common form of government in Africa is still that of the single party, often headed by a leader with charismatic appeal. For all its drawbacks, the single party has, in cases like Tanzania, Mali, and Guinea, been able to overcome ethnic and tribal divisions, forge national unity, and constitute an effective instrument of communication between the government and the people. So far, however, there has not been the evolution in the direction of party pluralism or the development of independent interest groups that was hoped for by early observers. It is true that trade unions had important roles in the overthrow of the governments of Upper Volta (1965) and the Congo-Brazzaville (1964) and have played a significant critical role in Nigeria. However, the result has been either a more radically authoritarian government (the Congo-Brazzaville) or military control.

The Role of the Military

The emergence of the military in the developing areas should come as no surprise to anyone familiar with the history of Latin American politics since independence in the early nineteenth century. In the face of the "revolution of rising frustrations" under civilian rule, the military, citing the corruption and inefficiency around them, step in to reform the government and administer it in the hierarchical fashion in which their own military establishment is organized. Little attempt is made to justify military control on ideological grounds except as a negative reaction to the excesses of the civilian governments which preceded them. A spirit

[31] This seems to be the assumption in the discussion "Party Charisma in the Afro-Asian Bloc," in Irving Louis Horowitz, *Three Worlds of Development* (London and New York: Oxford University Press, 1966), Chap. VIII.

of puritanism and sacrifice is urged upon the people and administrative and economic reforms are promised. In the case of Nasser, over a period of almost ten years a more complete ideology was developed, but most military men are content to rely on nationalism and promises of reform to gain the support of the people. The lack of a single military ideology is illustrated in the contrast between the two coups in Nigeria and Ghana in early 1966. In Nigeria, the military leaders promised increased centralization, and attempted to modify the Nigerian federal system; in Ghana, the National Liberation Council appointed a commission to draw up a constitution based on the separation of powers so as to prevent the concentration of power in the hands of a single individual.[32] It cannot even be said that the military are more likely to be pro-Western in their orientation. Nasser is not the only military leader prepared to use Communist assistance to weaken his enemies. Ayub Khan's British military training did not prevent him from effecting rapprochement with China when he saw this as useful in Pakistan's dispute with India. Perón in Argentina was also strongly anti-American by the end of his regime.

What can be said is that the military are likely to have a technocratic orientation, an inclination to use government resources to mobilize the country by the use or threat of coercion, and a deep distrust of civilian politicians. Conversely, military rulers often lack the ability to respond to the people's needs and desires as effectively as the civilian politician. And like his civilian counterpart, the military ruler often finds it difficult to resist the temptation to use his position to secure privileges for members of his profession.[33]

If it is difficult to discern a single pattern among the military of the new nations, a distinction can at least be made between conservatives and reformers in attitudes toward social change.

[32] See the statement by General J. A. Ankrah (below, pp. 263–68).

[33] On the role of the military, see John J. Johnson (ed.), *The Role of the Military in Underdeveloped Countries* (Princeton, N.J.: Princeton University Press, 1962); William Gutteridge, *Armed Forces in the New States* (London and New York: Oxford University Press, 1962); and Morris Janowitz, *The Military in the Political Development of New Nations* (Chicago: University of Chicago Press, 1964). On the military in specific regions, see Sydney N. Fisher (ed.), *The Military in Middle Eastern Society and Politics* (Columbus, Ohio: Ohio State University Press, 1963); and Edwin Lieuwen, *Arms and Politics in Latin America* (New York: Frederick A. Praeger, 1961), and *Generals vs. Presidents* (New York: Frederick A. Praeger, 1964).

Perón in Argentina, Nasser in the United Arab Republic, Ayub Khan in Pakistan, and Kemal Ataturk in Turkey are examples of military reformers who have worked with varying degrees of success to achieve modernization and social progress in their countries. Many others (especially in Latin America) could be cited who did not succeed or did not wish to succeed in making any changes in the traditional order of their societies. As the above examples indicate, however, there is no necessary connection between a military background and conservatism.

What does seem almost inevitable is a lack of sensitivity to political pressures which, necessary at times, may at other times lead to disaster. Nasser has recognized the need to supplement military rule by a mass party which will establish a two-way communication between the government and the people, and has repeatedly attempted to establish a single official party; the latest and most successful is the Arab Socialist Union, created in 1962. The incapacity of the Sudanese military rulers to deal with the two problems of the revolt in the south and the dissatisfaction of the university students in Khartoum led to the resignation of the military in that country in 1964 and a return to democratic government. In Latin America, the alternation of military and civilian governments has by now become an established pattern in countries like Argentina, Ecuador, and Guatemala.

In Africa, a similar but not identical pattern of alternation between civilian single-party governments and rule by military reformers may be emerging. Alternatively, the military or civilian leader may develop the necessary combination of sensitivity, demagogy, and ruthlessness which will enable him to remain in power for a considerable time. Recent events have demonstrated that there is no necessary connection, however, between a single party or a military regime and stability in government.

Regionalism

The relationship between stability and development, a delicate one in internal politics, is even more difficult in international and regional relations. In Africa, the emphasis in regional affairs has moved more and more in the direction of assuring stability even if this favors the more conservative nations. In Latin America, which has seen a long period of relative stability in its own regional relations, the pressures are building for a greater effort for political and economic development. The same kind of dichotomy, in the form of a choice between regional unity and opposition of the moderate and radical states, characterizes regional relations in the Middle East; in Asia the disparity of interests, ideology, and power have made any kind of regional organization impractical.

The most important change in regional relationships in Africa since the first edition of this book was published was the establishment of the Organization of African Unity at Addis Ababa in May, 1963. For a time, at least, this obscured the division between the radical Casablanca and the moderate Monrovia groups in African politics. It also established an instrument through which some important efforts at conciliation of disputes have been made (e.g., between Mauritania and Morocco, Algeria and Morocco, and Somalia, Kenya, and Ethiopia), and created a Liberation Committee to coordinate efforts to free the territories remaining under European domination.

Yet important differences remained, and were expressed in the organization in maneuvering for influence and policy. The Congo rebellion of 1964 and the accession of Moise Tshombe as Premier of the central government exacerbated the differences between those who wished to adhere to the OAU Charter's insistence on noninterference in the affairs of others and those who felt that the first requirement was to liberate Africa from neocolonialist and imperialist-dominated regimes. The result was the re-emergence, not of the entire Monrovia group, but of the French-speaking moderates in the African and Malagasy Common Organization (OCAM) in February, 1965, to provide an instrument for the closer cooperation of like-minded moderates in politics, economics, and international relations.[34]

In the ideology of Pan-Africanism, the aims of regional unity are to present a united front to outside powers, to regulate internal disputes, and to prevent Balkanization of the continent. All-African pressure has been brought to bear on issues relating to colonialism and white domination, although even on this question there

[34] The Charter of the Organization of African Unity is reproduced below (pp. 204–7). It appears to represent a victory for the moderates, who were in a majority at Addis Ababa. However, a Guinean, Diallo Telli, was elected Secretary General, and the Cairo meeting of 1964, from which Tshombe was excluded, seemed to convince the moderates that they should recreate their own organization. (See the communiqué of the first OCAM meeting, below, pp. 210–11.)

was serious division in early 1966 on the forcefulness of the measures to be taken against Rhodesia. Some disputes have been successfully mediated, although on the most serious problem, that of the Congo rebellion in 1964, the OAU efforts were largely ignored by the Congolese government and the Western powers. The issue of subversion became another source of division in 1965, when the OCAM powers accused Ghana of harboring revolutionaries working for their overthrow. With the military coup against Nkrumah this should no longer be a serious problem.

Other smaller regional associations are likely to develop in the future, within or outside of the OAU. The East African Common Market negotiations have been progressing more slowly than expected, largely because of fear of Kenyan domination (Kenya has 70 per cent of the industry in the area). The Entente, an association of French-speaking West African states under the leadership of the Ivory Coast, continues to function. Other efforts are likely to be made in West Africa to secure the advantages of closer association, particularly in the economic field. And the African caucus, with some thirty-six members, will continue to exert an important influence in the United Nations General Assembly.

When one turns to the Middle East, the differences between radicals and moderates emerge with even greater intensity. The Middle East continues to be divided between the United Arab Republic, Syria, and Iraq on the one hand, and Saudi Arabia, Jordan, Libya, and, to some extent, Lebanon on the other. A similar division exists in North Africa between Algeria and the more moderate states of Tunisia and Morocco. At one time the only bond between these states was a common opposition to the state of Israel, but even here the ranks have been broken by Bourguiba, who has advocated a compromise settlement. The emergence of smaller groups, such as a closer union of the North African (Maghreb) countries, or an Islamic-based organization led by Saudi Arabia, is a possibility in the future.

In Latin America, the situation is complicated by the existence of the Organization of American States, which unites the Latin American countries and the United States. Proposals continue to be made for a closer political union of the Latin American states without the participation of the United States (and even as a counterweight to it), but the fact that the OAS performs many of the functions of such a regional organization has limited initiatives in this direction.[35] In 1964, a Latin American Parliament was formed which held its first meeting in Lima in 1965, but the principal political activity on a regional basis takes place in the meetings of the Organization of American States. A notable example of this was the way in which the Latin American states met and acted as a bloc in the Panama preparatory meeting for the OAS Foreign Ministers Conference, held from February to April, 1966.

In the area of economic unity, pressure for closer ties continues to be exerted, especially under the leadership of Eduardo Frei, the Christian Democratic President of Chile. The Latin American Free Trade Association is still a very loose arrangement for mutual agreements on the reduction of tariffs on specific items, but the reports of the Economic Commission for Latin America, and the writings and speeches of many Latin American leaders, call for its strengthening in the future. The real success story in the area of regional economic cooperation has been the Central American Common Market, which in the few years of its existence has promoted a great economic expansion in that area, and perhaps provides a model for similar sub-regional associations in other parts of Latin America.[36] As in the political area, much of the important regional economic activity is carried on through the Organization of American States and through the Alliance for Progress, which is associated with it although still largely under American control. (Although the Alliance for Progress is simply the Latin American section of the Agency for International Development [AID], the advisory Inter-American Committee for the Alliance for Progress includes Latin Americans among its members; proposals have also been made to vest control of the Alliance in an OAS body such as the Economic and Social Council.)[37]

The division between radicals concerned with continental libera-

[35] See the Charter of Rio de Janeiro, drawn up by the Latin American Christian trade unions (below, pp. 405–9), for an expression of the desire for a Latin American political union.

[36] See Miguel S. Wionczek, *Latin American Economic Integration* (New York: Frederick A. Praeger, 1966); and Sydney Dell, *A Latin American Common Market?* (London and New York: Oxford University Press, 1966). The latter includes a letter by Eduardo Frei proposing a Latin American Common Market similar to that endorsed at the Punta del Este Presidents' meeting in April, 1967.

[37] See the speech by the Chilean Foreign Minister Gabriel Valdes at the OAS Foreign Ministers Conference in Rio de Janeiro in November, 1965, printed by the Chilean foreign ministry.

tion and moderates who favor nonintervention also exists in Latin America. The single advocate of the export of revolution to all parts of Latin America, Castro's Cuba, has been excluded from all organs of the Organization of American States. However, there still remain differences between those who wish the organization to take a more active role in the extension of democracy and human rights in the hemisphere and those who see the organization as committed to nonintervention. The conflict became even more confused in the wake of the Dominican intervention of 1965 when some of those most committed to democracy, such as Chile and Mexico, actively opposed the establishment of an OAS Inter-American Peace Force on the grounds that this was a violation of the principle of nonintervention. (Their real grounds seem to have been the fear of establishing a precedent for similar antirevolutionary forays by the OAS in the future.)

On a broader scale, the notion of a unity of interest and action among the Afro-Asians which was propagated at the Bandung Conference of 1955 has suffered some setbacks in recent years—the attempt to hold a second conference in Algiers in 1965 foundered on internal difficulties and problems related to the Sino-Soviet split. Efforts have also been made to establish a unity of action among the developing nations as a whole. The Communist-sponsored Tricontinental Solidarity Conference in Havana in January, 1966, established a provisional organization and called for another meeting in Cairo. A more important effort to establish solidarity among the countries of Asia, Africa, and Latin America was the creation of a permanent organization by the United Nations Conference on Trade and Development in June, 1964. References are already being made to "the Geneva 75," the group of less developed countries in the United Nations which are now beginning to act together to extract concessions from the developed nations.

Nonalignment in International Relations

Various international developments are making the concept of nonalignment increasingly obsolete. The division between the developed and the developing countries is beginning to overshadow the East-West division on which earlier concepts of nonalignment were based. The increasing intensity of the Sino-Soviet split and the divisions in the West make it difficult to analyze international relations in terms of a bipolar model. In addition, the less active role of the Soviet Union in the developing areas since the over-throw of Khrushchev, and disillusionment in the United States with foreign aid, have meant that there is less opportunity for less developed countries to exploit their nonaligned position. The Chinese attack on India in 1962 resulted in the shift of a leading exponent of nonalignment to a somewhat more favorable attitude to the West—although India continues to get considerable assist-ance from the Soviet Union.

Yet most countries in Africa and Asia (but not in Latin Amer-ica) continue to favor nonalignment, although there are various conceptions of what that position implies. For the radicals, it means the termination of all military relations with the former colonial power. For those who have agreements for military assist-ance (as do many of the former French colonies), it simply means nonmembership in an Eastern or Western bloc.[38] For both groups, however, nonalignment offers a way of opting out of the East-West struggle, and making an independent assessment of the individual questions related to it.

The role of the developing countries as peacemakers or media-tors between the big powers has also received less attention in re-cent years. It is true that the Africans and Asians have a clear majority on the U.N. Disarmament Committee, and that the Secretary General will in the future be drawn from one of the Afro-Asian countries. But it has become evident that the major powers prefer to settle their differences through bilateral negotia-tions, and that peace-making efforts by leaders of the developing nations have become less prominent than in the past.

The leaders of the developing countries have indicated their opposition to revolutionary or subversive activity by a major power of either bloc. Yet here, too, there is a difference between the atti-tudes of the radicals and the moderates. The Chinese lost support throughout Africa when their foreign minister announced that the continent was "ripe for revolution," but the Chinese attitude was

[38] Cf. the confusion over the list of invitees to the Belgrade and Cairo Con-ferences of Nonaligned Nations. On the definition of nonalignment, see Cecil V. Crabb, Jr., *The Elephants and the Grass* (New York: Frederick A. Praeger, 1965); and Doudou Thiam, *The Foreign Policy of African States* (London: Phoenix House; New York: Frederick A. Praeger, 1965). In addition to the discussions below by Nehru, Sukarno, Nyerere, Nasser, and others, see the documents on the subject collected in Paul Power (ed.), *Neutralism and Disengagement* (New York: Charles Scribner's, 1964).

denounced with particular vehemence by Houphouet-Boigny, the leader of the moderate French-speaking group. Western attempts at subversion tend to be the objects of attacks by the radicals, and it was as a Western plot that the overthrow of Nkrumah was seen by the more radical Africans. The distinction which has been made between "Western-oriented" and "pro-Eastern" leaders may be exaggerated, but it has some basis in fact, even though both groups claim to be objectively neutral.[39]

Modernizing Nationalism and Communism

The distinction between Communism and modernizing nationalism made in the earlier edition of this book has become still clearer in the intervening years. No state in the developing areas has joined the Communist world since Castro's decision to do so in 1960–61. It is true that Indonesia was working closely with China until September, 1965, and that Communist-oriented leadership has had considerable influence in the Congo (Brazzaville) and in Zanzibar (before it joined Tanganyika to form the Republic of Tanzania). The same is true of some, although not all, of the leaders of the rebellion in the Congo in 1964. Yet it is only in Vietnam that an early and clear identification of nationalism with Communism has enabled the Communist leadership to channel the appeal of modernization and nationalism in the direction of Communism. Elsewhere, nationalist leaders have been careful to develop their own ideologies and to maintain their independence, even when working closely with the Soviet Union or China or receiving considerable assistance from them.

Yet this does not exclude the possibility of a nationalist-Communist synthesis in other areas. As it becomes evident that not all of the promises of the nationalist leaders can be implemented, it is possible that revolutionary movements modeling themselves on the Chinese example may become more important in the developing areas. This has already become the case among guerrilla movements in Latin America, in such countries as Guatemala, Colombia, Venezuela, and Peru, where guerrilla movements with Chinese

[39] Thus the military leaders who overthrew Nkrumah in Ghana in February, 1966, did so in the name of nonalignment. (See General Ankrah's statement below, p. 267.) Similar considerations were voiced in the reversal of Sukarno's pro-Chinese policy in Indonesia in 1965 and 1966. Both countries have taken steps to improve their relations with the West.

sympathies have been active. Yet as the Venezuelan example indicates, a government which is reformist, nationalist, democratic, and decisive can overcome the revolutionary movement with time, effort, and public support. There is therefore no inevitability about a series of violent revolutions in the developing countries, although the Chinese strategists are counting on this for the future.

On the Soviet side, the hope has been that the "national democracies" described in the Moscow Declaration of eighty-one Communist Parties in 1960 will prepare the way for a gradual transition to "socialism" of the Soviet variety. The difficulty of both supporting such governments and preparing the way for their overthrow was illustrated at a recent meeting of the Communist Party of the Soviet Union, where the delegation of the National Liberation Front of Algeria walked out when it saw that the outlawed Algerian Communist Party had been seated in a place of honor. While there are similarities between the views and policies of the more radical states in the developing areas and those of the Communist world, there are still important differences between them, especially on the question of who is to control the government.[40]

Conclusion

There is no denying that a certain disillusionment has set in among those who have created the ideologies of the developing nations and those who have observed or participated in the effort to implement them. The dreams of a Golden Age characterized by equality, solidarity, unity, progress, and economic development have given way in many cases to the harsh realities of compromise, corruption, instability, and apathy. Yet the period of creative experimentation is not over. *Mystique* has not given way completely to *politique*, nor has bureaucratism and institutionalization totally replaced charisma and reform. There are still countries that have not yet been freed from colonial domination. There are still new areas of political and social innovation in which the new leadership

---

[40] See Richard Lowenthal, " 'National Democracy' and the Post-Colonial Revolution," in Kurt London (ed.), *New Nations in a Divided World* (New York: Frederick A. Praeger, 1964), pp. 56–74; Zbigniew Brzezinski, "Communism and the Emerging Nations," in J. Roland Pennock (ed.), *Self-Government in Modernizing Nations* (Englewood Cliffs, N.J.: Prentice-Hall, 1964), pp. 81–99; and Zbigniew Brzezinski (ed.), *Africa and the Communist World* (Stanford, Calif.: Stanford University Press, 1963).

can engage. And there are still challenges that can be met and overcome. And as long as man articulates his goals and the means by which he proposes to reach them, we will not have reached "the end of ideology." For the process of modernization and development is just beginning in many parts of the world and the way lies open:

> The frozen misery
> Of centuries breaks, cracks, begins to move,
> The thunder is the thunder of the floes,
> The thaw, the flood, the upstart Spring,
> Thank God our time is now when wrong
> Comes up to face us everywhere,
> Never to leave us till we take
> The longest stride of soul men ever took.[41]

---

[41] Christopher Fry, *A Sleep of Prisoners* (London and New York: Oxford University Press, 1951), p. 47; quoted by permission of Oxford University Press.

PART I

ASIA — AN Overview

It is far more difficult to generalize about ideology and politics in an area as vast and diverse as Asia than in the case of the other areas under consideration. Asians have much less in common with one another, and national traditions and cultures are stronger than in Africa, the Middle East, and Latin America. Moreover, the travail of securing and consolidating national independence is largely past in most Asian countries. Reasonably stable and permanent regimes to which the populace is loyal are in control in most Asian countries, making ideological appeals less necessary. In one instance, Japan, the rate of economic development has progressed to such a point that the nation can no longer be considered underdeveloped.

Yet, there are some common elements in Asian political psychology and ideology. Asian philosophy and political practice emphasize conciliation in the resolution of conflict, and this is expressed in the speeches and writings of Asian political leaders by the attempt to stress common elements in conflicting views and to achieve a consensus as a basis for policy. This consensus is often to be found or typified in a single leader, endowed with quasi-religious charismatic qualities.

The attempt to find agreement and to gloss over differences also characterizes the approach of Asian leaders to the East-West conflict. It is no accident that the philosophy of neutralism was first formulated by Nehru and Sukarno, although it should be noted that this philosophy is not operative in Asian countries where there is an immediate Communist threat to national integrity.

In economic development, a mixed economy predominates in

*practice, although Marxist anticapitalism has strongly influenced
the theories of the intellectuals and the speeches of political leaders. Today, two models of economic and political development,
those of China and of India, are in competition for Asian allegiance, symbolizing the choice between democratic planning in an
open society and forced growth under a totalitarian regime.*

*This competition is also one of cultural influence. India and
China have old and deeply rooted cultural traditions, and both
have been subjected to heavy Western influence, but they have
reacted in different ways. The urbane and civilized synthesis of
East and West typified by the character and personality of Nehru
contrasts with the crusading aggressiveness of the Chinese transformation of an ancient culture into a modern nation, following
the Soviet example, but making its own alterations and innovations.*

*Since the Bandung Conference in 1955, China has attempted
to develop its relations with other underdeveloped countries. More
recently, it has embarked upon a program of trade, aid, and propaganda in Asia and Africa that has capitalized on the desire of the
new nations to establish new contacts and learn from all national
experiences. Yet, thus far, the uncommitted nations, while accepting Chinese assistance, have been careful to maintain their
neutrality, and they continue to view China with suspicion. In its
competition with the Soviet Union for influence in the developing
nations, Chinese ideology has stressed the continuing necessity
for violent revolution to achieve needed social change—an appeal
not likely to be viewed with favor by the present leadership in
the newly independent countries.*

1. Mao Tse-tung

Mao Tse-tung, the Chairman of the Politbureau of the Chinese Communist Party, was born in 1893 in a village in northern China. The son of a peasant landowner, Mao wished to become a scholar. After his mother's death in 1918, he went to Peking University, where he worked as assistant librarian and came under the influence of two professors who were among the founders of the Chinese Communist Party. In 1921, he attended the first Congress of the Chinese Communist Party and was elected to its Central Committee. After the split between Chiang Kai-shek and the Communists, he established himself as political commissar of the Red Army, and by 1935 he had achieved supremacy in the Party. At this time, he led the Long March of the Communists from southeast to northwest China. Starting from a base in Yenan and gaining peasant support through a program of agrarian reform, he expanded his control of China. Finally, in 1949, Chiang Kai-shek was driven off the Chinese mainland. From then until 1959, Mao Tse-tung was President of the Chinese People's Republic. He resigned from this post, but continues to serve as Party Chairman.

In his On New Democracy, written in 1940, Mao saw the significance of the anticolonial revolution and tried to identify Communism with the desires of traditional societies for national independence and economic development. He also developed a theory of "joint dictatorship of all anti-imperialist classes" that departs from the classical Marxist belief in the dictatorship of the proletariat as the stage that follows capitalism. Although this dictatorship must be under the leadership of the proletariat, the peasants have a prominent place and a section of the bourgeoisie, as well as the revolutionary intellectuals, also is admitted. In On the Correct Handling of Contradictions Among the People, published in 1957, Mao distinguishes between antagonistic and nonantagonistic contradictions under socialism, and admits that disagreements and class differences of a "nonantagonistic" variety continue to exist in China. These differences are to be resolved by persuasion rather than coercion. As a result of this speech, a brief period of free criticism ensued (the "Hundred Flowers" campaign). In June, 1957, it was abruptly terminated, but the official Chinese ideology still endorses Mao's idea of nonantagonistic contradictions.* Since 1966, Mao has attempted to ensure the survival of his doctrines through the Great Proletarian Cultural Revolution—an effort to make his writings the sole basis for public and private life in China.

ON NEW DEMOCRACY (1940)†

The Chinese Revolution as Part of the World Revolution

The historical feature of the Chinese revolution consists in two steps, democracy and socialism; the first step is no longer democracy in a general sense, but democracy of the Chinese type, a new and special type—New Democracy. How, then, has this historical feature come into existence? Has it been in existence for the past hundred years, or is it of only recent birth?

If we make a study of the development of China and of the world, we shall see that this historical feature did not emerge as a consequence of the Opium War, but began to take shape only after the first imperialist world war and the October Revolution in Russia. Let us now study the process of its formation.

Evidently, the colonial, semicolonial, and semifeudal character of present-day Chinese society requires two steps in the Chinese revolution. The first step is to change a colonial, semicolonial, and semifeudal society into an independent, democratic society. The second is to push the revolution further and build a socialist society. The Chinese revolution at present is taking the first step. . . .

The Revolution of 1911 was the beginning of that revolution in a fuller sense. In its social character that revolution is bourgeois-democratic and not proletarian-socialist. It is not yet completed,

---

* On the relation of Mao's writings to Marxism-Leninism, see Arthur Cohen, "How Original is 'Maoism'?," Problems of Communism, X, No. 6 (November–December, 1961), 34–42.

† Excerpts from Mao Tse-tung, On New Democracy (Peking: Foreign Languages Press, 1960).

and great efforts are still required because its enemies remain very powerful. When Dr. Sun Yat-sen said, "The revolution is not yet completed; all my comrades must strive on," he was referring to the bourgeois-democratic revolution.

A change, however, occurred in the Chinese bourgeois-democratic revolution after the outbreak of the first imperialist World War in 1914 and the founding of a socialist state on one-sixth of the globe in consequence of the October Revolution in Russia in 1917. Before these events, the Chinese bourgeois-democratic revolution belonged to the category of the old bourgeois-democratic world revolution, and was part of it. After these events, the Chinese bourgeois-democratic revolution changes its character and comes within the category of the new bourgeois-democratic revolution and, so far as the revolutionary front is concerned, forms part of the proletarian-socialist world revolution.

Why? Because the first imperialist World War and the first victorious socialist revolution, the October Revolution, have changed the course of world history and marked a new historical era. This is an era in which the capitalist front has collapsed in one part— one-sixth—of the world and fully revealed its decadence in other parts; those parts still under capitalism cannot get along without depending more than ever on the colonies and semicolonies; a socialist state has come into being and has declared itself willing to help the liberation movement of all colonies and semicolonies; the proletariat of the capitalist countries is increasingly freeing itself from the social-imperialist influence of the social-democratic parties and has also declared itself in support of the liberation movement of the colonies and semicolonies. In this era, any revolution that takes place in a colony or semicolony against imperialism—that is, against the international bourgeoisie and international capitalism—belongs no longer to the old category of bourgeois-democratic world revolution. . . . Such revolutionary colonies and semicolonies should no longer be regarded as allies of the counterrevolutionary front of world capitalism: They have become allies of the revolutionary front of world socialism.

Although in its social character the first stage or step of such a revolution in a colonial and semicolonial country is still basically bourgeois-democratic, and although the task imposed on it by objective conditions is to clear the path for the development of capitalism, it is no longer a revolution of the old type led by the bourgeoisie and aimed at establishing a capitalist society and a state under bourgeois dictatorship, but one of the new type led by the proletariat and aimed at establishing in the first stage a New Democratic society and a state under the joint dictatorship of all revolutionary classes. Thus, this revolution will clear an even wider path for the development of socialism. In the course of its progress, such a revolution, owing to changes in the situation of its enemies and to changes of alignment within its own front, passes through several further stages; but its basic character remains unchanged.

This revolution attacks the very foundation of imperialism, and for this reason is disapproved and opposed by imperialism. But it is approved by socialism and supported by a socialist state and the international socialist proletariat. Therefore, such a revolution inevitably becomes part of the proletarian-socialist world revolution.

The correct formulation that the Chinese revolution is part of the world revolution was made as long ago as 1924–27, during China's first great revolution. It was made by the Chinese Communists and approved by all those taking part in the anti-imperialist and antifeudal struggle of the time. However, the theoretical implication of this formulation was not then fully expounded, and consequently the whole question was only vaguely understood.

The "world revolution" referred to here is no longer the old world revolution or the old bourgeois world revolution, for that ended long ago, but a new world revolution, the socialist world revolution. Similarly, the "part" is not a part of the old bourgeois revolution but of the new socialist revolution. This is a tremendous change unparalleled in the history of China and of the world.

This correct formulation made by the Chinese Communists is based on Stalin's theory. As early as 1918, Stalin wrote in an article commemorating the first anniversary of the October Revolution:

The great world-wide significance of the October Revolution chiefly consists in the fact that:

1. It has widened the scope of the national question and converted it from the particular question of combating national oppression in Europe into the general question of emancipating the oppressed peoples, colonies, and semicolonies from imperialism.

2. It has opened up wide possibilities for their emancipation and the right paths toward it, has thereby greatly facilitated the

cause of the emancipation of the oppressed peoples of the West and the East, and has drawn them into the common current of the victorious struggle against imperialism.

3. It has thereby erected a bridge between the socialist West and the enslaved East, having created a new front of revolutions against world imperialism, extending from the proletarians of the West, through the Russian Revolution, to the oppressed peoples of the East.*

Thus it can be seen that there are two kinds of world revolution, the first belonging to the bourgeois and capitalist category. The era of this kind of world revolution is long past, having come to an end as early as 1914, when the first imperialist World War broke out, and especially in 1917, when the October Revolution occurred in Russia. Since then, the second kind—namely, the proletarian-socialist world revolution—has started. The main force in this revolution is the proletariat of the capitalist countries, and it has as its allies the oppressed peoples of the colonies and semicolonies. No matter what classes, parties, or individuals in the oppressed nations join the revolution, and no matter whether or not they are conscious of this fact and fully understand it, so long as they oppose imperialism, their revolution becomes part of the proletarian-socialist world revolution, and they themselves become allies of this revolution.

Today, the Chinese revolution assumes an even greater significance. This is a time when the world is being plunged more and more deeply into the Second World War by the economic and political crises of capitalism; when the Soviet Union has reached the period of transition from socialism to Communism and is now capable of leading and helping the proletariat and oppressed nations of the world in their fight against imperialist war and capitalist reaction; when the proletariat of the capitalist countries is preparing to overthrow capitalism and establish socialism; and when China's proletariat, peasantry, intelligentsia, and other sections of the petty bourgeoisie have become a mighty independent political force under the leadership of the Chinese Communist Party. At such a juncture, are we not right in claiming that the Chinese revolution has assumed a greater significance in the world? I think we are. . . .

* Stalin, *Works* (Eng. ed.; Moscow, 1953), IV, 169-70.

The first stage of the Chinese revolution, which contains many subdivisions, belongs, so far as its social character is concerned, to a new type of bourgeois-democratic revolution which is not yet a proletarian-socialist revolution in itself, but it has long been part of the proletarian-socialist world revolution and is now even an important part of it and a powerful ally. The first step or stage of this revolution is certainly not, and cannot be, the establishment of a capitalist society under the dictatorship of the Chinese bourgeoisie, but will be the establishment of a New Democratic society under the joint dictatorship of all Chinese revolutionary classes headed by the Chinese proletariat. Then the revolution will develop into the second stage to establish a socialist society in China. . . .

New Democratic Politics

The Chinese national bourgeoisie, because it belongs to a colonial and semicolonial country and lives under imperialist oppression, retains, even in the era of imperialism, at certain periods and to a certain degree, a revolutionary quality as expressed in its opposition to foreign imperialism and the home governments of bureaucrats and war lords (instances of the latter can be found in the Revolution of 1911 and in the Northern Expedition), and can ally itself with the proletariat and the petty bourgeoisie to oppose those enemies whom it wants to oppose. This is the difference between the Chinese bourgeoisie and the bourgeoisie of old Czarist Russia. Since Czarist Russia was already a militarist and feudalist imperialist power which carried on aggression against other countries, her bourgeoisie was in no way revolutionary. In Czarist Russia, the task of the proletariat was to oppose the bourgeoisie, not to unite with it. On the other hand, because China is a colony and a semicolony suffering from aggression by others, her national bourgeoisie has at certain periods and to a certain degree a revolutionary quality. Thus, in China, the task of the proletariat is to take into account the revolutionary quality of the national bourgeoisie and form with it a united front against imperialism and the bureaucratic and war-lord regime. . . .

It is quite evident that whoever in China can lead the people to overthrow the imperialist and feudal forces will win the people's confidence, because these forces, especially imperialism, are the mortal enemies of the people. Today, whoever can lead the people to drive out Japanese imperialism and carry out democratic policies will be the savior of the people. History has proved that the Chinese bourgeoisie is incapable of fulfilling this responsibility, which consequently falls upon the shoulders of the proletariat.

Therefore, in all circumstances, the proletariat, the peasantry, the intelligentsia, and other sections of the petty bourgeoisie in China are the basic forces which decide China's fate. These classes, some already awakened and others on the point of awakening, will necessarily become the basic components of the state structure. The democratic republic of China, which we now want to establish, can only be a democratic republic under the joint dictatorship of all anti-imperialist and antifeudal people, led by the proletariat—that is, a New Democratic republic. . . .

While different from the old European-American form of capitalist republic under bourgeois dictatorship, which is now out of date, this New Democratic republic is also different from the socialist republic of the type of the U.S.S.R., the republic of the dictatorship of the proletariat. The socialist republic is already flourishing in the Soviet Union, and will be established in all the capitalist countries and undoubtedly become the dominant form in the structure of state and political power in all industrially advanced countries, but, during a given historical period, it is not yet suitable for revolutions in colonial and semicolonial countries. Therefore, a third form of state must be adopted . . . namely, the New Democratic republic. This is the form for a given historical period and therefore a transitional form, but it is the necessary form to which there is no alternative.

The multifarious types of state system in the world can be reduced to three basic kinds, according to the class character of their political power: (1) republics under bourgeois dictatorships; (2) republics under the dictatorship of the proletariat; and (3) republics under the joint dictatorship of several revolutionary classes.

The first kind includes the old democratic states. Today, after the outbreak of the second imperialist war, there is no longer even a trace of democracy in many of the capitalist countries, which have come under, or are coming under, the bloody militarist dictatorship of the bourgeoisie. Certain countries under the joint dictatorship of the landlords and the bourgeoisie can be classed with this kind.

The second kind exists in the Soviet Union, and conditions for its birth are ripening in all capitalist countries. In the future, it will become the dominant form throughout the world for a certain period.

The third kind is the transitional form of state to be adopted in revolutions in colonial and semicolonial countries. Of course, revolutions in different colonial and semicolonial countries necessarily have certain different characteristics, but these are only minor differences within a general framework of uniformity. So long as they are revolutions in colonies or semicolonies, the form of state and political power will of necessity be basically the same, a New Democratic state under the joint dictatorship of several anti-imperialist classes. . . .

As to the question of political structure, it concerns the structural form of political power, the form adopted by certain social classes in organizing their political power to protect themselves against their enemies. Without a suitable organ of political power, there would be nothing to represent the state. In China, we can adopt a system of people's congresses—the national people's congress, the provincial people's congress, the county people's congress, the district people's congress, down to the township people's congress, and let these congresses at various levels elect the organs of government. But a system of really universal and equal suffrage—irrespective of sex, creed, property, or education—must be introduced so that each revolutionary class can be equitably represented according to its status in the state, the people's will properly expressed, the revolutionary struggles properly directed, and the spirit of New Democracy properly embodied. This is the system of democratic centralism. Only a government of democratic centralism can fully express the will of all the revolutionary people and most effectively fight the enemies of the revolution. The spirit of the phrase "not to be monopolized by a few" must be embodied in the government and the army apparatus; without a genuinely democratic system, this aim can never be attained, and there will be a discrepancy between the political structure and the state system.

The state system—joint dictatorship of all revolutionary classes. The political structure—democratic centralism. This is New Democratic government; this is a republic of New Democracy. . . .

ON THE CORRECT HANDLING OF CONTRADICTIONS AMONG THE PEOPLE (1957)*

. . . We are confronted by two types of social contradictions—contradictions between ourselves and the enemy and contradictions among the people. These two types of contradictions are totally different in nature.

If we are to have a correct understanding of these two different types of contradictions, we must, first of all, make clear what is meant by "the people" and what is meant by "the enemy."

The term "the people" has different meanings in different countries, and in different historical periods in each country. Take our country for example. During the War of Resistance to Japanese Aggression, all those classes, strata, and social groups which opposed Japanese aggression belonged to the category of the people, while the Japanese imperialists, Chinese traitors, and the pro-Japanese elements belonged to the category of enemies of the people. During the War of Liberation, the United States imperialists and their henchmen—the bureaucrat-capitalists and landlord class—and the Kuomintang reactionaries, who represented these two classes, were the enemies of the people, while all other classes, strata, and social groups which opposed these enemies, belonged to the category of the people. At this stage of building socialism, all classes, strata, and social groups which approve, support, and work for the cause of socialist construction belong to the category of the people, while those social forces and groups which resist the socialist revolution, and are hostile to and try to wreck socialist construction, are enemies of the people.

The contradictions between ourselves and our enemies are antagonistic ones. Within the ranks of the people, contradictions among the working people are nonantagonistic, while those between the exploiters and the exploited classes have, apart from

* Excerpts from Mao Tse-tung, *On the Correct Handling of Contradictions Among the People* (Peking: Foreign Languages Press, 1960).

their antagonistic aspect, a nonantagonistic aspect. Contradictions among the people have always existed. But their content differs in each period of the revolution and during the building of socialism. In the conditions existing in China today, what we call contradictions among the people include the following: contradictions within the working class, contradictions within the peasantry, contradictions within the intelligentsia, contradictions between the working class and the peasantry, contradictions between the working class and peasantry on the one hand and the intelligentsia on the other, contradictions between the working class and other sections of the working people on the one hand and the national bourgeoisie on the other, contradictions within the national bourgeoisie, and so forth. Our people's government is a government that truly represents the interests of the people and serves the people, yet certain contradictions do exist between the government and the masses. These include contradictions between the interests of the state, collective interests, and individual interests; between democracy and centralism; between those in positions of leadership and the led, and contradictions arising from the bureaucratic practices of certain state functionaries in their relations with the masses. All these are contradictions among the people. Generally speaking, underlying the contradictions among the people is the basic identity of the interests of the people.

In our country, the contradiction between the working class and the national bourgeoisie is a contradiction among the people. The class struggle waged between the two is, by and large, a class struggle within the ranks of the people. This is because of the dual character of the national bourgeoisie in our country. In the years of the bourgeois-democratic revolution, there was a revolutionary side to their character; there was also a tendency to compromise with the enemy—this was the other side. In the period of the socialist revolution, exploitation of the working class to make profits is one side, while support of the Constitution and willingness to accept socialist transformation is the other. The national bourgeoisie differs from the imperialists, the landlords and the bureaucrat-capitalists. The contradiction between exploiter and exploited, which exists between the national bourgeoisie and the working class, is an antagonistic one. But, in the concrete conditions existing in China, such an antagonistic contradiction, if properly handled, can be transformed into a nonantagonistic one and resolved in a peaceful way. But if it is not properly handled, if, say, we do not follow a policy of uniting, criticizing, and educating the national bourgeoisie, or if the national bourgeoisie does not accept this policy, then the contradiction between the working class and the national bourgeoisie can turn into an antagonistic contradiction as between ourselves and the enemy.

Since the contradictions between ourselves and the enemy and those among the people differ in nature, they must be solved in different ways. To put it briefly, the former is a matter of drawing a line between us and our enemies, while the latter is a matter of distinguishing between right and wrong. It is, of course, true that drawing a line between ourselves and our enemies is also a question of distinguishing between right and wrong. For example, the question as to who is right, we or the reactionaries at home and abroad —that is, the imperialists, the feudalists, and bureaucrat-capitalists— is also a question of distinguishing between right and wrong, but it is different in nature from questions of right and wrong among the people.

Ours is a people's democratic dictatorship, led by the working class and based on the worker-peasant alliance. What is this dictatorship for? Its first function is to suppress the reactionary classes and elements and those exploiters in the country who range themselves against the socialist revolution, to suppress all those who try to wreck our socialist construction; that is to say, to solve the contradictions between ourselves and the enemy within the country. For instance, to arrest, try, and sentence certain counterrevolutionaries, and for a specified period of time to deprive landlords and bureaucrat-capitalists of their right to vote and freedom of speech— all this comes within the scope of our dictatorship. To maintain law and order and safeguard the interests of the people, it is likewise necessary to exercise dictatorship over robbers, swindlers, murderers, arsonists, hooligans, and other scoundrels who seriously disrupt social order.

The second function of this dictatorship is to protect our country from subversive activities and possible aggression by the external enemy. Should that happen, it is the task of this dictatorship to solve the external contradiction between ourselves and the enemy. The aim of this dictatorship is to protect all our people so that they can work in peace and build China into a socialist country with a modern industry, agriculture, science, and culture.

Who is to exercise this dictatorship? Naturally it must be the working class and the entire people led by it. Dictatorship does not apply in the ranks of the people. The people cannot possibly exercise dictatorship over themselves; nor should one section of them oppress another section. Lawbreaking elements among the people will be dealt with according to law, but this is different in principle from using the dictatorship to suppress enemies of the people. What applies among the people is democratic centralism. Our constitution lays it down that citizens of the People's Republic of China enjoy freedom of speech, of the press, of assembly, of association, of procession, of demonstration, of religious belief, and so on. Our constitution also provides that organs of state must practice democratic centralism and must rely on the masses; that the personnel of organs of state must serve the people. Our socialist democracy is democracy in the widest sense, such as is not to be found in any capitalist country. Our dictatorship is known as the people's democratic dictatorship, led by the working class and based on the worker-peasant alliance. That is to say, democracy operates within the ranks of the people, while the working class, uniting with all those enjoying civil rights, the peasantry in the first place, enforces dictatorship over the reactionary classes and elements and all those who resist socialist transformation and oppose socialist construction. . . .

While we stand for freedom with leadership and democracy under centralized guidance, in no sense do we mean that coercive measures should be taken to settle ideological matters and questions involving the distinction between right and wrong among the people. Any attempt to deal with ideological matters or questions involving right and wrong by administrative orders or coercive measures will not only be ineffective but harmful. We cannot abolish religion by administrative orders; nor can we force people not to believe in it. We cannot compel people to give up idealism, any more than we can force them to believe in Marxism. In settling matters of an ideological nature or controversial issues among the people, we can only use democratic methods, methods of discussion, of criticism, of persuasion and education, not coercive, highhanded methods. . . .

Contradictions in a socialist society are fundamentally different from contradictions in old societies, such as capitalist society. Contradictions in capitalist society find expression in acute antagonisms and conflicts, in sharp class struggle, which cannot be resolved by the capitalist system itself and can only be resolved by socialist revolution. Contradictions in socialist society are, on the contrary, not antagonistic and can be resolved one after the other by the socialist system itself. . . .

The socialist system has promoted the rapid development of the productive forces of our country—this is a fact that even our enemies abroad have had to acknowledge. But our socialist system has just been set up; it is not yet fully established, nor yet fully consolidated. In joint state-private industrial and commercial enterprises, capitalists still receive a fixed rate of interest on their capital, that is to say, exploitation still exists. So far as ownership is concerned, these enterprises are not yet completely socialist in character. Some of our agricultural and handicraft producers' cooperatives are still semisocialist, while even in the fully socialist cooperatives certain problems about ownership remain to be solved. . . .

Socialist relations of production have been established; they are suited to the development of the productive forces, but they are still far from perfect, and their imperfect aspects stand in contradiction to the development of the productive forces. There is conformity as well as contradiction between the relations of production and the development of the productive forces; similarly, there is conformity as well as contradiction between the superstructure and the economic base. The superstructure—our state institutions of people's democratic dictatorship and its laws, and socialist ideology under the guidance of Marxism-Leninism—has played a positive role in facilitating the victory of socialist transformation and establishment of a socialist organization of labor; it is suited to the socialist economic base, that is, socialist relations of production. But survivals of bourgeois ideology, bureaucratic ways of doing things in our state organs, and flaws in certain links of our state institutions stand in contradiction to the economic base of socialism. We must continue to resolve such contradictions in the light of specific conditions. . . .

2. Lin Piao

Marshal Lin Piao was born in 1908 in northern China. He came from a lower-middle-class family and was educated at the Whampoa Military Academy, where one of his teachers was Chou En-lai. In 1925, he joined the Communist Youth. One of the founders of the Red Army in 1928, he was named president of the Red Army Academy in 1937. In 1945, he was made Commander of the Northeast People's Liberation Army. After the Communist victory in China, he became Vice Premier of the People's Republic of China (1954) and Vice Chairman of the Central Committee and member of the Standing Committee of the Politburo of the Chinese Communist Party (1958). Since 1959, he has been Minister of National Defense.

In the selection that follows, extracted from an article published in all major Chinese newspapers on September 3, 1965, Marshal Lin attempts to associate the anticolonial revolution in Asia, Africa, and Latin America with the model provided by the Communist revolution and civil war in China. Just as the Chinese Communist armies, based in the countryside and supported by the peasantry, were able to overcome Chiang Kai-shek, who controlled the principal urban centers, so "the countryside of the world," Asia, Africa, and Latin America, will ultimately defeat "the cities," North America and Europe. Following the analogy of Mao's New Democracy, this would be carried out by a coalition of anti-imperialist groups under the leadership of the Communists. Attacking the "revisionists" in the Soviet Union for advocating peaceful coexistence, Marshal Lin promises Chinese support for "people's wars" in which he predicts that guerrilla forces will ultimately defeat the highly developed weaponry and technology of "U.S. imperialism and its lackeys." The article sums up the Chinese ideological justification for its policy of active espousal of violent revolution and guerrilla warfare throughout Asia, Africa, and Latin America.

THE VICTORY OF THE PEOPLE'S WAR*

. . . It was on the basis of the lessons derived from the people's wars in China that Comrade Mao Tse-tung, using the simplest and the most vivid language, advanced the famous thesis that "political power grows out of the barrel of a gun."

He clearly pointed out: The seizure of power by armed force, the settlement of the issue by war, is the central task and the highest form of revolution. This Marxist-Leninist principle of revolution holds good universally, for China and for all other countries.

War is the product of imperialism and the system of exploitation of man by man. Lenin said that "war is always and everywhere begun by the exploiters themselves, by the ruling and oppressing classes." So long as imperialism and the system of exploitation of man by man exist, the imperialists and reactionaries will invariably rely on armed force to maintain their reactionary rule and impose war on the oppressed nations and peoples. This is an objective law independent of man's will. . . .

In the last analysis, whether one dares to wage a tit-for-tat struggle against armed aggression and suppression by the imperialists and their lackeys, whether one dares to fight a people's war against them means whether one dares to embark on revolution. This is the most effective touchstone for distinguishing genuine from fake revolutionaries and Marxist-Leninists.

In view of the fact that some people were afflicted with the fear of the imperialists and reactionaries, Comrade Mao Tse-tung put forward his famous thesis that "the imperialists and all reactionaries are paper tigers. . . . In appearance the reactionaries are terrifying, but in reality they are not so powerful. From a long-term point of view, it is not the reactionaries but the people who are really powerful."

The history of people's war in China and other countries provides conclusive evidence that the growth of the people's revolutionary forces from weak and small beginnings into strong and large forces is a universal law of development of class struggle, a universal law of development of people's war. A people's war in-

* Excerpts from Lin Piao's article "Long Live the Victory of the People's War!"; text released by the New China News Agency, September, 1965.

evitably meets with many difficulties, with ups and downs and setbacks in the course of its development, but no force can alter its general trend toward inevitable triumph.

Comrade Mao Tse-tung points out that we must despise the enemy strategically and take full account of him tactically. To despise the enemy strategically is an elementary requirement for a revolutionary. Without the courage to despise the enemy and without daring to win, it will be simply impossible to make revolution and wage a people's war, let alone to achieve victory. . . .

The imperialists are extremely afraid of Comrade Mao Tse-tung's thesis that "imperialism and the reactionaries are paper tigers," and the revisionists are extremely hostile to it. They all oppose and attack this thesis and the Philistines follow suit by ridiculing it. But all this cannot in the least diminish its importance. The light of truth cannot be dimmed by anybody.

Comrade Mao Tse-tung's theory of people's war solves not only the problem of daring to fight a people's war, but also that of how to wage it.

Comrade Mao Tse-tung is a great statesman and military scientist, proficient at directing war in accordance with its laws. By the line and policies, the strategy and tactics he formulated for the people's war, he led the Chinese people in steering the ship of the people's war past all hidden reefs to the shores of victory in most complicated and difficult conditions.

It must be emphasized that Comrade Mao Tse-tung's theory of the establishment of rural revolutionary base areas and the encirclement of the cities from the countryside is of outstanding and universal practical importance for the present revolutionary struggles of all the oppressed nations and peoples in Asia, Africa, and Latin America against imperialism and its lackeys.

Many countries and peoples in Asia, Africa, and Latin America are now being subjected to aggression and enslavement on a serious scale by the imperialists headed by the United States and their lackeys. The basic political and economic conditions in many of these countries have many similarities to those that prevailed in old China. As in China, the peasant question is extremely important in these regions. The peasants constitute the main force of the national-democratic revolution against the imperialists and their lackeys.

In committing aggression against these countries, the imperialists usually begin by seizing the big cities and the main lines of communication, but they are unable to bring the vast countryside completely under their control. The countryside, and the countryside alone, can provide the broad areas in which the revolutionaries can maneuver freely. The countryside, and the countryside alone, can provide the revolutionary bases from which the revolutionaries can go forward to final victory. Precisely for this reason, Comrade Mao Tse-tung's theory of establishing revolutionary base areas in the rural districts and encircling the cities from the countryside is attracting more and more attention among the people in these regions.

Taking the entire globe, if North America and Western Europe can be called "the cities of the world," then Asia, Africa, and Latin America constitute "the rural areas of the world." Since World War II, the proletarian revolutionary movement has for various reasons been temporarily held back in the North American and Western European capitalist countries, while the people's revolutionary movement in Asia, Africa, and Latin America has been growing vigorously. In a sense, the contemporary world revolution also presents a picture of the encirclement of cities by the rural areas. . . .

The October Revolution opened up a new era in the revolution of the oppressed nations. The victory of the October Revolution built a bridge between the socialist revolution of the proletariat of the West and the national-democratic revolution of the colonial and semicolonial countries of the East. The Chinese revolution has successfully solved the problem of how to link up the national-democratic with the socialist revolution in the colonial and semicolonial countries.

Comrade Mao Tse-tung has pointed out that, in the epoch since the October Revolution, anti-imperialist revolution in any colonial or semicolonial country is no longer part of the old bourgeois, or capitalist, world revolution, but is part of the new world revolution, the proletarian-socialist world revolution.

Comrade Mao Tse-tung has formulated a complete theory of the new democratic revolution. He indicated that this revolution, which is different from all others, can only be, nay must be, a revolution against imperialism, feudalism, and bureaucratic capitalism waged by the broad masses of the people under the leadership of the proletariat.

This means that the revolution can only be, nay must be, led by the proletariat and the genuinely revolutionary party armed with Marxism-Leninism, and by no other class or party.

This means that the revolution embraces in its ranks not only the workers, peasants, and the urban petty bourgeoisie, but also the national bourgeoisie and other patriotic and anti-imperialist democrats.

This means, finally, that the revolution is directed against imperialism, feudalism, and bureaucratic capitalism.

The new democratic revolution leads to socialism, and not to capitalism.

Comrade Mao Tse-tung's theory of the new democratic revolution is the Marxist-Leninist theory of uninterrupted revolution.

Comrade Mao Tse-tung made a correct distinction between the two revolutionary stages, that is, the national-democratic and the socialist revolutions; at the same time, he correctly and closely linked the two. The national-democratic revolution is the necessary preparation for the socialist revolution, and the socialist revolution is the inevitable sequel to the national-democratic revolution. There is no great wall between the two revolutionary stages. But the socialist revolution is only possible after the completion of the national-democratic revolution. The more thorough the national-democratic revolution, the better the conditions for the socialist revolution.

The experience of the Chinese revolution shows that the tasks of the national-democratic revolution can be fulfilled only through long and tortuous struggles. In this stage of revolution, imperialism and its lackeys are the principal enemy. In the struggle against imperialism and its lackeys, it is necessary to rally all anti-imperialist patriotic forces, including the national bourgeoisie and all patriotic persons. All those patriotic persons from among the bourgeoisie and other exploiting classes who join the anti-imperialist struggle play a progressive historical role: they are not tolerated by imperialism but welcomed by the proletariat.

It is very harmful to confuse the two stages, that is, the national-democratic and the socialist revolutions. Comrade Mao Tse-tung criticized the wrong idea of "accomplishing both at one stroke," and pointed out that this utopian idea could only weaken the struggle against imperialism and its lackeys, the most urgent task at the time. The Kuomintang reactionaries and the Trotskyites they hired during the War of Resistance deliberately confused these two stages of the Chinese revolution, proclaiming the "theory of a single revolution" and preaching so-called socialism without any Communist Party. With this preposterous theory they attempted to swallow up the Communist Party, wipe out any revolution, and prevent the advance of the national-democratic revolution, and they used it as a pretext for their nonresistance and capitulation to imperialism. This reactionary theory was buried long ago by the history of the Chinese revolution.

The Khrushchev revisionists are now actively preaching that socialism can be built without the proletariat and without a genuinely revolutionary party armed with the advanced proletarian ideology, and they have cast the fundamental tenets of Marxism-Leninism to the four winds. The revisionists' purpose is solely to divert the oppressed nations from their struggle against imperialism and to sabotage their national-democratic solution, all in the service of imperialism.

The Chinese revolution provides a successful lesson for making a thoroughgoing national-democratic revolution under the leadership of the proletariat; it likewise provides a successful lesson for the timely transition from the national-democratic revolution to the socialist revolution under the leadership of the proletariat. . . .

Ours is the epoch in which world capitalism and imperialism are heading for their doom, and socialism and Communism are marching to victory. Comrade Mao Tse-tung's theory of people's war is not only a product of the Chinese revolution, but has also characteristics of our epoch. The new experience gained in the people's revolutionary struggles in various countries since World War II has provided continuous evidence that Mao Tse-tung's thought is a common asset of the revolutionary people of the whole world. This is the great international significance of the thought of Mao Tse-tung. . . .

The contradiction between the revolutionary peoples of Asia, Africa, and Latin America and the imperialists headed by the United States is the principal contradiction in the contemporary world. The development of this contradiction is promoting the struggle of the whole world against U.S. imperialism and its lackeys. . . .

The struggles waged by the different peoples against U.S. imperialism reinforce each other and merge into a torrential world-wide tide of opposition to U.S. imperialism. The more successful the development of people's war in a given region, the larger the number of U.S. imperialist forces that can be pinned down and depleted there. When the U.S. aggressors are hard pressed in one place, they have no alternative but to loosen their grip on others. Therefore, the conditions become more favorable for the people elsewhere to wage struggles against U.S. imperialism and its lackeys. . . .

However highly developed modern weapons and technical equipment may be and however complicated the methods of modern warfare, in the final analysis the outcome of a war will be decided by the sustained fighting of the ground forces, by the fighting at close quarters on battlefields, by the political consciousness of the men, by their courage and spirit of sacrifice. Here the weak points of U.S. imperialism will be completely laid bare, while the superiority of the revolutionary people will be brought into full play. The reactionary troops of U.S. imperialism cannot possibly be endowed with the courage and the spirit of sacrifice possessed by the revolutionary people. The spiritual atom bomb that the revolutionary people possess is a far more powerful and useful weapon than the physical atom bomb. . . .

Ever since Lenin led the great October Revolution to victory, the experience of innumerable revolutionary wars has borne out the truth that a revolutionary people who rise up with only their bare hands at the outset finally succeed in defeating the ruling classes who are armed to the teeth. The poorly armed have defeated the better armed. People's armed forces, beginning with only primitive swords, spears, rifles, hand-grenades, have in the end defeated the imperialist forces armed with modern airplanes, tanks, heavy artillery, and atom bombs. Guerrilla forces have ultimately defeated regular armies. "Amateurs" who were never trained in any military schools have eventually defeated "professionals" graduated from military academies. And so on and so forth. Things stubbornly develop in a way that runs counter to the assertions of the revisionists, and facts are slapping them in the face. . . .

We know that war brings destruction, sacrifice, and suffering on the people. But the destruction, sacrifice, and suffering will be much greater if no resistance is offered to imperialist armed aggression and the people become willing slaves. The sacrifice of a small number of people in revolutionary wars is repaid by security for whole nations, whole countries, and even the whole of mankind; temporary suffering is repaid by lasting or even perpetual peace and happiness. War can temper the people and push history forward. In this sense, war is a great school. . . .

In diametrical opposition to the Khrushchev revisionists, the Marxist-Leninists and revolutionary people never take a gloomy view of war. Our attitude toward imperialist wars of aggression has always been clear-cut. First, we are against them, and secondly, we are not afraid of them. We will destroy whoever attacks us. As for revolutionary wars waged by the oppressed nations and peoples, so far from opposing them, we invariably give them firm support and active aid. It has been so in the past, it remains so in the present and, when we grow in strength as time goes on, we will give them still more support and aid in the future. . . .

The peoples of the world now have the lessons of the October Revolution, the antifascist war, the Chinese people's war of resistance and war of liberation, the Korean people's war of resistance to U.S. aggression, the Vietnamese people's war of liberation and their war of resistance to U.S. aggression, and the people's revolutionary armed struggles in many other countries. Provided each people studies these lessons well and creatively integrates them with the concrete practice of revolution in their own country, there is no doubt that the revolutionary peoples of the world will stage still more powerful and splendid dramas in the theater of people's war in their countries and that they will wipe off the earth once and for all the common enemy of all the peoples, U.S. imperialism and its lackeys. . . .

3. Sukarno

Sukarno, the former President of Indonesia, was born in 1901 at Surabaya. He is the son of a village teacher. He attended a Dutch elementary school, and later was sent to secondary school by a nationalist friend of his father. He joined a nationalist organization, and entered the Engineering School at Bandung, where he received his degree in 1925. Subsequently, Sukarno helped form the Indonesian National Party (PNI). He was imprisoned by the Dutch in 1929, and again in 1933, when he was exiled to a remote part of Indonesia. He was freed by the Japanese in 1942. On August 17, 1945, before the return of the Dutch, Sukarno declared his country's independence. In 1949, after several years of fighting, sovereignty was finally transferred by the Dutch, and he became Indonesia's first President, a position he held until 1967 In 1963, he was declared President for Life, but this action was reversed by the People's Consultative Congress in 1966.

In 1960, Sukarno dissolved parliament and outlawed several of the political parties. He proceeded to rule according to the principles of "guided democracy"—through leadership by an elite, consultation with an advisory parliament that represents social and economic groups, and decision-making by discussion and consensus rather than by voting. He also called for unity of the nationalist, religious, and Communist groups (NASAKOM). His increasingly close cooperation with the Communists was indicated by his subsequent abandonment of the view of the world as divided into three groups in favor of a bipolar model (NEFO-OLDEFO). However, an unsuccessful Communist coup on October 1, 1965, led to their virtual elimination from Indonesian political life, a sharp reduction in the political power of Sukarno, and a great increase in that of the army. On March 12, 1967, the People's Consultative Congress "replaced" him as President with General Suharto, and took away his remaining executive power.

LECTURE TO THE STUDENTS OF HASANUDDIN UNIVERSITY*

Jefferson and Marx

. . . The British philosopher Bertrand Russell divides mankind at present into two groups, following two different philosophies. One group has faith in the Declaration of Independence of Thomas Jefferson, while the other group believes in the Communist Manifesto of Karl Marx. . . .

Bertrand Russell is not partial to one or the other group. He only hopes that the competition between the followers of these two philosophies would not be determined on the battlefield. It should not be solved through the destruction of men by men, because of the signs we see now and which have also been observed by themselves, but at the end they want to prove their stand by fighting one another, destroying one another in war.

Bertrand Russell said: Compete with each other, but do not try to reach a solution on the battlefield. Compete in a field that brings prosperity to mankind. Please compete and try to achieve prosperity of mankind by applying your respective ideas. Followers of Thomas Jefferson, please try to establish the prosperity of men according to your world of thought, and followers of Karl Marx, please try to bring prosperity to mankind. Those who will bring the greatest prosperity to men will prove to be the victors in this competition. . . .

I do not agree with Bertrand Russell when he said that humanity only consists of these two groups. There is a third group, which numbers more than a billion, maybe even more than one and a half billion people—namely, the people who live under the flags of nationalism in Asia and Africa.

Those are the people whose hearts throb eagerly, who are very anxious to realize their national independence by establishing a just and prosperous society without getting involved in any way with the two ways of thought mentioned by Bertrand Russell. These three groupings I regard as a phenomenon of the twentieth

* Translated and published by the Ministry of Information, Djakarta, Indonesia, 1959.

century: the group of Thomas Jefferson, the group adhering to the Communist Manifesto, and the group of Asian and African nationalism. . . . We not only advocate the coexistence of what is known as the Western bloc and the Communist bloc—the bloc of the United States and that of the Soviet Union, we not only want coexistence between these two blocs, but we also suggest that these two blocs should coexist with Asian-African nationalism. I suggest this because I have seen that Asian-African nationalism, the third group, is always disturbed and attacked by people from outside. It is not respected by people from outside. People even try to suppress and destroy it.

It is my sincere hope, and this hope I put on all the Indonesian students, that we should not, as a nation that has just been established as a state, that is eager to establish a just and prosperous society, a nation that is eager to build up, a nation that thus needs to look at the experiences of the outside world, indulge in too many theories and look for the small mistakes in other people's ideas, so that at the end we only see these mistakes. This attitude is useless. . . . We do not have to look deliberately for errors in the Declaration of Independence, concentrate and pounce on it when we have found one. Neither do we look only for the mistakes of Karl Marx and Friedrich Engels and doggedly criticize and analyze them. It is of no use for the community we are building. We are looking for the experience of other nations outside of Indonesia, especially in these later periods; we use their good experiences to build up our community and country, and cast away the bad experiences.

That is why it is so important to send our scientists, cadres, and youth to other parts of the world. If our government had enough money, I would ask Pak Prijono, the Minister of Education, to send as many students as possible to the United States, to the Soviet Union, to Canada, to the People's Republic of China—everywhere—to get experience.

Do not say first, I do not want to go to the United States, as it follows the world of thought of Thomas Jefferson. Or do not say, I do not want to go to the People's Republic of China, as it is within the world of thought of Karl Marx. This kind of opinion is wrong. I have mentioned earlier that the world of thought of Thomas Jefferson has a great number of followers. It is impossible for human beings not to be rational, not to see some good things in the world of thought of Thomas Jefferson. Because of the existence of some good points in the world of thought of Thomas Jefferson, that world of thought has tens of millions, hundreds of millions of followers, because human beings have sound minds. The same applies to Karl Marx. . . .

The problem our country faces now is in the first place to provide our people with a good living. Therefore, the present is no time for us for too much theorizing. We had better be practical and pick out whatever is good from the ideas of Thomas Jefferson as well as those from Karl Marx—without, however, taking sides. In politics, this attitude is known as our independent and active policy. But I would like this attitude to be taken in the field of science, too. . . .

Guided Democracy

For reconstruction, three basic requirements are needed:

Firstly, capital. It is clear that one cannot build up without capital. Furthermore, capital, if possible, should be our own capital—national capital—owned and raised by the Indonesian people themselves. If our own capital is not sufficient, we can contract loans from abroad. If we cannot obtain enough loans, then only can we invite foreign capital to invest here, but remember, my friends, I mention capital investment as number three here. Firstly, we have to get our own capital. Whenever it is not enough, there is nothing we can do except to borrow, to borrow capital which we will repay in terms. Only when it is necessary, foreign capital has to be imported.

Secondly, managerial know-how. One cannot build without the knowledge of how to organize. That is the reason why we make a blueprint, that is the reason why we established this university, to train and educate cadres—as many as possible. . . . We are grateful that at present we have 30,000 students in the whole of Indonesia. But that is not enough yet. I think that we need more than 150,000 students whose spirits are alert and whose minds are filled with practical, managerial, and applied sciences.

Thirdly, a political atmosphere which is conducive to reconstruction. Even though we possess capital (the first requirement), although we possess managerial know-how (the second requirement), if the political atmosphere is not conducive to reconstruction, development cannot be carried out smoothly. How is our political atmosphere at present? I have said over and over again, our political atmosphere is an unhealthy one, a liberal political atmosphere, an atmosphere of "free-fight liberalism." An atmosphere in which we continuously fight and quarrel, each claiming to be right, looking for mistakes of one another. It is a situation where there is no order and no unity, no one yielding to the other. One is eager to destroy the other. We must abandon this free-fight liberalism completely, if we want to develop and build up in the right way.

Indeed, the delegations which I sent have come back with an answer from the people of the countries they visited. Indonesia is richer than those countries. The Indonesians do not lack intelligence or brains. We also know that the Indonesian people have enough spirit. But why do we not build up speedily, why are we lagging behind? That is why, on the 17th of August, 1957, I said that the political atmosphere in Indonesia had to be changed. That is why I suggested that the free-fight liberalism which gives us this unhealthy atmosphere has to be abandoned. In order to draw up a blueprint, I suggested what is called democracy with leadership.

The day before yesterday, in Bogor, I was visited by a large delegation of 260, representing cooperative bodies of the whole of Indonesia. Their spokesman said the following: "Mr. President, with our cooperatives we have been able to raise the standard of living of the people a little. And for your knowledge, we would like to inform you that in the world of cooperatives, democracy with leadership or guided democracy is applied. In the world of co-operatives . . . we have a clear aim, a clear-cut way of working and distribution of profit—everything is clearly under leadership."

Within the world of cooperatives, then, guided democracy is applied. If the blueprint of the National Planning Council is finished, the execution thereof could not be carried out smoothly without guided democracy, without leadership. The number-one leader is the blueprint itself. One cannot carry out a blueprint and at the same time debate about it, after it has been approved by parliament. This blueprint becomes the property of the Indonesian people, becomes national property. . . . This blueprint has to be carried out, and its principles cannot be debated again.

I am myself a qualified engineer. Very often, when I was in the construction business, I received blueprints of things to be built. I carried out those blueprints as they were. I did not argue why, for instance, certain lines went a certain way, why a certain thing should be made of concrete and not of wood, why its stories were that high when they were not lower. It was a blueprint entrusted to me, for me to carry out, and I would carry it out. The blueprint was my guide, and I myself guided and led the employees. As a qualified engineer, I had under me superintendents and foremen. I was their leader, and I had conferences with them. But my conferences with them were not of that type of free-fight liberalism. I conferred with them about the execution of the blueprint. I asked the superintendents: These things have to be made out of concrete; what would be the best way to get them done? One superintendent would suggest: Pak, I think this is the best way; get stones, gravel, sand, and cement, call a lot of people—twenty, a hundred—and have everything mixed by hand. I then asked another superintendent what his opinion was. He answered: No, do not work by hand, Bung, this building is too large for that; buy a concrete mixer at once; with that we can mix concrete for this building and others. I conferred with my foremen—I practiced democracy with them—I asked for their opinion. I also discussed the choice of the materials; I conferred with my men. On all aspects of the execution of the blueprint, I held discussions, but these discussions were under guidance—the guidance of the blueprint, my guidance, the constructor of the building.

That is why it is wrong when people say that guided democracy is a false democracy, that it is a form of dictatorship. I even said in my statement of October 28, 1958, that democracy with leadership is a true Indonesian democracy. This is the danger you are facing, the danger that many of you become copyists. You have heard of the word "democracy"; democracy is indeed good. What does America say about democracy? It is to be found in certain American books. What does England say, France, the Netherlands, Germany? They each have their own reference books. Well, one of them must be the genuine democracy. Thus, you then try to apply in Indonesia democracy as it is practiced in America, Germany, France, England, the Netherlands, the U.S.S.R., or in other countries? You are only trying to copy!

No, as I have said before, we have to return to our own personality; we want to return to our own identity. Do not let us become a carbon-copy nation. We have had a democracy since olden times. I do not imply that we should remain as we were then.

But the things of former times are good material for us today to refer to, because we are going to establish democracy in our own country.

How was democracy of former times in Indonesia? It still is practiced today in the villages in Java, Minangkabau, Sulawesi, Lombok, Bali, and other places—namely, in their laws and their system of *musjawarah* and *mufakat* (discussion and agreement). Every village practices democracy. But do they in these village meetings apply the practice of voting? Of free-fight liberalism, where half plus one is always right? No, the *musjawarah* is held under the guidance of Lurah, the Chief of the Elders, of Nini Mamak, the guidance of whoever is leader. Everybody says something different until at one time a compromise is achieved out of all these different opinions, without voting. This is what is called *mufakat* (agreement)—that by *musjawarah* (discussion) without voting, a joint compromise is achieved. There is no dictatorship in *musjawarah* and *mufakat*. That is why democracy with leadership is a true, original Indonesian democracy. This is one of the most important sources for us from which we can draw material to find a new, clear democracy—not American democracy, Dutch, French, British, German, or Soviet, or anybody else's democracy. Let us find a democracy which is suitable for our own identity. And use sources and material which are to be found in our own country.

Regarding our own democracy, I initiated the idea, calling on the people to join to fight the diseases that were the results of free-fight liberalism. I called on the people to destroy free-fight liberalism completely, and to change it into Indonesian democracy, guided democracy, or democracy with leadership. If people asked me to explain in detail what it means, I would not be able to give a proper answer. No, I want this guided democracy to become the property of the Indonesian people again. That is why I suggest to the people, especially the experts, scientists, students, to think. Please think and rethink, make and remake. Think, carry it out so that as a joint result we can achieve a new democratic system which I call democracy with leadership, or guided democracy, which is suitable for conditions in Indonesia. . . .

NASAKOM AND NEFO*

The rhythm of Revolution! Yes, it was this notion that brought me to the idea of the romanticism of Revolution—the romanticism of my own personal struggle also. But in the very first place the romanticism of the national struggle, the romanticism of the struggle of mankind in the universal revolution of man, the romanticism of every great struggle that is revolutionary. How great is God who gave that sense of the romanticism of struggle to me when I, as a youth, physically sitting on a grass mat under the flickering rays of a rushlight, conducted a mental dialogue in the metaphysical world with the great strugglers of many different nations, with the thinkers of all nations who steered the course of history! Thus when, in consequence of that mental dialogue, I reached the conviction that no great struggle could be carried out without the sense of the romanticism of struggle, I never ceased from transferring that feeling of the romanticism of struggle to the people of Indonesia. All rising and falling tides of the struggle, all blows which we have and all blows which we took are the rhythm of struggle, the rhythm of Revolution. "Strike a blow—come on, march ahead! Struck by a blow—come on, march ahead!" The thunder of Revolution, sometimes resounding as shouts of applause, sometimes voicing suffering and sorrow, as a whole we hear as a song, a symphony, a chorus, like the roar of the waves of the tumultuous ocean pounding on the shore which we hear as a mighty chorus to God.

Nevertheless, there still are people who accuse Sukarno of "taking sides," who accuse Sukarno of "favoritism." Sukarno taking sides? Taking sides with whom? If it is against imperialism, feudalism, and the enemies of the Revolution in general, Yes! Certainly Sukarno is taking sides, certainly Sukarno has favorites, that is, he sides with the people and he sides with the Revolution itself. Have not I said before that a revolution cannot possibly be uncommitted, which means that a revolution must always be committed, it must take sides? Yes, indeed! If it is against imperialism,

---

* Speech delivered on August 17, 1964; translated and published by the Ministry of Information, Djakarta, Indonesia, 1964.

against feudalism, against the enemies of the Revolution in general, certainly I have favorites, certainly I take sides, because I cannot possibly favor imperialism and feudalism, I cannot possibly favor the lackeys of imperialism such as Tunku Abdul Rahman,* and therefore I have favorites and my favor is for the people, for the man of the masses, for the proletariat, for "the humiliated and the hungry."

I have been accused of bringing advantage to one group only among our big national family? My answer here is also, Yes. Yes, I am giving advantage to one group only, namely—the revolutionary group! I am a friend of the nationalists, but only the revolutionary nationalist! I am a friend of the religious group, but only the revolutionary religious group! I am a friend of the Communist, because the Communists are revolutionary people. . . .

All that I, as Great Leader of the Revolution, have done in leading the Revolution is a reflection of the progressiveness of the Indonesian Revolution. There is not a single aspect in my leadership that is conservative in nature, not a single thing that is "stagnant," not a single thing that is unprogressive.

Elements of this progressiveness are to be found in all layers of Indonesian society. Some are amongst the religious groups. Some are amongst the nationalists. Some are amongst the socialists-Communists. Isn't that so? Religion aspires to freedom and justice. The Indonesian nationalist strives for socionationalism and sociodemocracy.

The socialist-Communist wants freedom and socialism. Thus all three contain progressiveness. For that reason NASAKOM is a progressive necessity of the Indonesian Revolution. Whoever is opposed to NASAKOM is not progressive! Whoever is against NASAKOM in reality cripples the Revolution, disbalances the Revolution! Whoever is anti-NASAKOM is not fully revolutionary, nay, is historically even contrarevolutionary!

The tree of the Bandung Spirit is becoming deeper and deeper rooted into the soil! Its foliage is getting thicker and thicker! Its flowers are blossoming forth more and more radiantly! Its fruit has increased and is becoming more and more tasty! African-Asian solidarity has become stronger, and this forms the coral reef upon which there runs aground every reactionary and contrarevolution-

---

* The Prime Minister of Malaysia.—ED.

ary attempt of "nekolim." (This is General Yani's abbreviation for neocolonialism, colonialism, and imperialism.)

Not only is Asian-African solidarity ever growing in strength, but also the solidarity of the NEFO, the solidarity of the New Emerging Forces, the forces that encompass the trinity of the socialist states, the newly independent states, and the progressive forces within the capitalist states—this NEFO solidarity too materializes more day by day, ever growing, ever increasing in strength. When I corrected the theory of "the three forces and the third forces," and launched the theory of the New Emerging Forces (NEFO) contra the Old Established Forces (OLDEFO), there were people, and even some of our own friends, who could not immediately grasp it and thought this NEFO theory was "without substance." But then, really, these people have no historical outlook! . . .

So as to enable our opponents to hear it, I will now once more proclaim what I have said time and time again: Go to hell with your "Indonesia going to economic collapse"! Go to hell with your tale of Indonesia's economic destruction. Go to hell! Your psy-war is not effective! We consider your psy-war the barking of a dog. Tens of times you have claimed that Indonesia under Sukarno would flounder, would collapse, would be destroyed, but we are immune to your psy-war! Last year they "predicted" that at the beginning of 1964 the Indonesian economy would collapse. But at the beginning of 1964 Indonesia did not collapse! And they are saying again that in October of this year Indonesia will "collapse." Go to hell! Indonesia will never collapse!—God willing, Indonesia will never collapse! . . .

Clearly, then, my message to you is, flow on, O river of the Indonesian Revolution, flow on with the strength of romanticism and the progress of your dynamism in the direction and toward the goal that is determined by the dialectics of revolution; flow on, do not become stagnant, for in flowing on in the direction and toward the goal determined by your own dialectics you remain loyal to the message that the sufferings of the people have charged you with!

SPEECH TO THE PEOPLE'S
CONSULTATIVE CONGRESS*

. . . I realize that [Great Leader of the Revolution] is merely a title. However, I am fully convinced—and with me are all the progressive revolutionary forces in our society, which have never been absent in our revolutionary struggle—that it is an absolute prerequisite for every revolution to have national leadership. This is even more the case with our multicomplex National Revolution, which aims at Pantjasila† socialism. Such a revolution cannot possibly exist without leadership. And this leadership is clearly reflected in the three elements of RE-SO-PIM, namely, Revolution, Socialism, and Leadership. . . .

It would not be in accordance with the pure spirit and letter of the 1945 Constitution if the People's Consultative Congress should fall back again into the sphere of liberal democracy, where it loses itself in endless debate about the details of policy, where each group competes with the others to bring victory to the interest of its own group and to defeat the national interest, the interest of the multitude, the interest of our Revolution. . . .

In the second plenary session of the People's Consultative Congress, in May, 1963, you even made me President for Life. At that time I replied to that decision of yours in the following words: "How good it would be if the People's Congress of the future, that is the People's Congress which is the result of general elections, would reconsider this matter." Now I still adhere to this opinion.‡ . . .

* Excerpts from an Antara News Agency transcript of a speech delivered to the fourth plenary session of the People's Consultative Congress, June 22, 1966.

† Pantjasila: the five principles of nationalism, internationalism, representative government, social justice, and belief in God in a context of religious freedom. These were adopted in 1945 by a committee of sixty Indonesians, under the leadership of Sukarno, as the fundamental principles of the Indonesian state.—ED.

‡ Despite Sukarno's assertion that only an elected Congress should have the power to strip him of the life presidency, the appointed Consultative Congress did so in July, 1966.

In the economic crash program, which I herewith convey to you, you will read that self-reliance is not just an aim but, what is not less important, it is a principle by which we are to achieve that aim, the principle of realizing development without depending on assistance from other countries or nations. It is obvious that not being dependent does not mean that we do not wish to cooperate on the same footing and for mutual benefit.* It is in the context of such a policy of self-reliance that we must surmount our difficulties in the fields of economy, finance, and development, those which are connected with inflation as well as those connected with the payment of our foreign debts. . . .

Ever since the decree of July 5, 1959, our Revolution has been continuously moving forward at an accelerated speed and this again makes it imperative for our democratic institutions to accelerate their speed without deviating our guided democracy toward liberal democracy. . . . It should also be fully realized, both outside and inside the People's Consultative Congress, what the differences and similarities are between the People's Consultative Congress and the People's Congress which results from general elections in the future, so that together we can truly open the way toward purification of the implementation of the 1945 Constitution and thus open a new page in the history of our Pantjasila Revolution.

When I presented [my address] "The March of Our Revolution" (1960), I made it clear that we "should not be halfhearted" and that "based on revolutionary morals and the moral of the Revolution it is the duty of the authorities to attack and to destroy every power, whether foreign or not, native or not, endangering the security or the continuation of the Revolution." Then, expressing the voice of the heart of the people, which demanded justice and democracy, I prohibited the reactionary parties Masjumi and PSI,† and I also ordered that a number of yellow [news] papers which liked to act at will be suppressed. These actions objectively strengthened national unity and made it healthier.

In my address "The March of Our Revolution," I warned: "One

* This passage marks a reversal (under pressure from the military) of Sukarno's opposition to aid programs with the United States and Western-oriented economic organizations.—ED.

† Masjumi is an Islamic political party; PSI, the Indonesian Socialist Party.—ED.

of the characteristics of a person who is truly revolutionary is the oneness of words and deed, the oneness of what his lips say and what he does." I also explained about the "three big groups of revolutionary powers" whose "reality cannot be denied even by the Gods in heaven," and that therefore "the bundling together of the three large groups of revolutionary powers is a must in the struggle against imperialism and capitalism." I said at that time: "We should not be afflicted by the diseases of Islam-phobia, nationalist-phobia, or Communist-phobia," and "I work my fingers to the bone to unify all forces which are revolutionary"—"work my fingers to the bone to unify all NASAKOM forces, all nationalist, religious, and Communist forces!" . . .

4. Mohandas K. Gandhi

Mohandas K. Gandhi was born in 1869 in western India, a member of the merchant caste. He studied law in London, was admitted to the bar in 1891, and then returned to India to practice law. Two years later, he went to South Africa, where he organized his first passive-resistance campaign against racial discrimination. On his return to India in 1915, he became one of the most influential members of the Indian Congress Party. After World War I, he organized campaigns of passive resistance calling for an end to British rule over India. Between 1922 and 1942, Gandhi was repeatedly imprisoned, but gained a vast following both in India and abroad. In 1948, after Indian independence had been established, Gandhi was assassinated by a Hindu fanatic—thus becoming a martyr to his belief in tolerance for all religions.

The Indian Congress Party still accepts Gandhi's philosophy as the basis of its ideology, although it has taken a more favorable attitude toward industrialization. Kwame Nkrumah has also mentioned Gandhi as one of the important influences upon his thinking.

The following selections are from a pamphlet Gandhi wrote in 1909. They include his explanation of passive resistance, and his defense of village and home industries as a more appropriate economic system than the machine civilization of the West.

INDIAN HOME RULE*

True Civilization

Reader: You have denounced railways, lawyers, and doctors. I can see that you will discard all machinery. What, then, is civilization?

Editor: The answer to that question is not difficult. I believe that the civilization India has evolved is not to be beaten in the world. Nothing can equal the seeds sown by our ancestors. Rome went; Greece shared the same fate; the might of the Pharaohs was broken; Japan has become Westernized; of China, nothing can be said; but India is still, somehow or other, sound at the foundation. The people of Europe learn their lessons from the writings of the men of Greece or Rome, which exist no longer in their former glory. In trying to learn from them, the Europeans imagine that they will avoid the mistakes of Greece and Rome. Such is their pitiable condition. In the midst of all this, India remains immovable, and that is her glory. It is a charge against India that her people are so uncivilized, ignorant, and stolid that it is not possible to induce them to adopt any changes. It is a charge really against our merit. What we have tested and found true on the anvil of experience we dare not change. Many thrust their advice upon India, and she remains steady. This is her beauty; it is the sheet anchor of our hope.

Civilization is that mode of conduct which points out to man the path of duty. Performance of duty and observance of morality are convertible terms. To observe morality is to attain mastery over our mind and our passions. So doing, we know ourselves. The Gujarati equivalent for civilization means "good conduct."

If this definition be correct, then India, as so many writers have shown, has nothing to learn from anybody else, and this is as it should be. We notice that the mind is a restless bird; the more it gets the more it wants, and still remains unsatisfied. The more

* Excerpts from *Indian Home Rule* (Ahmedabad: Navajivan Trust, 1946); reprinted by permission.

we indulge our passions, the more unbridled they become. Our ancestors, therefore, set a limit to our indulgences. They saw that happiness was largely a mental condition. A man is not necessarily happy because he is rich, or unhappy because he is poor. The rich are often seen to be unhappy, the poor to be happy. Millions will always remain poor. Observing all this, our ancestors dissuaded us from luxuries and pleasures. We have managed with the same kind of plough as it existed thousands of years ago. We have retained the same kind of cottages that we had in former times, and our indigenous education remains the same as before. We have had no system of life-corroding competition. Each followed his own occupation or trade, and charged a regulation wage. It was not that we did not know how to invent machinery; but our forefathers knew that, if we set our hearts after such things, we would become slaves and lose our moral fiber. They therefore, after due deliberation, decided that we should only do what we could with our hands and feet. They saw that our real happiness and health consisted in a proper use of our hands and feet. They further reasoned that large cities were a snare and a useless encumbrance and that people would not be happy in them, that there would be gangs of thieves and robbers, prostitution, and vice flourishing in them, and that poor men would be robbed by rich men. They were, therefore, satisfied with small villages. They saw that kings and their swords were inferior to the sword of ethics, and they, therefore, held the sovereigns of the earth to be inferior to the rishis and the fakirs.* A nation with a constitution like this is more fit to teach others than to learn from others. This nation had courts, lawyers, and doctors, but they were all within bounds. Everybody knew that these professions were not particularly superior; moreover, they did not rob people; they were considered people's dependants, not their masters. Justice was tolerably fair. The ordinary rule was to avoid courts. There were not touts to lure people into them. This evil, too, was noticeable only in and around capitals. The common people lived independently and followed their agricultural occupation. They enjoyed true home rule.

And where this cursed modern civilization has not reached, India remains as it was before. The inhabitants of that part of India

---

* A rishi is an ancient sage of the Hindu religion; a fakir is a religious ascetic.—Ed.

will very properly laugh at your newfangled notions. The English do not rule over them, nor will you ever rule over them. Those whose name we speak we do not know, nor do they know us. I would certainly advise you and those like you who love the mother-land to go into the interior that has not yet been polluted by the railways, and to live there for six months; you might then be patriotic and speak of home rule.

Now you see what I consider to be real civilization. Those who want to change conditions such as I have described are enemies of the country and are sinners.

Reader: It would be all right if India were exactly as you de-scribed it, but it is also India where there are hundreds of child widows, where two-year-old babies are married, where twelve-year-old girls are mothers and housewives, where women practice poly-andry, where the practice of *niyog** obtains, where, in the name of religion, girls dedicate themselves to prostitution, and where, in the name of religion, sheep and goats are killed. Do you con-sider these also symbols of the civilization that you have described?

Editor: You make a mistake. The defects that you have shown are defects. Nobody mistakes them for ancient civilization. They remain in spite of it. Attempts have always been made, and will be made, to remove them. We may utilize the new spirit that is born in us for purging ourselves of these evils. But what I have described to you as emblems of modern civilization are accepted as such by its votaries. The Indian civilization, as described by me, has been so described by its votaries. In no part of the world, and under no civilization, have all men attained perfection. The tendency of Indian civilization is to elevate the moral being, that of the Western civilization is to propagate immorality. The lat-ter is godless, the former is based on a belief in God. So under-standing and so believing, it behooves every lover of India to cling to the old Indian civilization even as a child clings to its mother's breast. . . .

Passive Resistance

Reader: Is there any historical evidence as to the success of what you have called soul-force or truth-force? No instance seems to

---

* *Niyog* is a practice that permits the husband to have sexual intercourse with other women when his wife is ill or pregnant.—Ed.

have happened of any nation having risen through soul-force. I still think that the evildoers will not cease doing evil without physical punishment.

Editor: The poet Tulsidas has said: "Of religion, pity or love is the root, as egotism of the body. Therefore, we should not abandon pity so long as we are alive." This appears to me to be a scientific truth; I believe in it as much as I believe in two and two being four. The force of love is the same as the force of the soul or truth. We would disappear without the existence of that force. But you ask for historical evidence. It is therefore necessary to know what history means. The Gujarati equivalent means: "It so happened." If that is the meaning of history, it is possible to give copious evidence. But if it means the doings of kings and emperors, there can be no evidence of soul-force or passive resistance in such history. You cannot expect silver ore in a tin mine. History, as we know it, is a record of the wars of the world, and so there is a proverb among Englishmen that a nation which has no history—that is, no wars—is a happy nation. How kings played, how they became enemies of one another, and how they murdered one another is found accurately recorded in history; and, if this were all that had happened in the world, it would have been ended long ago. If the story of the universe had commenced with wars, not a man would have been found alive today. Those people who have been warred against have disappeared—as, for instance, the natives of Australia, of whom hardly a man was left alive by the intruders. Mark, please, that these natives did not use soul-force in self-defense, and it does not require much foresight to know that the Australians will share the same fate as their victims. "Those who wield the sword shall perish by the sword." With us, the proverb is that professional swimmers will find a watery grave.

The fact that there are so many men still alive in the world shows that it is based not on the force of arms, but on the force of truth or love. Therefore, the greatest and most unimpeachable evidence of the success of this force is to be found in the fact that, in spite of the wars of the world, it still lives on.

Thousands—indeed, tens of thousands—depend for their existence on a very active working of this force. Little quarrels of millions of families in their daily lives disappear before the exercise of this force. Hundreds of nations live in peace. History does not, and cannot, take note of this fact. History is really a record of every interruption of the even working of the force of love or of the soul. Two brothers quarrel; one of them repents and reawakens the love that was lying dormant in him; the two again begin to live in peace; nobody takes note of this. But if the two brothers, through the intervention of solicitors or some other reason, take up arms or go to law—which is another form of the exhibition of brute force—their doings would be immediately noticed in the press; they would be the talk of their neighbors, and would probably go down in history. And what is true of families and communities is true of nations. There is no reason to believe that there is one law for families, and another for nations. History, then, is a record of an interruption of the course of nature. Soul-force, being natural, is not noted in history.

Reader: According to what you say, it is plain that instances of this kind of passive resistance are not to be found in history. It is necessary to understand this passive resistance more fully. It will be better, therefore, if you enlarge upon it.

Editor: Passive resistance is a method of securing rights by personal suffering; it is the reverse of resistance by arms. When I refuse to do a thing that is repugnant to my conscience, I use soul-force. For instance, the government of the day has passed a law which is applicable to me. I do not like it. If, by using violence, I force the government to repeal the law, I am employing what may be termed body-force. If I do not obey the law, and accept the penalty for its breach, I use soul-force. It involves sacrifice of self.

Everybody admits that sacrifice of self is infinitely superior to sacrifice of others. Moreover, if this kind of force is used in a cause that is unjust, only the person using it suffers. He does not make others suffer for his mistakes. Men have before now done many things which were subsequently found to have been wrong. No man can claim to be absolutely in the right, or that a particular thing is wrong, because he thinks so, but it is wrong for him so long as that is his deliberate judgment. It is, therefore, meet that he should not do that which he knows to be wrong, and suffer the consequence whatever it may be. This is the key to the use of soul-force.

Reader: You would then disregard laws; this is rank disloyalty. We have always been considered a law-abiding nation. You seem to be going even beyond the extremists. They say that we must obey the laws that have been passed, but that, if the laws be bad, we must drive out the lawgivers even by force.

Editor: Whether I go beyond them or whether I do not is a

matter of no consequence to either of us. We simply want to find out what is right, and to act accordingly. The real meaning of the statement that we are a law-abiding nation is that we are passive resisters. When we do not like certain laws, we do not break the heads of lawgivers, but we suffer and do not submit to the laws. That we should obey laws, whether good or bad, is a newfangled notion. There was no such thing in former days. The people disregarded those laws they did not like, and suffered the penalties for their breach. It is contrary to our manhood if we obey laws repugnant to our conscience. Such teaching is opposed to religion and means slavery. If the government were to ask us to go about without any clothing, should we do so? If I were a passive resister, I would say to them that I would have nothing to do with their law. But we have so forgotten ourselves and become so compliant, that we do not mind any degrading law.

A man who has realized his manhood, who fears only God, will fear no one else. Man-made laws are not necessarily binding on him. Even the government do not expect any such things from us. They do not say: "You must do such and such a thing," but they say: "If you do not do it, we will punish you." We are sunk so low that we fancy that it is our duty and our religion to do what the law lays down. If man will only realize that it is unmanly to obey laws that are unjust, no man's tyranny will enslave him. This is the key to self-rule or home rule.

It is a superstition and an ungodly thing to believe that an act of a majority binds a minority. Many examples can be given in which acts of majorities will be found to have been wrong, and those of minorities to have been right. All reforms owe their origin to the initiation of minorities in opposition to majorities. If, among a band of robbers, a knowledge of robbing is obligatory, is a pious man to accept the obligation? So long as the superstition that men should obey unjust laws exists, so long will their slavery exist. And a passive resister alone can remove such a superstition.

To use brute force, to use gunpowder, is contrary to passive resistance, for it means that we want our opponent to do by force that which we desire but he does not. If such a use of force is justifiable, surely he is entitled to do likewise by us. And so we should never come to an agreement. We may simply fancy, like the blind horse moving in a circle around a mill, that we are making progress. Those who believe that they are not bound to obey laws which are repugnant to their conscience have only the remedy of passive resistance open to them. Any other must lead to disaster.

Reader: From what you say, I deduce that passive resistance is a splendid weapon of the weak, but that when they are strong, they may take up arms.

Editor: This is gross ignorance. Passive resistance—that is, soul-force—is matchless. It is superior to the force of arms. How, then, can it be considered only a weapon of the weak? Physical-force men are strangers to the courage that is requisite in a passive resister. Do you believe that a coward can ever disobey a law that he dislikes? Extremists are considered to be advocates of brute force. Why do they, then, talk about obeying laws? I do not blame them. They can say nothing else. When they succeed in driving out the English and they themselves become governors, they will want you and me to obey their laws. And that is a fitting thing for their constitutions. But a passive resister will say he will not obey a law that is against his conscience, even though he may be blown to pieces at the mouth of a cannon.

What do you think? Wherein is courage required—in blowing others to pieces from behind a cannon, or with a smiling face to approach a cannon and to be blown to pieces? Who is the true warrior—he who keeps death always as a bosom-friend, or he who controls the death of others? Believe me that a man devoid of courage and manhood can never be a passive resister.

This, however, I will admit: that even a man weak in body is capable of offering this resistance. One man can offer it just as well as millions. Both men and women can indulge in it. It does not require the training of an army; it needs no jujitsu. Control over the mind is alone necessary, and when that is attained, man is free like the king of the forest, and his very glance withers the enemy.

Passive resistance is an all-sided sword; it can be used any way; it blesses him who uses it and him against whom it is used. Without drawing a drop of blood, it produces far-reaching results. It never rusts and cannot be stolen. Competition between passive resisters does not exhaust. The sword of passive resistance does not require a scabbard. It is strange indeed that you should consider such a weapon to be a weapon merely of the weak.

Reader: You have said that passive resistance is a specialty of India. Have cannons never been used in India?

Editor: Evidently, in your opinion, India means its few princes. To me, it means its teeming millions, on whom depends the existence of the princes and our own.

Kings will always use their kingly weapons. To use force is bred in them. They want to command; but those who have to obey commands do not want guns, and these are in a majority throughout the world. They have to learn either body-force or soul-force. Where they learn the former, both the rulers and the ruled become like so many madmen, but where they learn soul-force, the commands of the rulers do not go beyond the point of their swords, for true men disregard unjust commands. Peasants have never been subdued by the sword, and never will be. They do not know the use of the sword, and they are not frightened by the use of it by others. That nation is great which rests its head upon death as its pillow. Those who defy death are free from all fear. For those who are laboring under the delusive charms of brute force, this picture is not overdrawn. The fact is that, in India, the nation at large has generally used passive resistance in all departments of life. We cease to cooperate with our rulers when they displease us. This is passive resistance.

I remember an instance when, in a small principality, the villagers were offended by some command issued by the prince. The former immediately began vacating the village. The prince became nervous, apologized to his subjects, and withdrew his command. Many such instances can be found in India. Real home rule is possible only where passive resistance is the guiding force of the people. Any other rule is foreign rule. . . .

Machinery

Reader: When you speak of driving out Western civilization, I suppose you will also say that we want no machinery.

Editor: By raising this question, you have opened the wound I had received. When I read Mr. Dutt's *Economic History of India,* I wept; and, as I think of it again, my heart sickens. It is machinery that has impoverished India. It is difficult to measure the harm that Manchester has done to us. It is due to Manchester that Indian handicraft has all but disappeared. . . .

Machinery has begun to desolate Europe. Ruination is now knocking at the English gates. Machinery is the chief symbol of modern civilization; it represents a great sin. The workers in the mills of Bombay have become slaves. The condition of the women working in the mills is shocking. When there were no mills, these women were not starving. If the machinery craze grows in our country, it will become an unhappy land. It may be considered a heresy, but I am bound to say that it were better for us to send money to Manchester and to use flimsy Manchester cloth, than to multiply mills in India. By using Manchester cloth, we would only waste our money, but by reproducing Manchester in India, we shall keep our money at the price of our blood, because our very moral being will be sapped, and I call in support of my statement the very mill hands as witnesses. And those who have amassed wealth out of factories are not likely to be better than other rich men. It would be folly to assume that an Indian Rockefeller would be better than the American Rockefeller. Impoverished India can become free, but it will be hard for any India made rich through immorality to regain its freedom. I fear we will have to admit that moneyed men support British rule; their interest is bound up with its stability. Money renders a man helpless. The other thing as harmful is sexual vice. Both are poison. A snake bite is a lesser poison than these two, because the former merely destroys the body, but the latter destroys body, mind, and soul. We need not, therefore, be pleased with the prospect of the growth of the mill industry.

Reader: Are the mills, then, to be closed down?

Editor: That is difficult. It is no easy task to do away with a thing that is established. We therefore say that the nonbeginning of a thing is supreme wisdom. We cannot condemn millowners; we can but pity them. It would be too much to expect them to give up their mills, but we may implore them not to increase them. If they would be good, they would gradually contract their business. They can establish in thousands of households the ancient and sacred hand looms, and they can buy out the cloth that may be thus woven. Whether the millowners do this or not, people can cease to use machine-made goods.

Reader: You have so far spoken about machine-made cloth, but there are innumerable machine-made things. We have either to import them or to introduce machinery into our country.

Editor: Indeed, our gods even are made in Germany. What need, then, to speak of matches, pins, and glassware? My answer can be only one. What did India do before these articles were introduced? Precisely the same should be done today. As long as we cannot make pins without machinery, so long we will do without them. The tinsel splendor of glassware we will have nothing to do with, and we will make wicks, as of old, with home-grown cotton, and use handmade earthen saucers for lamps. So doing, we shall have our eyes and money, and will support Swadeshi,* and so shall we attain home rule. It is not to be conceived that all men will do all these things at one time, or that some men will give up all machine-made things at once. But if the thought is sound, we will always find out what we can give up, and will gradually cease to use this. What a few may do, others will copy, and the movement will grow like the coconut of the mathematical problem. What the leaders do, the populace will gladly follow. The matter is neither complicated nor difficult. You and I shall not wait until we can carry others with us. Those will be the losers who will not do it, and those who will not do it—although they appreciate the truth—will deserve to be called cowards.

Reader: What, then, of the tramcars and electricity?

Editor: This question is now too late. It signifies nothing. If we are to do without the railways, we shall have to do without the tramcars. Machinery is like a snake hole which may contain from one to a hundred snakes. Where there is machinery, there are large cities; and where there are large cities, there are tramcars and railways; and there only does one see electric light. English villages do not boast of any of these things. Honest physicians will tell you that where means of artificial locomotion have increased, the health of the people has suffered. I remember that when, in a European town, there was a scarcity of money, the receipts of the tramway company, of the lawyers, and of the doctors went down, and the people were less unhealthy. I cannot recall a single good point in connection with machinery. Books can be written to demonstrate its evils.

Reader: Is it a good point or a bad one that all you are saying will be printed through machinery?

Editor: This is one of those instances which demonstrate that sometimes poison is used to kill poison. This, then, will not be a good point regarding machinery. As it expires, the machinery, as it were, says to us: "Beware and avoid me. You will derive no benefit

---

* Swadeshi was a program of the Indian nationalists to boycott British goods and to buy only Indian-made products.—ED.

from me, and the benefit that may accrue from printing will avail only those who are infected with the machinery craze." Do not, therefore, forget the main thing. It is necessary to realize that machinery is bad. We shall then be able gradually to do away with it. Nature has not provided any way whereby we may reach a desired goal all of a sudden. If, instead of welcoming machinery as a boon, we would look upon it as an evil, it would ultimately go.

5. Jawaharlal Nehru

Jawaharlal Nehru, the late Prime Minister of India, was born in Allahabad in 1889, the only son of a Kashmiri Brahmin. His father was a wealthy and successful lawyer, and he was sent to Britain for his schooling. He attended Harrow and then Cambridge, where he was graduated with honors in science in 1910. For the next two years, he studied law in London. When he returned to India, he met Gandhi at the annual conference of the Indian National Congress in 1916, and became his lifelong disciple. He became General Secretary of the Congress in 1923, and was elected President of the Congress several times. He was repeatedly imprisoned by the British for passive-resistance activities. During World War II, Nehru began the negotiations with Britain that culminated in Indian independence on August 15, 1947. From that time until his death in May, 1964, he was Indian Prime Minister and Minister of Foreign Affairs, supported by a large Congress majority in the Indian parliament. Although he asserted a major role for India in international relations, he was equally concerned with the problem of economic development. A socialist in his early days in England, as Prime Minister Nehru took a more pragmatic view, favoring a mixed economy as more effective in development.

The first group of selections below is taken from The Discovery of India, *a book that was written by Nehru in 1944. The contrast between his approach to modernization and economic development and that of Gandhi is evident in his discussion of his personal philosophy and his attitude toward industrialization. This is followed by a short selection illustrating the modification of his views on socialism.*

THE DISCOVERY OF INDIA*

Philosophy of Life

Often, as I look at this world, I have a sense of mysteries, of unknown depths. The urge to understand it, insofar as I can, comes to me; to be in tune with it and to experience it in its fullness. But the way to that understanding seems to me essentially in the way of science, the way of objective approach, though I realize that there can be no such thing as true objectiveness. If the subjective element is unavoidable and inevitable, it should be conditioned as far as possible by the scientific method.

What the mysterious is I do not know. I do not call it God because God has come to mean much that I do not believe in. I find myself incapable of thinking of a deity or of any unknown supreme power in anthropomorphic terms, and the fact that many people think so is continually a source of surprise to me. Any idea of a personal god seems very odd to me. Intellectually, I can appreciate to some extent the conception of monism, and I have been attracted toward the Advaita (nondualist) philosophy of the Vedanta, though I do not presume to understand it in all its depth and intricacy, and I realize that merely an intellectual appreciation of such matters does not carry one far. At the same time, the Vedanta and other similar approaches rather frighten me with their vague formless incursions into infinity. The diversity and fullness of nature stir me and produce a harmony of the spirit, and I can imagine myself feeling at home in the old Indian or Greek pagan and pantheistic atmosphere, but minus the conception of god or gods that was attached to it.

Some kind of ethical approach to life has a strong appeal for me, though it would be difficult for me to justify it logically. I have been attracted by Gandhi's stress on right means, and I think one of his greatest contributions to our public life has been this emphasis. The idea is by no means new, but this application of an ethical doctrine to large-scale public activity was certainly novel.

* Excerpts from Jawaharlal Nehru, *The Discovery of India* (New York: The John Day Company, 1946); copyright 1946 by The John Day Company; reprinted by permission of The John Day Company, Inc., publisher.

It is full of difficulty, and perhaps ends and means are not really separable and form together one organic whole. In a world which thinks almost exclusively of ends and ignores means, this emphasis on means seems odd and remarkable. How far it has succeeded in India I cannot say. But there is no doubt that it has created a deep and abiding impression on the minds of large numbers of people.

A study of Marx and Lenin produced a powerful effect on my mind and helped me to see history and current affairs in a new light. The long chain of history and of social development appeared to have some meaning, some sequence, and the future lost some of its obscurity. The practical achievements of the Soviet Union were also tremendously impressive. Often, I disliked or did not understand some development there, and it seemed to me to be too closely concerned with the opportunism of the moment or the power politics of the day. But despite all these developments and possible distortions of the original passion for human betterment, I had no doubt that the Soviet Revolution had advanced human society by a great leap and had lit a bright flame which could not be smothered, and that it had laid the foundations for that "new civilization" toward which the world would advance. I am too much of an individualist and believer in personal freedom to like overmuch regimentation. Yet it seemed to me obvious that in a complex social structure individual freedom had to be limited, and perhaps the only way to real personal freedom was through some such limitation in the social sphere. The lesser liberties may often need limitation in the interest of the larger freedom.

Much in the Marxist philosophical outlook I could accept without difficulty: its monism and nonduality of mind and matter, the dynamics of matter, and the dialectic of continuous change by evolution as well as leap—through action and interaction, cause and effect, thesis, antithesis, and synthesis. It did not satisfy me completely, nor did it answer all the questions in my mind, and almost unawares a vague idealist approach would creep into my mind, something rather akin to the Vedanta approach. It was not a difference between mind and matter, but rather of something that lay beyond the mind. Also, there was the background of ethics. I realized that the moral approach is a changing one and depends upon the growing mind and an advancing civilization; it is conditioned by the mental climate of the age. Yet there was something more to it than that, certain basic urges which had greater permanence. I did not like the frequent divorce—in Communist, as in other, practice—between action and these basic urges or principles. So there was an odd mixture in my mind which I could not rationally explain or resolve. There was a general tendency not to think too much of those fundamental questions which appear to be beyond reach, and rather to concentrate on the problems of life—to understand, in the narrower and more immediate sense, what should be done and how. Whatever ultimate reality may be, and whether we can ever grasp it in whole or in part, there certainly appear to be vast possibilities of increasing human knowledge, even though this may be partly or largely subjective, and of applying this to the advancement and betterment of human life and social organization.

There has been in the past, and there is to a lesser extent even today among some people, an absorption in finding an answer to the riddle of the universe. This leads them away from the individual and social problems of the day, and when they are unable to solve that riddle, they despair and turn to inaction and triviality, or find comfort in some dogmatic creed. Social evils, most of which are certainly capable of removal, are attributed to original sin, to the unalterableness of "human nature," or the social structure, or (in India) to the inevitable legacy of previous births. Thus one drifts away from even the attempt to think rationally and scientifically, and takes refuge in irrationalism, superstition, and unreasonable and inequitable social prejudices and practices. It is true that even rational and scientific thought does not always take us as far as we would like to go. There is an infinite number of factors and relations which influence and determine events in varying degrees, and it is impossible to grasp all of them. Still, we can try to pick out the dominating forces at work and, by observing external material reality and by experiment and practice, trial and error, grope our way to ever-widening knowledge and truth.

For this purpose, and within these limitations, the general Marxist approach, fitting in as it more or less did with the present state of scientific knowledge, seemed to me to offer considerable help. But even accepting that approach, the consequences that flow from it and the interpretation of past and present happenings were by no means always clear. Marx's general analysis of social development seems to have been remarkably correct, and yet many developments took place later which did not fit in with his outlook for the immediate future. Lenin successfully adapted the Marxian thesis to some of these subsequent developments, but again, since then, further remarkable changes have taken place—the rise of fascism and Nazism and all that lay behind them. The very rapid growth of technology and the practical application of vast developments in scientific knowledge are now changing the world picture with an amazing rapidity, leading to new problems. . . .

Industrialization and the Machine

The Congress, under Gandhi's leadership, had long championed the revival of village industries, especially hand spinning and hand weaving. At no time, however, had the Congress been opposed to the development of big industries, and whenever it had the chance —in the legislatures or elsewhere—it had encouraged this development. Congress provincial governments were eager to do so. In the twenties, when the Tata Steel and Iron Works were in difficulties, it was largely due to the insistence of the Congress Party in the central legislature that government aid was given to help to tide over a critical period. The development of Indian shipbuilding and shipping services had long been a sore point of conflict between nationalist opinion and the government. The Congress, as all other sections of Indian opinion, was anxious that every assistance should be given to Indian shipping; the government was equally anxious to protect the vested interests of powerful British shipping companies. Indian shipping was thus prevented from growing by official discrimination against it, although it had both capital and technical and managerial ability at its disposal. This kind of discrimination worked all along the line, whenever any British industrial, commercial, or financial interests were concerned. . . .

The Congress Party has thus always been in favor of the industrialization of India, and at the same time has emphasized the development of cottage industries and worked for this. Is there a conflict between these two approaches? Possibly there is a difference in emphasis, a realization of certain human and economic factors which were overlooked previously in India. Indian industrialists and the politicians who supported them thought too much in terms of the nineteenth-century development of capitalist industry in Europe and ignored many of the evil consequences that were obvious in the twentieth century. In India, because normal progress had been arrested for a hundred years, those consequences were likely to be more far-reaching. The kind of medium-scale industries that were being started in India under the prevailing economic system resulted not in absorbing labor, but in creating more unemployment. While capital accumulated at one end, poverty and unemployment increased at the other. Under a different system and with a stress on large-scale industries absorbing labor, and with planned development, this might well have been avoided.

This fact of increasing mass poverty influenced Gandhi powerfully. It is true, I think, that there is a fundamental difference between his outlook on life generally and what might be called the modern outlook. He is not enamored of ever-increasing standards of living and the growth of luxury at the cost of spiritual and moral values. He does not favor the soft life; for him, the straight way is the hard way, and the love of luxury leads to crookedness and loss of virtue. Above all, he is shocked at the vast gulf that stretches between the rich and the poor—in their ways of living and their opportunities of growth. For his own personal and psychological satisfaction, he crossed that gulf and went over to the side of the poor, adopting, with only such improvements as the poor themselves could afford, their ways of living, their dress or lack of dress. This vast difference between the few rich and the poverty-stricken masses seemed to him to be due to two principal causes: foreign rule and the exploitation that accompanied it, and the capitalist industrial civilization of the West, as embodied in the big machine. He reacted against both. He looked back with yearning to the days of the old autonomous and more or less self-contained village community where there had been an automatic balance between production, distribution, and consumption; where political or economic power was spread out and not concentrated as it is today; where a kind of simple democracy prevailed; where the gulf between the rich and the poor was not so marked; where the evils of great cities were absent, and people lived in contact with the life-giving soil and breathed the pure air of the open spaces.

There was all this basic difference in outlook as to the meaning of life itself between him and many others, and this difference colored his language as well as his activities. His language—vivid and powerful as it often was—drew its inspiration from the religious and moral teachings of the ages, principally of India, but also of other countries. Moral values must prevail; the ends can never justify unworthy means, or else the individual and the race perish.

And yet he was no dreamer living in some fantasy of his own creation, cut off from life and its problems. He came from Gujrat, the home of hardheaded businessmen, and he had an unrivaled knowledge of the Indian villages and the conditions of life that prevailed there. It was out of that personal experience that he evolved his program of the spinning wheel and village industry. If immediate relief was to be given to the vast numbers of the unemployed and partially employed; if the rot that was spreading throughout India and paralyzing the masses was to be stopped; if the villagers' standards were to be raised, however little, en masse; if they were to be taught self-reliance instead of waiting helplessly like derelicts for relief from others; if all this was to be done without much capital—then there seemed no other way. Apart from the evils inherent in foreign rule and exploitation, and the lack of freedom to initiate and carry through big schemes of reform, the problem of India was one of scarcity of capital and abundance of labor—how to utilize that wasted labor, that manpower that was producing nothing. Foolish comparisons are made between manpower and machine power; of course, a big machine can do the work of a thousand or ten thousand persons. But if those ten thousand sit idly by or starve, the introduction of that machine is not a social gain—except in long perspective which envisages a change in social conditions. When the big machine is not there at all, then no question of comparison arises; it is a net gain both from the individual and the national point of view to utilize manpower for production. There is no necessary conflict between this and the introduction of machinery on the largest scale, provided that machinery is used primarily for absorbing labor and not for creating fresh unemployment.

Gandhi's attitude to the use of machinery seemed to undergo a gradual change. "What I object to," he said, "is the craze for machinery, not machinery as such. . . . If we could have electricity in every village home, I should not mind villages plying their implements and tools with electricity." The big machine seemed to him to lead inevitably, at least in the circumstances of today, to the concentration of power and riches: "I consider it a sin and injustice to use machinery for the purpose of concentration of power and riches in the hands of the few. Today the machine is used in this way." He even came to accept the necessity of many kinds of heavy industries and large-scale key industries and public utilities, provided they were state-owned and did not interfere with some kinds of cottage industries which he considered essential. Referring to his own proposals, he said: "The whole of this program will be a structure on sand if it is not built on the solid foundation of economic equality."

Thus, even the enthusiastic advocates for cottage and small-scale industries recognize that large-scale industry is, to a certain extent, necessary and inevitable; only they would like to limit it as far as possible. Superficially, then, the question becomes one of emphasis and adjustment of the two forms of production and economy. It can hardly be challenged that, in the context of the modern world, no country can be politically and economically independent, even within the framework of international interdependence, unless it is highly industrialized and has developed its power resources to the utmost. Nor can it achieve or maintain high standards of living and liquidate poverty without the aid of modern technology in almost every sphere of life. An industrially backward country will continually upset the world equilibrium and encourage the aggressive tendencies of more developed countries. Even if it retains its political independence, this will be nominal only, and economic control will tend to pass to others. This control will inevitably upset its own small-scale economy which it has sought to preserve in pursuit of its own view of life. Thus an attempt to build up a country's economy largely on the basis of cottage and small-scale industries is doomed to failure. It will not solve the basic problems of the country or maintain freedom, nor will it fit in with the world framework, except as a colonial appendage.

Is it possible to have two entirely different kinds of economy in a country—one based on the big machine and industrialization, and the other mainly on cottage industries? This is hardly conceivable, for one must overcome the other, and there can be little doubt that the big machine will triumph unless it is forcibly prevented from doing so. Thus, it is not a mere question of adjustment of the two forms of production and economy. One must be dominating and paramount, with the other complementary to it, fitting in where it can. The economy based on the latest technical achievements of the day must necessarily be the dominating one.

If technology demands the big machine, as it does today in a large measure, then the big machine with all its implications and consequences must be accepted. Where it is possible in terms of that technology to decentralize production, this would be desirable. But in any event, the latest technique has to be followed. To adhere to outworn and out-of-date methods of production—except as a temporary and stopgap measure—is to arrest growth and development.

Any argument as to the relative merits of small-scale and large-scale industry seems strangely irrelevant today, when the world and the dominating facts of the situation that confront it have decided in favor of the latter. Even in India, that decision has been made by these facts themselves, and no one doubts that India will be rapidly industrialized in the near future. She has already gone a good way in that direction. The evils of unrestricted and unplanned industrialization are well recognized today. Whether these evils are necessary concomitants of big industry, or derive from the social and economic structure behind it, is another matter. If the economic structure is primarily responsible for them, then surely we should set about changing that structure, instead of blaming the inevitable and desirable developments in technique.

The real question is not one of quantitative adjustment and balancing of various incongruous elements and methods of production, but a qualitative changeover to something different and new, from which various social consequences flow. The economic and political aspects of this qualitative change are important, but equally important are the social and psychological aspects. In India especially, where we have been wedded far too long to past forms and modes of thought and action—new experiences, new processes, leading to new ideas and new horizons, are necessary. Thus, we will change the static character of our living and make it dynamic and vital, and our minds will become active and adventurous. New situations lead to new experiences, as the mind is compelled to deal with them and adapt itself to a changing environment.

It is well recognized now that a child's education should be intimately associated with some craft or manual activity. The mind is stimulated thereby, and there is a coordination between the activities of the mind and the hands. So also the mind of a growing boy or girl is stimulated by the machine. It grows under the machine's impact (under proper conditions, of course, and not as an exploited and unhappy worker in a factory) and opens out new horizons. Simple scientific experiments, peeps into the microscope, and an explanation of the ordinary phenomena of nature bring excitement in their train, an understanding of some of life's processes and a desire to experiment and find out instead of relying on set phrases and old formulas. Self-confidence and the cooperative spirit grow, and frustration—arising out of the miasma of the past—lessens. A civilization based on ever-changing and advancing mechanical techniques leads to this. Such a civilization is a marked change, a jump almost, from the older type, and is intimately connected with modern industrialization. Inevitably, it gives rise to new problems and difficulties, but it also shows the way to overcome them. . . .

India and the West

A nation, like an individual, has many personalities, many approaches to life. If there is a sufficiently strong organic bond between these different personalities, it is well; otherwise, those personalities split up and lead to disintegration and trouble. Normally, there is a continuous process of adjustment going on, and some kind of an equilibrium is established. If normal development is arrested, or sometimes if there is some rapid change which is not easily assimilated, then conflict arises between those different personalities. In the mind and spirit of India, below the surface of our superficial conflicts and divisions, there has been this fundamental conflict due to a long period of arrested growth. A society, if it is to be both stable and progressive, must have a certain more or less fixed foundation of principles, as well as a dynamic outlook. Both appear to be necessary. Without the dynamic outlook, there is a stagnation and decay; without some fixed basis of principle, there is likely to be disintegration and destruction.

In India, from the earliest days, there was a search for those basic principles—for the unchanging, the universal, the absolute. Yet the dynamic outlook was also present, and an appreciation of life and the changing world. On these two foundations, a stable and progressive society was built up, though the stress was always more on stability and security and the survival of the race. In later years, the dynamic aspect began to fade away, and in the name of eternal principles the social structure was made rigid and unchanging. It was, as a matter of fact, not wholly rigid, and it did change gradually and continuously. But the ideology behind it, and the general framework, continued unchanged. The group idea as represented by more or less autonomous castes, the joint family, and the communal self-governing life of the village were the main pillars of this system, and all these survived for so long because—in spite of their failings—they fulfilled some essential needs of human nature and society. They gave security and stability to each group, and a sense of group freedom. Caste survived because it continued to represent the general power relationships of society, and class privileges were maintained, not only because of the prevailing ideology, but also because they were supported by vigor, intelligence, and ability, as well as a capacity for self-sacrifice. That ideology was not based on a conflict of rights, but on the individual's obligations to others and a satisfactory performance of his duties, on cooperation within the group and between different groups, and essentially on the idea of promoting peace rather than war. While the social system was rigid, no limit was placed on the freedom of the mind.

Indian civilization achieved much that it was aiming at, but in that very achievement life began to fade away, for it is too dynamic to exist for long in a rigid, unchanging environment. Even those basic principles which are said to be unchanging lose their freshness and reality when they are taken for granted, and the search for them ceases. Ideas of truth, beauty, and freedom decay, and we become prisoners following a deadening routine.

The very thing India lacked, the modern West possessed—and possessed to excess. It had the dynamic outlook. It was engrossed in the changing world, caring little for ultimate principles, the unchanging, the universal. It paid little attention to duties and obligations, and emphasized rights. It was active, aggressive, acquisitive, seeking power and domination, living in the present and ignoring the future consequences of its actions. Because it was dynamic, it was progressive and full of life, but that life was a fevered one, and the temperature kept on rising progressively.

If Indian civilization went to seed because it became static, self-absorbed, and inclined to narcissism, the civilization of the modern West—with all its great and manifold achievements—does not appear to have been a conspicuous success or to have thus far solved the basic problems of life. Conflict is inherent in it, and periodically it indulges in self-destruction on a colossal scale. It seems to lack something to give it stability, some basic principles to give meaning to life, though what these are I cannot say. Yet, because it is dynamic and full of life and curiosity, there is hope for it.

India—as well as China—must learn from the West, for the modern West has much to teach, and the spirit of the ages is represented by the West. But the West is also obviously in need of learning much, and its advances in technology will bring it little comfort if it does not learn some of the deeper lessons of life which have absorbed the minds of thinkers in all ages and in all countries.

India had become static, and yet it would be utterly wrong to imagine that she was unchanging. No change at all means death. Her very survival as a highly evolved nation shows that there was some process of continuous adaptation going on. When the British came to India, though technologically somewhat backward, she was still among the advanced commercial nations of the world. Technical changes would undoubtedly have come and changed India as they had changed some Western countries. But her normal development was arrested by the British power. Industrial growth was checked, and, as a consequence, social growth was also arrested. The normal power relationships of society could not adjust themselves and find an equilibrium, as all power was concentrated in the alien authority, which based itself on force and encouraged groups and classes which had ceased to have any real significance. Indian life thus progressively became more artificial, for many of the individuals and groups who seemed to play an important role in it had no vital functions left and were there only because of the importance given to them by the alien power. They had long ago finished their role in history and would have been pushed aside by new forces if they had not been given foreign protection. They became straw-stuffed symbols or protégés of foreign authority, thereby cutting themselves further away from the living currents of the nation. Normally, they would have been weeded out or diverted to some more appropriate function by revolution or democratic process. But so long as foreign authoritarian rule continued, no such development could take place. And so India was cluttered up with these emblems of the past, and the real changes that were taking place were hidden behind an artificial façade. No true social balances or power relationships within society could develop or become evident, and unreal problems assumed an undue importance.

India must break with much of her past and not allow it to dominate the present. Our lives are encumbered with the dead-wood of this past; all that is dead and has served its purpose has to go. But that does not mean a break with or a forgetting of the vital and life-giving in that past. We can never forget the ideals that have moved our race: the dreams of the Indian people through the ages; the wisdom of the ancients; the buoyant energy and love of life and nature of our forefathers; their spirit of curiosity and mental adventure; the daring of their thought, their splendid achievements in literature, art, and culture; their love of truth, and beauty, and freedom; the basic values that they set up; their understanding of life's mysterious ways; their toleration of other ways than theirs; their capacity to absorb other peoples and their cultural accomplishments, synthesize them, and develop a varied and mixed culture. Nor can we forget the myriad experiences which have built up our ancient race and lie embedded in our subconscious minds. We will never forget them or cease to take pride in that noble heritage of ours. If India forgets them, she will no longer remain India, and much that has made her our joy and pride will cease to be.

It is not this that we have to break with, but all the dust and dirt of ages that have covered her up and hidden her inner beauty and significance, the excrescences and abortions that have twisted and petrified her spirit, set it in rigid frames, and stunted her growth. We have to cut away these excrescences, and remember afresh the core of that ancient wisdom, and adapt it to our present circumstances. We have to get out of traditional ways of thought and living which, for all the good they may have done in a past age—and there was much good in them—have ceased to have significance today. We have to make our own all the achievements of the human race and join up with others in the exciting adventure of man, more exciting today perhaps than in earlier ages—realizing that this has ceased to be governed by national boundaries of old divisions and is common to the race of man everywhere. We have to revive the passion for truth and beauty and freedom which gives meaning to life, and develop afresh that dynamic outlook and spirit of adventure which distinguished those of our race who, in ages past, built our house on these strong and enduring foundations. Old as we are, with memories stretching back to the early dawns of human history and endeavor, we have to grow young again, in tune with our present time, with the irrepressible spirit and joy of youth in the present and its faith in the future. . . .

The Caste System

Caste is the symbol and embodiment of exclusiveness among the Hindus. It is sometimes said that the basic idea of caste might remain, but its subsequent harmful development and ramifications should go; that it should not depend on birth but on merit. This approach is irrelevant and merely confuses the issue. In a historical context, a study of the growth of caste has some value, but obviously we cannot go back to the period when caste began; in the social organization of today, it has no place left. If merit is the only criterion and opportunity is thrown open to everybody, then caste loses all its present-day distinguishing features and, in fact, ends. Caste has in the past not only led to the suppression of certain groups but to a separation of theoretical and scholastic learning from craftsmanship and a divorce of philosophy from actual life and its problems. It was an aristocratic approach based on traditionalism. This outlook has to change completely, for it is wholly opposed to modern conditions and the democratic ideal. The functional organization of social groups in India may continue, but even that will undergo a vast change as the nature of modern industry creates new functions and puts an end to many old ones. The tendency today everywhere is toward a functional organization of society, and the concept of abstract rights is giving place to that of functions. This is in harmony with the old Indian ideal.

The spirit of the age is in favor of equality, though practice denies it almost everywhere. We have got rid of slavery in the narrow sense of the word—that a man can be the property of another. But a new slavery, in some ways worse than the old, has taken its place all over the world. In the name of individual freedom, political and economic systems exploit human beings and treat them as commodities. And again, though an individual cannot be the property of another, a country and a nation can still be the property of another nation, and thus group slavery is tolerated. Racialism also is a distinguishing feature of our times, and we have not only master nations but also master races.

Yet the spirit of the age will triumph. In India, at any rate, we must aim at equality. That does not and cannot mean that everybody is physically or intellectually or spiritually equal or can be made so. But it does mean equal opportunities for all and no political, economic, or social barrier in the way of any individual or group. It means a faith in humanity and a belief that there is no race or group that cannot advance and make good in its own way, given the chance to do so. It means a realization of the fact that the backwardness or degradation of any group is not due to inherent failings in it, but principally to lack of opportunities and long suppression by other groups. It should mean an understanding of the modern world, wherein real progress and advance, whether national or international, have become very much a joint affair and a backward group pulls back others. Therefore, not only must equal opportunities be given to all, but special opportunities for educational, economic, and cultural growth must be given to backward groups so as to enable them to catch up to those who are ahead of them. Any such attempt to open the doors of opportunity to all in India will release enormous energy and ability and transform the country with amazing spéed.

Democratic Collectivism

If the spirit of the age demands equality, it must necessarily also demand an economic system which fits in with it and encourages it. The present colonial system in India is the very antithesis of it. Absolutism is not only based on inequality, but must perpetuate it in every sphere of life. It suppresses the creative and regenerative forces of a nation, bottles up talent and capacity, and discourages the spirit of responsibility. Those who have to suffer under it lose their sense of dignity and self-reliance. The problems of India, complicated as they seem, are essentially due to an attempt to advance while preserving the political and economic structure more or less intact. Political advance is made subject to the preservation of this structure and existing vested interests. The two are incompatible.

Political change there must be, but economic change is equally necessary. That change will have to be in the direction of a democratically planned collectivism. "The choice," says R. H. Tawney, "is not between competition and monopoly, but between monopoly which is irresponsible and private and a monopoly which is responsible and public." Public monopolies are growing even in capitalist states, and they will continue to grow. The conflict between the idea underlying them and private monopoly will continue till the latter is liquidated. A democratic collectivism need not mean an abolition of private property, but it will mean the public ownership of the basic and major industries. It will mean the cooperative or collective control of the land. In India especially, it will be necessary to have, in addition to the big industries, cooperatively controlled small and village industries. Such a system of democratic collectivism will need careful and continuous planning and adaptation to the changing needs of the people. The aim should be the expansion of the productive capacity of the nation in every possible way, at the same time absorbing all the labor power of the nation in some activity or other and preventing unemployment. As far as possible, there should be freedom to choose one's occupation. An equalization of income will not result from all this, but there will be far more equitable sharing, and a progressive tendency toward equalization. In any event, the vast differences that exist today will disappear completely, and class distinctions, which are essentially based on differences in income, will begin to fade out.

Such a change would mean an upsetting of the present-day acquisitive society, based primarily on the profit motive. The profit motive may still continue to some extent, but it will not be the dominating urge, nor will it have the same scope as it has today. It would be absurd to say that the profit motive does not appeal to the average Indian, but it is nevertheless true that there is no such admiration for it in India as there is in the West. The possessor of money may be envied, but he is not particularly respected or admired. Respect and admiration still go to the man or woman who is considered good and wise, and especially to those who sacrifice themselves or what they possess for the public good. The Indian outlook, even of the masses, has never approved of the spirit of acquisitiveness. . . .

Behind these problems in India, as in many other countries, lies the real issue—which is not merely the establishment of democracy of the nineteenth-century European type, but also far-reaching social revolution. Democracy has itself become involved in that seemingly inevitable change, and hence among those who disapprove of the latter, doubts and denials arise about the feasibility of democracy, and this leads to fascist tendencies and the continuation of an imperialist outlook. All our present-day problems in India—the communal or minority problem, the Indian princes, vested interest of religious groups and the big landowners, and the entrenched interests of British authority and industry in India—ultimately resolve themselves into opposition to social change. And because any real democracy is likely to lead to such change, therefore democracy itself is objected to and considered unsuited to the peculiar conditions of India. So the problems of India—for all their seeming variety and difference from others—are of the same essential nature as the problems of China, or Spain, or many other countries of Europe and elsewhere. . . . Many of the resistance movements of Europe reflect these conflicts. Everywhere the old equilibrium of social forces has been upset, and till a new equilibrium is established, there will be tension, trouble, and conflict. From these problems of the moment, we are led to one of the central problems of our time: how to combine democracy with socialism, how to maintain individual freedom and initiative and yet have centralized social control and planning of the economic life of the people, on the national as well as the international plane. . . .

INDIAN SOCIALISM*

In a country like India—an underdeveloped country—socialism, a real socialist basis of society, can only come gradually. There is no help for it. Take the instance of China: They are very keen on changing their economy, and there are no such difficulties as we have—that is, parliamentary institutions and all kinds of "three readings" and select committees, which take a long time. They can pass a law overnight, if they want to. Even then, they go on saying that it will take them twenty years to lay the socialist basis of their society—to have a socialist economy—in spite of all the speed with which they may work. . . .

If by adopting some method which in theory appeals to us we reduce our production, then we are in effect undermining the growth toward socialism—although that particular step may be called a socialist step. For instance, I am quite clear in my mind that if we start nationalizing the existing institutions, industries,

* From a speech delivered by Nehru to the Congress Parliamentary Party on December 22, 1954; excerpted from *Towards a Socialistic State* (New Delhi: All-India Congress Committee, 1956).

etc., by giving compensation, we reduce our capacity to go ahead. Here you have to be clear about one thing in your minds. Are we going in for possible seizure, expropriation without compensation, or are we not? Generally speaking, if we go in for possible seizure, then we think out its consequences, the consequences of conflict, the consequences of suffering of large numbers. Now, so far as our Constitution is concerned, that is ruled out. Apart from the Constitution, our general policy has been opposed to it. . . .

People do not generally realize how many years it took the Soviet Union to get the machines running. We see Russia today, forty years after the Revolution. It took them years to get the machines moving. Take one simple instance. In their Constitution, they said, in a sense as we say, compulsory free primary education for everybody. As far as I remember, it took them fifteen years to do that, in spite of all the power of the state. These things do take time; you cannot help it, because it involves not only the money factor, but numerous other factors.

I think it is advantageous for the public sector to have a competitive private sector to keep it up to the mark. The public sector will grow. But I feel that, if the private sector is not there, if it is abolished completely, there is a risk of the public sector becoming slow, not having that urge and push behind it. It depends on men, of course. On the whole, it is a good thing to have a private sector, something where the surplus energies of people who are not employed in the public sector may have some play, provided, of course, we control that private sector in the interest of the National Plan. You can control it in a hundred ways. Control it by all means. But where you do not control, give them room to exercise initiative and bring results. That is only a sort of broad approach to this problem. I can understand that a government may gradually take steps which might be said to be in a wrong direction. It may strengthen the existing structure of society rather than weaken it. But in the final analysis, we want to break through the existing structure—the economic as well as the social—because it restricts progress. A country cannot grow if it allows rigid structures. . . . Similarly, we have to break through what might be called a capitalist structure and have something else. But breaking through it has to be in a way so as to replace it for all time, and to begin with—even while it exists—to control it.

PART II

THE ISLAMIC WORLD

The area of Islamic religion and culture extends from Morocco to Pakistan. There are also substantial Moslem elements in Malaya, Indonesia, and some African countries, but the common tie of the Arab language—which links areas as distant as Morocco and Iraq—is not present, and Islam does not have the political significance in these areas that it possesses in North Africa, the Middle East, and Pakistan.

In the Islamic world, as in Africa, nationalism has taken several forms. Where the nation-state was the product of artificial divisions imposed by the Europeans, loyalties have been directed to a Pan-Arab or even Pan-Islamic ideal as much as to the individual nation. In these areas, the binding force of culture, language, and religion gives a common universe of discourse to political leaders. These ties are the basis of efforts toward common consultation and action through such bodies as the Arab League or the projected Maghreb (North African) Federation. The appeal of the Pan-Arab ideal may also be used—as in the case of Nasser—to extend the influence of an individual national leader throughout the Middle East.

Yet divisions remain—whether caused by personal rivalries, ideological differences (e.g., between Nasser and Saudi Arabia), permanent competition for influence (as between Iraq and Egypt), or different geographical situations and contacts with outside influences. North Africa, while maintaining links with the Middle East, seems destined to pursue a separate course, and Pakistan looks to Asia as much as to the Arab world.

All these areas are currently facing a common political problem (which Catholic Europe had to face earlier, in the nineteenth century): the adjustment of a traditional religion having a deep hold

131

*on the population to the needs of the modern world.** This, in turn, is part of the larger problem of how to combine traditional culture and the European influences, to which the area has been subjected intensively during the last fifty years. In most Islamic countries, democracy has not functioned effectively, and reformist military rule has been more successful. Moreover, as the history of the Middle East—particularly the success of Nasser's policy and the failure of the Baghdad Pact—has demonstrated in the last decade, the Islamic world prefers a neutral position in the East-West conflict.*

Nasser's nationalization of a substantial sector of the Egyptian economy set off new discussions concerning the relationship of his "Arab socialism" and Islam. Nasser himself defends socialization as being in accord with the principles of the Prophet. While he has been both defended and criticized by Islamic leaders, his action is in accord with the modernizing elite's desire to assert political control over the production and distribution of goods in the interest of economic development and social reform.

The Islamic world spans Africa, the Middle East, and parts of Asia, linking three of the four major areas of the underdeveloped world. Its contacts with Latin America have thus far been limited, though observers have commented on similarities in the political psychology and ideological assumptions of Latin America and the Middle East—in their hostility to foreign imperialism, in the intensity of their emotional involvement in politics, and in the importance of military men in national politics. The Tricontinental Solidarity Conference held in Cuba in January, 1966, attempted to develop closer relations between Cuba and the Arab world; a second conference is scheduled to be held in Cairo. Cairo was the site of the second Conference of Nonaligned Nations in 1964, and is also the headquarters of the Afro-Asian Solidarity Organization.

* See Bourguiba's speech on Ramadan and Ayub Khan's speech on Islam in Pakistan.

6. Mohammed Ayub Khan

Mohammed Ayub Khan was born in 1908 in the northwest frontier province of British India. His father was a member of the British-trained Indian Army. He studied at the Moslem University of Aligarh and at Sandhurst (the equivalent of West Point in Britain). During World II, he commanded a battalion in Burma. Upon the partition of India in 1947, his regiment became part of the Pakistani Army. In 1951, Ayub became Commander-in-Chief of the Army, and in 1954–55, he served also as Minister of Defense. In 1958, Iskander Mirza, President of Pakistan, with Ayub Khan's support, abrogated the constitution and dissolved the political parties. A few weeks later, Mirza left the country and Ayub Khan took over the presidency and proclaimed martial law.

Under his rule, land reform has been instituted, and a system of "basic democracy" introduced (described in his article "Pakistan Perspective"). Pakistan is an Islamic state, and Ayub Khan is himself a devout Moslem. In his address to the assembly of Moslem legal and religious scholars (Ulema), Ayub Khan discusses the ways in which Islam can be modernized to meet the needs of a contemporary society.

ISLAM IN PAKISTAN*

. . . Islam came on earth by divine grace 1,400 years ago. It was not only a new religion but also a movement of great developing power that changed completely the conditions of human life and

* From a speech delivered by Ayub Khan to the Assembly of the Ulema on May 13, 1959; translated by the editor (by permission) from the French version in *Orient* (Paris), No. 12 (1959).

the realities of civilization. As long as that movement kept its fundamental vitality, Moslems demonstrated their greatness in the domains of theory, practice, and science. Gradually, however, the dynamic aspect of Islam was weakened, and its dogmatic aspect became stronger. The inevitable result of this was that life and religion became two absolutely separate worlds. This division extended to our entire existence. Islam, however, came to break down that difference.

If the link between life and religion weakens, life itself continues to pursue its course, one way or another, while religion becomes a silent and immobile idolatry, deprived of movement and flexibility, and imprisoned far from the world, in the mosques and monasteries. This, to some extent, is what has happened in Islam. Thanks to philosophy and science, the life of men today has progressed, while the progress of religion has been shackled for centuries. The miracle of Islam is that it ended idolatry, but Moslems have made an idol out of their religion.

One of the consequences of this situation is very dangerous for our community and civilization. Indeed, those Moslems who have accepted the new enlightenment and advanced with their times are called secular, and those who have remained in the shelter of traditional faith in the world of the past are called religious. To look to the future was soon considered an infraction of religion, and to look to the past a proof of love of religion. All new progress, new invention, and new education were suspect as contrary to Islam. This is why in past history most Moslem leaders who were too revolutionary were regarded as infidels.

Today I invite you to consider the content of the sermons read each Friday in all of the mosques in our country. In a good number of these sermons, exception is taken to the petty, inoffensive things of our day for the sole reason that these things are new. Thus Islam is considered as the enemy and rival of material progress, and to advance is the greatest crime that one can commit against Islam. Still worse, this crime falls on the young people who are Moslem and who want to remain Moslem in the modern world of today. To oblige twentieth-century man to go back some hundreds of years in the past in order to be Moslem is to perpetuate an injustice against the world and against the faith.

The question is to know now why and how this lack of progress has occurred in a religion as practical and dynamic as Islam. Is it because we have departed from our basic principles and have not been able to establish a social order and governmental regime that could survive in the midst of changing situations and values? Is it because, considering religion a collection of stories about spirits and angels, we have imprisoned it in all kinds of superstitions and, demanding a kind of servile imitation, have cut off the critical and creative faculties of human nature? Is it because of a type of mysticism that flees the world and tries to shut up life within the four walls of the monastery cell? Is it because of the erroneous belief that we can achieve salvation without taking action with our hands and feet? Have we forgotten that life in the other world is the fruit of this terrestrial life and that there we will receive our reward for our efforts and work accomplished on earth?

All these questions are basic. It is absolutely necessary to learn the reasons why the impatient soul of the youth of Islam has been forced into insensibility and lack of realism. In this search, many disagreeable and bitter things will become clear to us, but our moral duty is to overcome our bitterness and face this question honestly and courageously in order to find a proper solution.

One of the great reasons for confusion in the world of Islam is sectarianism. Whether it is right or wrong, it is a fact, and it is not wise to ignore it. Which sect is right? Which sect is wrong? Only evil can result from these differences. Instead of criticizing the beliefs of others, is it not preferable to declare that fundamentally we are all alike, since Allah is one, our Prophet is one, and our Holy Book is one? Development of this kind of correct sentiment is primarily in the hands of the doctors of Moslem law. You possess the treasure of wisdom. As to particular points of religion, your knowledge is very vast. But it is not right to limit this great knowledge to one single area. In this period of progress and evolution, it is indispensable that theologians also have some knowledge of philosophy, science, economics, history, and current events. It is likewise necessary that people have the benefit of modern education—so that they are not ignorant of the fundamental beliefs and principles of their religion. In your sermons, you should also insist that as far as possible, we should harmonize religious instruction and civic education. This point is still more important in this period. I have the firm hope that the Education Commission will give it particular attention. But even with the recommendations of the Education Commission, this matter will not be entirely resolved. The greatest responsibility to resolve it is on the shoulders of the religious and juridical leaders. And we will be thankful to you if in your perfect wisdom you present Islam in such language and in such a way that the scientists who carry out experiments in the laboratories, the professors who teach in the universities, the peasants who plow the fields, and the workers who work in the factories can understand Islam without difficulty and find their hearts revived and their souls lifted up in accordance with their capacities.

You know that the world today is divided into two hostile camps. This struggle is carried out not only on the material plane, but also on the ideological plane. The principal effort of Communism is to destroy all other ideologies and to impose itself on the whole world. Material values obviously have great importance for all, but not to such an extent that man must sacrifice himself for them. In these conditions, there is only one possible answer to Communism, and that answer is Islam. Between the ideology of Communism and the materialist conceptions of the West, Islam is the only point of view that can prevent the spirit of humanity from being destroyed. It is false to believe that Communism can be a danger only for Christian nations. The conditions of life that are developing in the Middle East show clearly that the Islamic world is in no way impervious to the attempts of Communism. To prevent that danger, it is necessary that Islam be taken out of the recesses of the past and presented to the world in a way and a language that are absolutely modern—not as an ideology, but as a true plan of political, civic, and spiritual action, because this is the fundamental meaning of Islam. For this effort, we also need the aid and the inspiration of religious and juridical leaders.

As to the affairs of Pakistan, there is no doubt that problems and difficulties—both internal and external—rise before us. By divine grace and mercy, many of these difficulties are being resolved. But the simplest method is still for you to have confidence in your own powers as spiritual guides both for yourselves and for others, and to carry out your different responsibilities with the greatest diligence. The law of nature decrees that man can work conscientiously only when a clear plan of action is presented before him.

We are not only Moslems; we are also Pakistanis. We are not only Pakistanis; among us there are Bengalis, Sinds, Punjabis, Baluchis, and Pathans. Our plan of action must be sufficiently broad to respond easily to all the local, national, and community aspects of the problems that we have to resolve. This can only be done if we carry on our lives according to the principles of fraternity, order, pity, nobility, courtesy, and honesty—that is, according to the principles in force in all countries and at all times. The most important thing is that these principles should also be those of Islam. If we conform to the principles of honesty and sincerity and if Allah wills it, Pakistan can become a model of peace and security, not only for ourselves, but also for the Islamic world and perhaps for the whole world. . . .

PAKISTAN PERSPECTIVE*

. . . It is a common fallacy to believe that the concept of Pakistan was formed in a poet's dream. The poet, Dr. Muhammad Iqbal, was no idle dreamer. Nor can countries like Pakistan (364,737 square miles; population 80 million) spring from the nebulous realm of poetry alone. Iqbal was in fact a philosopher of traditional as well as modern thought who had made a careful study of human affairs, both East and West, and focused the light of his inquiry on the causes of the economic and cultural subjugation to which the Moslems of India had been systematically subjected since their first abortive struggle for independence in 1857. It was in his presidential address to the annual session of the All-India Moslem League in 1930 that he spelled out the broad outlines of a plan under which the Moslems of India were led to aspire to an independent state in which they would be free to follow their own way of life.

The All-India Moslem League based its Charter on this idea and, under the leadership of Qaid-i-Azam Mohammed Ali Jinnah, launched a struggle which culminated in the establishment of Pakistan in August, 1947.

Iqbal's thesis—that in their free state the Moslems were to practice their own way of life—posed an ideological problem which was not easy to handle. On one hand, there were many outside Pakistan who charged us with planning to establish an obdurate theocracy in the medieval sense of the term. On the other,

* Reprinted, by special permission of the Council on Foreign Relations, from Mohammed Ayub Khan's article "Pakistan Perspective," in *Foreign Affairs*, XXXVIII, No. 4 (July, 1960), 547–56. Copyright by the Council on Foreign Relations, New York.

most of us within Pakistan itself were not quite clear how to go about welding our spiritual ideals into the business of statecraft. The result was a great deal of loose groping which infected our politics and our intellect alike.

Pakistan was thus involved in the paradox of almost losing its ideology in the very act of trying to fulfill it. This distraction was totally unwarranted, for Iqbal—one of the main creators of our ideology—had taken pains to define it in very clear terms: "In Islam, the spiritual and the temporal are not two distinct domains, and the nature of an act, however secular in its import, is determined by the attitude of mind with which the agent does it. It is the invisible mental background of the act which ultimately determines its character. An act is temporal or profane if it is done in a spirit of detachment from the infinite complexity of life behind it. It is spiritual if it is inspired by that complexity. In Islam, it is the same reality which appears as church looked at from one point of view and state from another."

According to this concept, the state owes a singular and specific duty to its people. "The essence of *Tauhid* [unity of God] as a working idea is equality, solidarity, and freedom," according to Iqbal. "The state, from the Islamic standpoint, is an endeavor to transform these ideals into space-time forces, an aspiration to realize them in a definite human organization."

It is this sort of human organization which Pakistan aspires to become, and one of my endeavors is to clear at least a part of the way by liberating the basic concept of our ideology from the dust of vagueness and ambiguities it has accumulated over the years. . . .

The British parliamentary system which we inherited and later adopted in the Constitution of 1956 is largely an unwritten law and takes for granted too many prerequisites which do not really exist in a country like Pakistan. Our rate of literacy is appallingly low. Our means of communication are poor—even primitive. The rural population, which constitutes over 80 per cent of the total, is hardly touched by the world outside the villages.

Just before independence, when Mr. Jinnah was anxious to put more and more of his party men in the Central and Provincial Assemblies of India to carry on the struggle for the idea of Pakistan, he issued an appeal: "Vote for a Moslem Leaguer even if it be a lamppost." People complied cheerfully—some even literally! When independence came, the gentlemen thus elected found themselves in a position of vantage to assume power in the new state of Pakistan, and the political system in their hands enabled them to keep delaying the making of a constitution for about eight years. The outgoing Parliament of Pakistan had eighty seats, with each member presuming to represent about a million of his countrymen for almost an indefinite period. Even under the Constitution of 1956, a member of the Provincial Assembly was required to be elected by more than 100,000 voters. Now this is the type of electoral college which just cannot work in Pakistan—or for that matter in any country where conditions like those of Pakistan obtain, as they do in many newly independent countries of Asia and Africa. An average villager with little or no education has no means of gaining any personal knowledge about a candidate who is mixed up in a population of 100,000 or more, spread over a large area without any advanced means of communication and contact. Votes cast under these circumstances cannot but be vague, wanton, and responsive to fear, coercion, temptation, and other modes of misguidance. This is exactly what had been happening in Pakistan. Whenever elections were held, they could be easily manipulated to return candidates with power to influence, money to bribe, and nuisance value to coerce. Conditions such as these reduce the practice of democracy to a farce.

But this does not dismay us. Nor should it be taken to imply that we can do—or wish to do—without democracy. The revolution of October 7, 1958, was not aimed against the institution of democracy as such. No, it was only against the manner in which its institutions were being worked. There are two main reasons why we in Pakistan cannot but adhere to a democratic pattern of life and government. In the first place, as Moslems, we are brought up on two basic ingredients of democracy—namely, equality and fraternity. Anything to the contrary would be the negation of our spiritual faith and practice. And secondly, we have to fight a long and arduous battle for progress and development in which every man, woman, and child of Pakistan must participate to the fullest possible extent. Democracy provides the only healthy and dignified way for arousing the willing cooperation of people and harnessing it to a sustained national endeavor.

We must, therefore, have democracy. The question then is: what type of democracy? The answer need not be sought in the theories and practices of other people alone. On the contrary, it must be found from within the book of Pakistan itself.

To my mind, there are four prerequisites for the success of any democratic system in a country like Pakistan:

1. It should be simple to understand, easy to work, and cheap to sustain.

2. It should put to the voter only such questions as he can answer in the light of his own personal knowledge and understanding without external prompting.

3. It should ensure the effective participation of all citizens in the affairs of the country up to the level of their mental horizon and intellectual caliber.

4. It should be able to produce reasonably strong and stable governments.

The scheme of "basic democracies" which has been launched in Pakistan is designed to meet most of these fundamental prerequisites. Under this scheme, the two wings of the country have each been divided into 40,000 constituencies with an average population of about 1,000. Every constituency elects one representative by universal franchise. In such a small and well-defined field of choice, voters of the meanest intelligence cannot go far wrong in putting their finger on the right type of candidate.

Ten such constituencies form a Union Council in the rural areas, and this elects its own chairman from among the elected members. Provision has also been made for nominated members to ensure, where necessary, the representation of special interests like women, minorities, etc. In towns and larger municipalities, organization follows a similar pattern.

The elected chairmen of Union Councils and Town Committees represent their areas on the next tier of administration, the *Thana* Council, which covers the entire area under the jurisdiction of a Police Station. From this stage, this system of associating the chosen representatives of the people with local administration travels upward, covering all intermediary tiers, like *tehsils*, districts, and divisions, up to the provincial level. This is designed to ensure a full sense of cooperation between the official and elected agencies at all stages of public administration.

The first elections to basic democracies were held last December, and I feel the results were quite heartening. The average percentage of votes cast was 67 per cent by men and 42 per cent by women. Those elected included 14 per cent university graduates,

78 per cent literate, and 8 per cent illiterate members. They came from the real hard core of the country, the majority of them being middle-class and lower middle-class agriculturists, lawyers, medical practitioners, businessmen, retired government servants, workers, and artisans.

One great lesson which these elections brought out was that, for the first time in Pakistan, it seemed possible for an average citizen to seek election purely on his or her personal merit, without the help of any financial, social, or political backing. Also for the first time, the elected candidate finds himself in a position to participate effectively and directly in the affairs of the country as they exist immediately around him.

The Union Councils and Town Committees have been given a wide charter of duties and responsibilities, ranging from local self-government to national reconstruction and development. Besides this, I am looking to this gigantic instrument of mass representation to achieve three other pressing objectives: First, to help create a fresh supply of local and national leaders. Second, to serve as a two-way traffic post between the government and the basic core of the people, and to bridge the gulf which under the best of systems is bound to exist between them in countries where education is limited, distances are large, and modern facilities for reaching the masses are not universal. And, third, I would personally like this body of 80,000 elected representatives to serve as the electoral college for the Parliament, and, possibly, for the President.* This is only my personal view, for I do not wish to prejudge the recommendations of the Constitution Commission, which is at the moment seized of this and other allied problems. . . .

An archaic type of feudalism which existed in Pakistan—particularly west Pakistan—had vested the entire political, economic, and social might of the country in a limited group of families. It was impossible to make any advance in any direction without first breaking this monopoly of power. Therefore, land reform was one of the first measures to be taken by the new regime. This was a major operation, but it was performed peacefully and scientifically, and was attended by no manner of tyranny or injustice. This is a

---

* The electors chosen in December, 1959, and January, 1960, elected Ayub Khan for a five-year term as President of Pakistan. In 1965 he was re-elected, defeating Fatimah Jinnah, the daughter of the founder of Pakistan.—ED.

far-reaching socio-economic change, and its full impact will be felt only with the passage of time.

Other fields in which reforms have been undertaken include education, public health, fiscal systems, law courts, civil administration, and the rehabilitation of refugees. The object is to get us to the starting point of development, whence we may be better able to grapple with some of the most pressing and immediate of our problems. These are: fighting the grave menace to the land of salinity and waterlogging; curbing the excessive rate of growth of population; and launching the next Five-Year Plan for national development—estimated to cost over 19 billion rupees (about $4 billion). According to experts, these figures are not astronomical, but only reasonable.

The next fifteen to twenty years are going to be most crucial for Pakistan. Either we "make the grade" in this period, or we do not. If we fail to make the grade, we are bound to be submerged under the tidal wave of Communism, which is constantly lashing its fury all around us. Since we do not seek this fate, we must move forward, and do so quickly. It is here that our eyes turn toward our friends and allies. They have already given us magnanimous aid, for which we are most grateful. But there are reasons of history which entitle us to claim still more. . . .

Moreover, in the context of present-day world politics, Pakistan has openly and unequivocally cast its lot with the West, and unlike several other countries around us, we have shut ourselves off almost completely from the possibility of any major assistance from the Communist bloc. We do not believe in hunting with the hound and running with the hare. We wish to follow, and are following, a clear and unambiguous path.*

All these factors lead to one conclusion: that the English-speaking world ought to feel a special responsibility to assist Pakistan in attaining a reasonable posture of advancement. It is not just a claim. It is in fact the dictate of history. . . .

---

* Since this article was written, Pakistan has developed closer relations with China, primarily as a counterweight to American military aid to India.—ED.

7. Gamal Abdel Nasser

Gamal Abdel Nasser, President of the United Arab Republic, was born in 1918, the son of a postal clerk in Alexandria. He went to secondary school in Cairo, studied law for a time, and then attended military school, receiving his commission in 1938. He served in the Sudan, and fought in the Israeli War. Nasser had been a nationalist since his secondary-school days, and the corruption and inefficiency of the Egyptian politicians at the time of the war against Israel led him to form a Free Officers' Committee, out of which grew the Council of Revolutionary Command, which seized power on July 23, 1952. General Naguib, the nominal head of the revolutionary junta, was removed in November, 1954, and Nasser took power as Premier and Chairman of the Council of Revolutionary Command. In 1956 he was elected President, and he has been re-elected twice, most recently in March, 1965. All elections have been uncontested.

After the seizure of power in 1952, Nasser wrote a series of articles for the Egyptian magazine Akhar Saa, *later published as* The Philosophy of the Revolution. *Nasser has outlawed all political parties except the government party, reorganized in 1962 as the Arab Socialist Union. In July, 1961, he nationalized most major business enterprises and placed limits on landholding. His program of "Arab socialism," which he described in a speech on May 21, 1962, rejects the Marxist view of the inevitability of the class struggle and calls for a mixed economy and the establishment of elected councils in factories and in local and national government.*

THE PHILOSOPHY OF THE REVOLUTION*

The Two Revolutions

Every people on earth go through two revolutions: a political revolution that helps them recover their right to self-government from the hands of a despot who had imposed himself upon them, or free themselves from the domination of alien armed forces which had installed themselves in the land against their will; and a social revolution—a class conflict that ultimately ends in the realization of social justice for all the inhabitants of the country.

People who preceded us on the path of human progress have all passed through those two revolutions, but not simultaneously. In certain cases, centuries have separated the one from the other. In our case, we are passing through the grueling ordeal of experiencing the two revolutions together. This ordeal, this acid test lies in the fact that each of these two revolutions has peculiar circumstances which are strangely conflicting and highly contradictory.

Unity, solidarity, and cooperation of all elements of the nation and self-denial and self-sacrifice on the part of the individual to ensure the safety, prosperity, and integrity of the motherland are the fundamental factors for the success of a *political* revolution. The disintegration of values, disruption of principles, dissension and discord among both classes and individuals, and domination of corruption, suspicion, and perversion of egoism form the foundation of *social* upheaval. Between these two millstones we find ourselves today, destined to go through two revolutions—one calling for unity, solidarity, self-sacrifice, and devotion to sacred duty, while the other imposes upon us, against our will, disunity, dissension, and nothing else but envy, hatred, vindictiveness, and egoism.

Between these two millstones, to cite a case in point, the 1919 Revolution failed to reach the results it ought to have realized. Hardly had the ranks designed to meet oppression been formed before they dispersed to engage in nothing else but strife. . . .

* Reprinted from *The Philosophy of the Revolution* (Cairo: Information Department, 1954).

Ignominious failure was the result; the oppressors tightened the screw, whether through the occupation forces or through their tools and instruments, who were then led by Sultan Fuad, and later by Farouk, his son. All that the people reaped was distrust, doubt, dissension, hatred, rancor, and strife among themselves— both classes and individuals. Thus faded the hope that was expected to be realized by the 1919 Revolution.

I said the hope faded. I did not say the hope disappeared, because the natural forces of resistance driven by the people's great hopes were still active and getting ready for yet another trial. Such was the situation that prevailed after 1919—a situation which made it imperative for the army to be the only force capable of any action.

In fact, the situation demanded a force concentrated within a framework that separates its members to a certain extent from the continual conflict between individuals and classes, a force drawn from the very heart of the people, whose members can trust one another and have full confidence in themselves—a force so equipped as to be capable of a swift and decisive action, and these conditions only prevailed in the army.

Thus it was not the army that determined the role it was to play in the course of events. The reverse was nearer to the truth. It was the events and their development that determined the army's part in the supreme struggle for the liberation of the homeland.

I realized from the outset that our success depended on our complete understanding of the nature of the circumstances in which we live in the present phase of our country's history. We could not with a mere stroke of the pen change these circumstances. We could not put back or forward the hands of the clock, and be masters of time. We also could not act the part of a traffic officer on the road of history, holding up the passage of one revolution to allow another revolution to pass through, and thus avert a collision. All that we could do was to act as best we could to escape being crushed between two millstones. There was no alternative to carrying out the two revolutions together.

In fact, the day we proceeded on the road to the political revolution and dethroned Farouk, we took a similar step on the road to the social revolution and limited the ownership of land. I still believe that the July 23 Revolution should continue to retain the initiative and its ability of rapid movement, so that it would be able to accomplish the miracle of carrying out the two revolutions simultaneously, no matter how contradictory our action may seem at times. . . .

Egypt at the Crossroads

Fate has decreed that we should stand at the world's crossroads. We have oftentimes been the invader's passageway and the adventurer's target. So numerous have been the circumstances through which we have lived that it would indeed be impossible to explain the factors latent in our people's souls unless these circumstances were taken into account.

In my opinion, Egypt's history under the Pharaohs cannot be overlooked. Then comes the interaction between the Greek culture and ours. The Roman invasion and the Islamic conquest, with the waves of Arab migration which followed, should also not be left out of the picture.

I am also of the opinion that we should dwell long on the circumstances through which we lived in the Middle Ages. It was those circumstances which brought about the situation in which we now are. If the Crusades marked the first dawnings of the Renaissance in Europe, they heralded the beginning of the ages of darkness in our country. Our people had borne alone almost the whole brunt of those battles, which left them completely impoverished and utterly helpless. And at the very time when they were shaking and tottering after the shattering blows of battle, it was their lot to suffer further humiliation and misery under the heels of Circassian tyrants and Mogul despots. . . .

My soul is torn with grief when I come to think, as I oftentimes do, of that period in our history in which a despotic feudalism was formed; a feudalism the sole object of which was to bleed the people white and deprive them of the last vestige of power and dignity. We shall indeed have to fight hard and long before we are able to rid ourselves completely of the deleterious effects of that system.

In fact, what still remains latent in our souls has on many an occasion provided me with an explanation of some of the aspects of our political life. It would seem to me sometimes, for instance, that many adopt toward the revolution the attitude of mere onlookers who are interested in nothing else but the result of a fight between two sides with whom they are in no way connected. . . .

Then what happened to us after the Mamelukes? There came the French expedition, the iron curtain drawn around us was smashed, new ideas followed, and horizons as yet invisible to us opened. The Mohammed Ali Dynasty inherited all the evils of the Mameluke regime, although it attempted to garb them in nineteenth-century garments. Our contacts with Europe and the whole world began anew. So also began our modern awakening, but it began with a new crisis.

In my opinion, our case very much resembled that of a sick man who had spent a long time in a closed room. The heat in that closed room had become so intense that the man was in anguish. Suddenly a violent storm blew, smashing all windows and doors, and strong currents of cold air began to lash the body of the sick man, who was still perspiring. The sick man needed a breath of air. Instead, a raging hurricane assailed him, and fever began to devour his feeble body. This was exactly the case of our society. It was indeed a dangerous case.

Undoubtedly, this state of affairs is responsible for the non-existence of a strong united public opinion in our country. The difference between one individual and another is vast; that between one generation and another is greater still.

There was a time when I complained that the people did not know what they were about, that they never agreed to follow the same road. I later realized, however, that I was asking for the impossible, that I had not taken the society in which we live into account. Actually, we live in a society which has not yet crystallized. It is still in a state of ferment and agitation and has not yet stabilized to continue its gradual development, like the other peoples who have gone before on the same road. I believe, with no intention to flatter the people in expressing such a belief, that our people have wrought a veritable miracle. Any other society subjected to the same severe trials as ours might have succumbed. It would have been swept by the powerful currents that had overtaken us. We have, however, weathered the tempest. It is true we have almost lost our balance, but we have not fallen down.

I sometimes consider the state of an average Egyptian family—one of the thousands of families which live in the capital of the country. The father, for example, is a turbaned *fellah*—a thoroughbred country fellow. The mother is a lady of Turkish descent. The sons and daughters attend schools following, respectively, the English and French educational systems—all this in an atmosphere

in which the thirteenth-century spirit and twentieth-century manifestations intermingle and interact.

I see all this and feel in my heart of hearts that I know the
cause of this bewildering perplexity which is torturing our minds
and this astounding confusion which is destroying our very existence. Then I say to myself, "Surely our society will crystallize;
surely it will be solidified; surely it will be welded into a strong
homogeneous whole. All that is required is to strain every nerve to
hold our ground during this period of transition."

The Three Circles

When I come to analyze the elements of our strength, I cannot
help being struck by three sources standing in bold relief, which
should be taken into account before everything else.

The first of these sources lies in the fact that we are a group of
neighboring nations welded into a homogeneous whole by every
possible material and moral tie that would unite any such group
of nations. Moreover, our peoples possess peculiarities, potentialities, and a civilization inspired by the spiritual principles of the
three divine religions which can never be overlooked in any attempt to build a new stable and peaceful world.

The second source is our land itself and the position it occu-
pies on the map of the world—that important strategic position
which rightly makes of it the world's crossroads, the main route of
its trade and the highway of its armies.

There remains the third source. This is oil—which is considered
the backbone of material civilization, and without which all the
world's largest factories, all means of land, sea, and air communication, all war weapons would become mere iron . . .

If I have succeeded in explaining the extent of the importance
of this vital element of strength, as I sincerely hope I have, it
would thus follow that we are strong—strong not through wailing,
shouting, or appealing for help at the top of our voices, but strong
through our composure or our correct estimation (supported by
figures) of our capacity for work, and our true understanding of
the strength of the ties that bind our peoples together, those ties
which make of our homeland an integral and indivisible whole,
which should be defended as such and not as an isolated unit. So
much for the First Circle—the Arab Circle, within the framework

of which we should endeavor to turn, move, and act with all our force.

As for the Second Circle—the African Continent Circle . . . we cannot, under any condition, even if we want to, stand aloof from the terrible and terrifying battle now raging in the heart of that continent between 5 million whites and 200 million Africans. We cannot stand aloof for one important and obvious reason—we ourselves are in Africa.

Surely the people of Africa will continue to look to us—we who are the guardians of the Continent's northern gate, we who constitute the connecting link between the Continent and the outer world. We certainly cannot, under any condition, relinquish our responsibility to help to our utmost in spreading the light of knowledge and civilization to the very depths of the virgin jungles of the continent.

There remains another equally important reason: The Nile, the life artery of our country, springs from the heart of the continent. And still one more reason: the beloved Sudan, whose boundaries extend to the heart of the continent and which is bound by neighborly relations with the sensitive spots in its center.

There is no denying the fact that Africa is now the scene of a strange and stirring commotion. The white man, who represents several European nations, is again trying to change the map of the continent. We surely cannot, under any condition, stand as mere onlookers, deluding ourselves into the belief that we are in no way concerned with these machinations.

Indeed, I shall continue to dream of the day on which I shall see in Cairo a great Africa institute, seeking to reveal to us the various aspects of the continent, to create in our minds an enlightened African consciousness, and to associate itself with all those working in all parts of the world for the progress, prosperity, and welfare of the peoples of Africa.

There remains the Third Circle—the circle encompassing continents and oceans—the Circle of our Brethren in Islam, who, wherever their place under the sun, turn with us toward the same *kiblah*,* their lips solemnly saying the same prayers.

My faith in the magnitude of the positive effectiveness that could result from strengthening the Islamic tie that binds all Mos-

* *Kiblah* means "direction"; the reference is to Mecca, which Moslems must face during prayer.—Ed.

lems grew stronger when I accompanied the Egyptian mission to Saudi Arabia to offer condolences on the death of its great King. As I stood before the Kaaba,* with my thoughts wandering around every part of the world which Islam has reached, I fully realized the need for a radical change of our conception of the pilgrimage. I said to myself: The journey to the Kaaba should no longer be construed as an admission card to paradise or as a crude attempt to buy forgiveness of sins after leading a dissipated life.

The pilgrimage should have a potential political power. The world press should hasten to follow and feature its news not by drawing attractive pen pictures of its rites and rituals for the delectation of readers, but by its representation as a periodic political conference at which the heads of all the Islamic states—leaders of opinion, scientists, eminent industrialists, and prominent businessmen—assemble to draw up at this world Islamic parliament the broad lines of the policies to be adopted by their respective countries, and lay down the principles ensuring their close cooperation until they have again gathered together in the following session.

They assemble, devout, but mighty; unambitious of power, but active and full of energy; submissive to divine will, but immutable in difficulties and implacable with their enemies.

They assemble, confirmed believers in the life to come, but equally convinced that they have a place under the sun which they should occupy in this life. . . .

ARAB SOCIALISM †

Political democracy cannot be separated from social democracy. No citizen can be regarded as free to vote unless he is given the following three guarantees:

1. He should be free from exploitation in all its forms.

* The Kaaba is the square structure in the center of the Great Mosque at Mecca which houses the sacred Black Stone.—ED.

† Excerpts from Nasser's speech on the draft charter, delivered on May 21, 1962; English translation published by the U.A.R. Information Department, Cairo.

2. He should enjoy an equal opportunity to have a fair share of the national wealth.

3. His mind should be free from all anxiety likely to undermine the security of his life in the future.

Only when a citizen possesses these three guarantees can he be said to have political freedom and can he take part, by means of his vote, in shaping the authority of the state he aspires to have.

Political democracy cannot exist under the domination of any one class. Democracy means, literally, the domination and sovereignty of the people—the entire people. The experiment started with the beginning of the organized revolutionary action has proved that it is indispensable that the revolution undertake to liquidate the force of reaction, deprive it of all its weapons, and prevent it from making any attempt to come back to power and subject the state machinery to the service of its own interests.

The bitterness and sanguinary nature of class strife, as well as the grave dangers likely to ensue, are in fact the creation of the force of reaction, which does not wish to give up the monopolies or privileged positions from which it continues to exploit the people. The force of reaction possesses the means of resistance; it possesses the power of the state, and if this is taken away from it, it turns to the power of capital. If, however, this is taken away from it, then it turns to its natural ally, imperialism.

Because of their monopoly of wealth, reactionary interests are bound to clash with the interest of the whole people. Consequently, the peaceful resolution of class struggle cannot be achieved unless the power of reaction is first and foremost deprived of all its weapons.

The removal of such clashes will pave the way to peaceful solutions to class struggles. It does not remove the contradictions in the rest of the social classes, but it creates a chance for the possibility of resolving them peacefully—namely, by means of democratic action. If, on the other hand, this clash of interests is allowed to remain, then it will not be resolved except by a civil war that will cause great damage to the country at a time of great international conflict and bitter Cold War.

The collaboration between the force of reaction and exploiting capital must, therefore, collapse. The road must then be paved for democratic interaction among the various powers of the working people—namely, the farmers, workers, soldiers, intellectuals, and national capital.

Cooperation among the powers representing the working people is the legitimate substitute for the collaboration between feudalism and exploiting capital. It alone is capable of replacing reactionary democracy by true democracy.

The national unity created by the cooperation between those representative powers of the people will be able to set up the Arab Socialist Union.* This union will constitute the authority representing the people and the driving force behind the possibilities of the revolution and the guardian of the values of true democracy.

These enormous popular powers—forming the Arab Socialist Union, and responsible for the unleashing of its energy and effectiveness—make it necessary that, when dealing with the form of the political organization of the state, the new constitution of the United Arab Republic must refer to a set of necessary guarantees:

1. The popular and political organizations based on free and direct election must truly and fairly represent the powers forming the majority of the population—the powers that have for long been exploited and have a deep interest in the Revolution, through their experience of deprivation. These powers are also naturally the storehouse of revolutionary energy, which is both dynamic and forceful.

This is only just and fair, since it means that the majority will be represented. It also provides a sure guarantee of the strength of the revolutionary impetus because it will then be springing from its genuine and natural sources.

It follows, then, that the new constitution must ensure that farmers and workers will get half the seats in political and popular organizations at all levels—including the house of representatives—since they form the majority of the people.† Moreover, they are the majority who have been longest deprived of their inalienable right to shape and direct their future.

---

* The creation of the Arab Socialist Union in 1962 marked Nasser's third attempt to establish an official political party. The two predecessors were the Liberation Rally (1953–57) and the National Union (1957–61).—Ed.

† In the March, 1964, legislative elections, two candidates were nominated and elected in each district, one of whom was a worker or peasant.—Ed.

2. The authority of the elected popular councils must be consolidated and raised above the authority of the executive machinery of the state, for that is the natural order regulating the sovereignty of the people, and ensures that the people will always lead national action. . . . Local government should gradually but resolutely transfer the authority of the state to the people, for they are in a better position to feel their own problems and find the proper solutions.

3. There is a dire need to create a new political organization within the framework of the Arab Socialist Union—recruiting the elements fit for leadership, organizing their efforts, clarifying the revolutionary motives of the masses, sounding their needs, and endeavoring to satisfy them.

4. Collective leadership is imperative in the period of the revolutionary drive. Collective leadership not only guards against the individual running loose, but also confirms and ensures the reign of democracy in its most sublime form.

Popular organizations, especially cooperatives and trade unions, can play an effective and influential role in promoting sound democracy. These organizations should form a vanguard force in the various fields of national democratic action. The development of the cooperative and trade-union movements provides an endless source to the conscious leadership that directly feels the reactions and responses of the masses. The pressure that stifled these organizations and paralyzed their movements has vanished.

Besides their productive role, the farmers' cooperatives are democratic organizations, capable of spotting and solving the problems of the farmers. So it is high time for agricultural labor unions to be established.

Industrial, commercial, and service trade unions were able, thanks to the July laws, to reach a position of leadership in the national struggle. The workers are no longer commodities in production processes. The forces of labor have become masters of the production process. They also share in its administration and profits, under the best terms of wages and working hours.

Criticism and self-criticism are among the most important guarantees to freedom. The greatest danger in the way of free criticism and self-criticism in political organizations is the infiltration of reactionary elements.

As a result of their control of economic interests, the reactionary forces controlled the press. Freedom of opinion was thus deprived of its most valuable instrument. The elimination of reaction puts an end to the dictatorship of one class and paves the way for the democracy of all the national powers of the people. It provides the surest guarantees for the freedom of assembly and freedom of discussion. . . .

Nationalization and Private Ownership

It is of prime importance that our outlook toward nationalization should be freed from the stigmas that private interests have tried to attach to it. Nationalization is but the transfer of the means of production from the sphere of private ownership to that of public ownership.

This is not a blow to individual initiative, as alleged by the enemies of socialism, but a guarantee to and an expansion of the range of general interest in cases affected by the socialist change, carried out for the benefit of the people.

Nationalization does not lead to a decrease in production. Experience has proved the ability of the public sector to shoulder the greatest responsibilities with maximum efficiency, whether in the achievement of the production targets or in the raising of the standard of its quality. Although some mistakes may occur during this great evolution, we must recall the new hands that have assumed the responsibility. At any rate it was inevitable that the major national interests should be handed over to the people even at the cost of facing temporary difficulties.

The great importance attached to the role of the public sector, however, cannot do away with the existence of the private sector. The private sector has its effective role in the development plan. It must be protected to fulfill that part. The private sector is now required to renovate itself and strike a new path of creative effort not dependent, as in the past, on parasitic exploitation.

The crisis which befell private capital before the Revolution actually stemmed from the fact that it had inherited the era of the foreign adventurers, who, in the nineteenth century, helped transfer abroad the wealth of Egypt. Private capital was accustomed to live under a protective trade policy that gave it benefits at the expense of the people. It was also accustomed to dominate the government with the aim of pursuing a policy of exploitation. . . . The people could not forever remain indifferent to maneuvers to direct the government to favor the minority controlling wealth, and to guarantee the maintenance of their privileged position at the expense of the people's interests.

Progress through socialism is a consolidation of the bases of sound democracy, the democracy of all the people. . . .

Moreover, the maintenance of the role of the private sector beside that of the public sector renders control over public ownership more effective. By encouraging free competition within the framework of the general economic planning, the private sector is also an invigorating element to the public sector. The July, 1961, revolutionary laws did not aim at destroying the private sector, but had two basic aims: The creation of some form of economic equality among citizens that ensures legitimate rights and removes the effects of a minority's monopolizing all opportunities at the expense of the majority contributes to the dissolution of class distinctions in a way that enhances the possibilities of a peaceful struggle between them, and paves the way for democratic solutions to the major problems confronting the process of development. The second objective is to step up the efficiency of the public sector, owned by the people, to consolidate its capacity to shoulder the responsibility of planning, and to enable it to play its leading role in industrial development on a socialist basis. These two objectives have been crowned with sweeping success, confirming the power of the revolutionary drive and the depth of national unity.

The realization of these two objectives wipes out the residue of the complexes (created by exploitation) that cast a shadow of doubt on the role of the private sector. Consequently, the path open to this sector today, to promote the process of development, is only restricted by the socialist laws now in force or by the steps deemed necessary by the popular authorities elected in future. . . .

Foreign Capital

Foreign capital is regarded with dark doubts in underdeveloped countries—particularly those which were colonized. The sovereignty of the people over their land and their restoration to the helm allow them to set the conditions under which foreign capital may be invested in the country.

The matter calls for the setting up of a system of priority, drawn from the essence of the national experience. It also takes into account the nature of world capital—always striving after unexploited raw materials in areas not yet ready for any economic or social revival, where it can obtain the highest share of profit.

In the first place, in the process of national evolution, all foreign aid with no strings attached is accepted to help attain the national objectives. The aid is accepted with sincere gratitude for those who offer it regardless of the colors of their flags.

In the second place, all unconditional loans are accepted, provided they can be refunded without difficulty or strain. Experience shows that loans are a clear operation; their problem ends with their amortization and the reimbursement of their interest.

In the third place, the participation of foreign capital as investment is accepted in indispensable operations, especially those requiring experience difficult to find in the national domain. Acceptance of foreign investment implies that a foreigner would participate in the administration. It also implies that a share of the annual profits would be transferred to the investors indefinitely. This matter should not be left without limitation.

First priority goes to unconditional aid. The second place is reserved to unconditional loans. Then follows the acceptance of foreign investment (in unavoidable circumstances) in aspects of modern evolution requiring international experience.

In their conscious revolutionary outlook, our people consider it the duty of the advanced states to offer aid to those still struggling for development. In their conception of history, our people believe the states with a colonialist past are, more than others, compelled to offer to the nations aspiring to development part of the national wealth they sapped when that wealth was a booty for all looters. . . .

The Class Struggle

We must clearly realize that no individual can be free unless he is first liberated from the shackles of exploitation. It is this fact that makes social freedom a way—in fact, the only way—to achieve political freedom.

Our immediate aim is to do away with exploitation and to make possible the exercise of the natural right of equal opportunity; to dissolve class distinctions and to end the domination of one class, and hence remove the struggle between classes, which constitutes a threat to the freedom of the individual citizen and even to freedom of the whole of the country by violating the rights of the people, and which creates the chance of exposing the country to the lurking dangers of foreign forces, vigilantly on the lookout to drag it to the arena of the Cold War and make of it its battlefield and of its people fodder for their guns. The removal of the struggle between classes which arises out of interests that can never be reconciled, between those who exercise exploitation and those crushed by exploitation in the past society, cannot overnight lead to the dissolution of all class distinctions, or lead to social freedom and true democracy.

Yet, the removal of the struggle between classes makes it possible—by eliminating the exploiting class—to dissolve class distinctions peacefully and to open the gates for democratic exchange, which brings the whole society nearer the age of true freedom. That was one of the great social objectives of the July laws, which directed a deadly blow at the centers of exploitation and monopolies. That great revolutionary action made it possible to have democracy for the first time in Egypt.

Land Reform

The Arab application of socialism in the domain of agriculture does not call for nationalizing the land and transforming it into the domain of public ownership. From experience and study, it believes in individual ownership of land within limits that do not allow for feudalism.

This conclusion is not just a response to the longing of the farmers for ownership of land. It is derived from the real circumstances of the agricultural problem in Egypt. These circumstances have confirmed the ability of the Egyptian farmer to work creatively if he is given favorable conditions. The efficiency of the Egyptian farmer throughout history has been able to exploit the land, especially when the opportunity is provided to benefit from scientific agricultural advances. Moreover, Egyptian agriculture long ago arrived at sound socialist solutions to its most complicated problems. Foremost among these were irrigation and drainage, which in Egypt are now and have been for a long time within the framework of the public services.

Thus the correct solution to the agricultural problem does not lie in transferring land to public ownership but requires individual ownership of land and the expansion of ownership by providing this opportunity to the largest number of wage-earners—and supporting this ownership by means of agricultural cooperation in all the stages of agricultural production.

Agricultural cooperation is much more than the simple credit to which it was confined until recently. It starts with the process of pooling agricultural exploitation which has proved to be very successful. It also involves the financial process which protects the farmer and liberates him from usurers and middlemen who take the largest part of the fruit of his labor. Cooperation also enables the farmer to use the most modern machines and scientific means to raise production. It helps the farmer in marketing, enabling him to obtain the highest return for his lengthy labor and toil.

The revolutionary solution to the land problem in Egypt is to increase the number of landowners. This was the aim of the land reform laws of 1952 and 1961.

It was also—in addition to the aim of raising production—one of the reasons for the great irrigation projects, the powerful symbol of which is the High Aswan Dam, for which the people of Egypt have suffered all kinds of military, economic, and psychological hardships. The dam has become the symbol of the will and determination of the people to fashion their lives. It is also a symbol of their will to provide the right of land ownership to large numbers of farmers for whom this opportunity was never provided through centuries of continuous feudal rule.

The success of this revolutionary attempt to solve the agricultural problem by increasing the number of landowners cannot be consolidated except by agricultural cooperation and the expansion of its scope to provide a strong and vital economy for small landholdings. . . .

8. The Ba'th Party

Although many of its ideas are similar to those of Nasser, the Ba'th (Arab Resurrection Socialist) Party differs from him on a number of significant issues. The party was founded by Michel Aflaq and Salah Bitar in 1943; in 1953, it merged with the Syrian Socialist Party. It is committed to Arab unity, neutralism, constitutional democracy, and socialism. Originally suspicious of Nasser, the party supported the union of Egypt and Syria in the United

Arab Republic in 1958. When it became evident that Nasser was interested in Arab unity only under his own auspices, the Ba'thists withdrew their support and supported the Syrian secession in 1961.

The Ba'th Party is active in several Middle Eastern countries in addition to Syria: Ba'thists have held power in Iraq, and in Jordan they make up part of the opposition. Since one of its founders is a Christian, Ba'thist ideology does not emphasize the role of Islam in forging Arab unity. As the principles enumerated below demonstrate, Ba'thism is committed to freedom of speech, organization, and expression, and to an independent judiciary. Its socialism provides for guarantees for small property holders but limits the size and nature of individual economic activity. At the present time, it is Nasser's chief rival for ideological leadership in the Middle East.

THE CONSTITUTION OF THE ARAB RESURRECTION SOCIALIST PARTY*

FUNDAMENTAL PRINCIPLES

The first principle: The unity and freedom of the Arab nation.

The Arabs are a single nation, having a natural right to exist within a single state and to be free to realize all its potentialities.

To these ends, the Arab Resurrection Socialist Party declares:

1. The Arab homeland is an indivisible politico-economic unit. It is impossible for any of the Arab regions to perfect the conditions of its life in isolation from the rest.

2. The Arab nation is a cultural unit. All of the differences among its members are artificial accidents which will cease to exist as a consequence of the awakening of Arab consciousness.

3. The Arab homeland belongs to the Arabs. They alone have the right to utilize its resources and its wealth, and to control its potentialities.

The second principle: The special character of the Arab nation.

The Arab nation is distinguished by its special merit, revealed in its repeated awakenings; it is marked by the abundance of its

* Reprinted by permission from the *Middle East Journal*, XIII (Spring, 1959), 195–200; translated by Leonard Binder.

vitality and inventiveness, and its tendency toward reform and resurgence. Its resurgence is ever related to the growth of individual freedom and the (extension of the) scope of harmony between individual freedom and the national interest.

Therefore, the Arab Resurrection Socialist Party declares that:

1. Freedom of speech, of association, of belief, and of science are sacred, and may not be limited by any government whatsoever.

2. The value of members of the nation is to be assessed—after they have been granted an adequate opportunity—exclusively on the basis of their efforts on behalf of the Arab nation and its efflorescence.

The third principle: The mission of the Arab nation.

The Arab nation is characterized by an eternal mission which manifests itself in the form of a complete regeneration through the stage of history, leading to the reformation of human existence, the advancement of human progress, and the enhancement of harmony and cooperation among nations.

Therefore, the Arab Resurrection Socialist Party declares that:

1. Colonialism and everything connected therewith is an evil which will be opposed by the Arabs by every possible means. They will make continuous and substantial efforts, within their capacity, to aid all people who are striving for freedom.

2. All humanity is mutually responsible for its common welfare, and collectively responsible for its protection and civilization. The Arabs benefit from world civilization, and they contribute to it in turn. The Arabs will extend a brotherly hand to the other nations and will cooperate with them in bringing about the rule of justice, guaranteeing to all peoples peace, well-being, and moral and spiritual elevation.

GENERAL PROVISIONS

Article 1. The party is a universal Arab party, branches of which will be established in all the rest of the Arab regions. It will not pursue a regional policy, except out of regard for the higher Arab interest.

Article 2. The general headquarters of the party is in the district of Damascus, but it may be transferred to any other Arab country if the national interest so determines.

Article 3. The Arab Resurrection Socialist Party is nationalist, holding that nationalism has a truly permanent existence, and that the precious feeling of nationalism which firmly ties the individual to his nation is a sacred sentiment, full of creative power, encouraging sacrifice, reawakening the sense of responsibility, and striving to channel the individual personality purposefully, efficiently, and gloriously.

The nationalist idea which the party preaches is the will of the Arab people to be free and united; that the Arab people be given an opportunity to realize the Arab character in history; and that it cooperate with the rest of the nations on whatever will assure humanity's unswerving progress toward goodness and well-being.

Article 4. The Arab Resurrection Socialist Party is socialist, believing that socialism is necessarily derived from genuine Arab nationalism because it is the exemplary system which will permit the Arab people to realize its own potentialities. Socialism will cause the Arab genius to unfold in the most complete manner. Socialism will guarantee the continuous growth of the nation in its spiritual and material development; and it will guarantee close fraternization among its individual members.

Article 5. The Arab Resurrection Socialist Party is populist, believing that dominion belongs to the people, that they alone are the origin of all government and leadership, and that the value of the state derives from the will of the masses, even as its sanctity is in proportion to the extent of their freedom in choosing the government. Therefore the party depends upon the people for the accomplishment of its mission, and endeavors to tie itself closely to the people, and to raise their intellectual, moral, economic, and hygienic levels in order to increase their sense of individuality and to increase the exercise of their rights in the individualistic (sphere) of national life.

Article 6. The Arab Resurrection Socialist Party is revolutionary, believing that its principal goals of reawakening Arab nationalism and building socialism cannot be achieved except by revolution and strife. The party believes that dependence upon gradual change and contentment with superficial (because) partial amelioration will defeat these ends (through faintheartedness and loss of opportunities). Therefore the party decides to: (a) struggle against foreign colonialism in order to achieve absolute freedom for the Arab homeland; (b) struggle to achieve a union of Arabs in a single independent state; (c) rebel against existing evils affecting all intellectual, economic, social, and political aspects of life.

Article 7. The Arab national homeland is that part of the earth inhabited by the Arab people and which lies between the Taurus Mountains, the Zagros mountains, the Persian Gulf, the Arabian Sea, the mountains of Ethiopia, the Sahara Desert, the Atlas range, and the Mediterranean Sea.

Article 8. The official language of the state and the language of its people, authorized for publication and instruction, is the Arabic language.

Article 9. The subjects of the Arab state are the subjects of the Arab revolt which was begun in the year 1916 for the purpose of freeing and uniting the Arab people.

Article 10. An Arab is anyone whose language is Arabic, who lives in the Arab homeland or aspires to live therein, and who believes in his connection with the Arab people.

Article 11. Whoever agitates on behalf of or is connected with a racial group opposed to the Arabs, or whoever immigrates into the Arab homeland for the purpose of colonization, will be expelled from the Arab homeland.

Article 12. Arab women will enjoy all the rights of citizenship. The party will strive to raise the status of women so that they become worthy of these rights.

Article 13. In order that the citizens demonstrate their abilities in their true light and to their fullest extent in all fields of human activity, a true beginning is to be made with the equalization of educational and economic opportunity.

PROGRAM

The Domestic Policy of the Party

Article 14. The system of government in the Arab state will be representative and constitutional. The executive authority will be responsible to the legislative authority, which is to be directly elected by the people.

Article 15. The national tie will be the sole (social) bond existing in the Arab state. It will guarantee harmony among the citizens and it will guarantee their fusion in the crucible of a single nationality. It will combat all other denominational, factional, tribal, parochial, or regional loyalties.

Article 16. The system of administration in the Arab state will be decentralized.

Article 17. The party will strive to make the populist spirit prevail, and to make it a living reality in the life of the individual. The party will strive to enact a constitution for the state which will guarantee absolute equality before the law to Arab citizens; which will guarantee the complete freedom of the expression of their will and the choice of their representatives in honest elections; thus organizing for them a life of freedom within the limits of the laws.

Article 18. A single legislative code, in harmony with the spirit of the contemporary period and based upon the experience of the Arab nation in the past, will be enacted for the Arab state in complete freedom.

Article 19. The judicial authority will be protected from and independent of every other authority and it will enjoy complete immunity.

Article 20. Full rights of citizenship will be bestowed upon every citizen living in the Arab homeland who identifies himself solely with the Arab homeland and disassociates himself from every racial group.

Article 21. Military service will be compulsory in the Arab homeland.

The Foreign Policy of the Party

Article 22. The foreign policy of the Arab state will be inspired by the Arab national interest and the eternal Arab mission, and it will be aimed at cooperation with other nations in improving the harmony, freedom, faith, and righteousness of the world and its continuous progress.

Article 23. The Arabs will struggle with all their power to undermine the supports of colonialism and foreign occupation and all foreign political or economic influence in their country.

Article 24. When the Arab people alone become the source of all authority, all trade agreements and conventions made by the present governments which infringe upon the absolute sovereignty of the Arabs will be abrogated.

Article 25. The Arab foreign policy will be revealed to have received its correct form from the will of the Arabs to live in freedom, and from their desire to see all other nations similarly enjoying freedom.

The Economic Policy of the Party

Article 26. The Arab Resurrection Socialist Party is socialist, believing that the economic wealth of the homeland is the property of the nation.

Article 27. The distribution of immovable (landed) property in the Arab homeland is unjust, and therefore this distribution will be re-examined and (such property) will be redistributed among the citizens on a just basis.

Article 28. All citizens are to be recognized as equal in their capacity as human beings; therefore the party will prevent the exploitation of the labor of others.

Article 29. Public utilities, enterprises based on great natural resources, large-scale industries, and means of transport are the property of the nation to be administered directly by the state. All (relevant) foreign companies and concessions are to be abolished.

Article 30. Agricultural ownership will be limited in accordance with the capacity of the owner for proper exploitation and within the framework of the general economic plan, rather than (as presently regulated by) the exploitation of the labor of others by the dignitaries of the state.

Article 31. The ownership of small industries will be regulated in accordance with the economic level enjoyed by the rest of the citizens of the state.

Article 32. The workers will be associated with the administration of (their) factory, and the sum of their wages will be determined by the state in a proportion, also to be determined by the state, to the value of their work.

Article 33. The ownership of real property or buildings will be permitted to all citizens, provided that they will not have the right to rent it out nor to exploit it at the expense of others: moreover the government will guarantee a minimum of real property to all citizens.

Article 34. Ownership and inheritance are national and protected rights within the limits of the national interest.

Article 35. Lending at interest among the citizens will be abolished, and a single bank will be established which will issue banknotes guaranteed by national production, and which will apply (credit) to essential agricultural and industrial enterprises.

Article 36. The state will supervise domestic and foreign commerce directly in order to eliminate exploitation between producer and consumer to protect them both, to protect national production from the competition of foreign production, and to maintain a balance between exports and imports.

Article 37. A comprehensive plan will be drawn up in the light of experience and on the basis of economic theory for the purpose of industrializing the Arab homeland, increasing national production, opening new (economic) horizons to it, and in order to direct the economy in all spheres in accordance with its capacity and in order to fulfill desired priorities.

The Social Policy of the Party

Article 38. The family, children, and marriage:

a) The family is the basic unit of the nation; its protection, development, and welfare are responsibilities devolving upon the state.

b) Children are first the responsibility of the family and secondly of the state. It is incumbent upon both to strive to increase their number and to care for their health and education.

c) Marriage is essential to the nation; its encouragement, facilitation, and regulation is the duty of the state.

Article 39. Public health: The state will establish, at its own expense, institutions of preventive medicine, clinics, and dispensaries which will supply the needs of all the citizens in accordance with the highest standards, and which will guarantee scrupulous medical treatment to them.

Article 40. Labor:

a) Work is to be required of all who are capable of it, and the state will guarantee either intellectual or physical employment to all citizens.

b) The product of labor must guarantee its producer at least a proper standard of living.

c) The state will provide for the subsistence of invalids out of the total national product.

d) Just labor legislation will be enacted, limiting the daily hours of the worker, granting him weekly and annual paid vacations, safeguarding his rights, guaranteeing him old age insurance, and compensating partial or complete unemployment (occurring) during the course of work.

e) Free syndicates will be organized for workers and peasants. These syndicates will be encouraged to become beneficial instruments for defending their rights, raising their standards (of living), looking after their needs, increasing their opportunities, creating a spirit of mutual responsibility among them, and representing them in the high labor tribunal.

f) A tribunal specifically concerned with labor will be organized, in which the state and the worker and peasant syndicates will be represented, and which will decide in cases of disputes occurring among the latter (the syndicates), management, and the representatives of the state.

Article 41. The culture of the public:

a) The party will strive to create a general culture for the Arab homeland which will be nationalist, Arab, free, progressive, comprehensive, profound, and humane in its goals, and the party will cause it to prevail among all sections of the people.

b) The state will be responsible for protecting the freedoms of speech, publishing, association, protest, and of the press within the limits of the higher interest of the Arab nation; and the state will be responsible for promoting all instrumentalities which may assure these freedoms.

c) Intellectual work is of the most sacred kind of labor, and it will be incumbent upon the state to protect intellectuals and ulema and to encourage them.

d) There will be freedom—within the limits of Arab nationalist ideology—in the establishment of clubs, the formation of associations, parties, popular organizations, and institutions for travel, and in utilizing the benefits of the cinema, of broadcasting and television, and all the means of modern civilization for diffusing the national culture and improving the lot of the people.

Article 42. Manifestations and distinctions of class resulting in corrupted social conditions will be abolished. To that end the party will struggle in the ranks of the oppressed toiling classes of the public until such manifestation and distinction cease, until their full human dignity is restored to them, and until they will be enabled to live under a just social order without discrimination between one citizen and another except in the adequacy of the intellect and the skill of the hand.

Article 43. Nomadism: Nomadism is a primitive social state which weakens national productivity and renders a large part of the nation a paralyzed limb, hindering its growth and progress.

The party will strive to settle the Bedouin and to grant them lands; and the party will strive to abolish the tribal system and the adaptation of the laws of the state thereto.

The Educational and Instructional Policy of the Party

The educational policy of the party will be aimed at the creation of a new generation of Arabs which will believe in the unity of its nation and the permanence of its mission, which will seize hold of scientific thought free of the fetters of superstition and retrograde authority, which will be filled with the spirit of optimism and mutual responsibility with their fellow citizens in striving for a true, universal, Arab revolution and for human progress.

To this end the party decides that:

Article 44. Every manifestation of intellectual, economic, political, cultural, and artistic life will be stamped with the impress of Arab nationalism to remind the nation of its connection with its glorious history, and to direct it to advance toward a more glorious and exemplary future.

Article 45. Education is the function of the government alone; therefore all private or foreign institutions of learning will be abolished.

Article 46. Education, at all levels, will be free for all citizens, and compulsory in the primary and secondary levels.

Article 47. Higher professional schools will be established along the most modern lines, and instruction therein will be free.

Article 48. The teaching profession and all functions related thereto, except higher education, will be restricted to Arab nationals. . . .

9. *Munif al-Razzaz*

Munif al-Razzaz was born in Jordan in 1919. He studied at Amman Secondary School and did his university work in Beirut and Cairo. In 1949 he joined the Ba'th Party. During the last ten years he has held various positions of leadership in the party, most recently that of Secretary General. In February, 1966, he was imprisoned in Syria following a military coup by a splinter group within the party. He has written three books: Features of Arab Life (1953), which won the Arab League prize as the best book on the Arab world; The Evolution of the Meaning of Nationalism (1960), which was published in English in 1963; and Freedom and Its Problems in Underdeveloped Countries (1965), from which the following selection is taken.

The argument contained in this selection is an important criticism of the apologists for the one-party and the no-party state. Its defense of the rights of opposition parties has added significance because it was written at the time when the Ba'th Party was in power in Syria. Unlike some critics of the single party, al-Razzaz is a socialist and strongly anti-Western, but he is also deeply committed to freedom of expression and meaningful democracy. His work is typical of the reassessment of the claims of the strong man and the single party which has taken place in recent years in many parts of Asia, the Middle East, and Africa.

PARTIES—A PRECONDITION
OF FREEDOM*

There is no doubt that freedom in these [underdeveloped] countries is passing through a severe crisis. . . . The gap between hope and actual fulfillment is enormous. . . . Hence the masses' general feeling of disappointment and loss wherever you turn. . . . It is in order to disguise this stifling crisis, to deceive the masses, and to counter feelings of loss and disappointment that ruling authorities in these countries, and opposition movements as well, have resorted to employing the word "freedom" in a way which it was not intended to mean and cannot possibly signify. Freedom has been used to refer to systems that have the forms of parliamentarism but lack all other expressions of freedom; reactionary systems in which economic exploitation and political tyranny have been carried to the extreme; systems that have realized a measure

* Excerpts from al-Hurriyah wa-mushkilatuhā fī al-buldān al-mutakhallifah (Freedom and Its Problems in Underdeveloped Countries) (Beirut, 1965); translated by John Mikhail.

of economic emancipation but have repressed all aspects of political freedom; and Communist systems that are no more than one-party dictatorships. In short, the word "freedom" has been used to describe both reactionary rightist and dictatorial leftist regimes. Most of the time the word "freedom" has come to be no more than a slogan disguising one or another form of dictatorship.

Has "freedom" lost its meaning? Has it become merely a propaganda symbol?

Because of the genuine crisis that the underdeveloped countries, including our Arab homeland, are going through, because of this continuous distortion in the use of the word "freedom" by both right and left, I have been induced to attempt to write this book. My aim is twofold: first, to restore to the word its [true] meaning lest it be lost in the labyrinth of assertion and counterassertion; second, to discuss the crisis of freedom in our country and countries with similar problems, out of a belief that discussion of these causes can indicate the way to overcome this crisis. . . .

Perhaps the understanding of freedom was initially dim and superficial, but it began to crystallize as a result of experience during the various phases that these countries passed through, especially after independence. There was first the realization that the democratic freedoms which nationalist governments had established in all these countries did not bring the masses closer to the fulfillment of their hopes for economic and social progress, despite the fact that imperialism, which they had imagined to be the sole obstacle to such progress, had been defeated. Then came the realization that in the absence of democracy and political freedom, economic progress, if achieved, is only achieved at the expense of the citizen's dignity and feeling of individuality, identity, freedom, and worth; his participation in bearing public responsibility; and his right to express his opinion and to determine his destiny.

The very crisis of freedom that these countries are passing through is, therefore, the way to educate the public as to the true meaning of freedom, and to bring it to the mature realization that freedom is indivisible, that it is impossible to realize economic freedom in the shadow of political tyranny, or political freedom in the shadow of economic enslavement. . . .

Disagreement as to the prerequisites of freedom has been greatest on the subject of parties. . . . Western democratic states have considered the existence of several parties as a guarantee of the expression of public opinion and an indispensable basis for political freedom. Communist thought, on the other hand, has considered the multiparty system in capitalist societies as an expression of the multiplicity of classes, and has thus championed the philosophy of the single party representing the single class.

As for the underdeveloped countries, most of them adopted the Western multiparty system at the time of independence. However, political life was dominated by one principal party—the party that personified the struggle for independence. After the collapse of democratic government, these countries went in one of two ways: either one-party rule, or the abolition of party activity and a call for government by the people without parties.

Parties are instruments for the organized expression of political opinion by the citizens. No political life can exist in any country without expressing itself in functioning parties. If party life is absent, then the participation of the people in charting their political destiny is absent.

The claim that parties are class expressions is a result of the rigid class theory of Marx, in which a class replaces man. Starting from the unity of interest, Marx arrives at the unity of opinion. Within any class, however, there is neither a single interest nor a unanimity of opinion. Otherwise, we would not have seen the intense differences among Communist parties themselves in Russia, Yugoslavia, and China. The mere existence of these differences is proof that disagreement is possible not only within a single class but also within a single-class party.

The claim that the people as a whole take the place of parties is further from the truth than the claim that parties are merely expressions of class interests. The people necessarily have greater contradictions and differences among themselves than has a given class. If a given class or its ideological representatives cannot agree, how can the whole people do so? The overwhelming majority of a people or class may come to an agreement about ultimate ends, but beyond that, disagreement is inevitable. Such disagreements cannot find expression except through party life.

Most underdeveloped countries in which democratic systems have collapsed have suffered greatly from anarchy, corruption, and internal conflict among the parties. There is no doubt that most of the parties that prevailed in Asia and Africa soon after independence were capitalist or feudalist parties that represented the interests of the exploiters. Having assumed power they used their positions for exploitation and destruction, thus discrediting party life in general and forcing the people to put an end to these parties when they revolted, as they often did.

However, granting that they can be instruments of anarchy and corruption, still parties are the only way to express a people's vitality, enthusiasm, and energy. We must remember that the struggle which the people undertook before and after independence was carried out by militant parties that have proved party organization to be the only means of organization capable of mobilizing the people, especially its militant elements.

Putting an end to all party life is quite a different matter from putting an end to corrupt parties. To end parties is to end the direct participation of the people in the determination of its destiny; it is to destroy the people's spirit of struggle which finds its expression in party organization, replacing it with a feeling of weariness, indifference, and irresponsibility among the citizenry. If in the West parties are an instrument for the expression of opinion, in the struggling underdeveloped countries they are something else. They are the way in which the people participate in the struggle.

The party has a function in awakening the people, associating them with responsibility, involving them in their future and in the politics of their country—a function that cannot be carried out by the state regardless of the means and organizations at its disposal. Moreover, a party cannot be imposed on a people from above. For a party is a conscious, voluntary, popular organization, and joining the party is an act that demands that the citizen be prepared to bear the responsibility of struggle, participation, and awakening.

A one-party system by its nature cannot be democratic, especially if the party itself is not democratic in its organization. A one-party state means domination by an organization in the name of the people. As for government without parties, it means the abolition of popular political life for the citizens and the replacement of the people by the state.

Many revolutions in the countries of Asia and Africa have found themselves faced with a choice between going back to the corrupt party life that prevailed during the period of reactionary rule, and abolishing political parties. They were forced to make the second choice.

However, there is a great difference between being forced to abolish political parties because they are corrupt, conspiratorial, and exploitative and considering the abolition of parties as an ideological starting point and a new basis for government.

Understanding the true meaning of party life and its fundamental importance is one of the conditions for passing from this crisis of freedom to true freedom. When a government is forced to abolish party activity or to be satisfied with one party, one must begin by introducing democratic procedures in the party itself where it exists and then permit the establishment of liberal democratic parties provided that their goals are not incompatible with the ultimate aims of the backward countries.

The claim that the party is the people, or that the government is the people, is a feeble attempt to disguise the dictatorial nature of the government. If over a short period of time such a claim is true, the longer run inevitably exposes this claim [as false]. . . .

The realization of freedom is a human as well as a national problem. Freedom cannot be fully realized in one country while it breaks down in another, for the threat to freedom in any country is a threat to freedom throughout the world. Similarly, the realization of freedom in any country is an example and a guide for the realization of freedom in other countries. For this reason the promotion of freedom is a service to the world. The promotion of freedom anywhere is a part of the promotion of freedom in one's own country. It is not enough that one country rid itself of imperialism and tyranny, but it must help to fight imperialism and tyranny wherever they may be. . . .

The realization of freedom is not an easy task. It will not be realized by issuing laws. It will not be realized over a short period of time. It will be realized only through continuous work and a permanent struggle. The underdeveloped countries themselves are faced with a reality that is full of contradictions. But they are also faced with a goal that is inextricably linked to their destiny. Setting out to realize freedom may call for lowering the ideal goal to the level of stubborn reality at which point improvement can commence. But it must also call for raising the level of reality to approach the ideal goal. Continuous interaction between the present reality and its demands, and the ideal goal and its requirements, given faith and will, is the guarantee for moving toward progress and freedom.

10. Habib Bourguiba

Habib Bourguiba was born in 1903, in a small fishing village in Tunisia. His father had been an officer in the army of the Bey of Tunis, but had resigned in protest against the establishment of the French protectorate. Bourguiba was educated at French schools in Tunis and at the Faculty of Law in Paris. On his return to Tunis, in 1928, he became active in the nationalist movement. In 1934, Bourguiba organized the Neo-Destour Party, which stood for complete independence of Tunisia. From 1934 until 1952, he was repeatedly imprisoned by the French for nationalist activities, but when Tunisia received internal autonomy in 1956, he became Prime Minister. When full independence was accorded a year later, he became President.

A modernizing Moslem, Bourguiba has campaigned—with only limited success—to persuade the Tunisians to abandon the traditional fast of Ramadan as not suited to a country trying to develop as rapidly as possible. Sometimes regarded as pro-Western, Bourguiba describes his policy as one of nonalignment and gradualism (Bourguibism). These policies are defended in the following selections from his speeches.

THE FAST OF RAMADAN*

...The cause of these obstacles to our progress and of the paralysis of our minds is not the Moslem religion. As I know it, as I have studied it and learned it—as it was lived and practiced by the

* From a speech delivered by Bourguiba on February 6, 1961; translated and published by the Tunisian Secretariat of State for Information.

earliest members and by the Prophet himself, his companions, contemporaries, and successors—the Moslem religion is not a doctrine of intellectual asphyxia.

The first leaders of Islam were infinitely bolder and infinitely freer in the application of the principles of their religion, in their creativeness and adaptation to circumstances than our Ulema of the period of decadence. The Prophet's life and history are witness of this. They did not hesitate to suspend the effects of a Koranic edict. The caliph Omar suspended the application of certain penalties because of special circumstances. The Prophet himself had done likewise before him.

Why should such boldness be forbidden today? Why should we always be bound by what so and so said or someone else forbade?

I do not want you to agree with me blindly. I shall be satisfied if the question is studied, thought about, and freely discussed. What surprises and pains me at the same time is to hear that problems of this sort are outside the field of reason. Here we see the poverty of the chained mind. "How can we discuss this problem, since it has never been discussed before?" This is the supreme argument. I cannot accept it. We must discuss it, with complete freedom. Allah has given us brains. Let us use them to discuss and understand his commands. After all, we allow ourselves to discuss his existence.

Let us see what all the talk is about. It is said that I want to abolish Ramadan and want to force civil servants, among others, not to fast. There has never been any question of this. Need I say that the Ramadan fast is perfectly valid. The institution of fasting is to be found in other religions. Its beneficial effects are well known: self-mastery, improvement perhaps of physical condition, treatment of certain illness. All this is reasonable, and we subscribe to it.

But, as we said, we are living today in special circumstances. Neither the Prophet nor the first Moslems would ever have imagined that this nation, which Allah said was the best ever to have existed among men, should be far behind the other nations and reduced to its present fate. You need only look around you. . . .

Thus, as soon as we took power, we considered it of the utmost importance to set resolutely to work. Work and still more work: productive, rational, and methodically organized work, undertaken to create new wealth and cause an upheaval comparable to what the Arabs achieved in passing from the pre-Islamic to the Islamic era.

I am convinced that the greatest contribution made by Islam is in the liberation of the human mind. The first Moslem Arabs owe their extraordinary advance to this liberation. In reading the *Koran* and the *Life of the Prophet*, we are struck by the boldness and the exceptional power of the thought expressed.

It is only natural that, in talking to the mass of believers, Islam should have made attractive promises and terrible threats. Paradise and hell were both described in minute detail. Of course, for the Arabs of that time, paradise represented every imaginable form of beauty: gently murmuring springs, trees, and gardens watered by rivers. The inhabitants of a harsh, bare country could imagine no greater delight than water and a green landscape. To this picture, a few houris were added, as well as rivers flowing with honey and melted butter—in fact, all that was needed for perfect happiness.

On the other side, however, there were the flames and burning coals of hell. One might imagine that, once the sinner was burned to ashes, his tortures would be ended. Far from it! His flesh would be reconstituted and his sufferings start all over again an infinite number of times.

In this way, primitive people were induced to behave well, so as to avoid hell and make themselves worthy of paradise.

However, when a higher outlook came into being—as during the golden age of Moslem civilization—the great doctrinal masters, such as Ghazali and others, taught that this belief is at a lower level than that of the faith which expects neither heavenly nor earthly reward for good works, but seeks only peace of conscience. The accomplishment of duty, the practice of charity, the forgiveness of injuries, all these Moslem virtues are gifts of self designed to bring the believer close to Allah.

At the same time, we should note that by working solely to deserve paradise and avoid hell, scrupulously carrying out divine teachings, man works for his happiness here on earth. This is of the utmost importance. After all, religion is made for men and to keep man from being a "wolf to man." There was no state organization at that time, but religion held out the prospect of reward or punishment so that men would do good and refrain from evil. By observing the commandments, abstaining from theft, drink, etc., by practicing charity and doing good around them, men were contributing to social harmony. When the Last Judgment sounded, they would have won happiness in heaven as well as here on earth. As for those who are skeptical about the afterlife, they would have accomplished their duty; they would have produced and triumphed; their consciences would be at peace.

Then, spiritual decay set in. There was a tendency to disregard essential truths and abandon the substance while clinging to the form. And the Moslem world entered on a period of decadence.

As head of the state, responsible for the progress of the nation in the world, in the same way the Prophet was responsible for the Moslems of his day, I must think of every possible way of strengthening and building up the nation, making it creative and energetic. I must impress on you the need for a new approach to the problem of achieving national renewal. The means we use must be treated as sacred and as categorical obligations, like religious commands. Thus, work and behavior will no longer be dictated by the fear of the police or of the law, but will be ordered with the conviction that they come under the authority of religion, society, and individual conscience. Any disharmony between conscience, reason, and religious teaching would lead to complete disorganization.

I have developed these ideas as an introduction to the remarks I want to make today about Ramadan. This question has led to heated discussion and is being exploited in bad faith by a certain group. The seeds of doubt and hesitation are being sown in the minds of the unlearned, so that they will become agents of destruction and civil war.

Today, I shall repeat what I have already said about the fast of Ramadan. This practice was imposed by Islam. It is still so imposed today, as it will be till the end of time. However, Allah has allowed certain dispensations, which are laid down in the *Koran*. In certain circumstances, a man is not obliged to observe the fast. These dispensations are well known and have been thoroughly studied. In the Tunisian schools, they are not mentioned in certain teachings, but they are nonetheless authentic and valid. Originally, dispensations were only allowed in cases of sickness or when traveling. Then the Jihad (or holy war) was included. Later on, with the agreement of the Ulema, the risk of illness was added, by extension of principle.

If we study the question thoroughly and analyze the reasons given for the dispensations, we see that they have a common purpose—that of relieving Moslems of the obligation to fast if the effort involved is excessively arduous. For example, traveling was included in the dispensations because it was originally very tiring.

Under these circumstances, a traveler was not bound to observe the fast. He was excused because Allah did not want him to suffer excessively. If there were no dispensation, there would be a serious risk that Moslems would abstain from traveling during the month of Ramadan. This would reduce their means, and force idleness and unemployment upon them. But, far from encouraging laziness, religion gives dispensation from fasting in cases where it would stand in the way of traveling, that is to say, of work and effort.

Another case for dispensation is sickness. Why? Because fasting is likely to aggravate an illness, since the physical condition of a sick person is such that it is dangerous to deprive him of food. In fact, instead of fasting, he needs to eat properly.

If we meditate over these Koranic provisions and examine them closely, we realize how much trouble Islam has taken to spare men unnecessary causes of fatigue and impediments to their activity. You all know the origin of the dispensation allowed for the Jihad. The day before the capture of Mecca, Mohammed ordered the faithful to break their fast, so that they would be in the best physical condition to meet the enemy.

From a careful study of the purposes of the fast, the circumstances which surround this practice, the dispensations allowed, and the reasons for them, we find there is no room for hesitation. There are good grounds today for not observing the fast of Ramadan.

The *Koran* prescribes fasting, so as to accustom men to controlling their senses and appetites. But if fasting involves a risk, is harmful or impairs a man's physical condition, health, or working capacity, or lowers his potentialities or those of the Moslem community, he is dispensed from fasting.

We must keep a sense of proportion. Thus, traveling is one of the reasons for dispensation. But traveling is no longer as tiring today as it used to be. Today, we travel by air, ensconced in a comfortable seat. Modern travel bears no comparison with journeys across the desert by camel. All the same, some people argue that the dispensation allowed to travelers still holds good. Personally, I think that traveling today no longer gives dispensation from fasting. These same people maintain that no dispensation can be allowed to workers even when they toil to the point of fainting. Why should an allowance be made for a traveler surrounded by the most up-to-date comfort, and refused to an underfed worker with a weak constitution? The latter, it is argued, may only break his fast after fainting for the second time. Is this logical?

I invite the Tunisian people, its Ulema, and sheiks to study the whole problem from the point of view of the purpose of the fast and the reasons for dispensation. Everyone must acquaint himself with the problem of how to interpret divine law properly. Allah gave man his reasoning faculty so that he would be able to distinguish good from evil.

At a time when we are fighting against poverty and drawing up programs and plans to remedy our underdevelopment, when we contemplate calling to account those who do not produce enough, and restricting individual freedom, when the recovery of the Moslem nation depends on strenuous work—I urge you to make use of a dispensation which is based on a sound conception of religious law.

BOURGUIBISM*

The policy which has been described as Bourguibism is not a matter of accepting charity from the colonizing country and then begging for more. It is more like a war for positions, which consists of directing the weight of the attack against strategic points. This is the meaning of our policy of stages, each of which should facilitate accession to the next, until we achieve our final goal of independence, without which there can be no dignity.

This has been our concern from the very beginning. Since 1930, I have accepted many things: cosovereignty; participation in a ministry—most of whose members were tools of the colonialists—which we eventually left in order to take up armed resistance; internal autonomy, from which we achieved incomplete independence, which, in turn, enabled us to obtain partial evacuation. We have achieved all this after only seven years, starting with a regime of direct French administration, the like of which neither Syria, Lebanon, nor any other Middle East country has known. For although these countries have experienced French colonization, it had nothing in common with the regime installed in Tunisia. The form they knew did indeed make use of ruse, perfidy, and division in order to maintain its position, but the regime knew it was provisional because it was authorized by mandate. Here things were

* From a speech delivered by Bourguiba on October 12, 1961; translated and published by the Tunisian Secretariat of State for Information.

quite different. We experienced colonization by settlement. This came to an end barely seven years ago. All of you here and most of those listening to me remember this period. The protectorate which Tunisia underwent was harsher than was imposed on any other Arab country. In Egypt, for instance, the English protectorate came to an end in 1922, yet total evacuation was not obtained until 1957—over thirty years, in stages. Our stages barely lasted seven years, while our situation was much worse to start with.

We do not say this in order to boast of our successes, but only to give a comparable example, illustrating Bourguibism—which has sometimes been badly understood, to the extent of likening it to a policy of collusion or complicity with colonialism. It is nevertheless the policy of our means, the one which follows from our geographical position, our history, and the form of colonization imposed on us. . . .

My method is to advance by steps, thinking out every step as I go. Speed does not mean hasty, unthought-out actions. In the past, when I was a school child and had quarrels with my schoolfellows, I did not rush to fight the enemy, but on the contrary I needed a certain amount of time to ponder and watch the situation evolve. It is too serious a matter for me to allow myself to throw the whole nation in with one bloc or another, with the excuse of French aggression.* In spite of the aggression we have suffered, we must not brutally change our policies. Naturally we must foresee matters, temper our policies, and allow them to evolve according to both circumstances and the means at our disposal.

We ourselves were fed on and formed by French culture. Through it, we found the principles of humanity, liberty, and dignity. We have always harbored feelings of affection for French culture and the French people and nation. We were even searching for explanations for the French attitude by saying that it is not possible for the French people to commit acts of aggression such as this. We distinguished between the French people and the supporters of colonialism. In spite of all this, the French used cultural relations as an object for low bargaining. We must refuse all bargaining. This refusal could lead to the reshaping of our programs. We may even have to envisage the use of a language other than French, and thus look toward other civilizations, countries, and

* Bourguiba is referring here to the Bizerte crisis.—Ed.

friends. The problem is still of great importance and must be seriously examined and thought out.

Our decisions will be taken calmly by stages, in the light of our interests and the interests of the Tunisian state, and according to what suits our best interests. . . .

THE AGRICULTURAL ASPECT OF THE ECONOMIC BATTLE *

We are not inspired by any considerations of demagogy in the field of agrarian reform, a tempting formula covering a very simple operation: parceling out lands and distributing them. A regime which carries out such measures aims at gaining the support of the masses by satisfying those who are worst off. It is not greatly concerned with the effect of the reform on the curve of production. In fact, no thought is given to this. Agrarian reforms of this sort are generally accompanied by a vast propaganda campaign in which there is talk of social justice, of poor people to whom rights are restored, and of rich men despoiled—to the delirious applause of the populace.

What is important to me is the level of production. Admittedly, in some special cases, individual estates may be as much as 15,000 to 25,000 acres—which one man cannot farm properly. The state may intervene to help him and improve working conditions. If it decides to confiscate part of the estate, this is not done out of a desire for revenge. To create a hate psychosis like this would be contrary to the general interest. Poor and rich, we are one family. The state's role is to maintain the nation's unity. However, when a landowner has an agricultural estate which is too large for him to manage properly—or in conditions corresponding to the community's interest—it is the state's duty to dispossess him in whole or in part. The state performs its duty in the interest of all, whether poor or rich. It is concerned solely with the community's interest. An owner who has part of his lands confiscated must not feel he is being despoiled. In any case, the increase in production which would result from confiscation would help to raise the general level of the community. As a member of this community, a

---

*From a speech delivered by Bourguiba on October 27, 1961; translated and published by the Tunisian Secretariat of State for Information.

dispossessed owner will have his share of the general income. The sense of fraternity and association uniting the nation will be strengthened thereby. Sacrifices are accepted all the more readily if they are seen to be in the general interest. We do nothing with the intention of restricting the freedom of individuals. We do not apply any pressure. We do not impair individual freedom or the right of ownership, except in the general interest.

This is the path we have chosen in order to achieve socialism. Our method is based on respect for the individual, not on class hatred or the dictatorship of the poor over the rich. Our sole guide is the interest of the country, in which we are united for better or worse.

How can we compare the sacrifice of a few interests, a few minor rights, a few relatively unimportant freedoms, to the deportation, imprisonment, and death to which Tunisians were exposed in the past, and to which they are still prepared to expose themselves anew should the country be threatened once again?

If the state, which is in a position to weigh the situation, decides on measures implying a restriction of a given freedom, the reconversion of a given crop, the redivision of certain agricultural lands, it is because it has been led to do so for imperative reasons of general interest.

In carrying out this gigantic task, using the method of Neo-Destourian socialism,* we are at the same time respecting the dignity of the individual. The latter must be convinced that the sacrifice he accepts, by agreeing to the restriction of some of his freedoms, is in his country's interest. He is not so different from a conscript who relinquishes his individual freedom when he is called up. He makes this sacrifice willingly.

Freely accepted discipline is the motive power of progress. We must realize this and fully familiarize ourselves with the idea that the individual's interest lies in the progress and well-being of the community.

---

* Bourguiba only began to speak favorably of socialism in 1961. In October, 1964, his commitment to the doctrine became formalized when he changed the name of his party from the Neo-Destour to the Destourian Socialist Party.—ED.

THE NEED FOR BIRTH CONTROL*

· · · · The disequilibrium between births and available resources is still considerable and we must look for a solution to the problem of the birthrate in our country.

I should like you to realize how serious this problem is. In twenty years' time we shall number 6 million, perhaps more. Think of the new wealth we shall have to create in order to feed all these mouths. Think of the number of classes that will be needed in order to provide education for all children of school age. This is the underlying reason for planning, which many people still do not understand. However, every Tunisian must come to realize how necessary and urgent it is. We cannot help but feel some apprehension at the human tide rising implacably at a speed much greater than the rate of increase of subsistence.

Here arises the problem of birth control which preoccupies many countries in Latin America, Asia, and Africa. This is an endless task. The babies grow more rapidly than our food resources. What is the use of increasing our agricultural production and our mineral wealth, what is the use of raising our national income in order to bring about a fair distribution of wealth, if the population is to go on rising in a frenzied, uncontrolled manner? We should have achieved nothing, for we run the risk of dropping, in spite of all our efforts, to a general level lower than our point of departure.

We must find a solution to this vital problem. First of all, on the psychological level we must free ourselves from the archaic ideas that men and women in Tunisia hold on the subject of procreation. It is readily believed that the question is beyond us and is a matter solely of the divine will. We must stop abdicating our own will. By the use of reason, humanity has managed to master nature and progressively conquer disease, has created tools and changed the face of the world, and is able to govern itself and control the rate of procreation.

We must also discard the popular belief that Allah has endowed each newborn baby with its share of wealth, its subsistence. This is a false and dangerous opinion, and can only unduly aggravate the state's burdens.

* From a speech delivered by Bourguiba on December 26, 1962; translated and published by the Tunisian Secretariat of State for Information.

But I should like to clarify my thought further. What we want is not to do away with or hinder procreation, but only to discipline it, so that men and women should be able to procreate by an act of their will, in the light of reason. If a household can support seven, eight, or ten children, so much the better. But if it does not have the means to support more than two, we should help it to understand that it is not in its interest to exceed this limit and that it can effectively keep within it. . . .

We therefore do not aim to limit procreation systematically, but rather to improve the quality of our human potential. In any given society, what is important is not so much the number as the quality of the men. And quality is determined both by physical and moral health and by the standard of living. . . .

11. Bechir Ben Yahmed

Bechir Ben Yahmed is the general manager of Jeune Afrique, *a journal of news and opinion published in Tunis and Paris and distributed in many parts of French-speaking Africa. Ben Yahmed was born in Djerba, Tunisia. The Minister of Information in the first Bourguiba government, he resigned after a year and has subsequently devoted himself to business and journalism.* Jeune Afrique, *like its predecessor,* Afrique Action, *has been increasingly critical of the concentration of power in the hands of Bourguiba. In 1963 and 1964, it devoted several issues to a general debate on the advantages and disadvantages of the African single-party system. The debate was concluded with the article translated below giving Ben Yahmed's own views in favor of a two-party system— a position not widely shared by African ideologists today.*

FOR OR AGAINST
THE SINGLE PARTY?*

One of the merits of the debate begun in these columns under the above title has been to reveal or confirm several truths.

1. If the African countries live under governments which are dominated by a single party with all power, it is because this corresponds to a social and economic situation which demanded this solution at the time of independence. The colonizer constantly tried to break down the unity of our national movements. When we achieved independence, we thirsted for unity. We were haunted by the nightmare of our old divisions and also, I should note, by the spectacle of impotence and ridicule provided by the multiparty system of the French Fourth Republic between 1950 and 1958. When we became masters of our destinies, we also regarded independence as only a means to allow us to build a modern state and undertake the real battle for development. For this a strong, stable government, endowed with special powers, was necessary. We had confidence in those governments; we accepted the sacrifice of the liberties we had just acquired all the more readily because we were entrusting our fate to those who had liberated us from colonialism.

2. There is the single party which is an instrument of progress (at least in its early years) and the single party which, from the time of its creation, is a mask for immobilism and sterile dictatorship, an instrument of the domination of a single social group over the rest of the nation.

The single party means an unusual concentration of power in the hands of one man, aided and influenced by a group. What that man and group who monopolize power and the means of expression will do depends almost entirely upon their ideology, their force of character, and their capacity to resist the easy solution. Since they have force at their disposal, they have little need for persuasion. What they think is good for the country, they do. What in the long run is fatal is that even in their own consciences

* From "Pour ou contre le parti unique," *Jeune Afrique* (Tunis and Paris), No. 166 (January 13–19, 1964), p. 5. Translated by the editor, by permission.

they identify what is good for them with what is good for the country. In the party and in the nation they become an interest group instead of a government.

The result is that *in the optimal situation* the single party and personal power can only be helpful to a country during a transition period—that of the construction of the state, the consolidation of national unity, and the establishment of new economic structures. After that phase, the single party becomes unbearable, a factor making for sterility of thought, social immobility, and even political disorder.

3. Once the single party is established in power, it is the last to perceive the need for a change or for its own disappearance. It is practically incapable of democratizing itself or the country. It is accustomed to silencing the opposition and is persuaded that it represents the general interest; it therefore does not understand the need for concessions and is afraid to initiate them.

In these conditions what was the motor becomes the brake. The state just created is corrupted. The traditions which have hardly been established begin to decay. Confidence among companions in the struggle breaks down. The prisons fill up; the youth are alienated and revolt. The future becomes uncertain.

The single party and the leader who incarnates the state and the nation thus seem to be a sort of historical necessity for underdeveloped countries as they become independent. Directed by men who have sprung from the people and have been formed in battle, the party, when it establishes national goals, can be an incomparable instrument of progress for several years. After that, unable to see that its mission is ended, it becomes an obstacle to progress.

To go from the phase of the single party to that of democracy is in a way to go from underdevelopment to development, from the tribal phase to that of the nation, from the agricultural state to the industrial state. Just as one cannot modernize and industrialize a country without social dislocation, so one cannot democratize it without disagreement and adjustment.

Democracy is the result of education, and fortunately education is spreading through Africa like wildfire. Education produces citizenship and national horizons. Rather than plotting to overthrow a man or a group so as to replace them—fatally—with another man and another group, let us strive, we the youth, for a better and more widespread education of those below us. Just as our elders have struggled and suffered for independence, let us struggle and suffer, if necessary, for democracy.

When we say the word democracy, some of our elders . . . throw in our faces the formalism of Western democracy, the multi-party system of the French Fourth Republic, and stories about old man Queuille.*

Let us give a reasonable reply to that facile response—a form of government in which democracy does not prevent stability and efficiency in the state. We do not need to invent this form. It exists and has been tested by experience. It is the only one which has succeeded historically—that of a majority party in government and an opposition *united in a single organization* which checks the government and is prepared to take its place.

They will say that we are not sufficiently developed to adopt such a form of government. But when will we be?

12. Frantz Fanon

Frantz Fanon was born in Martinique in 1925. He studied medicine and psychiatry in France and practiced in Blida, Algeria, where he treated both colonizers and natives. He joined the National Liberation Front at the time of its founding, and later served as Ambassador to Ghana for the Algerian Provisional Government. He died of leukemia in 1961, at the age of thirty-six.

Fanon was known among leaders and intellectuals of the French-speaking world for his moving books on the Algerian Revolution and the anticolonial movement. His best-known work, translated into English as The Wretched of the Earth (*a reference to the second line of the "International"*), *endows the violence of the revolution with a mystical liberating quality. Writing from a radical nationalist point of view, Fanon was critical of the economic arrangements which many African governments have made with*

---

*Henri Queuille, twice Premier under the Fourth Republic. He was known for his ability to maintain himself in power by inaction.—Ed.

the former colonial powers, interpreting them as a "sell-out" to capitalism and neocolonialism by the national bourgeoisie. His criticisms of the regime of the single party and the demagogy of the nationalist leader are similar in content to the more Western-oriented comments of Bechir Ben Yahmed.

This selection, showing the influence of the Algerian War but in no way Islamic in content, may be seen as an introduction to the African selections which follow, underscoring Algeria's dual orientation toward the Arab world and Africa. (Fanon's discussion of the revolutionary role of the slum-dwellers has also been favorably received by some of the more radical leaders of the civil rights movement in the United States.)

THE WRETCHED OF THE EARTH*

. . . The originality of the colonial context is that economic reality, inequality, and the immense difference of ways of life never come to mask the human realities. When you examine at close quarters the colonial context, it is evident that what parcels out the world is to begin with the fact of belonging to or not belonging to a given race, a given species. In the colonies the economic substructure is also a superstructure. The cause is the consequence; you are rich because you are white, you are white because you are rich. This is why Marxist analysis should always be slightly stretched every time we have to do with the colonial problem.

Everything up to and including the very nature of precapitalist society, so well explained by Marx, must here be thought out again. The serf is in essence different from the knight, but a reference to divine right is necessary to legitimize this statutory difference. In the colonies, the foreigner coming from another country imposed his rule by means of guns and machines. In defiance of his successful transplantation, in spite of his appropriation, the settler still remains a foreigner. It is neither the act of owning factories, nor estates, nor a bank balance which distinguishes the gov-

---

* Excerpts from *The Wretched of the Earth* (New York: Grove Press; London: McGibbon and Kee, 1965). Translated by Constance Farrington from *Les Damnés de la Terre*. Reprinted by permission of Grove Press, Inc. and McGibbon and Kee Ltd. Copyright 1963 by Présence Africaine.

erning classes. The governing race is first and foremost those who come from elsewhere, those who are unlike the original inhabitants, "the others."

The violence which has ruled over the ordering of the colonial world, which has ceaselessly drummed the rhythm for the destruction of native social forms and broken up without reserve the systems of reference of the economy, the customs of dress and external life, that same violence will be claimed and taken over by the native at the moment when, deciding to embody history in his own person, he surges into the forbidden quarters. To wreck the colonial world is henceforward a mental picture of action which is very clear, very easy to understand, and which may be assumed by each one of the individuals which constitute the colonized people. To break up the colonial world does not mean that after the frontiers have been abolished lines of communication will be set up between the two zones. The destruction of the colonial world is no more and no less than the abolition of one zone, its burial in the depths of the earth, or its expulsion from the country. . . .

The Revolutionary Role of the Peasants

What are the forces which in the colonial period open up new outlets and engender new aims for the violence of colonized peoples? In the first place there are the political parties and the intellectual or commercial elites. Now, the characteristic feature of certain political structures is that they proclaim abstract principles but refrain from issuing definite commands. The entire action of these nationalist political parties during the colonial period is action of the electoral type: a string of philosophico-political dissertations on the themes of the rights of peoples to self-determination, the rights of man to freedom from hunger and human dignity, and the unceasing affirmation of the principle: "One man, one vote." The national political parties never lay stress upon the necessity of a trial of armed strength, for the good reason that their objective is not the radical overthrowing of the system. Pacifists and legalists, they are in fact partisans of order, the new order— but to the colonialist bourgeoisie they put bluntly enough the demand which to them is the main one: "Give us more power." On the specific question of violence, the elite are ambiguous. They are violent in their words and reformist in their attitudes. When the nationalist political leaders *say* something, they make quite clear that they do not really *think* it.

This characteristic on the part of the nationalist political parties should be interpreted in the light both of the make-up of their leaders and the nature of their followings. The rank-and-file of a nationalist party is urban. The workers, primary schoolteachers, artisans and small shopkeepers who have begun to profit—at a discount, to be sure—from the colonial setup, have special interests at heart. What this sort of following demands is the betterment of their particular lot: increased salaries, for example. The dialogue between these political parties and colonialism is never broken off. Improvements are discussed, such as full electoral representation, the liberty of the press, and liberty of association. Reforms are debated. Thus it need not astonish anyone to notice that a large number of natives are militant members of the branches of political parties which stem from the mother country. These natives fight under an abstract watchword, "Government by the workers," and they forget that in their country it should be *nationalist* watchwords which are first in the field. The native intellectual has clothed his aggressiveness in his barely veiled desire to assimilate himself to the colonial world. He has used his aggressiveness to serve his own individual interests.

Thus there is very easily brought into being a kind of class of enfranchised slaves, or slaves who are individually free. What the intellectual demands is the right to multiply the emancipated, and the opportunity to organize a genuine class of emancipated citizens. On the other hand, the mass of the people have no intention of standing by and watching individuals increase their chances of success. What they demand is not the settler's position of status, but the settler's place. The immense majority of natives want the settler's farm. For them, there is no question of entering into competition with the settler. They want to take his place.

The peasantry is systematically disregarded for the most part by the propaganda put out by the nationalist parties. And it is clear that in the colonial countries the peasants alone are revolutionary, for they have nothing to lose and everything to gain. The starving peasant, outside of the class system, is the first among the exploited to discover that only violence pays. For him there is no compromise, no possible coming to terms; colonization and decolonization are simply a question of relative strength. The exploited man sees that his liberation implies the use of all means, and that of force first and foremost. When in 1956, after the capitulation of M. Guy Mollet to the settlers in Algeria, the National Liberation Front, in a famous leaflet, stated that colonialism only loosens its hold when the knife is at its throat, no Algerian really found these terms too violent. The leaflet only expressed what every Algerian felt at heart: colonialism is not a thinking machine, nor a body endowed with reasoning faculties. It is violence in its natural state, and it will only yield when confronted with greater violence.

At the decisive moment, the colonialist bourgeoisie, which up till then has remained inactive, comes into the field. It introduces that new idea which is in proper parlance a creation of the colonial situation: nonviolence. In its simplest form this nonviolence signifies to the intellectual and economic elite of the colonized country that the bourgeoisie has the same interests as they and that it is therefore urgent and indispensable to come to terms for the public good. Nonviolence is an attempt to settle the colonial problem around a green baize table, before any regrettable act has been performed or irreparable gesture made, before any blood has been shed. But if the masses, without waiting for the chairs to be arranged around the baize table, listen to their own voice and begin committing outrages and setting fire to buildings, the elites and the nationalist bourgeois parties will be seen rushing to the colonialists to exclaim "This is very serious! We do not know how it will end; we must find a solution—some sort of compromise."

This idea of compromise is very important in the phenomenon of decolonization, for it is very far from being a simple one. Compromise involves the colonial system and the young nationalist bourgeoisie at one and the same time. The partisans of the colonial system discover that the masses may destroy everything. Blown-up bridges, ravaged farms, repressions, and fighting harshly disrupt the economy. Compromise is equally attractive to the nationalist bourgeoisie, who, since they are not clearly aware of the possible consequences of the rising storm, are genuinely afraid of being swept away by this huge hurricane and never stop saying to the settlers: "We are still capable of stopping the slaughter; the masses still have confidence in us; act quickly if you do not want to put everything in jeopardy." One step more, and the leader of the nationalist party keeps his distance with regard to that violence. He loudly proclaims that he has nothing to do with these Mau Mau, these terrorists, these throat-slitters. At best, he shuts himself off in a no man's land between the terrorists and the settlers and willingly offers his services as go-between; that is to say, that as the settlers cannot discuss terms with these Mau Mau, he himself will be quite willing to begin negotiations. Thus it is that the rear guard of the national struggle, that very party of people who have never ceased to be on the other side in the fight, find themselves somersaulted into the van of negotiations and compromise—precisely because that party has taken very good care never to break contact with colonialism. . . .

. . . The militant nationalist who decides to throw in his lot with the country people instead of playing at hide-and-seek with the police in urban centers will lose nothing. The peasant's cloak will wrap him around with a gentleness and firmness that he never suspected. These men, who are in fact exiled to the backwoods, who are cut off from the urban background against which they had defined their ideas of the nation and of the political fight, these men have in fact become "Maquisards." Since they are obliged to move about the whole time in order to escape from the police, often at night so as not to attract attention, they will have good reason to wander through their country and to get to know it. The cafés are forgotten; so are the arguments about the next elections or the spitefulness of some policeman or other. Their ears hear the true voice of the country, and their eyes take in the great and infinite poverty of their people. They realize the precious time that has been wasted in useless commentaries upon the colonial regime. They finally come to understand that the changeover will not be a reform, nor a bettering of things. They come to understand, with a sort of bewilderment that will from henceforth never quite leave them, that political action in the towns will always be powerless to modify or overthrow the colonial regime.

These men get used to talking to the peasants. They discover that the mass of the country people have never ceased to think of the problem of their liberation except in terms of violence, in terms of taking back the land from the foreigners, in terms of national struggle and of armed insurrection. It is all very simple. These men discover a coherent people who go on living, as it were, statically, but who keep their moral values and their devotion to the nation intact. They discover a people that is generous, ready to sacrifice themselves completely, an impatient people with a stony pride. It is understandable that the meeting between these militants with the police on their track and these mettlesome masses of people, who are rebels by instinct, can produce an explosive mixture of unusual potentiality. The men coming from the towns learn their lessons in the hard school of the people; and at the same time these men open classes for the people in military and political education. The people furbish up their weapons; but in fact the classes do not last long, for the masses come to know once again the strength of their own muscles, and push the leaders on to prompt action. The armed struggle has begun. . . .

Moreover, the first overtures which the men of the Maquis make toward their former friends—precisely those whom they consider to be the most toward the left—will confirm their fears and will take away even the wish to see their old companions again. In fact the rebellion, which began in the country districts, will filter into the towns through that fraction of the peasant population which is blocked on the outer fringe of the urban centers, that fraction which has not yet succeeded in finding a bone to gnaw in the colonial system. The men whom the growing population of the country districts and colonial expropriation have brought to desert their family holdings circle tirelessly around the different towns, hoping that one day or another they will be allowed inside. It is within this mass of humanity, this people of the shanty towns, at the core of the *lumpenproletariat* that the rebellion will find its urban spearhead. For the *lumpenproletariat*, that horde of starving men, uprooted from their tribe and from their clan, constitutes one of the most spontaneous and the most radically revolutionary forces of a colonized people. . . .

So long as the uncertainty of colonialism continues, the national cause goes on progressing, and becomes the cause of each and all. The plans for liberation are sketched out; already they include the whole country. During this period spontaneity is king, and initiative is localized. On every hill a government in miniature is formed and takes over power. Everywhere—in the valleys and in the forests, in the jungle and in the villages—we find a national authority. Each man or woman brings the nation to life by his or her action, and is pledged to ensure its triumph in their locality. We are dealing with a strategy of immediacy which is both radical and totalitarian: the aim and the program of each locally constituted group is local liberation. If the nation is everywhere, then she is here. One step further, and only here is she to be found. Tactics are mistaken for strategy. The art of politics is simply transformed into the art of war; the political militant is the rebel. To fight the war and to take part in politics: the two things become one and the same. . . .

The National Bourgeoisie

The national middle class which takes over power at the end of the colonial regime is an underdeveloped middle class. It has practically no economic power, and in any case it is in no way commensurate with the bourgeoisie of the mother country which it hopes to replace. In its willful narcissism, the national middle class is easily convinced that it can advantageously replace the middle class of the mother country. But that same independence which literally drives it into a corner will give rise within its ranks to catastrophic reactions, and will oblige it to send out frenzied appeals for help to the former mother country. The university and merchant classes, which make up the most enlightened section of the new state, are in fact characterized by the smallness of their number and their being concentrated in the capital, and the type of activities in which they are engaged: business, agriculture, and the liberal professions. Neither financiers nor industrial magnates are to be found within this national middle class. The national bourgeoisie of underdeveloped countries is not engaged in production, nor in invention, nor building, nor labor; it is completely canalized into activities of the intermediary type. Its innermost vocation seems to be to keep in the running and to be part of the racket. The psychology of the national bourgeoisie is that of the businessman, not that of a captain of industry; and it is only too true that the greed of the settlers and the system of embargoes set up by colonialism has hardly left them any other choice.

Under the colonial system, a middle class which accumulates capital is an impossible phenomenon. Now, precisely, it would seem that the historical vocation of an authentic national middle class in an underdeveloped country is to repudiate its own nature insofar as it is bourgeois, that is to say, insofar as it is the tool of capitalism, and to make itself the willing slave of that revolutionary capital which is the people.

In an underdeveloped country an authentic national middle class ought to consider it as its bounden duty to betray the calling fate has marked out for it, and to put itself to school with the people: in other words to put at the people's disposal the intellectual and technical capital that it has snatched when going through the colonial universities. But, unhappily, we shall see that very often the national middle class does not follow this heroic, positive, fruitful, and just path; rather, it disappears with its soul set at peace into the shocking ways—shocking because antinational —of a traditional bourgeoisie, of a bourgeoisie which is stupidly, contemptibly, cynically bourgeois.

The objective of nationalist parties as from a certain given period is, we have seen, strictly national. They mobilize the people with slogans of independence, and for the rest leave it to future events. When such parties are questioned on the economic program of the state that they are clamoring for, or on the nature of the regime which they propose to install, they are incapable of replying, because, precisely, they are completely ignorant of the economy of their own country.

This economy has always developed outside the limits of their knowledge. They have nothing more than an approximate, bookish acquaintance with the actual and potential resources of their country's soil and mineral deposits; and therefore they can only speak of these resources on a general and abstract plane. After independence this underdeveloped middle class, reduced in numbers and without capital, which refuses to follow the path of revolution, will fall into deplorable stagnation. It is unable to give free rein to its genius, which, as it was formerly wont to lament, though rather too glibly, was held in check by colonial domination. The precariousness of its resources and the paucity of its managerial class forces it back for years into an artisanal economy. From its point of view, which is inevitably a very limited one, a national economy is an economy based on what may be called local products. Long speeches will be made about the artisan class. Since the middle classes find it impossible to set up factories that would be more profit-earning both for themselves and for the country as a whole, they will surround the artisan class with a chauvinistic tenderness in keeping with the new awareness of national dignity, and which moreover will bring them in quite a lot of money. This cult of local products and this incapability to seek out new systems of management will be equally manifested by the bogging down of the national middle class in the methods of agricultural production which were characteristic of the colonial period.

The national economy of the period of independence is not set on a new footing. It is still concerned with the peanut harvest, with the cocoa crop, and the olive yield. In the same way there is no change in the marketing of basic products, and not a single industry is set up in the country. We go on sending out raw materials;

we go on being Europe's small farmers, who specialize in unfinished products.

Yet the national middle class constantly demands the nationalization of the economy and of the trading sectors. This is because, from their point of view, nationalization does not mean placing the whole economy at the service of the nation and deciding to satisfy the needs of the nation. For them, nationalization does not mean governing the state with regard to the new social relations whose growth it has been decided to encourage. To them, nationalization quite simply means the transfer into native hands of those unfair advantages which are a legacy of the colonial period.

Since the middle class has neither sufficient material nor intellectual resources (by intellectual resources we mean engineers and technicians), it limits its claims to the taking over of business offices and commercial houses formerly occupied by the settlers. The national bourgeoisie steps into the shoes of the former European settlement: doctors, barristers, traders, commercial travelers, general agents, and transport agents. It considers that the dignity of the country and its own welfare require that it should occupy all these posts. From now on it will insist that all the big foreign companies should pass through its hands, whether these companies wish to keep on their connections with the country, or to open it up. The national middle class discovers its historic mission: that of intermediary. . . .

As regards internal affairs and in the sphere of institutions, the national bourgeoisie will give equal proof of its incapacity. In a certain number of underdeveloped countries the parliamentary game is faked from the beginning. Powerless economically, unable to bring about the existence of coherent social relations, and standing on the principle of its domination as a class, the bourgeoisie chooses the solution that seems to it the easiest, that of the single party. It does not yet have the quiet conscience and the calm that economic power and the control of the state machine alone can give. It does not create a state that reassures the ordinary citizen, but rather one that rouses his anxiety.

The state, which by its strength and discretion ought to inspire confidence and disarm and lull everybody to sleep, on the contrary seeks to impose itself in spectacular fashion. It makes a display, it jostles people and bullies them, thus intimating to the citizen that he is in continual danger. The single party is the modern form of the dictatorship of the bourgeoisie, unmasked, unpainted, unscrupulous, and cynical.

It is true that such a dictatorship does not go very far. It cannot halt the processes of its own contradictions. Since the bourgeoisie has not the economic means to ensure its domination and to throw a few crumbs to the rest of the country, since, moreover, it is preoccupied with filling its pockets as rapidly as possible but also as prosaically as possible, the country sinks all the more deeply into stagnation. And in order to hide this stagnation and to mask this regression, to reassure itself and to give itself something to boast about, the bourgeoisie can find nothing better to do than to erect grandiose buildings in the capital and to lay out money on what are called prestige expenses.

The national bourgeoisie turns its back more and more on the interior and on the real facts of its undeveloped country, and tends to look toward the former mother country and the foreign capitalists who count on its obliging compliance. As it does not share its profits with the people, and in no way allows them to enjoy any of the dues that are paid to it by the big foreign companies, it will discover the need for a popular leader to whom will fall the dual role of stabilizing the regime and of perpetuating the domination of the bourgeoisie. The bourgeois dictatorship of underdeveloped countries draws its strength from the existence of a leader. We know that in the well-developed countries the bourgeois dictatorship is the result of the economic power of the bourgeoisie. In the underdeveloped countries, on the contrary, the leader stands for moral power, in whose shelter the thin and poverty-stricken bourgeoisie of the young nation decides to get rich.

The people who for years on end have seen this leader and heard him speak, who from a distance in a kind of dream have followed his contests with the colonial power, spontaneously put their trust in this patriot. Before independence, the leader generally embodies the aspirations of the people for independence, political liberty, and national dignity. But as soon as independence is declared, far from embodying in concrete form the needs of the people in what touches bread, land, and the restoration of the country to the sacred hands of the people, the leader will reveal his inner purpose: to become the general president of that company of profiteers impatient for their returns which is known as the national bourgeoisie. . . .

The economic channels of the young state sink back inevitably into neocolonialist lines. The national economy, formerly protected, is today literally controlled. The budget is balanced through loans and gifts, while every three or four months the chief ministers themselves or else their governmental delegations come to the erstwhile mother countries or elsewhere, fishing for capital. . . .

From time to time the leader makes an effort; he speaks on the radio or makes a tour of the country to pacify the people, to calm them and bemuse them. The leader is all the more necessary in that there is no party. During the period of the struggle for independence there was a party led by the present leader. But since then this party has sadly disintegrated; nothing is left but the shell of a party, the name, the emblem, and the motto. The living party, which ought to make possible the free exchange of ideas which have been elaborated according to the real needs of the mass of the people, has been transformed into a trade union of individual interests. Since the proclamation of independence, the party no longer helps the people to set out its demands, to become more aware of its needs and better able to establish its power. Today, the party's mission is to deliver to the people the instructions which issue from the summit. There no longer exists the fruitful give-and-take from the bottom to the top and from the top to the bottom which creates and guarantees democracy in a party. Quite the contrary, the party has made itself into a screen between the masses and the leaders. There is no longer any party life, for the branches which were set up during the colonial period are today completely demobilized. . . .

Europe and the Third World

The Third World today faces Europe like a colossal mass whose aim should be to try to resolve the problems to which Europe has not been able to find the answers.

But let us be clear: what matters is to stop talking about output, and intensification, and the rhythm of work.

No, there is no question of a return to Nature. It is simply a very concrete question of not dragging men toward mutilation, of not imposing upon the brain rhythms which very quickly obliterate it and wreck it. The pretext of catching up must not be used to push man around, to tear him away from himself or from his· privacy, to break and kill him.

No, we do not want to catch up with anyone. What we want

to do is to go forward all the time, night and day, in the company of man, in the company of all men. The caravan should not be stretched out, for in that case each line will hardly see those who precede it; and men who no longer recognize each other meet less and less together, and talk to each other less and less.

It is a question of the Third World starting a new history of man, a history which will have regard to the sometimes prodigious theses which Europe has put forward, but which will also not forget Europe's crimes, of which the most horrible was committed in the heart of man, and consisted of the pathological tearing apart of his functions and the crumbling away of his unity. And in the framework of the collectivity there were the differentiations, the stratification, and the bloodthirsty tensions fed by classes; and finally, on the immense scale of humanity, there were racial hatreds, slavery, exploitation, and above all the bloodless genocide which consisted in the setting aside of fifteen billion men.

So, comrades, let us not pay tribute to Europe by creating states, institutions, and societies which draw their inspiration from her.

Humanity is waiting for something other from us than such an imitation, which would be almost an obscene caricature.

If we want to turn Africa into a new Europe, and America into a new Europe, then let us leave the destiny of our countries to Europeans. They will know how to do it better than the most gifted among us.

But if we want humanity to advance a step further, if we want to bring it up to a different level than that which Europe has shown it, then we must invent and we must make discoveries.

If we wish to live up to our people's expectations, we must seek the response elsewhere than in Europe.

Moreover, if we wish to reply to the expectations of the people of Europe, it is no good sending them back a reflection, even an ideal reflection, of their society and their thought with which from time to time they feel immeasurably sickened.

For Europe, for ourselves, and for humanity, comrades, we must turn over a new leaf, we must work out new concepts, and try to set afoot a new man.

PART III

AFRICA

African political and social thought, like African nationalism, has developed only in recent years. Yet, it has already made some important contributions to the common ideological stock of modernizing nationalism. In London and in Paris and in the African capitals, African students, intellectuals, and political leaders have drawn on Western democratic thought, on Marxism, on Gandhiism, and (in the case of those studying in America) on Black Nationalism and combined them with a romanticized version of the African cultural heritage and history to produce a common Pan-African ideology shared by most African nationalist leaders—however much they may differ on its practical implementation.

The African nationalists face many of the same problems of underdevelopment as their counterparts in the Middle East, Asia, and Latin America, but there are also important differences. Since much of Africa has only recently achieved independence, no entrenched military class or feudal oligarchy impedes national development. In some areas, tribalism has broken down, either because cooperation with the colonizing power has discredited the traditional tribal leadership or because urbanization has loosened traditional loyalties. The nationalist leaders have thus been presented with a ready-made following, responsive to nationalistic and anti-colonial appeals.

Yet, the vast majority of Africans remain enmeshed in tribal and traditional structures of authority. The modernizing elite finds itself caught between the goals of democracy and development. The objective of modernization is by no means certain to win a majority.

The theory of the democratic single party—perhaps the distinctive African contribution to the ideology of modernizing nationalism—offers a way out of this dilemma. Utilizing the slogans of development and national unity, the party educates a largely illiterate population to desire the goals that the modernizing elite considers desirable, at the same time making it possible for at least minimal controls to be exercised over the leadership by party members. Although it has not been universally accepted by African leaders, the theory of the single party has received its best formulation in the writings and speeches of African nationalists such as Sékou Touré, Julius Nyerere, and Madeira Keita, and its influence is wide.

In economic thought, the attempt to find a middle way between the individualism of the West and the collectivism of the Soviet bloc has received eloquent expression in Senghor's "African Socialism." A similar conception also underlies Julius Nyerere's emphasis on the harmony of the individual and the group in African social life.

The revival of African culture under the labels of Negritude and "the African personality" has a political as well as a cultural significance in the support it gives to the ideal of African unity. Already, however, there is among the Pan-Africanists a division, derived partly from varying conceptions of the method to reach African unity, partly from differing views regarding internal development and external ties, and partly from power rivalries.

There is no disagreement on the desirability of national independence, of the liberation of the remaining colonial territories, or of a nonaligned position in international relations. Above all, modernization and development are the objectives agreed upon by all educated Africans as the goals of African national and regional policy. This process has been termed "Westernization," but African leaders specifically reject some aspects of Western life—for example, its racialism, its individualism, and, in many instances, its political forms. Yet, the categories of their thought—the nation, the party, and the concept of modernization itself—are derived from Western sources and modified to fit African political and social realities.

The relations of Africa with the other developing areas are especially important in the United Nations. Voting records indicate that there is no clearly defined Afro-Asian bloc, but consultation does go on among Africans, Asians, and Middle Easterners. At the Bandung Conference of 1955, which was the first attempt to bring together the leaders of African and Asian governments, Ghana and

Liberia were the only African nations represented. Many more—though by no means all—African nations attended the Belgrade Conference of Unaligned Nations in September, 1961. There is also a bridge to the Islamic world, through the North African countries and the United Arab Republic. The Algerians cultivated African support throughout the lengthy history of their revolt, and Nasser has harbored anticolonial African leaders in Cairo for many years. Gandhi's system of thought has exercised influence upon a number of African leaders, but Indian-African relations may be strained in the future by the position of the Indian traders in East Africa.

The rise of Africa to self-assertion and independence has brought with it new contributions to the political theory of modernizing nationalism. While there has been a recent decline in the importance of ideology in some African states, as practical problems consume the energies of the leadership, or nontheoretical military men seize power, in others ideology remains a guiding force and a principal determinant of action.

13. The Organization of African Unity (OAU)

One of the most powerful currents in African thinking has been that favoring African unity. All African leaders have endorsed the concept but there has been some disagreement on how to achieve it. Kwame Nkrumah took the lead in the early days of African independence, calling a Conference of Independent African States in April, 1958, and later in the same year forging a rather vague union with Guinea (Guinea later provided him with refuge when he was overthrown). In 1959, Senegal and the French-speaking Sudan (now the Republic of Mali) formed the Federation of Mali, which split apart a year later. In the same year the Ivory Coast and its French-speaking neighbors formed the Entente, a loose organization for economic cooperation. In December, 1960, all the French-speaking states (except Guinea and Mali) met at Brazzaville; the following year they established the African and Malagasy Union. The 1961 Conferences at Casablanca and at Monrovia seemed to make more permanent the rapidly emerging split between radicals and moderates.* Yet in May, 1963, all the African states, meeting at Addis Ababa, agreed upon a Charter of African Unity which established the Organization of African Unity (OAU). The voting power of the moderates is evident in the Charter's emphasis on noninterference and its condemnation of subversion. In addition to setting up a Mediation Commission, which has already done important work in settling disputes involving Morocco, Algeria, and Mauritania and Somalia, Ethiopia, and

* Neither Morocco, the organizer of the Casablanca Conference, nor Libya, which also participated, can properly be described as radical. The character of the meeting was determined by the other participants: Ghana, Guinea, Mali, the United Arab Republic, and the Algerian Provisional Government.

Kenya, the Addis Ababa Conference also established a Liberation Committee to supervise and coordinate Pan-African support for independence movements in the remaining colonial territories in Africa.

CHARTER OF THE ORGANIZATION OF AFRICAN UNITY*

We, the Heads of African and Malagasy States and Governments assembled in the city of Addis Ababa, Ethiopia;

Convinced that it is the inalienable right of all people to control their own destiny;

Conscious of the fact that freedom, equality, justice, and dignity are essential objectives for the achievement of the legitimate aspirations of the African peoples;

Conscious of our responsibility to harness the natural and human resources of our continent for the total advancement of our peoples in spheres of human endeavor;

Inspired by a common determination to promote understanding and collaboration among our States in response to the aspirations of our peoples for brotherhood and solidarity, in a larger unity transcending ethnic and national differences;

Convinced that, in order to translate this determination into a dynamic force in the cause of human progress, conditions for peace and security must be established and maintained;

Determined to safeguard and consolidate the hard-won independence as well as the sovereignty and territorial integrity of our States, and to resist neocolonialism in all its forms;

Dedicated to the general progress of Africa;

Persuaded that the Charter of the United Nations and the Universal Declaration of Human Rights, to the principles of which we reaffirm our adherence, provide a solid foundation for peaceful and positive cooperation among States;

Desirous that all African and Malagasy States should henceforth unite so that the welfare and well-being of their peoples can be assured;

* From OAU Provisional Secretariat, *Organization of African Unity, Basic Documents and Resolutions* (Addis Ababa, 1963).

Resolved to reinforce the links between our States by establishing and strengthening common institutions;

Have agreed to the present Charter.

ESTABLISHMENT

Article I

The High Contracting Parties do by the present Charter establish an Organization to be known as the Organization of African and Malagasy States.

PURPOSES

Article II

1. The Organization shall have the following purposes: (a) to promote the unity and solidarity of the African and Malagasy States; (b) to coordinate and intensify their collaboration and efforts to achieve a better life for the peoples of Africa; (c) to defend their sovereignty, their territorial integrity, and independence; (d) to eradicate all forms of colonialism from the continent of Africa; and (e) to promote international cooperation, having due regard to the Charter of the United Nations and the Universal Declaration of Human Rights.

2. To these ends, the Member States shall coordinate and harmonize their general policies, especially in the following fields: (a) political and diplomatic cooperation; (b) economic cooperation, including transport and communications; (c) educational and cultural cooperation; (d) health, sanitation, and nutritional cooperation; (e) scientific and technical cooperation; (f) cooperation for defense and security.

PRINCIPLES

Article III

The Member States, in pursuit of the purposes stated in Article II, solemnly affirm and declare their adherence to the following principles: (1) the sovereign equality of all African and Malagasy States; (2) noninterference in the internal affairs of States; (3) respect for the sovereignty and territorial integrity of each State and for its inalienable right to independent existence; (4) peaceful settlement of disputes by negotiation, mediation, conciliation, or arbitration; (5) unreserved condemnation, in all its forms, of political assassination as well as of subversive activities on the part of neighboring states or any other states; (6) absolute dedication to the total emancipation of the African territories which are still dependent; (7) affirmation of a policy of nonalignment with regard to all blocs.

MEMBERSHIP
Article IV

Each independent sovereign African and Malagasy State shall be entitled to become a Member of the Organization.

RIGHTS AND DUTIES OF MEMBER STATES
Article V

All Member States shall enjoy equal rights and have equal duties.

Article VI

The Member States pledge themselves to observe scrupulously the principles enumerated in Article III of the present Charter.

INSTITUTIONS
Article VII

The Organization shall accomplish its purposes through the following principal institutions: (1) the Assembly of Heads of State and Government; (2) the Council of Ministers; (3) the General Secretariat; (4) the Commission of Mediation, Conciliation, and Arbitration. . . .

COMMISSION OF MEDIATION, CONCILIATION, AND ARBITRATION
Article XIX

Member States pledge to settle all disputes among themselves by peaceful means and, to this end, agree to conclude a separate treaty establishing a Commission of Mediation, Conciliation, and Arbitration. Said treaty shall be regarded as forming an integral part of the present Charter.

SPECIALIZED COMMISSIONS

Article XX

The Assembly shall establish such Specialized Commissions as it may deem necessary, including the following: (1) Economic and Social Commission; (2) Educational and Cultural Commission; (3) Health, Sanitation, and Nutrition Commission; (4) Defense Commission; (5) Scientific, Technical, and Research Commission.

DECOLONIZATION RESOLUTION*

The summit conference of Independent African and Malagasy States meeting in Addis Ababa, Ethiopia, from 22 May to 25 May 1963; having considered all aspects of the questions of decolonization; unanimously convinced of the imperious and urgent necessity of coordinating and intensifying their efforts to accelerate the unconditional attainment of national independence by all African territories still under foreign domination; reaffirming that it is the duty of all African Independent States to support dependent people in Africa in their struggle for freedom and independence; noting with deep concern that most of the remaining dependent territories in Africa are dominated by foreign settlers; convinced that the colonial powers by their forcible imposition of the settlers to control the governments and administration of those territories are thus establishing colonial bases in the heart of Africa; have agreed unanimously to concert and coordinate their efforts and action in this field, and to this end have decided on the following measures:

Declares that the forcible imposition by the colonial powers of the settlers to control the governments and administration of the dependent territories is a flagrant violation of the inalienable rights of the legitimate inhabitants of the territories concerned;

Invites the colonial powers to take the necessary measures for the immediate application of the declaration on the granting of independence to colonial countries and peoples by insisting on

* From OAU Provisional Secretariat, *Organization of African Unity, Basic Documents and Resolutions* (Addis Ababa, 1963).

the fact that their determination to maintain colonies or semi-colonies in Africa constitutes a menace to the peace of the continent. . . .

Asks for an effective boycott of the foreign trade of Portugal and South Africa by : (a) prohibiting the import of goods from those two countries, (b) closing African ports and airports to their ships and planes, and (c) forbidding the planes of those two countries to overfly the territories of all African States;

Earnestly invites all national liberation movements to coordinate their efforts by establishing common action fronts wherever necessary so as to strengthen the effectiveness of their struggle and the rational use of the concerted assistance given them;

Establishes a coordinating committee consisting of Ethiopia, Algeria, Uganda, U.A.R., Tanganyika, Congo (Léopoldville), Guinea, Senegal, and Nigeria with headquarters in Dar-es-Salaam responsible for harmonizing assistance from African States and for managing the special fund to be set up for that purpose;

Establishes a special fund to be contributed by Member States to supply the necessary practical and financial aid to the various African national liberation movements. . . .

Receives, on the territories of Independent African States nationalists from liberation movements in order to give them training in all sectors, and afford young people all the assistance they need for their education and vocational training;

Promotes, in each state, the establishment of a body of volunteers in various fields, with a view to providing the various African national liberation movements with the assistance they need. . . .

14. The African and Malagasy Common Organization (OCAM)

At the 1963 meeting in Addis Ababa, it was understood that the various political groups already in existence would be dissolved or would fuse with the OAU. The French-speaking moderates, however, were reluctant to abandon the organization they had set up among themselves—the African and Malagasy Union. In 1964, they replaced it with an organization for economic cooperation (UAMCE). A recurrence of difficulties over the Congo exacerbated the differences between the moderates and radicals within the OAU, and in February, 1965, a new organization—the African and Malagasy Common Organization (OCAM)—was formed. Although the OCAM acts within the framework of the OAU, it has taken political action on its own—notably the recognition of the Tshombe government in the Congo (an action particularly abhorrent to the radicals) and an attack on Ghana for harboring and encouraging subversives working for the overthrow of neighboring states. The formation of OCAM marked a re-emergence of the earlier division between those who favored a Pan-African movement largely confined to technical and functional cooperation (the former Monrovia group) and those who saw it as an instrument for the encouragement and ultimate union of "progressive" forces throughout the continent (the former Casablanca group).

STATEMENT OF THE FIRST OCAM CONFERENCE*

The conference of chiefs of state convened by His Excellency Mokhtar Ould Daddah, President of the Islamic Republic of Mauritania, was held in Nouakchott from February 10 to 12, 1965. Its purpose was to examine the condition of the organization formed by the fourteen states involved in the light of the African and international situations, as had been done previously at the Cotonou and Dakar conferences.

The conference discussions took place in an atmosphere of complete frankness and cordiality. The participants were able, after careful examination of the African and international situation, to arrive at positive conclusions which will give a new impetus to their organization. The new organization, the OCAM (Organisation Commune Africaine et Malgache [African and Malagasy Common Organization]), is a regrouping of African states within the framework of the OAU. Its objective is to strengthen cooperation and solidarity among the African and Malagasy states in order to speed up their political, economic, social, technical, and cultural development. The new organization, with headquarters in Yaoundé, will concentrate its activities under the authority of one administrative secretary general. The conference took note of the decision of the states of the Entente to establish "multinationality."

With regard to the African situation:

Considering that the malaise from which the OAU is suffering derives essentially from the lack of respect given to its Charter;

Considering that respect for the sovereignty of the states and noninterference in their internal affairs constitute the sine qua non conditions for peace and development in Africa;

Considering that the situation in Congo-Léopoldville and the intensification of the Cold War between the two blocs in Africa constitute a permanent threat to the existence of the OAU and the independence of the African countries;

Considering that covetous designs from abroad are increasing in Africa,

* Translated in *Africa Report*, X, No. 3 (March, 1965), 10.

The chiefs of state of the Organization recommend prudence and vigilance to all.

They solemnly affirm the urgent necessity of bringing peace back to Congo-Léopoldville through aid to the legal government to hasten national reconciliation in order and liberty, in accordance with the resolutions of the Addis Ababa conference and the [United Nations] Security Council. They advocate at the same time the reconciliation of Congo-Léopoldville with its neighbors. They energetically condemn the action of certain states, notably Ghana, which harbor agents of subversion and organize training camps on their national territory.

They have decided, in consequence, to inform the OAU [of the problem] and make an appeal to the African feeling of all the chiefs of state of the continent in order that a climate of cooperation among equals can be substituted as soon as possible for the present climate of mistrust and false leadership through intervention in the internal affairs of the other states. . . .

15. Sékou Touré

Sékou Touré was born in 1922 in Kan-Kan, Guinea, of peasant parents. He received a primary education, but was expelled from a trade school for leading a food strike at the age of fifteen. He then secured a civil-service job and became active in Guinean trade unionism, becoming leader of the Guinean branch of the Confédération Générale du Travail (CGT), the Communist-influenced French trade-union federation. Touré organized the Parti Démocratique de Guinée (PDG), as the Guinean branch of the Rassemblement Démocratique Africain; his party lost the apparently rigged elections of 1954, but won complete control of the Guinea Assembly in 1957. He then broke ties with the CGT and formed an African trade-union federation. Using the French grant of internal autonomy to consolidate his political control and break the power of tribal chieftains, he was able to secure a 95 per cent en-

*dorsement of his position for immediate independence in the refer-
endum of September, 1958—at a time when all other French-speaking African territories were voting by equally lopsided margins for
continued association with France. Since 1958, Sékou Touré has
pursued a policy that is regarded as one of the furthest left of any
of the African states, in both internal and international politics.
Those who had considered Guinea a member of the Soviet bloc
were surprised, however, when Touré expelled the Soviet Ambassador in December, 1961.*

*The selection below is taken from his speech to the congress of
the Parti Démocratique de Guinée, delivered on September 14,
1959, a year after independence. It explains how the PDG operates
as the single party in Guinea, and defends Touré's version of
"democratic centralism."*

AFRICAN EMANCIPATION*

The Contradictions of Colonialism

If the problem of the individual is a central concern in other continents—in countries that are free and independent—the first and
the only true problem for the colonial peoples is that of the attainment of independence. It is consequently a collective problem, a
political reality engendered by nationalist sentiments.

But if our party has been more successful than the other fraternal parties of Senegal, of the (French) Sudan, of Niger, etc.,
in guiding our country to its independence, it is because it has
found itself in favorable objective conditions. Political struggle involves laws, power relationships, a given level of maturity,
problems of unity, etc.—a number of objective conditions which,
combined, produce the rise of the dependent countries and govern
the rhythm of their political development.

The expansion of our political movement was achieved because

*Excerpts from *La Lutte du Parti Démocratique de Guinée pour l'Emanci-
pation Africaine* (Conakry: Imprimerie Nationale, 1959); translated by the
editor.

of the many contradictions between the interests of the people and the interests of the colonial regime. The principal contradiction was between the African interest and the interests of French imperialism, which had repercussions in all areas of social life. In addition to the moral domain (that of the dignity of our people) and the juridical domain, by which the illegitimate occupation of our country established by the colonial power was firmly entrenched, there were practices on the economic level and on the level of public activity, on the military level, and on the social level which constantly revealed these conflicts of interest. It was on the basis of these oppositions and in terms of these dichotomies that the struggle was organized and conducted, against both the colonial regime and those who by their actions, consciously or unconsciously, favored the programs of that regime.

Internal contradictions also existed. In the first place, the peasants—who constitute 80 per cent of the population of Guinea —turned against feudalism, which, perverted by the colonial regime, had ceased to be the true expression of the thought of our national social units. Created, supported, and used by the colonial regime, this feudalism, in opposition to the interests of the people, was better known under the name of "cantonal chiefdom." The chiefs lived on the exploitation of the peasant masses, and they justified the colonialist practices with which their own interests were intimately linked. There were still other internal contradictions, which were less apparent, but which had to be eliminated rapidly in order to reinforce the unity of the people. There was, notably, the nascent opposition between what we can call the intellectual elite on the one side and the peasant masses on the other. The education that was given to us was designed to assimilate us, to depersonalize us, to Westernize us—to present our civilization, our culture, our own sociological and philosophical conceptions, even our humanism as the expression of a savage and almost unconscious primitivism—in order to create a number of complexes in us which would drive us to become more French than the French themselves. In addition to this, there were the advantages and security of the material surroundings of the intellectual elite, which were absolutely foreign to the life of the immense majority of the people and constituted a privileged situation in comparison with general conditions. The satisfaction of the requirements of one group appeared immediately as a new obligation, a new burden on the others, who constituted not only the majority of the population, but also the most disinherited strata.

Contradictions existed in the economic domain, as they exist elsewhere in all colonial and imperialist regimes. Appropriate structures were used to facilitate the exploitation by the colonialists of the two aspects of the market: import and export. The shameful system of trading functioned through practices that none could deny because they were too simple and too apparent. There was speculation, with produce handled at three stages: purchase, storage, and resale to the producer in time of need. The difference between the cost of imported merchandise and the price to the consumer was exorbitant.

The feudal regime (despite the fact that the land is the first and natural property of the people) annexed the land and, under the name "national property," made it the property of the French state. The military regime contained the same contradictions because the African soldier had neither the material nor the moral advantages of his French colleague—just as the African veteran was treated in an inferior fashion in relation to his French counterpart. Finally, the administrative structure could be summed up by this simple formula: The French administration, the sole origin of all decisions involving the destiny of the country, was in fact the guarantor and manager of the interests of the colonialists. . . .

In its military organization, as in its administrative, economic, and political structure, assimilationist colonialism decreed laws that were to be applied unilaterally throughout the whole empire, without taking account of the particular characteristics of each part, or of its economic and social conditions or political evolution. This unification policy, the corollary of the aim of assimilation, created a feeling of equality in misery, and was bound to result in the emergence of an identity of interests of all those under colonial rule—whether in the north, south, or west of Africa. Thus the military and administrative organizations, with their broader and more general structures involving the whole of the former French empire, created new institutions favoring the unity of action of those under colonial rule against a common oppressor. . . .

Our party is a committed party which does not look for the golden mean between truth and falsehood. It is aware of the backwardness of the African peoples and does not want to lose time in useless evasions. From the moment that it has decided on a goal, it wants to attain that goal with the support and action of the people. Hence the anticolonial struggle did not end on the 28th

of September;* it has only started again with more power as a
double struggle against the consequences of the colonial regime
(by the adaptation of methods, structures, spirit and population to
the new requirements of a free national life) and against the
colonial domination that still weighs upon a good part of Africa.

We are aware that as long as all Africa is not free, Guinea will
feel threatened. Consider the man who has injured a finger. The
finger alone does not feel pain; if there is pain, it is the whole body
of the man that feels it. Guinea feels the pain of the colonized
people of Africa. In order to attempt to eliminate the pain of
soul and body of the inhabitants of Africa, whose welfare constitutes the object and the reason for our combat, we must first examine the state of the instruments—the Democratic Party of
Guinea, and its institutions, the people and their political, social,
economic, and cultural practices—that serve to lead us to victory
in the combat.

Principles of the PDG and Their Application

The Democratic Party of Guinea is a national movement grouping together (without distinction of race or sex) all those of good
will who are determined to work against colonialism and for the
building up of a solid democratic state in Guinea. There should
be no astonishment that in Guinea there is only one single national
party, the PDG. I want to emphasize that political unity is not an
end. It is only a means to develop a progressive movement that
serves the general interest. This unity can be maintained and developed to serve the national interest only if it involves unity of
action on the part of the whole population, mobilized for positive
ends and constantly confirming the democratic character of the
development of our country. We can also say that the life of a
society, of a social unit, or of a nation is not essentially governed
by laws, decrees, or regulations. The life of a society is governed
by habits, customs, historic traditions, and the necessity for its
maintenance and development. Thus, the value of a government
is determined by the balanced development it assures on the
national level. The various changes in living conditions that result

* September 28, 1958 was the date of the referendum on the Constitution
of the Fifth Republic of France. By voting "no" on the constitution and
thus refusing to join the new French Community, Guinea became the first
of the French colonies in sub-Sahara Africa to achieve independence.—ED.

from our progress clash with the conservative forces of the present
and the reactionary forces of the past, the former representing
vested interests and privileges and the latter the interests and
privileges that have been lost. These forces are not working for
the general interest because their demands only involve particular
and special cases which are, by their nature, opposed to social
justice and the national interest.

The most progressive and revolutionary law will remain without
application if it is not understood by the people and if the attitudes
and habits of the people are contrary to that law. Similarly, if the
principles of the party are not well understood by the party membership, and especially by all the leaders, the party will only list
its principles at its congresses without ever translating them into
reality in the living conditions of the nation. We must constantly
recall that the Democratic Party of Guinea is a popular movement,
uniting the entire mass of the population who wish to work together for the realization of its program in the general interest.
The party should not change its political line if this line remains
in conformity with the national interest. The essential principle
that we should never forget is that the Democratic Party of Guinea
is different from the ethnic movements we formerly knew in
Guinea. Our party operates scientifically—by analyzing concrete
situations to determine the objectives and forms of its action.

We constantly reiterate that the PDG is a party of men who
place their intelligence at the service of the masses. When we say
they are "intellectuals," it is in the true sense of the word. It is not
a question of those who know how to read and write, but of those
who determine their action on the basis of reason, starting out with
concrete study; of those who, guided by intelligence, can know
at any moment what has already been accomplished and what has
not yet been carried out; of those who can appreciate the real
value of the action of our party, so as to make it more efficient;
in short, of those men and women who look for the truth—starting
out with historic and present facts, determining their action by
the objectives that have been assigned to them. This intelligence
is found among peasants, workers, civil servants, laborers, women,
and children.

In the world today, there are three types of organizations and
movements. There is the party that speaks of the past and lives
on the basis of the past. The members of this party continually

say, "We have done such and such a thing in 1900, we have done such and such in 1910"; they are not capable of saying, "This is what we have done today, and this is what we should do tomorrow." The second category lives only in the present, and its workers are concerned exclusively with day-to-day problems and make no effort to analyze these problems or carry out the changes that would resolve them in the future. The Democratic Party of Guinea belongs neither to the first nor to the second category. Not forgetting what has taken place in the past, and keeping in mind what is taking place today, it is also concerned with what should take place tomorrow. Indeed, it is insofar as one is concerned with what will take place tomorrow that one can take the appropriate measures to make the future of the country more happy and prosperous. Party workers who only think of what is taking place today are those who are often surprised, have no general view, and are very quickly discouraged, for, at the least unhappy and unexpected event, they are disoriented and suffer panic, thus distorting the real significance of the party. When something happens that they cannot work out, they are immediately discouraged and lose all desire to continue their activity. It is the opposite with the worker who thinks of the program of the future while keeping in mind the present. Mistakes—far from discouraging him or limiting his action—are sources of profit, because once he has discovered them, thanks to criticism and self-criticism, he can henceforth avoid them in carrying out his future actions.

Indeed, it is when we discover a mistake committed by the whole party or by a worker or leader, that we seek to know its nature, its causes, and its consequences. There is no action without mistakes. Only a party that carries on no activity can avoid mistakes. Just as one cannot develop knowledge without study and apprenticeship, one cannot learn anything without the possibility of mistakes. That is why the party should stimulate action every day on the part of its workers. The officeholders and party workers ought to know that action feeds the intelligence and gives practical effect to the thinking of the party. We have often said that practice is superior to thought and theory. Suppose that the members of the party establish a program which everyone approves. Even when there is agreement on the program, it is action that will determine what part of the program is possible for the country and in the interest of the party, and what should be corrected, modified, or abandoned. The superiority of practice over theory is attainable only in action and results. Hence, the party should be organized at all levels—in the local districts, in the villages, in the administrative divisions, and at a national level—a perfect organization of militant activity, so that each one can contribute effectively to the realization of the party program.

When we say that the party works for democracy and the unity of the country, and against colonialism, this is only the general framework and spirit in which all daily actions should be taken, and a statement of future activities. On the level of local and village committees, as well as those of the sections and districts, there should be general assemblies and conferences to study and establish a concrete program, to work for the permanent mobilization of the energies of the PDG. Without a concrete and definite program according to the respective possibilities of the different branches of the party, action can be carried out in the abstract and come to an end before any positive result is attained. . . .

The workers ought to give an account of what they have done and an evaluation of the progress that has been realized every day. Action is necessary, but it is only possible within the framework of a program, and how is this program established? It is not the Political Bureau that establishes it. The Political Bureau only prepares a project, and the General Assembly discusses and determines it. Thus each one can understand its value and its implications.

It is necessary also to popularize the program among the masses, but it is not just a question of discussion of the program or of adopting it and understanding it. It is also a matter of distributing assignments; and the party must exercise some check over the carrying out of the tasks undertaken by each one.

For example, a delegation of the Political Bureau recently went into the regions of the interior. Its accounting, observation, and notes were discussed, after which a statement was made and circulars were sent out to the various sections, which drew lessons from this visit and determined new directives for action. The party should let no phenomenon or action take place without an appropriate analysis for the purpose of drawing from it a positive conclusion and determining the political line of its further activities. One can say that confidence does not exclude the review of action. When you benefit from the unlimited confidence of the masses, you have to act in such a way that the masses are aware that they have made a good decision, that they were not mistaken in granting you their confidence. . . .

In following the principles of the party, the officers of a local committee ought to have a meeting every evening and bring together all their information, review the execution of assignments, establish a program, distribute new assignments to be fulfilled, and, finally, organize a general assembly. At the assembly, everyone who is absent should be noted. If review is made in a rigorous manner, methodically and democratically, only real workers will continue in the party, for the bad elements will be eliminated of themselves.

When you cease to have criticism and self-criticism in the party, the party will die little by little. Everyone, as a matter of principle, must serve the party, and no one must serve himself. If there is no criticism and self-criticism, one cannot determine what is good and what is evil; one cannot locate mistakes that have been committed or evaluate the consequences; one cannot act against the enemies of the party, who are making use of it to operate against its objectives. . . .

Political Supremacy and Democratic Dictatorship

For the argument from force which the old colonialist state used, our new democratic state intends to substitute another basis of authority and draw its strength from arguments and from its guiding principles. Thus, the supremacy of political action is the consequence, the reality, of the political democracy that we have chosen for ourselves and have wished to be as real as possible and as vivid as the popular desire for a general revival in our country.

Democracy has different natures indeed and is interpreted in different ways, according to whether it is inspired by one or another form of thought, objective, or social force. We do not have to carry our analysis very far to become aware of the different social conceptions that utilize the name "democracy." Christianity acts politically under the name "Christian democracy," the bourgeoisie operate under the name "bourgeois democracy," and some social sectors talk about a "social democracy." Thus, if democracy represents a conception of the organization of society and peoples, its real content can be perverted or interpreted in different fashions.

As for ourselves, we are in favor of a democracy as real and as complete as possible and based solely on the interests of the people. This is the only form of democracy we recognize, the only interpretation we give to the word "democracy." . . .

Whether we are concerned with the democratic or nondemocratic state, both are governed by a man or a group of men who exercise power over the whole population. Both are dictatorships. Dictatorship is the concentration of powers exercised by a man or group of men over the whole. We can say, following that definition, that the driver of a vehicle imposes a dictatorship on the passengers of the vehicle. In a trade union, in a youth organization, in a women's organization, in an athletic team, there is this type of dictatorship. We can say, therefore, that states are democratic or nondemocratic—but whatever their nature, their direction toward specific objectives set out in advance necessarily implies a dictatorship.

To define the nature of this dictatorship, which is exercised differently in democratic states and nondemocratic states, we must consider the objective conditions surrounding the exercise of dictatorship to determine whether a state is democratic. . . . If the dictatorship exercised by the governmental apparatus emanates directly from the whole of the people, this dictatorship is popular in nature and the state is a democratic state—democracy being the exercise of national sovereignty by the people. It is power exercised of the people, by the people, and for the people.

A democratic state comes from the will of the people. Its program is therefore necessarily in conformance with the interests of the people. Likewise, its force, its authority, the powers it exercises, the discipline it imposes—in short, the dictatorship it exercises—arise exclusively from the interests, the requirements, and the principles of popular sovereignty. For every human society, democracy always corresponds in its form to given conditions and requirements, which are the result of the economic and social level at which the society has arrived. Hence, democracy can be more or less developed, more or less advanced. Democratic dictatorship—that is, the concentration of powers of the sovereignty of the people at the level of the people—can be more or less great and more or less developed. Thus, a state whose program of work and whose political power are determined, not in the interests of one level or part of the population, but exclusively in the interests of the whole people is a democratic state.

This means that on the level of the governing apparatus, there is an obligation to assure direct and free representation of the whole population, without discrimination of any sort. In a democratic state, the sovereign power is exercised directly by representatives whom the people have chosen freely.

But if the dictatorship is exercised by a king, a part of the population, a coalition of interests, or a feudal economic power, and if there is an interest other than the general interest operating in the exercise of the sovereignty, the dictatorship ceases to be exercised in the interests of the people. Economic dictatorship, financial dictatorship, personal dictatorship, military dictatorship are nothing else than the exercise of national sovereignty for the economic, financial, and personal benefit of one caste or social class. The state ceases to be democratic when the dictatorship it exercises arises solely out of the interests of the king, a social class, or any other group that does not represent the whole population. . . .

In a democratic state, sovereignty is the property of the nation as a whole. The responsibilities involved in running the state are, by the nature of its structure, shared collectively. Thus, all intelligence, all values, and all energies are mobilized for the benefit of the whole, so as to assure the best possible ways of achieving progress, creating the best conditions for the development of the country, and bringing about the maximum guarantee of the expansion of the society and the security of each of its members. . . .

On the other hand, there are states that are democratic in form, ruled by ministers, parliamentarians, and responsible people in power, elected according to sometimes quite complicated procedures; but the dictatorship practiced by these states is not democratic in fact, since it is exercised by one feudal group or coalition of private interests, or even by a clan or social caste. This is a dictatorship one can call ethnic or factional.

A first requirement for democracy is liberty. If men are to be considered as equals and are to participate with equal concern and involvement in the life of the nation, they must first be free. Without effective liberty, there is no possibility for men or societies to determine themselves freely. . . .

The Exercise of Democracy

We can say that our state is democratic, unitary, and progressive. We want Guinea to be a viable national entity. In three or four years, no one will think any longer of the tribal, ethnic, and religious rivalries that have in the past caused so much evil for our country and population. A considerable decentralization of administration and policy has been permitted on the level of electoral districts, and the district council has all authority to decide what needs to be done. But there is also a perfect concentration of powers in the national institutions: the assembly and the government. Our constitution has authorized this concentration of powers by stipulating that the chief of the state is also the chief of the army—as he is the one who names the ministers and can at any point remove them. Obviously, if we did not understand that behind the state there is a higher entity, the party, we could not comprehend the political value of the provisions of the Guinean constitution. That is why the party assumes a directing role in the life of the nation and exercises all the powers of the nation. Political, judiciary, administrative, economic, and technical powers are in the hands of the Democratic Party of Guinea. It is the party that designates the chief of state, by direct universal suffrage. The deputies to the National Assembly are elected for five years, directly by the population, under the same conditions as the chief of the state. Every seven years . . . popular elections take place for the selection of the President of the republic. . . .

There are contradictions in all societies. We refuse to regard them passively, for we want to direct our evolution in a harmonious and just fashion. But to govern is to choose, and to choose is to use authority for the realization of previously determined objectives. To govern is to apply a dictatorship. When an aroused people has chosen its future, it must follow the line that leads it efficiently and rapidly to that future. But to impose a discipline in the framework of principles set up in advance is to agree to subordinate oneself to the authority of principles and to accept the dictatorship that flows from them. Our fundamental principles are simple. We recognize as valuable only what serves the cause of the people and develops the history of the nation. This is the discipline to which we submit ourselves freely, and this orientation constitutes the principal task of a forward-looking party and a democratic state. This is the nature of the dictatorship. It can have a different content if it is applied by one man who considers himself superior to all others, or if it is the people themselves who have conceived its program of development and chosen the methods by which it will accomplish its daily tasks. Depending on how it is applied, dictatorship can be antidemocratic or democratic. As for ourselves, we say that in giving supremacy to the people and making them participate directly in all important decisions involving the nation, we want a popular democratic dictatorship.

For our decision to be more than a theoretical one—for it to be applied in every aspect of the life of every citizen and every branch of the state—we must immediately struggle against ourselves, against whatever in us is in contradiction to the decision we have taken. Thus, more than ever, there is a task of education on all levels and stages of thought, conception, and action. That is why, in the political field, the party has decided that our state, as a democratic state, will be at the same time a unitary and communitarian state.

Many nations in the world have 100–200 million inhabitants and are centuries ahead of us, disposing of enormous riches, which we do not have, and utilizing modern methods, which we lack today. We are just beginning, and our first chance to raise ourselves to the level of modern states in the world consists in our unity. Our desire for progress will be fruitless if individual wills are not identical and do not aim at attaining the same objectives, for internal contradiction will become more and more violent and hold us back, endangering our very independence. That is why we have said that at all levels the party must be extremely vigilant, intransigent, and severe, in order to force the unitary and dynamic character of its policy into the awareness and action of every citizen. . . .

The Unification of the Youth of Guinea

The constant concern of the Democratic Party of Guinea has been to . . . place all the institutions of the country at the service of the population. Thanks to its integral and solid structure, it has brought all organizations under its control. . . . It was the only party to choose independence in the name of the people of Guinea and of all of colonial Africa, by rejecting the French Community in a massive and historic vote.

Youth will play a primary role in the immense task of construction that we have begun since our accession to full sovereignty. It is important for each worker of the party, and particularly for the youth, that the specific problems of young people be approached with a clear conception of the general objectives of the nation. More than ever, the actions of young people must necessarily reflect the essential concerns of the country. We are guided by the central principle that the party has always considered of great importance—the absolute necessity of carrying out the program of youth on a national level, in the framework of the general program of the party. Youth ought to have an active part in the nation, be aware of its responsibilities, and be ready to play the dynamic role we assign to it.

The unification of youth movements was a response to the necessity of putting an end to the dispersion of energies that paralyzed the youth and prevented it from playing a worthy role as a front-ranking part of the Guinean people in the struggle for the emancipation of Africa. When the officers of the PDG, at the Congress of the JRDA* in March, 1959, emphasized the weakness of youth organizations in the fields of sport and art, they were right in thinking that it was urgent to abolish the individualism and mediocrity inherited from the colonial system and to place sport and art on the level of the most noble institutions of our nation. Henceforth, the spirit of competition should be developed among young people on the basis of an aroused sentiment of national pride. The PDG has therefore acted perfectly well in unifying the youth movements and in concretely realizing, within the JRDA, the unity of action of all the young people of the country. . . .

The Principles of Democratic Centralism

Democratic centralism consists of the following principles:

1. All the leaders of the party are directly elected, democratically, by the party workers, who have complete freedom of conscience and expression within the party.

2. The concerns of the state of Guinea are the concerns of all the citizens of Guinea. The program of the party is discussed democratically. As long as a decision has not been taken, each one is free to say what he thinks or wishes. But when—after a long discussion in the Congress or Assembly—the decisions have been taken by a unanimous vote or by a majority, the workers and the leaders are required to apply them faithfully.

3. There is no sharing of the responsibility of the leaders— only of the responsibility for a decision. Thus, discipline will not be undermined.

Democracy and the freedom of all party workers are expressed

* Jeunesse du Rassemblement Démocratique Africain, the youth section of the PDG.—ED.

in the framing of problems, in their discussion, and in the choice of solutions for them. On the other hand, the leadership of the party has complete liberty in the execution of assigned responsibilities and in the evaluation of the forms of action appropriate for the objective conditions of their execution. Thus, at certain points, the leadership of the PDG has said to the masses: "Do not create any incidents. Even in the case of flagrant provocation, do not respond." Then, at other moments, when the power relationships and the development of the struggle required a strong attitude, the same leaders invited the militant masses to respond with force to the blows of the adversaries. Each movement of retreat or offense was linked to the political context of the moment. In other words, once the decisions had been democratically arrived at, it was up to the leadership to study the situation, the conditions, and the means, and to adopt the tactic to be employed to carry out effectively and efficiently the tasks assigned to the party. The choice of tactics to be employed was up to the leadership of the party. This required that the authority of the leadership be complete. If the leaders of the party abdicated their authority, if they were neither heard nor respected, what would the authority of the party be? If the party were without authority, what would be the character of the authority of the government or of the state of Guinea? Without the authority of the party, where would the government derive its own authority? The country would soon fall into disorder and anarchy, and rapidly lose its independence. As far as authority is concerned, there is no isolated problem. Everything holds together and makes one body. In the subdivisions of the party, if the leaders are without authority, there is no reason to be surprised if inefficient and mediocre administration results. There is no reason to be surprised if taxes are collected with difficulty, if human investment* is not fully carried out, and if discord arises. All that is normal. When supremacy is given to the party, nothing can go well in the places where the party is insufficient or lacks authority. The party ought to be continually mobilized if it wants the country to develop rapidly at an extraordinary rate of social, economic, and cultural progress.

---

* *Investissement Humain* is the title of the program organized by the PDG in Guinea in which the inhabitants of villages, towns, and other social units donate their free time to collective-work projects organized by the party.—ED.

In order to maintain this indispensable supremacy of the party, we have decided that the general secretaries of the local committees of Conakry are henceforth the official representatives of the mayor. No public act can take place in the future without the authorization of the party. In the local subdivisions (*quartiers*), the general secretary is the representative of the mayor. He represents him at the administrative and political level, at the level of authority and of public order. . . .

Conclusion

The foreign policy of our state is based on positive neutralism with regard to the antagonistic blocs that at present dominate the world with their influence. This is in order to safeguard the chance of the Republic of Guinea to lead the struggle for African independence to success. Indeed, Africa cannot accept the organic extension of any political or ideological system that does not respect its personality, its civilization, and its proper structure. And, as we have said recently at the Indian Congress of Transvaal, "Africa, land of the oppressed, cannot become, against its ardent will for liberation, a place for oppression." In its struggle for reconquest, there is no demand other than that its people have the right to life and to possession of their land, their sun, their sky, and to free utilization and free disposal of their goods. If Africa is a place of asylum for all those who have a sacred respect for man and wish to develop human society, it cannot allow brute force, exaction, and discrimination to be the laws governing the relations of men, people, and races. Against the old divisive practices utilized by the colonial dominators, against the continual diversionary maneuvers that attempt to reduce all coordinated action by arousing internal oppositions among the exploited and oppressed masses, we will respond with firmer cohesion and a renewed determination to assure the triumph of justice, dignity, and liberty.

16. Madeira Keita

Madeira Keita was born in 1917. Although a native of Mali (formerly the French Sudan), he was active in the politics of Guinea before it acquired independence in 1958. A founder of the Democratic Party of Guinea, he collaborated closely with Sékou Touré. More recently, he has been engaged in the building up of the local organizations of the Union Soudanaise, the governing party in Mali. In April, 1959, he became Interior Minister of Mali. He is now Minister of Justice. In Mali politics, he is considered somewhat to the left of President Modibo Keita in political orientation. The selection below, from a speech Madeira Keita gave in Paris at a meeting organized by the journal Présence Africaine in early 1960, is the classic defense of the single party. (It concludes with brief comments by others present at the meeting.)

THE SINGLE PARTY IN AFRICA*

Before 1945, there was a colonial regime with government by decree, the regime of the *indigénat*. The *indigénat* form of government permitted the colonial administration to put Africans in prison without any trial. Sometimes you were put in prison for two weeks because you did not greet the administrator or the commander. You were happy enough if they did not throw stones at you or send you to a work camp, because there was also forced labor at that time. In 1947, I met French journalists who were very surprised to learn that forced labor was nonvoluntary and not

* Excerpts from Madeira Keita, "Le Parti Unique en Afrique," *Présence Africaine*, No. 30 (February–March, 1960); translated by the editor, by permission.

paid for. Transportation was not even covered; nor were food and lodging. The only thing that was covered was work.

Then Africa began political life. When I say Africa, I mean Negro Africa, West Africa, French-speaking Africa. In 1945, we were asked to participate in political life. Naturally, Senegal was an exception. We should not lose sight of the fact that in Senegal, Africans have been rather directly involved in the public life of France since the French Revolution. . . . They were French citizens, and could elect a municipal council and send one representative to the French National Assembly. But the others, the great mass of Senegalese (since the electors constituted a minority), began political life with the elections in 1945. And this was going to create difficulties which African political leaders and political parties would have to take time to remove, because we began political life with elections and we did not have much experience in the first elections of September, 1945. In the second elections, in November, 1945, we were not aware for the most part of the intervention of the administrative apparatus of France, which gave administrative support to its candidates.

Little by little, with increasing awareness, we saw more clearly what the situation was, and we perceived the contradictions between the declarations on the subject of liberty and democracy and the reality. . . .

I saw French colonialists (to the extent that colonialism can be honest) who were revolted by the elections, which they said were a caricature of democracy. Honesty and electoral freedom were not respected; methods that degraded the parliamentary regime and would hurt Africa were used. I do not think it necessary to speak longer on what has been called *élections à l'Algérienne*.

If I speak on this subject, it is in order to underline the fact that, from the beginning, Africans were rather disturbed to perceive the contradictions that existed between theoretical definitions and realities in Africa. Now we have progressed rather far. England, in the meantime, has granted independence in a peaceful way. The Gold Coast has taken the glorious name of the old empire of Ghana. Tunisia and Morocco have acquired their independence. All of this has stimulated the desire of the African peoples under colonial rule to achieve full sovereignty.

Thus, in 1956—because the English were planning to grant independence to Nigeria (after having done so in Ghana), and because the Soviet Union, with its political and social regime, had become a factor in the political consciousness of peoples who aspired to liberty and wanted to free themselves from the bonds of slavery—France, some of whose political leaders had accused England and the Soviet Union of sabotaging the French empire and wishing to liquidate it, created the *loi-cadre*.* Many of our African comrades and militants thought that it was an error to accept the *loi-cadre*. . . . Personally, I think that although it included erroneous conceptions—especially as far as the "Balkanization" and division of French West Africa were concerned—the *loi-cadre* also had positive aspects.

The most stable governments (and I am not now talking about the most efficient governments) were those constituted by a single party that had a very large majority. This was the situation in the Ivory Coast, in Senegal, and in the Sudan.† (I am mentioning these particular territories because they stand for different political doctrines.) The governments created under the *loi-cadre* had very little in the way of disturbances or crises. However, in countries such as Upper Volta, which had the good fortune to have a remarkable man at its head—the late President Ouezzin Coulibaly—the government underwent an extremely long and difficult ministerial crisis, and only three parties made up a coalition government. In Dahomey, likewise, we had a coalition government. In Chad, as well as in Ubangui-Chari,‡ with the late President Boganda, there was government by a single party, the government of the MSA (*Mouvement Socialiste Africain*). These governments under the *loi-cadre* were a valuable education for Africans. We became aware that in the present historical conditions of Africa, it was not impossible, but extremely difficult, to take over successfully the responsibility of carrying on public affairs under coalition governments. We left the colonial system and took a part of our affairs into our own hands, and we likewise left what one might call the evil period of electoralism.

I want to emphasize that the elections had the effect of dividing Africans and of weakening the consciousness of the masses, since, in the absence of organized parties, the leaders—who wanted votes and wished to sit in councils and territorial assemblies and in the French Parliament—were obliged to play on regionalism

* The *loi-cadre* was a French law permitting considerable internal autonomy to African territorial governments.—ED.

† Now the Republic of Mali.—ED.

‡ Now the Central African Republic.—ED.

and on what we have called internal racism. It was useful to set regions and ethnic groups in opposition to each other in the same electoral areas, and for a time we were obliged to act this way.

In the beginning, the French administration supported a certain number of politicians, who did not, however, always follow the directions given by that administration or by the interest groups which the French administration was trying to defend. These politicians were sometimes confused and tried more and more to involve Africa in purely electoral stands that were caricatures of democracy, for what was important for them was to have a majority for their party and to get positions they considered honorific or lucrative. Thus I must say that we had very great difficulties to surmount, both within and among the parties.

Now all African countries have finally taken the road toward independence. This situation creates a certain number of problems to be resolved by African political leaders. We are the so-called underdeveloped countries. We are aware of our economic backwardness. We are aware of our cultural backwardness. Nevertheless, we want to move very quickly. In general, our European friends and our French friends do not always understand the African position. Perhaps this is because they do not know Africa well. This may be the situation because the French, proud of their own country and their own culture, want to suggest their own institutions as a model. Thus, when we speak of democracy and liberty, I have the impression, sometimes, that we are not in complete agreement with our friends the French. For us, the essential thing is to mobilize all the forces of the country to advance, and we do not think that liberty is threatened in Africa. We think that we are acting with complete respect for democratic rules.

Does democracy necessarily imply several parties? We say no. We think that there are democratic forms without political parties. We think also that if a political party is the political expression of a class, the class itself representing economic interests, that, though we cannot assert that the society of Negro Africa is a classless society, we can say that the differentiation of classes in Africa does not arise from a diversification of [economic] interests and especially not from an opposition of interests.

In 1946, the dominant and most relevant concern was the union of all social levels against colonialism and for an increase in liberty, without religious or social distinction. With a few exceptions, the African leaders—if one classified them by the criteria of the French—would have been in the category of the petty bourgeoisie. And it is very interesting to note that these leaders are neither bankers nor industrialists—that M. Senghor, M. Modibo Keita, and M. Sékou Touré, if they have bank accounts, have them only for their salaries, that very few have shares in corporations, and that if they do, it is merely a reflection of their [governmental] responsibilities, a device to create confidence in one corporation or another. Such shares represent insurance for these corporations. The rare cases that I know involve the mixed companies, those established by private capital and the public authority. There is a very definite tendency on the part of large companies—a little frightened by the rapid evolution of the countries of Africa and wishing to invest—to prefer the mixed form, since the government and the nationals of the country can take out shares, and this, they think, constitutes a solid guarantee and an assured climate.

As to the religious problem, this does not constitute a major reason for division among Africans. In particular, the Africans are avoiding the involvement of religion in politics. On this subject, we should be very clear since, in general, when we take positions that are considered advanced, people speak of Communism. These last weeks, we have seen a great prelate of the Roman Catholic Church coldly compare Islam and Communism. On the level of African politics, no religious problems exist. Moslems in Mali, some 70 per cent of the population, live in peace, and the other Africans are very tolerant. A hundred years ago, of course, Islam could be used as a pretext by some conquerors in Nigeria—or even in Western Sudan, Senegal, or Guinea—to carve out empires. But today, all religions are in competition in Negro Africa, and we are very concerned about this. We refuse to allow religious rivalries to become operative on the political level. . . .

The Africans tolerate their neighbors, and in our political parties up to the present time no Catholic or animist has ever been ostracized because of his religious convictions. Naturally, the Moslems are in a majority in the country, but our leadership is chosen purely according to democratic criteria—that is, on the basis of capacity, merit, and devotion within the party.

Therefore, we do not have the same reasons as France, Italy, and Belgium for having several parties, and for experiencing the luxury of a ministerial crisis every six months. Our position is completely different. It is true that we must have more experience in order to analyze African problems. We are no longer like the countries of the Middle East or Latin America who, even at a time when the number of parties was limited, had many revolutions and government turnovers. We think that these revolutions, these uprisings, these *coups d'état* do not correspond to our needs.

There is still the question of the organization of democracy in the action of the party. And since we have no reason to increase the number of parties, since the differentiation of interests is not very great, the most important problem for the countries of Africa arises from aspirations for unity—both for the countries that have been deprived of freedom and for those countries that only experienced freedom of association fifteen years ago. The most important problem is that of international independence and sovereignty. We have very clear objectives for the most part, although the awareness of some people is confused, but we all agree that Africa will only have the possibility of developing rapidly in very large groupings. Philosophical, religious, and ideological problems do not divide us. The only objective that animates us is that of finding the way to put the apparatus of the state in the service of economic, cultural, and social development. We are looking for the methods that will permit us to carry out this development as rapidly as possible.

If we analyze the situation carefully, even keeping in mind that the electoral system of colonialism divided Africans by its fraud and deceit, we can note that there is no fundamental opposition among us. Certainly, we played the game for a long time. But when one considers the programs and resolutions of the party congresses, one can see our agreement on all points. Nevertheless, we carried our battle to the death, passionately, furiously—and the word "passion" expresses for Africans, for men of the land of the sun, all the violence of our struggles and oppositions.

Since we agreed on the essentials and pursued the same objectives, was there any reason to remain divided and split into parties that fought one another? It was by reason of this thinking that the countries began to move progressively toward the formula of the unified party. I started out by talking about the *single* party, but I have ended by using President Senghor's expression "unified." Language contains many nuances; the word "unified" has been adopted because it allows for the juridical possibility of the formation of other parties. We say "unified" because other parties and other political groups have voluntarily sacrificed themselves for the sake of unity. . . .

Now, since our objectives are common ones and we are in agreement on methods, we must create a single party. It is necessary to create a single party to be efficient, to remedy the situation, and not to give aid to the anonymous adversary, colonialism, which up to the present has been instrumental in the division of our country. We must have the unified party in order to limit the possibilities of corruption and to attempt to destroy opportunism, for these constitute dangers that threaten the African parties and the action of the governments and parliaments.

But how to safeguard the ideals of liberty and democracy in the single party? As to the meaning of democracy, I have already said that we understood it in its naïvely original sense. Democracy is the exercise of public authority in conformance with the will of the masses. But if we want to remedy the situation and deprive the colonialists and adversaries of the weapon of division, if we want to prevent corruption and give more assurance to the leadership, we must recognize that the system of the single party is not without dangers.

There is one aspect of the problem of African life that I want to emphasize—our sincerity with ourselves. If there is one party, it is necessary, first of all, that it be the true expression of the aspirations of the people. It is not sufficient that it be the expression of true aspirations for one moment; it must continue to be so. This is only possible to the degree that the party is solidly organized and there is a real discipline within the party, so that decisions are taken only after lengthy debate and free discussion. I would add that the system of the unified party demands more honesty, more disinterest, and more devotion from the leadership. In addition, one can remain a leader in Africa for a long time only if one is really acting effectively.

I want to give some examples of internal democracy in our parties. The press has emphasized the freedom of speech, which the eminent leaders of French politics noted in September, 1957, at the third interterritorial congress of the RDA* at Bamako. I saw our friends, the students, denounce us violently at that time

* Rassemblement Démocratique Africain, a political party organized in many French African territories before independence.—ED.

because we accepted the *loi-cadre*. I saw them very much impressed by the discussions of the Fifth Congress of the Union Soudanaise in August, 1958, because the discussions were absolutely free. There are other examples at the present time. When Modibo Keita makes a decision, it is generally thought that it is immediately accepted by the Union Soudanaise or, when it is a matter of the opinion of Senghor, by the Parti Fédéraliste Africain (PFA). Those who think that one can do what one wishes in the PFA, or in Mali, are sadly mistaken. As for those two men, I can assert that they are very disciplined party militants. Moreover, the highest body in the Union Soudanaise is the Political Bureau. In the PFA, it is the Executive Bureau and the Directing Committee. And without giving away any secrets, I can tell you that the leaders are obliged to follow the advice of the majority. They are obliged to execute the decisions taken by the majority.

In the case of the unified party, I believe that the leaders not only ought to be capable, but also ought to encourage discussions and give examples of party discipline. The party ought to be very well organized, since—if universal suffrage is a criterion of democracy—we have to change the parliaments continuously through elections.

Nevertheless, our democracy does not end there. First of all, it was necessary in Guinea and Sudan, when the political development and the development of awareness allowed, to replace a part of the leadership set up by the colonial regime and to modify the basic structure of the administration profoundly by suppressing the chiefdom, the chiefs of the local districts in Guinea and Sudan, and by changing the chiefs, as has just been done in Senegal. This latter change was carried out by giving them the full status of civil servants and establishing them in administrative posts, henceforth to be called *arrondissements*, and also by changing the electoral districts.

Structural reform is very important. In Sudan, we established an elective council in the villages. Naturally, we have enumerated the functions of the chief—whom the government has the power to name, on the advice of the elective council—and we have also enumerated the functions of the elective council, so that the chief cannot do anything without consulting it. In other words, the chief and the elective council must make decisions in common. Soon we expect to establish by universal suffrage provincial elective councils, which will be responsible for local interests.

The organizer of all this is the party. For not only the Congress but the Political Bureau can add a certain number of leaders to establish the Directing Committee and make not a national conference (since Sudan is a territory, a province of Mali) but a territorial conference.* In each electoral district, we have a political bureau on the model of the central Political Bureau, and in each village we have a political committee. And so that the political committee and the elective council of the village will not enter into conflicts of influence, rivalry, and personal opposition, the most outstanding and competent party leaders are elected to the village council to act as liaison, to coordinate and harmonize, with the party always remaining the organizer.

In a recent resolution (adopted during our last conference), we asserted the superiority of the political apparatus to the administrative one. Also, we placed clerks at the head of each electoral district—African administrative officials who had already given proof of their administrative efficiency when they headed political sections or trade unions.

Thus, from the point of view of internal democracy with freedom of discussion, party discipline, democratic election of not only the top organs of the party but also the legislative and representative organs such as the provincial assemblies and the village councils, we think that the criteria of democracy are respected.

In the present historical situation in Africa, there is no need to multiply parties. There is no need to indulge in the luxury of a sterile and fratricidal opposition. There is no need to have a ministerial crisis every three months if we have decided to move to independence and to consolidate the independence of the African states, and if we wish to realize African unity and raise Africa economically and culturally to the level of other countries and peoples.

Evidently, the unified party has effects on other democratic organizations. But if the party is the expression of the true aspirations of the people, if it is the spokesman and instrument for the realization of the state, there is no reason why trade-union organizations, whose program constitutes part of the program of the political party, should not find themselves in harmony with the political organization. For the same reasons, it is not impossible

* This speech was given before the union of Sudan and Senegal in the Mali Federation broke up and Sudan became the Republic of Mali.—ED.

that youth organizations, women's organizations, and democratic movements such as the Peace Movement should not find a way to collaborate with the leading force in the country, the unified political party. And this is much easier for the African countries since the dominant ideas and aspirations today are independence, unity, and rapid realization of economic and social progress.

You must travel in the country and participate in the meetings of the village committees and the political bureaus and the subdivisions, in the discussion groups, in the meetings of the central Political Bureau to understand that the system of a unified party such as exists today in Guinea and in Sudan, is a really democratic system. I am not going to spend time on the reasons for the effectiveness of the unified party. We refuse to fight on the ideological territory of the West. Journalists, businessmen, French intellectuals—in Paris or traveling in our countries—have expressed their fears to us. "Be careful," they tell us. "Do not follow the example of Guinea, which has relations with the countries of the East. Be careful. Do not leave the West. You are going to be independent, and you will have to choose your way. We believe that it is in your interest to locate yourself in the camp of the West." My personal opinion is that it is not desirable for us to establish ourselves in this position. When we see France, England, and the United States exchanging numerous tourists and missions with the Soviet Union, and we see the Soviet Union and other countries of the East planning commercial agreements with all countries of the West, we wonder why they fear our having contacts with these countries. We are aware that it is because of a lack of confidence. They tell us that they are very clever—as if France could without difficulty have contacts with Poland and Yugoslavia while there would be a mortal danger for Guinea or Mali tomorrow to establish the same contacts with the same countries. When one asks these people if they think that we are not sufficiently mature to defend our interests ourselves, they protest, "That isn't what we meant to say!"

I say that Africa should not fight on the ideological battleground of the West because we do not have religious and philosophical problems that divide us in the administration of civic life. . . . As for economic and cultural development, even right-wing economists now admit that the underdeveloped countries can only advance rapidly and develop themselves sufficiently through planning. Even the old industrialized countries now think that they will overcome their backwardness by planning. When a man like Nehru, who seems to me like a good British bourgeois from the City,* asserts that the underdeveloped countries, which have recently achieved independence after a long period of colonial regime, cannot develop without the methods of socialist planning, I believe that this is a very important indication. From the point of view of development, it is the countries in which a single party is in power that make the most evident progress. On the other hand, countries in which the new leaders are content to replace the colonial regime without changing the structure in any way or reforming it, without bringing new methods or giving a new conception and orientation to the economy and to the program of education, without adapting the new needs to the real situation of the country, and without adapting the actions of the government and parliament to the true aspiration of the masses—these countries, in spite of every kind of aid that can be given to them, will be marking time so long as they have not adopted new, revolutionary methods.

We have been much criticized since 1946, but all this propaganda has remained without effect and has not prevented us from advancing. The important thing for us is to know what we want and to decide how we shall reach our objective. The important thing for us is to find our inspiration in all experience—in the success of industrial civilization in the United States and France; but one cannot prevent us, and we will not allow ourselves to be prevented, from studying the Chinese experience and the Soviet experience, or the experience of Israel, and taking everything that is adaptable to the conditions of our country, and using all these experiences to try to work effectively for the benefit of our country. . . .

Cheikh Anta Diop: You have spoken of the single party. As others have already underlined, when this is the incarnation of national goals, it is a very good idea. But when it dominates the entire political life of the nation, all the national life, and orients it to its own pleasure without taking into account the aspirations of the people, the single party can have very serious consequences. On this point, my opinion is the following: The single parties we are going to create may be parties of the Latin American type

* The financial district of London.—ED.

—that is, there is danger that we will create petty, ephemeral dictatorships that will be dominated by foreign capital in a very insidious fashion. Then Africa will live in a state of division and permanent weakness exactly as Latin America does. The single party is a very good formula for the purpose of dominating a little territory and safeguarding personal interests by making them, for all practical purposes, permanent. Or, on the other hand, we can orient Africa toward federation. In this case, another political form and another political conception are relevant. First of all, we must indicate our intentions very clearly now, without waiting for political frontiers to be established—for it will be more difficult afterward, perhaps too late, to federate the African continent.

Madeira Keita: The political unification of the African continent poses the problem of membership in the Community or membership in the Commonwealth, and likewise the problem of time. That is why I insist on this question. When we federate from the Sahara to the Cape, from the Atlantic Ocean to the Indian Ocean, to become a great power which, from the point of view of potential economic power, will be as strong as the Soviet Union or America, we must show the former mother countries that we are not ignoring them. Their interests will continue to be safeguarded, but not in the way they hoped for. . . .

M. Ben Barka: If you will allow, I would like to add the following observations. The first concerns the worry that certain of those present have expressed that there may be a bundle of contradictions in these unified parties which will render the parties absolutely ineffective. We think that the social classes that are trying to reconstitute feudal domination or are open to foreign domination do not necessarily belong in these organizations and ought not to be considered as an integral part of this organizing force in the people working toward its unification. Therefore, there should be more concern for unanimity in the establishment of this organizing party necessary for all development.

A second observation relates to the attitude of the unified party with regard to other syndical organizations of youth and other groups. In my opinion, the unified party would be wrong to attribute to itself a monopoly of political conceptions and political activity. Certainly, since it includes the members of these organizations, it is their political expression. But it ought to allow youth organizations, women's organizations, and trade unions to play their political roles as well, in order to realize the democratic synthesis sought in the conception of the unified political party.

Finally, the religious problem raised by certain of those here is not a problem, as you said, for Africans. It is created from outside, by those who want to make use of it as a means of penetration. We need not congratulate ourselves on the allegiance of religious leaders who, seeing which way the wind was blowing, now appeal to the new leaders. If they rally to us, so much the better. But we should not consider their allegiance as a positive factor for the future of our countries. We do not have to approve that religious phenomenon by giving a preponderant place to religious leaders who have been discredited during the colonial period. We want to arouse and form our youth without destroying the religious foundation of each community, and to give it a common revolutionary education which ought to be the ferment of the union of all of Africa.

17. Léopold Sédar Senghor

Léopold Sédar Senghor, President of Senegal, was born in 1907. He was educated at Catholic schools in Senegal, and at the Lycée Louis-le-Grand and the Sorbonne in Paris. Senghor was the first African to receive the prized agrégation *degree. In World War II, he served with the French infantry and was imprisoned for four years by the Germans. After the war, he became active in French African politics, was elected four times as a Senegalese representative in the French National Assembly, and held cabinet posts in French governments. In 1951, he organized the Bloc Démocratique Sénégalais, which received a majority of the seats in the 1957 internal elections for a representative assembly in Senegal. In 1958, his party joined with the Senegalese Socialists under Lamine Gueyé to form the Union Progressiste Sénégalaise (UPS). The following year, Senegal joined French-speaking Sudan in the short-lived*

Federation of Mali, which broke apart in 1960. In 1960, Senghor was elected President of Senegal, a position he has held since that time. Although Senghor has been critical of the one-party state, the UPS is the only party in Senegal, following its fusion with the single opposition party in 1966.

The first selection below—detailing Senghor's program for a humanistic, democratic "African socialism"—is taken from an abridged English translation of Senghor's report to a party congress in Dakar (then the capital of the Mali Federation) on July 1, 1959. (The full French text is available under the title Nation et Voie Africaine du Socialisme *[Paris: Présence Africaine, 1961].)*

Senghor has also published four volumes of poetry, as well as an anthology of African poets. He is one of the leading spokesmen for the cultural revival associated with the concept of Negritude, and writes for the publication of the Society for African Culture, Présence Africaine. *The selection on this subject is taken from a speech Senghor delivered at Oxford University in October, 1961.*

AFRICAN SOCIALISM*

In the respective programs of our former parties, all of us used to proclaim our attachment to socialism. This was a good thing, but it was not enough. Most of the time, we were satisfied with stereotyped formulas and vague aspirations, which we called scientific socialism—as if socialism did not mean a return to original sources. Above all, we need to make an effort to rethink the basic texts in the light of Negro African realities.

The antifederalists† have accused us of being atheists, Marxists, and of outlawing religion. Though this smacks of propaganda, it poses a fundamental question. Can we integrate Negro African cultural values, especially religious values, into socialism? We must answer that question once and for all with an unequivocal "Yes."

We are not "Marxists" in the sense given the word today, in so

* Excerpts from Léopold Sédar Senghor, *African Socialism*, translated by Mercer Cook (New York: American Society of African Culture, 1959); reprinted by permission.

† Those opposed to the Federation of Mali (now defunct).—ED.

far as Marxism is presented as atheistic metaphysics, a total and totalitarian view of the world, a *Weltanschauung*. In this sense, Marx himself once said: "As for me, I am not a Marxist." We are socialists. In other words, we shall exclude neither Marx nor Engels from our sources; we shall start from their works as from those of the "utopian socialists," and we shall add to these sources the works of their successors and commentators. But we shall retain only the method and the ideas: the method, which can help us to analyze our situation; the ideas, which can help us to solve our problems.

We shall start from Marx and Engels. Whatever their limitations, their inadequacies, or their errors, they, more than all others, revolutionized political and economic thought of the nineteenth century. . . .

We may wonder, first of all, whether the socialism, the economics of Marx, is really "scientific." Yes and no. No, if one means by science the exact knowledge and formulation of economic facts in laws which permit one to foresee and to organize a balanced economy. *Yes*, if science is defined as comprehension of the real, if it consists of deciphering the complexities basic to economic facts, especially man's reactions to these facts, and if its aim is to unveil "the economic law of motion of modern society."

So we must not seek in Marx—not even in *Capital*—an exposé of economic laws. Considering them more or less as contingent "appearances," Marx was not interested in them. Moreover, he went so far as to predict changes that have not occurred.

In *Conflit du Siècle*, Fritz Sternberg has analyzed almost all the changes that have taken place in economic, social, and political reality since the publication of *Capital*. They are impressive and have been listed by other writers. In our résumé of Marx's theories, we have skipped over most of them, and we shall now mention only a few, while noting the recent studies made in France by the Autonomous Socialist Party:

1. The class struggle is much more complex than Marx thought. In fact, the working class is not a simple reality. Moreover, it is diminishing while the several categories of salaried workers with dissimilar interests are increasing.

2. The peasants, whom Marx considered more or less impervious to revolutionary ferment and dedicated "to the stupidity of

rural life," have belied his judgment in underdeveloped countries.

3. The theory of capitalist concentration has not been verified by the facts. On the contrary, the number of small and medium-sized businesses continues to grow in Western European countries.

4. Though periodic economic crises have not ceased, they are becoming rarer, and we cannot reasonably foresee a general cataclysm ending the capitalist system, which is adjusting to economic and social evolution.

5. "Socialism" has not triumphed, as Marx predicted, in the industrial nations of Western Europe, but in the underdeveloped nations of Eastern Europe and Asia.

By excessive simplification of the theory of class struggle—a more precise translation of *Klassenkampf* would be a "class war"—Marx overestimated the role of the determinism of things and underestimated man's freedom and the organizing power of the capitalist state. In fact, thanks to trade-union activity and a more enlightened middle class, the capitalistic state, by a policy of intervention and rational organization, has been able progressively to reduce the surplus value. This surplus value, reduced by more equitable taxation, has permitted the productive investments of the postwar era and the institution of social security. Marx advocated social legislation; in his opinion, it would lead to increased unemployment, bitter class antagonism, and, finally, to the revolution. However, social reforms have produced quite the opposite effects.

We may also observe, in passing, that he did not pay enough attention to the role of cooperatives, as preached by the utopian socialists. We know that these have proved their worth in the Scandinavian socialist democracies. Thus, a will to reform has replaced—in Western labor unions—the will to revolt. In the Communist countries, the "dictatorship of the proletariat," contrary to the teachings of Marx, has made the state an omnipotent, soulless monster, has stifled the natural freedoms of the human being, and has dried up the sources of art, without which life is not worth living.

One final word on this point. In Marx's day, colonialism was just beginning. He could not foresee its universal development during the second half of the nineteenth century. He spoke, of course, about "the modern theory of colonization,"* but merely in the etymological sense of the word. He had in mind only European colonization of the United States. Moreover, his macroeconomic theory, his almost blind confidence in proletarian generosity and conscience prevented him from anticipating the opposition that would develop between colonizing and colonized countries, between the well fed and the famished. It is a fact, now commonplace, that the standard of living of the European masses has been able to rise only at the expense of the standard of living of the masses in Asia and Africa. The economy of European nations consists fundamentally of selling manufactured products to underdeveloped countries at high prices and buying raw materials from them at the lowest possible cost. And I am not talking about the United States. The problem is different in France, but if the prices paid for raw materials in African countries are supported, it is no less true that French prices are generally the highest in Western Europe. This compensates for that. In a word, the European proletariat has profited from the colonial system; therefore, it has never really—I mean effectively—opposed it.

There we have a series of facts that we must think about, we men from underdeveloped countries, we men inspired by socialism. We must not consider Marx as an economist like Keynes, but as a sociologist, a philosopher. This is something that would have astonished the founder of "scientific socialism," since he refrained from "philosophizing." And yet his thought remains that of a philosopher. Beyond the economic "appearances," it dives into the human reality that causes them. For the *factual* view of things, Marx substitutes a profound insight into human needs. His is a new humanism, new because it is *incarnate*.

Humanism, *philosophy of humanism*, rather than economics— this is the basic character, the positive contribution of Marxian thought. As we said earlier, Marx does not formulate economic facts; he defines "the economic law of motion of modern society," which is a social "tendency" rather than a law. In his analysis, he advances by *postulates* and theories which explain the facts. . . .

For an African Type of Socialism

Let us recapitulate Marx's positive contributions. They are: the

* *Capital*, IV, 314–28.

philosophy of humanism, economic theory, dialectical method. To these we may add trade unionism, planning, and also federalism and cooperation, which come to us from the French idealistic socialists: Saint Simon, Proudhon, and Fourier—to name only the outstanding ones.

Thus, we are not Communists. Does this mean that we shall practice anti-Communism? Certainly not. Anti-Communism, the "witch hunt," can have but one result: increased tension between East and West and a continuation of the Cold War at the obvious risk of unleashing a third global conflict, from which humanity would not recover. We are not Communists for a theoretical reason. Lenin's definition of matter proceeds from a one-sided concept, from a purely materialistic and deterministic postulate. At the beginning of *Anarchy and Socialism*, Stalin goes even further: "Marxism is not only a theory of socialism, it is a definitive view of the world, a philosophical system."

We are not Communists for a practical reason. The anxiety for human dignity, the need for freedom—man's freedom, the freedoms of collectivities—which animate Marx's thought and provide its revolutionary ferment—this anxiety and this need are unknown to Communism, whose major deviation is Stalinism. The "dictatorship of the proletariat," which was to be only temporary, becomes the dictatorship of the party and state by perpetuating itself. "The Soviet Union," said Mamadou Dia on his return from Moscow, "has succeeded in building socialism, but at the sacrifice of religion, of the soul."

The paradox of socialistic construction in Communist countries —in the Soviet Union at least—is that it increasingly resembles capitalistic construction in the United States, the American way of life, with high salaries, refrigerators, washing machines, and television sets. And it has less art and freedom of thought. Nevertheless, we shall not be won over by a regime of liberal capitalism and free enterprise. We cannot close our eyes to segregation, although the government combats it; nor can we accept the elevation of material success to a way of life.

We stand for a middle course, for a *democratic socialism* which goes so far as to integrate spiritual values, a socialism which ties in with the old ethical current of the French socialists. Historically and culturally, we belong to the current. Besides, the French socialists—from Saint Simon to the Léon Blum of *A l'Echelle hu-*

maine—are not so utopian as they are reputed to be. In so far as they are idealists, they fulfill the requirements of the Negro African soul, the requirements of men of all races and countries. *Not by Bread Alone*—this is the title of a novel by Dudintsev, a citizen of the Soviet Union, and the Russians read this book avidly. Khrushchev was not mistaken: "De-Stalinization was imposed by the people by the thirst for freedom, the hunger for spiritual nourishment."

Concluding his report on the German Democratic Republic [East Germany], Michel Bosquet writes: "But when I ask him [the head of a labor union] what the workers demand, he replies: 'Today they want TV sets and motorcycles. When they get them, they will demand a shorter work week. And then? . . . I can only answer for myself. What I would like, what I miss, is more good literature.' "* This fact is not unrelated to a phenomenon observed in America: the appeal of the contemplative life, as a reaction against the surrounding machinism. Among American Catholics, the proportion of priests to laity is one of the highest in the world.

This thirst for freedom, this hunger for spiritual nourishment, strengthened by the moral tradition of French socialism, explains why numerous French Marxists in recent years have shunned Stalinism and even Communism: Henri Lefebvre, Pierre Fougeyrollas, and Edgar Morin, among others, who have stated their reasons lately in sorrowful but lucid volumes.† The major reason, common to all of them, is that the Party has come to submerge the individual under the collectivity, the person under the class, to hide reality behind the screen of ideology. If we reflect about these cases, we shall discover that not only Marxism but Marx himself is "called to question"—except perhaps by Lefebvre. For, if the person is submerged, it is because Marx did not pay sufficient attention to the "natural determination"—namely, the *nation*—that is not effaced by class.

Marx underestimated political and national idealism, which, born in France upon the ruins of provincial fatherlands with the Revolution of 1789, won over the world. "Justice," Marx writes, "humanity, liberty, equality, fraternity, independence . . . these

* *L'Express,* June 4, 1959, p. 24.

† Cf. Lefebvre, *La Somme et le reste* (La Nef de Paris); Fougeyrollas, *Le Marxisme en question* (Editions du Seuil); Morin, *Autocritique* (Julliard).

relatively moral categories which sound so nice, but which, in historical and political questions, prove absolutely nothing." I repeat: independence. If the creator of scientific sociology returned to this earth, he would perceive with amazement that these "chimeras," as he called them, and above all the concept of *nation*, are living realities in the twentieth century.

What is left of the 1789 Revolution? A political doctrine and technique, accepted nowadays even by the devout. . . . From Marxism there will surely remain an economic doctrine and technique, inasmuch as they do not contradict the teachings of Christianity and Islam—far from it.

But a third revolution is taking place, as a reaction against capitalistic and Communistic materialism—one that will integrate moral, if not religious, values with the political and economic contributions of the two great revolutions. In this revolution, the colored peoples, including the African Negro, must play their part; they must bring their contribution to the construction of the new planetary civilization. As Aimé Césaire says: "They will not come empty-handed to the rendezvous of give-and-take." Between the two world wars, Paul Morand observed: "The Negroes have rendered an enormous service to America. But for them, one might have thought that men could not live without a bank account and a bathtub."

For a Strong Federal Democracy

Our democracy will be *federal*. . . . We do not need to remind you that local diversities, with their complementary qualities, will enrich the federation. Conversely, the federation will preserve those diversities. The decentralized federal structure will be extended, within the framework of the federal state, to regional and communal collectivities, even into economic and social areas. The Yugoslavian structures, adapted to our realities, will, in this instance, serve as a model.

Thus we shall fill the dangerous void now existing between the federal state and the village. Our leaders are bored with their freedom from responsibility. Even when they fill this void by the political formation of militants, they tend to devote their activity to contention over slogans. Regional and communal assemblies, among others, would give them a practical opportunity to exercise their responsibilities. A revolution remains ideological, therefore ineffective, so long as it is not translated into concrete action which, by transforming the structure, raises the standard of living and culture of the citizens. . . .

A federal democracy, yes . . . but a strong democracy. As the Secretary General suggests in his report, it is a question of avoiding two dangers: on the one hand, fascist dictatorship, which one observes in the antifederalist states; on the other hand, governmental instability, which was common in France during the Third and Fourth Republics. Both deviations are signs of weakness; in the long run, they provoke the revolt of the people and the disintegration of the state.

The Federation of Mali, like the federated states, will be a democracy.* The electoral law will continue to be impartial . . . not a law of circumstance, cut to the measure of the government or the majority party. Freedom of opinion, speech, press, assembly, and association is guaranteed by the constitutions of Mali and the federated states—in the antifederalist states also. But, with us, these freedoms do not exist only on paper; they are effectively enjoyed and will continue to be so. Above all, the right of *free settlement* of the citizens will be assured, whether or not they were born in Mali. A democratic policy pays dividends; in addition, it conforms to our humanitarian ideal. Already, public opinion in black Africa and France is grateful to us. This is excellent propaganda for Mali.

The rights of the minority, of the opposition, will therefore be respected in Mali. They will find their natural and legal limits in the rights of the majority, the popular will, which is sovereign; in other words, in the rights of the nation-state. For we are a quasi nation, as François Perroux says.

The stability of the executive is guaranteed by our constitutions. We need to assure it in actual political practice. It is necessary that governments govern, that they, along with the legislative assemblies, take the initiative of making laws within the framework of the doctrine and program of the majority party. Governments must apply the law firmly, and legislative assemblies must check on the action of the government. It is necessary that the party (congress, executive committee, and officers) have the final word in matters of control. Yet, to be effective, the various controls will be

---

* In August, 1960, after this report was made, the Federation of Mali separated into its component parts, Senegal and the Sudan (which took the name of the Republic of Mali).—ED.

general and *a posteriori*. Meddling and harassing controls would not work. Here again, we shall avoid two dangers: granting government action a blank check, and taking away the executive power. The controls must be political, not technical.

Let us return to the rights of the opposition. Their role, certainly, is to criticize. But "criticism" means critical spirit, not spirit of criticism, systematic carping. In a democracy, criticism must be constructive and serve the general, not factional, interest. At any rate, one cannot grant the opposition more rights than the majority enjoys. The law also applies to the opposition, which is likewise required to observe it. Under the control of the majority party, the governments will take all necessary steps to curb demagogic opposition. They will not tolerate violations of the law, appeals to illegality or to violence, whether the pretexts be religious or racial. This is the democratic sense that we attach to the "dictatorship of the proletariat."

WHAT IS "NEGRITUDE"?*

Paradoxically, it was the French who first forced us to seek its essence, and who then showed us where it lay . . . when they enforced their policy of assimilation and thus deepened our despair. . . . Earlier, we had become aware within ourselves that assimilation was a failure; we could assimilate mathematics or the French language, but we could never strip off our black skins or root out black souls. And so we set out on a fervent quest for the "holy grail": our collective soul. And we came upon it.

It was not revealed to us by the "official France" of the politicians who, out of self-interest and political conviction, defended the policy of assimilation. Its whereabouts was pointed out to us by that handful of free-lance thinkers—writers, artists, ethnologists, and prehistorians—who bring about cultural revolutions in France. It was, to be quite precise, our teachers of ethnology who introduced us to the considerable body of work already achieved in the understanding of Africa, by the University of Oxford.

What did we learn from all those writers, artists, and teachers?

* Excerpts from a speech delivered by Senghor at Oxford University in October, 1961; reprinted, by permission, from *West Africa*, November 4, 1961.

That the early years of colonization and especially, even before colonization, the slave trade had ravaged black Africa like a bush fire, wiping out images and values in one vast carnage. That Negroid civilization had flourished in the Upper Paleolithic Age, and that the Neolithic revolution could not be explained without them. That their roots retained their vigor and would one day produce new grass and green branches . . .

Negritude is the *whole complex of civilized values—cultural, economic, social, and political—which characterize the black peoples,* or, more precisely, the Negro-African world. All these values are essentially informed by intuitive reason, because this sentient reason, the reason which comes to grips, expresses itself emotionally, through that self-surrender, that coalescence of subject and object; through myths, by which I mean the archetypal images of the collective soul; and, above all, through primordial rhythms, synchronized with those of the cosmos. In other words, the sense of communion, the gift of mythmaking, the gift of rhythm, such are the essential elements of Negritude, which you will find indelibly stamped on all the works and activities of the black man. . . .

In opposition to European racialism, of which the Nazis were the symbol, we set up an "antiracial racialism." The very excesses of Nazism, and the catastrophes it engendered, were soon to bring us to our senses. Such hatred, such violence, above all, such weeping and such shedding of blood produced a feeling of revulsion. It was so foreign to our continent's genius: our *need to love.* And then the anthropologists taught us that there is no such thing as a pure race: Scientifically speaking—races do not exist. They went one better and forecast that, with a mere 200 million people, we would in the end disappear as a "black race," through miscegenation. At the same time, they did offer us some consolation. "The focal points of human development," wrote Teilhard de Chardin in 1939, "always seem to coincide with the points of contact and anastomosis of several nerve paths"—that is, in the ordinary man's language, of several races.* If, then, we were justified in fostering the values of Negritude and arousing the energy slumbering within us, it must be in order to pour them into the mainstream of cultural miscegenation (the biological process taking place spontane-

* On the relation of Teilhard de Chardin and Negritude, see Senghor's *Pierre Teilhard de Chardin et la Politique Africaine* (Paris: Editions du Seuil, 1962).—Ed.

ously). They must flow toward the meeting point of all humanity; they must be our contribution to the civilization of the universal.

Biological miscegenation, then, takes place spontaneously, provoked by the very laws which govern life, and in the face of all policies of apartheid. It is a different matter in the realm of culture. Here, we remain wholly free to cooperate or not, to provoke or prevent the synthesis of cultures. This is an important point. For, as certain biologists point out, the psychological mutations brought about by education are incorporated in our genes and are then transmitted by heredity. Hence the major role played by culture.

Seen within this prospect of the civilization of the universal, the colonial policies of Great Britain and France have proved successful complements to each other, and black Africa has benefited. The policies of the former tended to reinforce the traditional native civilization. As for France's policy, although we have often reviled it in the past, it too ended with a credit balance, through forcing us actively to assimilate European civilization. This fertilized our sense of Negritude. Today, our Negritude no longer expresses itself as opposition to European values, but as a *complement* to them. Henceforth, its militants will be concerned, as I have often said, *not to be assimilated, but to assimilate*. They will use European values to arouse the slumbering values of Negritude, which they will bring as their contribution to the civilization of the universal.

Nevertheless, we still disagree with Europe: not with its values any longer (with the exception of capitalism), but with its theory of the civilization of the universal. . . . In the eyes of the Europeans, the "exotic civilizations" are static in character, being content to live by means of archetypal images, which they repeat indefinitely. The most serious criticism is that they have no idea of the *pre-eminent dignity of the human person*. My reply is this: Just as much as black Africa, Europe and its North American offspring live by means of archetypal images. For what are free enterprise, democracy, and Communism but *myths*, around which hundreds of millions of men and women organize their lives? Negritude itself is a myth (I am not using the word in any pejorative sense), but a living, dynamic one, which evolves with its circumstances into a form of humanism. Actually, our criticism of the [European] thesis is that it is monstrously antihumanist. For if European civilization were to be imposed, unmodified, on all peoples and continents, it could only be by force. That is its first disadvantage. A more serious one is that it would not be *humanistic*, for it would cut itself off from the complementary values of the greater part of humanity. As I have said elsewhere, it would be a universal civilization; it would not be the civilization of the universal.

Our revised Negritude is humanistic. I repeat, it welcomes the complementary values of Europe and the white man, and, indeed, of all other races and continents. But it welcomes them in order to fertilize and reinvigorate its own values, which it then offers for the construction of a civilization which shall embrace all mankind. The neohumanism of the twentieth century stands at the point where the paths of all nations, races, and continents cross, "where the four winds of the spirit blow."

18. *Kwame Nkrumah*

Kwame Nkrumah was born in the Gold Coast, near the Ivory Coast border, in 1909. He was baptized a Catholic and attended mission schools for eight years. A German priest sent him to Achimota College—a secondary school near Accra—where he first acquired nationalist sentiments. After several years of teaching in the Gold Coast, he borrowed enough money to get to the United States where, in 1935, he received a scholarship from Lincoln University in Pennsylvania. After graduation, he taught political science at Lincoln University, and at the same time did graduate work toward advanced degrees at the University of Pennsylvania. In 1945, he went to England, where he became active in the nationalist movement. Two years later, he returned to the Gold Coast as organizing secretary of the United Gold Coast Convention, under J. B. Danquah. In 1949, he organized his own party, the Convention People's Party, which won all subsequent elections (including one in which Nkrumah campaigned while in prison, in 1951). On March 6, 1957, the Gold Coast was

*granted independence under the name of Ghana, and Nkrumah
became its Prime Minister. In 1960, Ghana became a republic, and
Nkrumah was elected President. In 1964, Ghana was officially declared a one-party state. Nkrumah's increasingly dictatorial exercise
of power and Ghana's worsening economic situation led to an
army coup d'état on February 24, 1966, while Nkrumah was on a
state visit to China.*

*The selection below from Nkrumah's autobiography describes
the principal influences on his political outlook and the methods
that led to the independence of Ghana. It is followed by an excerpt
from Consciencism, a recent attempt to develop an ideology of
African revolution. Its contents give an indication of the increasingly radical character of Nkrumah's thinking before his overthrow
in 1966. His obsession with neocolonialism reflects a widespread
belief by the African left that nothing has really been changed by
the granting of political independence.*

BACKGROUND TO INDEPENDENCE*

Independence for the Gold Coast was my aim. It was a colony,
and I have always regarded colonialism as the policy by which a
foreign power binds territories to herself by political ties, with the
primary object of promoting her own economic advantage. No
one need be surprised if this system has led to disturbances and
political tension in many territories. There are few people who
would not rid themselves of such domination if they could.

At this time, I devoted much energy to the study of revolutionaries and their methods. Those who interested me most were
Hannibal, Cromwell, Napoleon, Lenin, Mazzini, Gandhi, Mus-
solini, and Hitler. I found much of value to be gleaned and many
ideas that were useful to me later in my own campaign against
imperialism.

At first I could not understand how Gandhi's philosophy of
nonviolence could possibly be effective. It seemed to me to be

* Excerpts from *Ghana: The Autobiography of Kwame Nkrumah* (New
York: Thomas Nelson and Sons, 1957; copyright by Thomas Nelson and
Sons, 1957); reprinted by permission.

utterly feeble and without hope of success. The solution of the colonial problem, as I saw it at that time, lay in armed rebellion. How is it possible, I asked myself, for a revolution to succeed without arms and ammunition? After months of studying Gandhi's policy and watching the effect it had, I began to see that, when backed by a strong political organization, it could be the solution to the colonial problem. In Jawaharlal Nehru's rise to power I recognized the success of one who, pledged to socialism, was able to interpret Gandhi's philosophy in practical terms.

The Gold Coast revolt against colonialism is not a new thing. Its roots are deep. There was the Confederation of 1868, when certain chiefs came together to defend themselves not only against their tribal kin, the Ashantis, but also against political encroachments from abroad. After the bond of 1844, which gave Britain trading rights, the Gold Coast had come increasingly under her control.

The next great move of political cohesion and conscience was the formation of the Aborigines Rights Protection Society by chiefs and literate Africans with the object of defending Gold Coast land. When this collapsed—because of an ever-widening rift between the chiefs and the educated people—the latter, binding themselves together and supported by their educated brothers in other West African territories, established the National Congress of British West Africa. This was the first indication of West African nationalism. However, because it lacked the support of the masses, it disintegrated in 1930.

The vacuum that this left in Gold Coast politics was eventually filled by the formation of the United Gold Coast Convention by the merchant and lawyer class of the country. It was when I realized that this movement was doomed to failure because it ignored the interests of the masses that I broke away, in 1949, and formed the Convention People's Party.

I saw that the whole solution to this problem lay in political freedom for our people; for it is only when a people are politically free that other races can give them the respect that is due them. It is impossible to talk of equality of races in any other terms. No people without a government of their own can expect to be treated on the same level as peoples of independent sovereign states. It is far better to be free to govern or misgovern yourself than to be governed by anybody else.

The formation of the CPP coincided with a political reawakening among the workers and young people of the country. Ex-service-men who had taken part in World War II returned to the Gold Coast dissatisfied with their position after having been given the chance of comparing their lot with that of other peoples, and they were prepared to take up any line which would better their conditions. There was a general dissatisfaction with the British colonial policy that had been adopted until that time, especially the policy of indirect rule which so encouraged tribal feudalism. Again, the Russian Revolution and its aftermath had left its mark by spreading ideas of workers' solidarity, trade-union movements, freedom and independence. Events in Asia also added a glow to the political awakening.

The CPP was not merely a mass movement. Mass movements are well and good, but they cannot act with purpose unless they are led and guided by a vanguard political party. And when the time comes for a ruling power to accord self-government, it will do so more willingly if it can hand over to a properly constituted political party with a majority backing, rather than to a revolutionary nationalist movement. Rallying around me all those who genuinely wished for progress, I resisted both the opportunist element and the reactionary forces, and sought to establish the CPP as the democratic instrument of the people's will and aspirations. We were freely elected to power in 1951. Three years later, and again in 1956, the same confidence was shown by the country.

The first objective then is political independence, for which I believe the organization itself must take two forms. First there is the period of "positive action"—a combination of nonviolent methods with effective and disciplined political action. At this stage, open conflict with the existing colonial regime is inevitable, and this is a test of strength for the organization. Since it is marked by nonviolence, and since the forces of might are on the side of the colonial power, there is little chance of complete success in this period.

The second stage is one of "tactical action"—a sort of contest of wits. From now on, the movement must make its ideology clear and convincing. The ideology of my party may be formulated as follows: No race, no people, no nation can exist freely and be respected at home and abroad without political freedom.

Once this freedom is gained, a greater task comes into view. All dependent territories are backward in education, in science, in agriculture, and in industry. The economic independence that should follow and maintain political independence demands every effort from the people, a total mobilization of brain and manpower resources. What other countries have taken three hundred years to achieve, a once dependent territory must try to accomplish in a generation if it is to survive. Unless it is, as it were, "jet-propelled," it will lag behind and thus risk everything for which it has fought.

Capitalism is too complicated a system for a newly independent nation. Hence the need for a socialistic society. But even a system based on social justice and a democratic constitution may need backing up, during the period following independence, by emergency measures of a totalitarian kind. Without discipline, true freedom cannot survive. In any event, the basis must be a loyal, honest, hard-working, and responsible civil service on which the party in power can rely. Armed forces must also be consolidated for defense. . . .

I concentrated on finding a formula by which the whole colonial question and the problem of imperialism could be solved. I read Hegel, Marx, Engels, Lenin, and Mazzini. The writings of these men did much to influence me in my revolutionary ideas and activities, and Marx and Lenin particularly impressed me as I felt sure that their philosophy was capable of solving these problems. But I think that of all the literature that I studied, the book that did more than any other to fire my enthusiasm was *The Philosophy and Opinions of Marcus Garvey* . . . with his philosophy of "Africa for the Africans" and his "Back to Africa" movement.

CONSCIENCISM*

. . . Whereas capitalism is a development by refinement from slavery and feudalism, socialism is obviously not a development from capitalism. In order that socialism should be a development from capitalism, it needs to share a fundamental principle, that of exploitation, with capitalism. Socialism most avowedly has no

* Excerpts from *Consciencism: Philosophy and Ideology for Decolonization and Development* (London: Heinemann Educational Books; New York: Monthly Review Press, 1964); reprinted by permission of Heinemann Educational Books Ltd. and the Monthly Review Press.

share in this principle. Hence socialism cannot develop from capitalism. Rather it stands for the negation of that very principle wherein capitalism has its being, lives, and thrives, that principle which unites capitalism with slavery and feudalism.

If one seeks the social-political ancestor of socialism, one must go to communalism. Socialism stands to communalism as capitalism stands to slavery. In socialism, the principles underlying communalism are given expression in modern circumstances. Thus, whereas communalism in an untechnical society can be *laissez faire*, in a technical society where sophisticated means of production are at hand, if the underlying principles of communalism are not given centralized and correlated expression, class cleavages will arise, which are connected with economic disparities, and thereby with political inequalities. Socialism, therefore, can be and is the defense of the principles of communalism in a modern setting. Socialism is a form of social organization which, guided by the principles underlying Communism, adopts procedures and measures made necessary by demographic and technological developments.

These considerations throw great light on the bearing of revolution and reform on socialism. The passage from the ancestral line of slavery via feudalism and capitalism to socialism can only lie through revolution: it cannot lie through reform. For in reform, fundamental principles are held constant and the details of their expression modified. In the words of Marx, it leaves the pillars of the building intact. Indeed, sometimes reform itself may be initiated by the necessities of preserving identical fundamental principles. Reform is a tactic of self-preservation.

Revolution is thus an indispensable avenue to socialism, where the antecedent social-political structure is animated by principles which are a negation of those of socialism, as in a capitalist structure (and therefore also in a colonialist structure, for a colonialist structure is essentially ancillary to capitalism). Indeed, I distinguish between two colonialisms, between a domestic one and an external one. Capitalism at home is domestic colonialism.

But from the ancestral line of communalism, the passage to socialism lies in reform, because the underlying principles are the same. But when this passage carries one through colonialism the reform is revolutionary since the passage from colonialism to genuine independence is an act of revolution. But because of the continuity of communalism with socialism, in communalistic societies, socialism is not a revolutionary creed, but a restatement in contemporary idiom of the principles underlying communalism. The passage from a noncommunalistic society to socialism is a revolutionary one which is guided by the principles underlying Communism.

In my autobiography, I said that capitalism might prove too complicated a system for a newly independent country. I wish to add to this the fact that the presuppositions and purposes of capitalism are contrary to those of African society. Capitalism would be a betrayal of the personality and conscience of Africa.

I have explained how society's desire to transform nature reflects itself in different social-political theories. I wish now to suggest how the same desire reflects itself in philosophy. Just as social-political theories, to the extent that they deploy forces for the harnessing and development of nature, fall into two lots, so do philosophies. From this standpoint, the two real social-political alternatives facing society are either that one section should produce, and another section batten thereon, or that all sections should produce and all sections should be fulfilled by the value created by labor.

In the same way, there are two real philosophical alternatives. These alternatives coincide with idealism and materialism. In the preceding chapter, I explained how idealism was connected with a tiered society, how through its mode of explaining nature and social phenomena by reference to spirit, idealism favored a class structure of a horizontal sort, in which one class sat upon the neck of another.

I also explained there how materialism, on the other hand, was connected with a humanist organization, how through its being monistic, and its referring all natural processes to matter and its laws, it inspired an egalitarian organization of society. The unity and fundamental identity of nature suggests the unity and fundamental identity of man in society. Idealism favors an oligarchy, materialism favors an egalitarianism.

Individuals have both idealist and materialist tendencies in them. So have societies both idealist and materialist streaks. But these streaks do not exist in equipoise. They are connected by a conflict in which now one streak predominates, now the other.

By reason of the connection of idealism with an oligarchy and of materialism with an egalitarianism, the opposition of idealism and materialism in the same society is paralleled by the opposition of conservative and progressive forces on the social level. When in the dialectical opposition of capitalism to socialism, the former for a time becomes triumphant, social progress is not thereby altogether arrested, though it is seriously attenuated. But since it is not arrested, it is hardly cause for wonder that the workers of today in many respects enjoy better circumstances of life than even a good many feudal lords of the past. To confess to this degree of progress is not to say, however, that capitalism has been without its shantytowns and slums, its captive workers languishing and finally dying in public squares, victims of hunger, cold, and disease.

The question is not whether there has been discernible progress under capitalism, but rather whether what progress is admitted can be said to be adequate. . . .

Practice without thought is blind; thought without practice is empty. The three segments of African society . . . the traditional, the Western, and the Islamic, coexist uneasily; the principles animating them are often in conflict with one another. I have in illustration tried to show how the principles which inform capitalism are in conflict with the socialist·egalitarianism of the traditional African society.

What is to be done then? I have stressed that the two other segments, in order to be rightly seen, must be accommodated only as experiences of the traditional African society. If we fail to do this our society will be racked by the most malignant schizophrenia.

Our attitude to the Western and the Islamic experience must be purposeful. It must also be guided by thought, for practice without thought is blind. What is called for as a first step is a body of connected thought which will determine the general nature of our action in unifying the society which we have inherited, this unification to take account, at all times, of the elevated ideals underlying the traditional African society. Social revolution must therefore have, standing firmly behind it, an intellectual revolution, a revolution in which our thinking and philosophy are directed towards the redemption of our society. Our philosophy must find its weapons in the environment and living conditions of the African people. It is from those conditions that the intellectual content of our philosophy must be created. The emancipation of the African continent is the emancipation of man. This requires two aims: first, the restitution of the egalitarianism of human society, and, second, the logistic mobilization of all our resources towards the attainment of that restitution.

The philosophy that must stand behind this social revolution is that which I have once referred to as philosophical consciencism; consciencism is the map in intellectual terms of the disposition of forces which will enable African society to digest the Western and the Islamic and the Euro-Christian elements in Africa, and develop them in such a way that they fit into the African personality. The African personality is itself defined by the cluster of humanist principles which underlie the traditional African society. Philosophical consciencism is that philosophical standpoint which, taking its start from the present content of the African conscience, indicates the way in which progress is forged out of the conflict in that conscience. . . .

Just as the placid appearance of matter only disguises the tension of forces underlying that appearance, like the bow of Heraclitus, so in a colonial territory, an opposition of reactionary and revolutionary forces can nevertheless give an impression of final and acquiescent subjugation. But just as a quality can be changed by quantitative (measurable) changes of a critical nature in matter, so this acquiescent impression can be obliterated by a change in the relation of the social forces. These opposing sets of forces are dynamic, in the sense that they seek and tend to establish some social condition. One may therefore refer to them by the name of action in order to make their dynamic nature explicit. In that case, one may say that in a colonial situation positive action and negative action can be discerned. Positive action will represent the sum of those forces seeking social justice in terms of the destruction of oligarchic exploitation and oppression. Negative action will correspondingly represent the sum of those forces tending to prolong colonial subjugation and exploitation. Positive action is revolutionary and negative action is reactionary.

It ought to be recognized at the outset that the introduced terms of positive and negative action are abstractions. But the ground for them is in social reality. It is quite possible by means of statistical analysis to discover the ways in which positive action and negative action are related in any given society. The statistical analysis will be of such facts as production, distribution, income, etc. Any such analysis must reveal one of three possible situations. Positive action may exceed negative action, or negative action may exceed positive action, or they may form an unstable equilibrium.

In a colonial situation, negative action undoubtedly outweighs positive action. In order that true independence should be won, it is necessary that positive action should come to overwhelm negative action. Admittedly, a semblance of true independence is possible without this specific relation. When this happens, we say that neocolonialism has set in, for neocolonialism is a guise adopted by negative action in order to give the impression that it has been overcome by positive action. Neocolonialism is negative action playing possum.

In order to forestall this, it is necessary for positive action to be backed by a mass party, and qualitatively to improve this mass so that by education and an increase in its degree of consciousness, its aptitude for positive action becomes heightened. We can therefore say that in a colonial territory, positive action must be backed by a mass party, complete with its instruments of education. This was why the Convention People's Party of Ghana developed from an early stage its education wing, workers' wing, farmers' wing, youth wing, women's wing, etc. In this way, the people received constant political education, their self-awareness was increased and such a self-image was formed as ruthlessly excluded colonialism in all its guises. It is also in the backing of millions of members and supporters, united by a common radical purpose, that the revolutionary character of the Convention People's Party consists, and not merely in the piquancy of its programs. Its mass and national support made it possible to think in realistic terms of instituting changes of a fundamental nature in the social hotchpotch bequeathed by colonialism.

A people's parliamentary democracy with a one-party system is better able to express and satisfy the common aspirations of a nation as a whole, than a multiple-party parliamentary system, which is in fact only a ruse for perpetuating, and covers up, the inherent struggle between the "haves" and the "have-nots." . . .

Any oblique attempt of a foreign power to thwart, balk, corrupt, or otherwise pervert the true independence of a sovereign people is neocolonialist. It is neocolonialist because it seeks, notwithstanding the acknowledged sovereignty of a people, to subordinate their interests to those of a foreign power.

A colonialist country can in fact offer independence to a people, not with the intention which such an act might be thought to imply, but in the hope that the positive and progressive forces thus appeased and quietened, the people might be exploited with greater serenity and comfort.

Neocolonialism is a greater danger to independent countries than is colonialism. Colonialism is crude, essentially overt, and apt to be overcome by a purposeful concert of national effort. In neocolonialism, however, the people are divided from their leaders and, instead of providing true leadership and guidance which is informed at every point by the ideal of the general welfare, leaders come to neglect the very people who put them in power and incautiously become instruments of suppression on behalf of the neocolonialists.

It is far easier for the proverbial camel to pass through the needle's eye, hump and all, than for an erstwhile colonial administration to give sound and honest counsel of a *political* nature to its liberated territory. To allow a foreign country, especially one which is loaded with economic interests in our continent, to tell us what *political* decisions to take, what *political* courses to follow, is indeed for us to hand back our independence to the oppressor on a silver platter.

Likewise, since the motivation of colonialism, whatever protean forms it may take, is well and truly economic, colonialism itself being but the institution of political bonds fastening colonies to a colonialist country, with the primary object of the metropolitan economic advantages, it is essential that a liberated territory should not bind her economy to that of the ousted rulers. The liberation of a people institutes principles which enjoin the recognition and destruction of imperialistic domination, whether it is political, economic, social, or cultural. To destroy imperialistic domination in these forms, political, economic, social, and cultural action must always have reference to the needs and nature of the liberated territory, and it is from these needs and nature that the action must derive authenticity. Unless this self-reference is religiously maintained, a liberated territory will welcome with open arms the very foe which it has sought to destroy at cost of terrible suffering. . . .

19. J. A. Ankrah

Lieutenant General Joseph A. Ankrah is Chairman of the National Liberation Council of Ghana, which overthrew Kwame Nkrumah on February 24, 1966. He was born in 1915 and attended the Methodist Secondary School in Accra, from which he was graduated in 1937. After a short period in the Gold Coast civil service, he joined the Royal West African Frontier Force, rising to the rank of warrant officer. Following cadet training in Britain in 1946–47, he received his commission and returned to the Gold Coast, where he served with various units of the army, including two years with the U.N. Peace-keeping Force in the Congo in 1960–61. Returning to Ghana, he supervised the "Ghanaianization" of the Army Command that followed the removal of its British general in 1962.

The following selection is taken from Ankrah's broadcast to the nation four days after the army took power. In it he denounced the dictatorial actions of Nkrumah, placing special emphasis on the economic problems the Ghanaian President's policies had created. He also reaffirmed the policy of nonalignment and promised an end to the policy of subversion of other African states for which Nkrumah was frequently criticized. Also worthy of note are Ankrah's references to the tribal practice of "destooling" incompetent rulers, and his reassurances to the Ghanaian chiefs, who had sometimes opposed Nkrumah's attempts to substitute rule by the party for that of traditional authorities. The influence of the United States Constitution is evident in the instructions of the National Liberation Council to the Constitutional Reform Commission, directing it to draft a constitution based on the separation of powers.

BROADCAST TO THE NATION*

Four days ago, on Thursday, February 24, 1966, the Ghana Armed Forces, in cooperation with the Ghana Police Service, took over the reins of government of this country after a successful overthrow of the regime of Kwame Nkrumah in what may be truly described as one of the most historic and boldest ventures in the history of this country. Following upon this epoch-making event, the National Liberation Council has been established to run the affairs of this country until true democracy based on the popular will of the people, and not on the will of one man alone, has been fully restored to this country.

Your calmness and restraint at this most critical period, your congratulatory messages, and your demonstrations of support for this long-awaited change assure us, the members of the National Liberation Council, that the takeover is a popular desire and encourage us in our determined effort to pave the way for the achievement of a better life for all our people.

It is necessary that at the very outset you should know and understand the reasons which have necessitated the overthrow of the old government and be informed in no uncertain terms of the policies which the National Liberation Council intends to pursue to put this country on the right road to national prosperity.

This grave step was taken because no other means was available to restore to the people of Ghana the blessings of liberty, justice, happiness, and prosperity for which we all have struggled for so long.

In taking this bold step, the Ghana Armed Forces and the Ghana Police Service acted in accord with the oldest and most treasured tradition of the people of Ghana, the tradition that a leader who loses the confidence and support of his people and resorts to the arbitrary use of power should be deposed.

No one can doubt that Kwame Nkrumah has completely lost the trust and confidence of the people of this country through his capricious use of power and the draconian measures he resorted to

* Excerpts from *The Rebirth of Ghana—The End of Tyranny* (Accra: Ministry of Information, 1966).

at the expense of our national institutions. It is not necessary for me, in the short time available to me for this broadcast, to recount the whole catalogue of the acts of maladministration of the old government led by Kwame Nkrumah and his band of lackeys, cronies, sycophants, and political renegades.

It is known to all of you that Kwame Nkrumah was entrusted with the leadership and government of this country in the sincere hope that with the attainment of independence, he would pilot the affairs of this country on sound democratic lines and tackle the task of reconstruction of our economy in the right way for the establishment of a welfare state. In the exercise of this trust, so unreservedly reposed in him by the people of this country, he took advantage of the pure faith of his people to establish by intimidation, exemplified in the pernicious weapon of detention, a one-man dictatorship based on a so-called democratic centralism.

A mere eighteen years ago, the United Kingdom Government, which had ruled this country for over a century, began to release the strings of government to the people of Ghana. The country then was blessed, on the final attainment of political independence, with an adequate exchequer and an able and competent personnel in all our departments of state, who could successfully continue the intricate work of government after the departure of the British colonial officials.

We believed then, as we believe now, that the people of Ghana with their own destiny in their hands could develop this country into a happy state and under a constitution based on popular will and support. It was never anticipated nor was it the wish of the Ghanaian people that the powers of the state should derive from one man, or that the representatives of the people should share one political ideology.

Until the historic coup last Thursday, one man had collected all power into his own hands with the pretentious claim that he enjoyed the unqualified and absolute support of the 7 million people of this country. This man was Kwame Nkrumah, Africa's number one tyrant and dictator. The rights of the people to vote at a free general election for their own chosen candidates were reduced to a formal and farcical privilege of sanctioning the election of such candidates as Kwame Nkrumah himself nominated.

His love for the arbitrary use of power, as is well known to you all, led him to whittle away gradually the independence of the judiciary, and to suppress academic freedom, fundamentals upon which the rights and freedom of the individual are based.

He brought Ghana to the brink of economic disaster by mismanagement, waste, and unwise spending. Incomes are falling, the cost of living is rising, unemployment has struck many families. The basic necessities of life are often either unavailable or can be obtained only at cutthroat prices. Yet Ghana is rich in natural resources.

It is against this general background of maladministration, mismanagement, the loss of individual freedom, and economic chaos into which the country has been plunged by Kwame Nkrumah and his band that I have come here to outline to you, and the people of Ghana, the policies which the National Liberation Council wishes to adopt to put the country on an even keel, politically, socially, and economically. The task will by no means be an easy one.

The economic problems facing the country are many and diverse. The foreign reserves of the country have all disappeared as a result of the implementation of costly prestige projects and undertakings, uncontrolled expenditure by the ex-President, unnecessary costly foreign adventures aimed at enhancing his own personal prestige.

Let me give you a few examples. The State House project, known as Job 600, cost us more than 20 million cedis [$24 million]. What have we gained from it? I leave it to you to answer. We have a number of airplanes standing idle at the Accra airport; yet we are all the time paying for them and their pilots. Massive sums of money are spent every month to maintain an unnecessarily large force of so-called security officers whose duty is ostensibly to provide for the security of the state but really to secure Nkrumah's own personal safety.

He established a private army of his own, at an annual cost of over half a million pounds, in flagrant violation of a constitution which he himself had foisted on the country, to serve as a counterpoise to the Ghana Armed Forces.

All these have been going on at a time when most of us cannot get ordinary food to buy to eat. Let us consider the present prices of cassava, tomatoes, pepper, rice, milk, bread. How many of us are able to buy these basic needs with our incomes which have dwindled in terms of real value with the rising prices over the past years? We are very close to famine and starvation.

Unemployment has been rising fast over the years. With our population showing a relatively high growth rate, policies should have been pursued to create more job openings for the people. You all know the frustrations which those who have been going to the employment centers have felt. The unemployed have been spending their times at the new resting spots of Accra on empty stomachs. . . .

With regard to Ghana's policy on African affairs, I wish to assure all members of the OAU that Ghana will continue to maintain friendly relations with them. If the old regime had offended any independent African state either by means of press vilification, subversion, or through diplomatic misconduct, the National Liberation Council of Ghana wishes to make it clear that a new leaf has been opened as from February 24, 1966.

To this end one of the first acts of the National Liberation Council will be to re-establish good relations between Ghana, Togo, Ivory Coast, Upper Volta, and Niger. We shall be sending special missions to our sister neighboring states as soon as possible.

The members of the Council and myself are pledged to honor the Charter of the Organization of African Unity and abide strictly by the Organization of African Unity resolutions on political refugees and on subversion. The days of harboring and training political refugees to subvert other states are over. The Council has already given instructions that all known political refugees from independent African states will only be allowed to remain in Ghana if they abide very strictly by the Organization of African Unity resolutions on political refugees. The Council has further directed that all other subversive elements from independent African states should leave Ghana forthwith.

As already announced, the National Liberation Council of Ghana will work toward the strengthening of the Organization of African Unity. The new Ghana accepts all member states as equals. Ghana will respect the sovereignty and territorial integrity of each state. If Ghana has any disputes with other African states these will be settled peacefully by negotiation, mediation, conciliation, and arbitration.

In accordance with the Organization of African Unity Charter, Ghana will support all legitimate efforts to promote the unity and solidarity of African states and to coordinate and intensify genuine efforts to achieve a better life for the peoples of Africa. Ghana will pay her contributions to the Organization of African Unity Liberation Committee and assist in the liberation of the remaining colonial territories in Africa.

In this spirit of brotherhood and genuine friendship the new Ghana sincerely hopes that all other independent African states will reciprocate our efforts and thus jointly help to bring a new order and life not only in Ghana, but also in Africa.

As the National Liberation Council has already stated, Ghana will not automatically change her foreign policy at this stage and to that end we shall continue to follow a policy of nonalignment.

In the past, as you all know, mere lip service was paid to this policy of nonalignment by the now deposed tyrant and autocrat. The National Liberation Council will, on its part, adhere strictly to this policy of neutrality both in theory and in practice, always guided by the highest interests of the state.

We have a gigantic task before us to build our country and to resuscitate its economy. We shall direct all our energies toward this goal. In pursuance of this policy, we should not be misunderstood as adopting a neutral attitude toward world problems. Ghana will continue to work for world peace and will associate herself with every effort designed to promote international harmony and friendship among nations. . . .

As already announced repeatedly on Radio Ghana, the armed forces and the police who put their lives at stake to bring about this long-awaited change from Nkrumah's oppressive regime to a democratic form of government have no ambition whatsoever to rule this country indefinitely. This is why the National Liberation Council has announced its intention to appoint a Constitutional Reform Commission to produce a draft constitution acceptable to all sections of our people.* The recommendations of the Constitutional Reform Commission for a new constitution will be presented to the nation for adoption at a referendum. . . .

The new regime headed by me wishes to assure all the people of Ghana that it will not seek to antagonize any section of the population and that every effort will be made by the National Liberation Council to pacify the people of Ghana for the wrongs and injustices perpetrated by the corrupt and dictatorial regime which has now been ousted.

In this connection the National Liberation Council has decided that following the disbandment of the Convention People's Party,

---

* On February 26, 1966, the National Liberation Council announced that the Commission would be directed to prepare "a constitution in which the sovereign powers of the state are fairly and judiciously shared between the three principal organs of the state—the legislature, executive, and judiciary," so as to "make it impossible for power to be concentrated in the hands of a single individual."—ED.

the dissolution of the National Assembly, and the suspension of the Constitution, the Convention People's Party flag which was so whimsically imposed on the country as the national flag shall cease forthwith to be the national flag of Ghana. The National Liberation Council is accordingly taking the necessary steps to restore the original national flag of Ghana consisting of three equal horizontal stripes, the upper stripe being red, the middle stripe yellow, and the lower stripe green, with a black star in the center of the yellow stripe.

Fellow Ghanaians and Friends, I give every assurance to all members of the public service—the civil service, the judiciary, the armed forces, the police and prison services, the local government service, statutory boards and corporations, and all institutions of higher education—that they will be left in peace to carry out their tasks without unnecessary interference. I extend also to our traditional rulers an assurance that we shall respect the institution of chieftaincy and recognize the role which the chiefs will play in the development of the new Ghana. In the same spirit we appeal to all Ghanaian refugees now outside Ghana who suffered in diverse ways at the hand of the old regime to return home to help in our task of nation-building on sounder democratic lines.

Finally, we appeal to our hard-working farmers, fishermen, artisans, and workers, all commercial houses, private businessmen in all sectors of the economy to give us their full support in our task of reconstructing the economy of Ghana to bring real happiness and prosperity to all our people.

20. The Cabinet of Kenya

While nearly all African leaders subscribe to the doctrine of African socialism, it is not always clear what they mean by the term. Senghor, Nkrumah, and Nyerere have made attempts to define it; in Kenya, the definition has been a joint effort of the entire cabinet under the leadership of President Jomo Kenyatta. Originally drafted in the Ministry of Economic Planning under Tom Mboya, the

Sessional Paper on African Socialism was discussed, modified, and approved by the cabinet and subsequently endorsed by the Kenya Parliament.

The document attempts to spell out the implications of a commitment to African socialism for the future economic development of Kenya. As in the writings of other Africans, both Marxism and laissez-faire capitalism are criticized as antiquated and inapplicable to African problems. Socialism is seen as implying political democracy, social responsibility, and limits on the ownership of land. However, the paper indicates a wide range of choices available to the government as to the specific means to be utilized in developing the country. In terms perhaps stronger than those of any other socialist statement, the paper lists the reasons against a policy of nationalization, but recognizes that in some cases it may be necessary. There is also support for the creation of a single trade union, despite the fact that Kenya has specifically decided against the creation of a one-party state. (In 1966, an opposition party broke away from the Kenya African National Union [KANU] and elected several members to Parliament in a special by-election.)

AFRICAN SOCIALISM AND ITS APPLICATION TO PLANNING IN KENYA*

. . . The system adopted in Kenya is African socialism, but the characteristics of the system and the economic mechanisms it implies have never been spelled out fully in an agreed form.

In the phrase "African socialism," the word "African" is not introduced to describe a continent to which a foreign ideology is to be transplanted. It is meant to convey the African roots of a system that is itself African in its characteristics. African socialism is a term describing an African political and economic system that is positively African, not being imported from any country or being a blueprint of any foreign ideology, but capable of incorporating useful and compatible techniques from whatever source. The principal conditions the system must satisfy are: (i) it must draw

* Published by the Government of Kenya, Nairobi, 1965.

on the best of African traditions; (ii) it must be adaptable to new and rapidly changing circumstances; and (iii) it must not rest for its success on a satellite relationship with any other country or group of countries.

African Traditions

There are two African traditions which form an essential basis for African socialism—political democracy and mutual social responsibility. Political democracy implies that each member of society is equal in his political rights and that no individual or group will be permitted to exert undue influence on the policies of the state. The state, therefore, can never become the tool of special interests, catering to the desires of a minority at the expense of the needs of the majority. The state will represent all of the people and will do so impartially and without prejudice.

Political democracy in the African traditional sense provided a genuine hedge against the exercise of disproportionate political power by economic power groups. In African society a man was born politically free and equal and his voice and counsel were heard and respected regardless of the economic wealth he possessed. Even where traditional leaders appeared to have greater wealth and hold disproportionate political influence over their tribal or clan community, there were traditional checks and balances including sanctions against any possible abuse of such power. In fact, traditional leaders were regarded as trustees whose influence was circumscribed both in customary law and religion. In the traditional African society, an individual needed only to be a mature member of it to participate fully and equally in political affairs. Political rights did not derive from or relate to economic wealth or status. When this is translated into our modern state it means that to participate in political matters and party activities as an equal, the individual must prove nothing beyond age and citizenship and need take no oath beyond allegiance to country.

Political democracy in the African tradition would not, therefore, countenance a party of the elite, stern tests or discriminatory criteria for party membership, degrees of party membership, or first and second class citizens. In African socialism every member of society is important and equal; every mature citizen can belong to the party without restriction or discrimination; and the party will entertain and accommodate different points of view. African socialism rests on full, equal, and unfettered democracy. Thus,

African socialism differs politically from Communism because it ensures every mature citizen equal political rights and from capitalism because it prevents the exercise of disproportionate political influence by economic power groups. Another fundamental force in African traditional life was religion, which provided a strict moral code for the community. This will be a prominent feature of African socialism.

Mutual social responsibility is an extension of the African family spirit to the nation as a whole, with the hope that ultimately the same spirit can be extended to ever larger areas. It implies a mutual responsibility by society and its members to do their very best for each other with the full knowledge and understanding that if society prospers its members will share in that prosperity and that society cannot prosper without the full cooperation of its members. The state has an obligation to ensure equal opportunities to all its citizens, eliminate exploitation and discrimination, and provide needed social services such as education, medical care, and social security.

To ensure success in the endeavors of the government, all citizens must contribute, to the degree they are able, to the rapid development of the economy and society. Every member of African traditional society had a duty to work. This duty was acknowledged and willingly accepted by members because the mechanism for sharing society's benefits, the reciprocal response of society to the individual's contribution, was definite, automatic, and universally recognized. But the response of society was not simply a passive one. African society had the power and duty to impose sanctions on those who refused to contribute their fair share of hard work to the common endeavor.

Drawing on this background, African socialism expects the members of the modern state to contribute willingly and without stint to the development of the nation. Society, in turn, will reward these efforts and at the same time will take measures against those who refuse to participate in the nation's efforts to grow. Sending needed capital abroad, allowing land to lie idle and undeveloped, misusing the nation's limited resources, and conspicuous consumption when the nation needs savings are examples of antisocial behavior that African socialism will not countenance.

While the modern economy is more complex than traditional society, the principle remains that to be successful, society and its members must each acknowledge fully and willingly its responsibility to the other. But the movement toward a modern, monetary economy changes the nature of these responsibilities and the mechanisms by which a member contributes to society and society shares benefits among its members. The people must be continually and carefully informed of what society expects of them and how these efforts will promote the welfare of all. . . .

Economic Nonalignment

. . . Ideologies and the theoretical systems on which they are based are rigid and uncompromising while the development over time of all viable practical systems has been marked by adaptability to change, frequently of substantial proportions. Marxian socialism and laissez-faire capitalism are both theoretical economic organizations designed to ensure the use of resources for the benefit of society. Both settled on the ownership of property as the critical factor in economic organization and advocated rigid systems based in the one case on state ownership and in the other on private ownership. But ownership is not an absolute, indivisible right subject only to complete control or none. Practical systems have demonstrated that the resources of society are best guided into proper uses by a range of sensitive controls each specifically designed for the task to be performed. . . .

As predictive models of what would happen to factory-system societies, both Marxian socialism and laissez-faire capitalism have been failures. The economic systems in actual use throughout the world today bear little resemblance to either model. The Industrial Revolution quickly led to the social protest of which Marx was a part and this in turn resulted in sweeping political and economic changes as the systems of the world adapted to the new state of technological change. Political democracy was achieved; private property rights were diluted; the state accepted increasing responsibilities for social services, planning, guidance, and control; taxes were made progressive to distribute benefits more widely. Capitalism did not evolve into Marxian socialism, as Marx predicted, but was indeed modified in directions that Marx might well have approved.

The adaptability of these systems has a parallel in those countries that have attempted to follow Marx. To become effective, these systems, too, have had to demonstrate an ability to adapt to changing circumstances. They have adopted wage differentials and management incentives, permitted various forms of ownership, and utilized interest rates or the equivalent in their planning procedures. All practical economic systems, regardless of their origin, have demonstrated adaptability. The problems of today are not the problems of a century ago. African socialism is designed to be a working system in a modern setting, fully prepared to adapt itself to changing circumstances and new problems. . . .

Relationships with Other Countries

. . . Economic nonalignment does not mean a policy of isolation, any more than political nonalignment implies a refusal to participate in world affairs. On the contrary it means a willingness and a desire: (i) to borrow technological knowledge and proven economic methods from any country—without commitment; (ii) to seek and accept technical and financial assistance from any source—without strings; and (iii) to participate fully in world trade —without political domination.

The ability of Africa to borrow advanced technological knowledge, modern methods of industrial organization, and economic techniques of control and guidance from more advanced countries provides the opportunity to leap over many of the hurdles that have restrained development in these modern societies in the past. It means also that African socialism as a system can profit from the mistakes of others. Unlike many countries that have eliminated many successful economic mechanisms on narrow ideological grounds, Kenya is free to pick and choose those methods that have been proven in practice and are adaptable to Kenya conditions regardless of the ideologies that others may attach to them. Kenya, therefore, is free to choose, among other things: (i) a wages-and-incomes policy that recognizes the need for differential incentives as well as an equitable distribution of income; (ii) techniques of production that combine efficiencies of scale with diffused ownership; (iii) various forms of ownership—state, cooperative, corporate and individual—that are efficient for different sectors or that compete with each other provided only that the form promotes the objectives of government; and (iv) techniques of control that vary with the needs of society and its members. . . .

African Socialism and Land Ownership

There is some conflict of opinion with regard to the traditional attitude toward rights to land. Some allege that land was essentially communally or tribally owned; others claim that individual rights were the distinguishing feature; still others suggest that ownership did not really exist in any modern context in many African tribes. Undoubtedly these traditions differed substantially from one tribe to another. In every case, however, and in sharp contrast to the European tradition, ownership was not an absolute indivisible bundle of rights. The ultimate right of disposal outside the tribe was essentially tribal and in this land was tribally owned. It must be remembered, however, that the political arrangements within the tribe were such that every mature member of the tribe would have a say in such a decision. Short of this right, others were assigned or allocated to clans, families, and individuals, including the right to transfer and reclaim property within the clan. Rights to use land were, in effect, assigned in perpetuity to various groups within the tribe, subject always, however, and this is significant to an understanding of African socialism, to the condition that resources must be properly used and their benefits appropriately distributed, not merely held idle, abused or misused, or the benefits hoarded. The rights normally associated in Europe with ownership as such scarcely mattered.

What does emerge with clarity and force and as a single, unifying principle from these discussions of traditional property rights is that land and other productive assets, no matter who owned or managed them, were expected to be *used*, and used for the general welfare. No individual family or clan could treat productive assets as private property unless the uses to which those assets were put were regarded as consonant with the general welfare. Unlike the traditional European approach to ownership, no person could treat a piece of land as his own with the freedom to use it or not as he chose. It is worth noting that over the past century, the European tradition of absolute ownership has gradually been eroded so that today the right of the state to guide, plan, and even order the uses to which property will be put is universally recognized and unquestioned.

These African traditions cannot be carried over indiscriminately to a modern, monetary economy. The need to develop and invest requires credit and a credit economy rests heavily on a system of land titles and their registration. The ownership of land must, therefore, be made more definite and explicit if land consolidation and development are to be fully successful. It does not follow, however, that society will also give up its stake in how resources are used. Indeed, it is a fundamental characteristic of African socialism that society has a duty to plan, guide, and control the uses of all productive resources.

Control of Resource Use

Under African socialism the power to control resource use resides with the state. To imagine, however, that the use of resources can only be controlled through their ownership or that the appropriate ownership will guarantee the proper use of productive assets are errors of great magnitude. Ownership can be abused whether private or public and ways must be found to control resource use in either case. African socialism must rely on planning to determine the appropriate uses of productive resources on a range of controls to ensure that plans are carried out. . . .

Class Problem

The sharp class divisions that once existed in Europe have no place in African socialism and no parallel in African society. No class problem arose in the traditional African society and none exists today among Africans. The class problem in Africa, therefore, is largely one of prevention, in particular: (i) to eliminate the risk of foreign economic domination; and (ii) to plan development so as to prevent the emergence of antagonistic classes. In addition, Kenya has the special problem of eliminating classes that have arisen largely on the basis of race.

The class divisions that Marx deplored in Europe a century ago were supported and strengthened by three factors: (i) a concentration of economic power; (ii) the treatment of private ownership as an absolute, unrestricted right; and (iii) the close relationship between economic power and political influence. The concept of political equality in Africa rules out in principle the use of economic power as a political base. The vigorous implementation of traditional political democracy in the modern setting will eliminate, therefore, one of the critical factors promoting class divisions. The policy of African socialism to control by various means how productive resources are used eliminates the second of the factors supporting a class system. Without its two supporting allies, the concentration of economic power cannot be the threat it once was, but African socialism proposes to restrict and guard against this factor as well with regard to both foreign and domestic concentrations.

Foreign Investors

Foreigners have no vote and can only have a political voice, now that independence has been achieved, by enlisting the support of Kenya citizens. Nevertheless, the foreign ownership and management of productive assets could mean that economic decisions in Kenya might be dominated by foreign rather than domestic considerations. Foreign investors should therefore be prepared to accept the spirit of mutual social responsibility, for example: (i) by making shares in the company available to Africans who wish to buy them; (ii) by employing Africans at managerial levels as soon as qualified people can be found; and (iii) by providing training facilities for Africans. . . .

Nationalization

Nationalization is a useful tool that has already been used in Kenya and will be used again when circumstances require. The pertinent questions are at what cost, for what purpose, and when. The Constitution and the KANU Manifesto make it clear that African socialism in Kenya does not imply a commitment to indiscriminate nationalization. These documents do commit the government to prompt payment of full compensation whenever nationalization is used. Kenya's policy with respect to nationalization should be more clearly defined within these stipulations.

It should be recognized that if the nation's limited domestic capital is used to buy existing land, livestock, buildings, machinery, and equipment, the nation has no more productive assets than before—only their ownership has changed. What may be lost are the new resources that could have been purchased instead—the new schools, hospitals, roads, water supplies, irrigation schemes, rolling stock, land surveys, housing, lodges, airports, and harbor development—and the employment opportunities and added output that these new developments would create. Further, the money paid for nationalized resources and the people who managed them before nationalization would most likely leave the country, increasing our foreign-exchange and skilled-manpower problems. There is also the firm likelihood that nationalization would discourage additional private investment, thus reducing further the rate of growth of the economy. It is also the case that the use of domestic capital to nationalize would reduce our ability to match foreign-aid funds leading to an even greater reduction in development expenditure. Finally, some speak of nationalization as though it should be applicable only to non-African enterprises. If the policy were applied to an economic activity, such as bus transportation, it would affect everyone, African and otherwise, owning productive resources in the industry.

Though the cost is great, there may be circumstances when nationalization will be needed: (i) when the assets in private hands threaten the security or undermine the integrity of the nation; or (ii) when productive resources are being wasted; or (iii) when the operation of an industry by private concerns has a serious detrimental effect on the public interest; and (iv) when other less costly means of control are not available or are not effective.

It must also be clear that, in most cases, when an industry is nationalized it must be operated efficiently, cover its costs, and earn a profit at least equivalent to the taxes paid when operated privately. If taxes must be used year after year to subsidize its operation, the nation has gained little if anything by the act of nationalization. . . .

Trade Unions

The rights of industrial workers must be fully protected as development takes place and much of this work can be left to responsible unions. But the unions now represent only a small minority of Kenya's adult population and they cannot be permitted to benefit these few at the expense of large numbers of less fortunate brothers. Experience in all developing countries has shown that in the interests of stability and good industrial relations government cannot permit the existence of more than one central organization for trade unions in the country. It is also desirable to have one central organization for employers.

The first responsibility of the unions must be to develop a disciplined, skilled, and responsible labor force. The nation's welfare and that of the workers depend much more on hard, productive work than on strikes and walkouts. Unions must concern themselves with training programs, apprentice programs, and workers' discipline and productivity. In addition, trade unions assisted by government should take an active role in organizing consumer cooperatives, generating savings for development, promoting cooperative housing development, initiating producer cooperatives, and making workers aware of their contribution to the development of the nation.

Strikes cost the nation output, the workers wages, the companies profits, and the government taxes. Wages in excess of those warranted by productivity increase the unemployment, encourage the substitution of capital for labor, and lead to bankruptcies. In order to avoid these drags on development, legislation will be needed providing for the compulsory arbitration of major issues not resolved through the regular bargaining process. Special legislation may be needed in sensitive industries and the government to avoid the economic paralysis that could result from work stoppages in these areas.

The Government will assume the responsibility for holding down the prices of basic commodities so that workers, farmers, and unemployed are not confronted with a rising cost of living. . . .

21. Julius Nyerere

Julius Nyerere, the President of the Republic of Tanzania, was born in 1922, the son of a Tanganyikan tribal chief. He was educated in Catholic schools, received his B.A. from Makerere College in Uganda, and his M.A. from the University of Edinburgh. After his return to Tanganyika, he became President of the Tanganyika African Association, which he transformed in 1954 into the Tanganyika African National Union (TANU). As Tanganyika moved toward independence, TANU virtually monopolized political activity, and when independence was granted in October, 1961, Nyerere became Prime Minister. In November, 1962, after a change in the Constitution, he was elected President of the Tanganyika Republic; when Zanzibar joined Tanganyika in the Republic of Tanzania in 1964, he became President of the new state, a position to which he was re-elected without opposition in September, 1965.

His writing and speeches on African subjects have been prolific and original. One of the leaders of the Pan-African movement, he has been critical of both East and West in what he sees as their attempts to dominate independent Africa. In his attempt to define African socialism, Nyerere has related the concept to traditional notions of familyhood, advocating limits on land ownership and an extension of the family sense of mutual responsibility to the nation and ultimately to the world. In his view, capitalism is the attempt to dominate others; he believes that ownership must be conditioned and limited by the good of society.

Nyerere's most distinctive contribution is his defense of the one-party state in Africa. Arguing that a multiplicity of parties is the result of class conflicts, which are absent in Africa, he advocates a single "National Movement" in which there is complete freedom of individual criticism and action but no organized factions. His thinking received concrete application in the recommendations of a 1965 Presidential Commission that the party give the voter a choice by nominating several candidates in each constituency (although only one for President). In the elections carried out under this system in September, 1965, several cabinet ministers were defeated.

THE ROLE OF AFRICAN TRADE UNIONS*

I think the time has come to re-examine our ideas about the trade-union movement in Africa and its relationship with the nationalist movements. Here again, we are in danger of accepting, without thought, the Western pattern, regardless of the fact that it makes little or no sense in Africa.

In Great Britain and in America, the trade unionists have come to believe that the trade-union movement must be "independent of any political party." Superficially, this sounds attractive; any slogan that can bring in the word "independence" always does sound attractive, so that its very appeal to the emotions automatically tends to stifle further thought about what it means. Let us try to find out how this idea of independence from the political parties grew, and what it does mean.

A great deal of the confused thinking on the part of those who

* Reprinted from *Labour* (Accra), June, 1961.

pontificate about African trade unions stems from their having forgotten a very important fact—that the trade unions and the labor, or socialist, parties of Europe are two wings of the same labor movement. Trade unionism first came into being as a result of the industrial revolution and the division of the Western countries between "labor" and "capital."

At first, unorganized labor was completely at the mercy of the employers, by whom it was exploited in more than one sense of the word. The workers then decided that they must organize themselves for the purpose of collective bargaining with the employers; to put it bluntly, they realized that they must fight for their rights against their exploiters, and that to do so they must organize.

It was not long before the workers found that their trade unions alone were not enough. In industry, the unions could bargain with the employers; but the employers still had the last word, for they were also the rulers of the country.

If the new labor movement was to have any influence over the laws affecting industrial conditions, it must have a voice in parliament. The workers must organize themselves into political parties as well as into trade unions; when the political prong had been added to the industrial one, the labor movement was complete.

In those early days there was no confusion of thought. The Labour Party in England, for instance, was quite clearly part of the same movement as the trade unions, and if anybody then had talked of the need for trade unions to be "independent of any political party," he would have been told he was talking nonsense.

If, on the other hand, he had said the trade-union movement must be independent of the government, he would merely have been stating the obvious; because at that time the "government" was the same thing as the industrialists—the exploiters—against whom the whole movement had been organized. The need for the labor movement to be free from any control by the capitalists is not a doctrine; it is a self-evident definition.

This fact, however, has gradually been forgotten, and forgetting it has led to some ridiculous results. In Britain, for instance, one would have expected that when once the labor movement succeeded in forming a government of its own, the whole movement would rejoice. But no! When this did eventually happen, only one prong of the labor movement rejoiced—the political prong. The other, the industrial prong, from long force of habit remained sulky and suspicious! . . .

·Habit, no less than emotion, has an unhappy tendency to stop people from thinking. The rule that you must not allow yourself to be controlled by the enemy springs from the very definition of "enemy." The labor movement applied this rule correctly in the days when Britain was controlled by the capitalists. But then, somehow, the rule slipped imperceptibly into some general doctrine of the independence of trade unions from *any* political control.

As a result, when the labor movement won its resounding victory after the end of World War II, the victory, instead of being seen in its true light as a victory of the whole movement, was looked at as only a Labour Party victory. . . . They [the unions] had for so long accepted the doctrine that trade unions must be independent and suspicious of the government that they had come to believe this meant *any* government—including, I suppose, a government 100 per cent trade unionist.

A socialist government either is socialist or it is not. A trade-union movement either is socialist or it is not. If a government *is* a socialist government, representing the working peoples of the country, then it must be acknowledged and treated as such, not only by the capitalists, but by the workers themselves. The workers can no more be independent of it than it can be independent of the workers.

Of course, if the particular individuals who happen at any given time to form the government do not carry out the policies for which the labor movement as a whole stands, they can be replaced, in the normal democratic way, by the labor movement itself. But there can be no logic in any *part* of the labor movement trying to have it both ways. . . .

I said the time had come to re-examine our ideas about the trade-union movement in Africa. So far, I have been dealing with European, and particularly British, trade unions. I have done this deliberately, in order to bring out one thing: that particular patterns or traditions grow up in different countries because of the historical circumstances peculiar to those countries during the period of growth, and that these habits of thought tend to become accepted as essential to trade unionism when, in fact, they are not.

I have tried to indicate why, in the case of Great Britain especially, the doctrine or habit of trade unions being independent of political control is the result of the original necessity for their independence from what was then a capitalist government, and how this habit of thought has slipped into a meaningless formula of independence from political control generally.

In Britain, the fact that the formula is meaningless saves it from doing much harm, for the British are accustomed to taking their political slogans with a pinch of salt, with a ruling class of industrialists or employers associated with political power, against whom it has been necessary for the workers to organize first an industrial and then a political movement. Our development has been the other way around. When, six years ago, we established our nationalist movement, its first aim was political—independence from colonialism. Within this nationalist movement, and very much a part of it, one of our objectives was to help the growth of a trade-union movement.

We have an officer in the organization whose special duty it was to stimulate and help the growth of trade unionism. Once firmly established, the trade-union movement was, and is, part and parcel of the whole nationalist movement. In the early days, when a trade union went on strike, for instance, and its members were in direct need of funds to keep them going, we saw no doctrine that would be abrogated by our giving financial support from the political wing to the industrial wing of the same nationalist movement.

It was simply a case of the right hand helping the left hand, or vice versa. It would clearly have been ridiculous to preach an imported doctrine of independence of the Tanganyika Federation of Labour from political control, and so to deny them the assistance they needed from the Tanganyika African Nationalist Union.*

NATIONALISM AND PAN-AFRICANISM†

You have asked me to speak on African unity. I am an advocate of African unity. I believe firmly that, just as unity was necessary for the achievement of independence in Tanganyika or any other nation, unity is equally necessary to consolidate and maintain the

---

* In 1964, the Tanganyika Federation of Labour was reorganized as the National Union of Tanganyika Workers and directly affiliated with TANU. —Ed.

† Excerpts from a speech delivered by Nyerere to the Second Pan-African Seminar, World Assembly of Youth. Reprinted, by permission, from WAY Forum, No. 40 (September, 1961).

independence which we are now achieving in different parts of Africa.

I believe that, left to ourselves, we can achieve unity on the African continent. But I don't believe that we are going to be left to ourselves! I believe that the phase through which we are emerging successfully is the phase of the first scramble for Africa—and Africa's reaction to it. We are now entering a new phase. It is the phase of the second scramble for Africa. And just as in the first one tribe was divided against another tribe to make the division of Africa easier, in the second the technique will be to try to divide one nation against another nation, to make it easier to control Africa by making her weak and divided against herself.

It is for this reason, therefore, that before we can talk complacently about "African unity," we should examine carefully the external ideas that are likely to be imposed upon us, imposed not for the purpose of uniting us, but for the purpose of dividing us!

Two Blocs

Today the world is divided into two blocs—what one might call the "capitalist bloc" and the "socialist bloc," but generally referred to as the "Western bloc" and the "Eastern bloc." I have said "capitalist" and "socialist" for a good reason—it makes it easier to understand the forces behind these divisions.

What is wrong with capitalism? To my mind, capitalism went wrong when it divorced wealth from its true purpose. The true purpose of wealth is to satisfy very simple needs: the need for food, the need for shelter, the need for education, and so on. In other words, the end of wealth is the banishment of poverty—and wealth is to poverty what light is to darkness.

There is enough wealth in every state for every individual to satisfy these simple needs. But the moment individuals in any single state begin to use wealth not for the satisfaction of those needs, not for the banishment of poverty, but for the purpose of acquiring power and prestige—then there is no longer enough. Then wealth tolerates poverty; then wealth is no longer to poverty what light is to darkness. For there is not enough wealth in any nation to satisfy the desire for power and the prestige of every individual.

So what happens? There is then ruthless competition between individuals—not to get wealth to feed themselves, or to clothe themselves, or to house themselves, but to seize enough wealth to give themselves more power, more prestige than their fellows, i.e., wealth that exceeds their real needs and will enable them to dominate other individuals. When that stage is reached, one millionaire is prepared to spend millions simply in order to destroy another millionaire.

I believe that the purpose of socialism was to remove this sin of capitalism and to return wealth to its original use—the satisfaction of simple human needs, the banishment of poverty. I think it would be hypocrisy on the part of the capitalist countries—not to recognize the fact that this is happening in the socialist countries; that, within those countries, personal wealth is not a symbol of power or prestige, and wealth is used to banish poverty.

But I believe that the socialist countries themselves, considered as individuals in the larger society of nations, are now committing the same crime that was committed by capitalists before. I believe that, on the international level, they are now beginning to use wealth for the purpose of acquiring power and prestige! It would be equally hypocritical on the part of the socialist countries to deny this. Internationally, they are now engaged in using wealth in exactly the same way as the capitalist countries—for power and prestige.

And socialist countries, no less than capitalist countries, are prepared to behave like the millionaire—to use millions to destroy another millionaire; and it need not necessarily be a capitalist millionaire—it is just as likely to be a socialist millionaire. In other words, socialist wealth now tolerates poverty—which is an even more unforgivable crime!

Lure of Slogans

I believe that no underdeveloped country can afford to be anything but socialist. I think, therefore, that we in Africa are bound to organize ourselves on a socialist pattern. But let us at least provide another corrective to socialism, and prevent the wealth we are beginning to build in our own countries from being used for the purpose of acquiring national power or prestige. Let us make sure that it is used solely for raising the standards of our people. Let us not allow the wealth that we are creating to live side by side with poverty, and tolerate that poverty.

. . . I have said already that socialism arose to remedy the mistakes capitalism had made. Karl Marx felt there was an inevitable clash between the rich of one society and the poor of that society. In that, I believe, Karl Marx was right. But today it is the international scene which is going to have a greater impact on the lives of individuals than what is happening within Tanganyika or withiri Uganda. And when you look at the international scene, you must admit that the world is still divided between the "haves" and the "have-nots." This division is not a division between capitalists and socialists, or between capitalists and Communists; this is a division between the poor countries of the world and the rich countries of the world.

The poor countries of the world should be very careful not to allow themselves to be used as the "tools" of any of the rich countries of the world, however much the rich countries may seek to fool them that they are on their side! And don't forget that the rich countries of the world today may be found on either side of the division between capitalist and socialist countries.

I have said all this as a rather long introduction to what I am going to say about African unity. I believe the danger to African unity is going to come from these external forces and slogans which bear no relation to the facts of the world today; from the fact that today the rich countries of the world—both capitalist and socialist—are using their wealth to dominate the poor countries. And they are ready to try to weaken and divide the poor countries for that purpose of domination. That is why I said at the beginning that if we in Africa were left on our own, we would achieve unity on our continent—but that I do not believe we are going to be left alone. And I have explained why I think we are not going to be left alone.

But there is no need for fear. All we need to do is to use our intellect, to know what is good for us. We need to listen to the outside world, to accept from them what we believe is in the best interests of Africa and of African unity, and to reject—and reject in no uncertain terms—what we believe is not in the best interests of Africa and of African unity. And that includes all those attractive but misleading slogans about "democracy" and "socialism" which are too often used to cloak the real designs of the power-hungry. These old slogans bear no relation at all to what Africa is doing, and they are generally used for the purpose of dividing Africa into camps.

Artificial Nations

At the beginning, I used the phrase "the second scramble for Africa." It may sound farfetched, in the context of the Africa of the 1960's. . . . But anybody who thinks this is farfetched has been completely blind to what is happening on the African continent. Take, for example, the Congo: There were obvious weaknesses in the Congo situation, but those weaknesses were deliberately used in a scramble for the control of the Congo.

There are obvious weaknesses on the African continent. We have artificial "nations" carved out at the Berlin Conference;* we are struggling to build these nations into stable units of human society. And these weaknesses, too, are being exploited. We are being reminded daily of these weaknesses. We are told that tribalism will not allow us to build nations. But when we try to take measures to deal with tribalism, we are accused of dictatorship.

Whenever we try to talk in terms of larger units on the African continent, we are told that it can't be done; we are told that the units we would so create would be "artificial." As if they could be any more artificial than the "national" units on which we are now building! Some of the people who say this are genuinely pointing to a difficulty; but I believe many of them are deliberately emphasizing the difficulties on our continent for the express purpose of maintaining them and sabotaging any move to unite Africa.

The technique is very simple. One power bloc labels a move for unity a "Communist plot"—not because it is Communist, but because they don't like it. Another power bloc labels another move for unity an "imperialist plot"—not because it is so, but because they don't like it. What annoys me is not the use of these slogans by power-hungry nations, for this is something we do expect; but what does infuriate me is that they should expect us to allow ourselves to be treated as if we were a bunch of idiots!

So I believe that the second scramble for Africa has begun in real earnest. And it is going to be a much more dangerous scramble than the first one. For what happened in the first scramble? One imperialist power fought another imperialist power for the booty. What do you think is going to happen in the second scramble? No imperialist power is going to fight another imperialist power for

* The Berlin Conference of 1884–85 agreed on the basic principles governing the partition of Africa among the European colonial powers.—ED.

the control of Africa; that would be too crude a method in the context of the 1960's. No. This time, one imperialist power is going to arm one African nation, and another imperialist power is going to arm another African nation, and African brother is going to slaughter African brother—not in the interests of Africa, but in the interests of the imperialists both old and new!

That is why I have often thought we must try and find a method which will enable us, in Africa, to avoid the weaknesses of the "national" state. We have the example of Europe before us, where one national state arms itself against another national state. In the world as it is today, nobody could seriously suggest that an African state can arm itself, or be armed, in order to defend itself against one of the great powers of the world. If an African state is armed realistically, it can only be armed against another African state. I think we should be very careful about this. We must not find ourselves committing the same mistakes committed by the nation-states of other continents; arming ourselves against ourselves, destroying our chances not only of raising the standards of living of our people—which is what we are here for—but also destroying forever the chances of African unity.

African Command

That is why, during the difficulties in the Congo, when the idea of an African Command was first proposed, I was very taken with it. I do think we in Africa should think very seriously of a method by which that idea could be put into practice. All that we need within our national boundaries are sufficient police forces for the purpose of maintaining law and order within those boundaries. As far as large military commitments are concerned, these should be on an African basis.

If such a thing could be done, it would achieve two objectives at least. First, it removes the danger I have already referred to— the danger of arming ourselves against ourselves, and thus depriving ourselves of the chance of achieving African unity, as well as of the materials for raising our people's standards of living. And secondly, it provides a real force for the defense of Africa against external aggression. Once again, I know, people have said that this is impossible, that it can't be done; but I believe it can be done.

What can be the role of the young people of Africa in all this? First, I would like to say that Africa is a young continent in two respects. Internationally, its nations are young nations. But Africa is also young in another sense—it is governed by young people. I think one of the troubles in the modern world is that nuclear power is being handled by people who were born in the nineteenth century and educated in the nineteenth century—people with a Victorian turn of mind who have been overtaken by the achievement of science and by modern ideas about human society.

They have not been able to adjust themselves; and while they repeat some of the slogans which sound very "modern" (and I have already said that many of the ones they shout are not modern at all), their actions are the actions of the past. They talk "unity" —and they divide. One advantage of youth is that it doesn't have this dichotomy. The young have had an education which is a present-day education; their ideas are present-day ideas. Youth, bred from the prejudices of the past, should be able to put into action the ideas which modern society demands—but to which the slogan-shouters do little more than pay lip service. Young leaders everywhere in the world find they are having to fight that Victorian attitude, and you can help them.

I believe that you, the youth of Africa, can understand that the role of African nationalism is different—or should be different— from the nationalism of the past; that the African national state is an instrument for the unification of Africa, and not for dividing Africa; that African nationalism is meaningless, is dangerous, is anachronistic, if it is not at the same time Pan-Africanism.

"UJAMAA": THE BASIS OF AFRICAN SOCIALISM*

. . . In the individual, as in the society, it is an attitude of mind which distinguishes the socialist from the nonsocialist. It has nothing to do with possession or nonpossession of wealth. Destitute people can be potential capitalists—exploiters of their fellow human beings. A millionaire can equally well be a socialist; he may value his wealth only because it can be used in the service of his

* Excerpts from a pamphlet published by the *Tanganyika Standard*, Dar-es-Salaam, 1962.

fellow men. But the man who uses wealth for the purpose of dominating any of his fellows is a capitalist. So is the man who would if he could! . . .

Defenders of capitalism claim that the millionaire's wealth is the just reward for his ability or enterprise. But this claim is not borne out by the facts. The wealth of the millionaire depends as little on the enterprise or abilities of the millionaire himself as the power of a feudal monarch depended on his own efforts, enterprise, or brain. Both are users, exploiters, of the abilities and enterprise of other people. Even when you have an exceptionally intelligent and hard-working millionaire, the difference between his intelligence, his enterprise, his hard work, and those of other members of society, cannot possibly be proportionate to the difference between their "rewards". . . .

Acquisitiveness for the purpose of gaining power and prestige is unsocialist. In an acquisitive society wealth tends to corrupt those who possess it. It tends to breed in them a desire to live more comfortably than their fellows, to dress better, and in every way to outdo them. They begin to feel they must climb as far above their neighbors as they can. The visible contrast between their own comfort and the comparative discomfort of the rest of society becomes almost essential to the enjoyment of their wealth, and this sets off the spiral of personal competition—which is then antisocial.

Apart from the antisocial effects of the accumulation of personal wealth, the very desire to accumulate it must be interpreted as a vote of "no confidence" in the social system. For when a society is so organized that it cares about its individuals, then, provided he is willing to work, no individual within that society should worry about what will happen to him tomorrow if he does not hoard wealth today. Society itself should look after him, or his widow, or his orphans. This is exactly what traditional African society succeeded in doing. Both the "rich" and the "poor" individual were completely secure in African society. Natural catastrophe brought famine, but it brought famine to everybody—"poor" or "rich." Nobody starved, either of food or of human dignity, because he lacked personal wealth; he could depend on the weal possessed by the community of which he was a member. That was socialism. That *is* socialism. There can be no such thing as acquisitive socialism, for that would be another contradiction in terms. Socialism is essentially distributive. Its concern is to see that those who sow reap a fair share of what they sow. . . .

In traditional African society *everybody* was a worker. There was no other way of earning a living for the community. Even the Elder, who appeared to be enjoying himself without doing any work and for whom everybody else appeared to be working, had, in fact, worked hard all his younger days. The wealth he now appeared to possess was not *his*, personally; it was only "his" as the Elder of the group which had produced it. He was its guardian. The wealth itself gave him neither power nor prestige. The respect paid to him by the young was his because he was older than they, and had served his community longer; and the "poor" Elder enjoyed as much respect in our society as the "rich" Elder.

When I say that in traditional African society everybody was a worker, I do not use the word "worker" simply as opposed to "employer" but also as opposed to "loiterer" or "idler." One of the most socialistic achievements of our society was the sense of security it gave to its members, and the universal hospitality on which they could rely. But it is too often forgotten, nowadays, that the basis of this great socialistic achievement was this: that it was taken for granted that every member of society—barring only the children and the infirm—contributed his fair share of effort toward the production of its wealth. Not only was the capitalist, or the landed exploiter, unknown to traditional African society, but we did not have that other form of modern parasite—the loiterer, or idler, who accepts the hospitality of society as his right but gives nothing in return! Capitalistic exploitation was impossible. Loitering was an unthinkable disgrace. . . .

. . . In the old days, the African had never aspired to the possession of personal wealth for the purpose of dominating any of his fellows. He had never had laborers or factory hands to do his work for him. But then came the foreign capitalists. They were wealthy. They were powerful. And the African naturally started wanting to be wealthy too. There is nothing wrong in our wanting to be wealthy; nor is it a bad thing for us to want to acquire the power which wealth brings with it. But it most certainly is wrong if we want the wealth and the power so that we can dominate somebody else. Unfortunately there are some of us who have already learned to covet wealth for that purpose—and who would like to use the methods which the capitalist uses in acquiring it. That is to say, some of us would like to use, or exploit, our brothers for the purpose of building up our own personal power and prestige. This is completely foreign to us, and it is incompatible with the socialist society we want to build here.

Our first step, therefore, must be to re-educate ourselves; to regain our former attitude of mind. In our traditional African society we were individuals within a community. We took care of the community, and the community took care of us. We neither needed nor wished to exploit our fellow men.

And in rejecting the capitalist attitude of mind which colonization brought into Africa, we must reject also the capitalist methods which go with it. One of these is the individual ownership of land. To us in Africa, land was always recognized as belonging to the community. Each individual within our society had a right to the use of land, because otherwise he could not earn his living and one cannot have the right to life without also having the right to some means of maintaining life. But the African's right to land was simply the right to *use* it; he had no other right to it, nor did it occur to him to try and claim one.

The foreigner introduced a completely different concept—the concept of land as a marketable commodity. According to this system, a person could claim a piece of land as his own private property *whether he intended to use it or not.* I could take a few square miles of land, call them "mine," and then go off to the moon. All I had to do to gain a living from "my" land was to charge a rent to the people who wanted to use it. If this piece of land was in an urban area, I had no need to develop it at all; I could leave it to the fools who were prepared to develop all the other pieces of land surrounding "my" piece, and in doing so automatically to raise the market value of mine. Then I could come down from the moon and demand that these fools pay me through the nose for the high value of "my" land; a value which they themselves had created for me while I was enjoying myself on the moon! Such a system is not only foreign to us, it is completely wrong. Landlords, in a society which recognizes individual ownership of land, can be—and they usually are—in the same class as the loiterers I was talking about: the class of parasites.

We must not allow the growth of parasites here in Tanganyika. The TANU [Tanganyika African National Union] government must go back to the traditional African custom of landholding. That is to say, a member of society will be entitled to a piece of land *on condition that he uses it.* Unconditional, or freehold, ownership of land (which leads to speculation and parasitism) must be abolished. We must, as I have said, regain our former attitude of mind—our traditional African socialism—and apply it to the new societies we are building today. . . .

There are bound to be certain groups which, by virtue of the market value of their particular industry's products, *will* contribute more to the nation's income than others. But the others may actually be producing goods or services which are of equal, or greater, *intrinsic* value although they do not happen to command such a high *artificial* value. For example, the food produced by the peasant farmer is of greater social value than the diamonds mined at Mwadui. But the mineworkers of Mwadui could claim, quite correctly, that their labor was yielding greater financial profits to the community than that of the farmers. If, however, they went on to demand that they should therefore be given most of that extra profit for themselves, and that no share of it should be spent on helping the farmers, they would be potential capitalists!

This is exactly where the attitude of mind comes in. It is one of the purposes of trade unions to ensure for the workers a fair share of the profits of their labor. But a "fair" share must be fair in relation to the whole society. If it is greater than the country can afford without having to penalize some other section of society, then it is *not* a fair share. Trade-union leaders and their followers, as long as they are true socialists, will not need to be coerced by the government into keeping their demands within the limits imposed by the needs of society as a whole. Only if there are potential capitalists among them will the socialist government have to step in and prevent them from putting their capitalist ideas into practice!

As with groups, so with individuals. There are certain skills, certain qualifications, which, for good reasons, command a higher rate of salary for their possessors than others. But, here again, the true socialist will demand only that return for his skilled work which he knows to be a fair one in proportion to the wealth or poverty of the whole society to which he belongs. He will not, unless he is a would-be capitalist, attempt to blackmail the community by demanding a salary equal to that paid to his counterpart in some far wealthier society.

European socialism was born of the Agrarian Revolution and the Industrial Revolution which followed it. The former created the "landed" and the "landless" classes in society; the latter produced the modern capitalist and the industrial proletariat.

These two revolutions planted the seeds of conflict within society, and not only was European socialism born of that conflict, but its apostles sanctified the conflict itself into a philosophy. Civil war was no longer looked upon as something evil, or something unfortunate, but as something good and necessary. As prayer is to Christianity or to Islam, so civil war (which they call "class war") is to the European version of socialism—a means inseparable from the end. Each becomes the basis of a whole way of life. The European socialist cannot think of his socialism without its father —capitalism! . . .

African socialism, on the other hand, did not have the "benefit" of the Agrarian Revolution or the Industrial Revolution. It did not start from the existence of conflicting classes in society. Indeed, I doubt if the equivalent for the word "class" exists in any indigenous African language; for language describes the ideas of those who speak it, and the idea of "class" or "caste" was nonexistent in African society.

The foundation, and the objective, of African socialism is the extended family. The true African socialist does not look on one class of men as his brethren and another as his natural enemies. He does not form an alliance with the brethren for the extermination of the nonbrethren. He rather regards *all* men as his brethren— as members of his ever extending family. . . .

Ujamaa, then, or "familyhood," describes our socialism. It is opposed to capitalism, which seeks to build a happy society on the basis of the exploitation of man by man; and it is equally opposed to doctrinaire socialism which seeks to build its happy society on a philosophy of inevitable conflict between man and man.

We, in Africa, have no more need of being "converted" to socialism than we have of being "taught" democracy. Both are rooted in our own past—in the traditional society which produced us. Modern African socialism can draw from its traditional heritage the recognition of society as an extension of the basic family unit. But it can no longer confine the idea of the social family within the limits of the tribe, nor, indeed, of the nation. For no true African socialist can look at a line drawn on a map and say, "The people on this side of that line are my brothers, but those who happen to live on the other side of it can have no claim on me"; every individual on this continent is his brother.

It was in the struggle to break the grip of colonialism that we learned the need for unity. We came to recognize that the same socialist attitude of mind, which in the tribal days gave to every individual the security that comes of belonging to a widely extended family, must be preserved within the still wider society of

the nation. But we should not stop there. Our recognition of the
family to which we all belong must be extended yet further—
beyond the tribe, the community, the nation, or even the continent—to embrace the whole society of mankind. This is the only
logical conclusion for true socialism.

DEMOCRACY AND THE PARTY SYSTEM*

. . . Democracy, in Africa or anywhere else, is government by the
people. Ideally, it is a form of government whereby the people—*all*
the people—settle their affairs through free discussion. The appropriate setting for this basic, or pure, democracy is a small community. The city-states of ancient Greece, for example, practiced
it. And in African society, the traditional method of conducting
affairs is by free discussion. Mr. Guy Clutton-Brock, writing about
a typical African village community, puts it neatly: . . . "The
Elders sit under the big tree, and talk until they agree." In larger
communities, however, government by the people is possible only
in a modified form.

After pure democracy, the next best thing is government by the
people's representatives. Where it is the affairs of several million
people that are to be settled by discussion, it is obviously not possible for all the people to come together and take a direct part
in the discussion. So instead, we have a Parliament in which a
number of spokesmen, or representatives, conduct the discussion
on their behalf. And if these representatives are truly to represent
the people, they must be freely chosen by the people from among
themselves. So free elections are the essential instruments of
representative democracy.

The purpose of a general election, then, is to elect these people's representatives. But, because of the historical circumstances
of the countries in which representative democracy has been most
highly developed, such elections are usually organized on a party
basis. The electorate is offered a choice between contending
parties. It could be said that the object is not so much to elect
representatives as to elect a representative party. The countries

* Excerpts from a pamphlet published by the *Tanganyika Standard*,
Dar-es-Salaam, 1962.

where this system works most successfully are those which have
two major political parties. Now the two-party system requires
certain disciplines. I will mention two in particular which are
relevant to the case I want to argue. These affect elections and
debate—both vital aspects of any form of democracy.

First, where one party is fighting an election against another, it
cannot afford to allow more than one of its members to contest
the same seat. If it did, it would split the votes of its own supporters and risk handing an easy victory to the rival party. So the
first thing such a party must do is select its official candidate,
usually by means of some kind of preliminary balloting within its
own organization. Once this has been done, *all* party members
must support the official candidates only, and fight the public elections as a united group. On this point party discipline is very strict.

Secondly, party candidates who have won the elections and
taken their seats in Parliament must remain bound by the rules of
party discipline. Once their own leaders have decided on a particular line of policy (even though it may be the purely negative line
of opposing the policies of another party), the backbenchers must
follow that line, for fear that they might increase the strength
or prestige of the rival party by appearing to agree with it.

These disciplines, however, do not apply when each party is
conducting what is purely party business. When, for instance,
party officials are elected, any member may freely oppose another
member, or when the official party candidates for election to national bodies are being selected from within the party organization,
fellow members may compete with one another for adoption. The
American primary is a typical example of this democratic freedom
within a party. Another freedom follows from this: when debate
takes place within party circles, it is a free and very often heated
debate—each member saying exactly what he feels. The British
Labour Party goes as far as allowing this kind of debate to be conducted in public. The Conservatives are more reticent, but it may
be presumed that their private debates are just as free and, no
doubt, at times as heated.

Those whose political thinking has been molded by the Western
parliamentary tradition have now become so used to the two-party
system that they cannot imagine democracy without it. It is no
good telling them that when a group of a hundred people have sat
together as equals and talked until they agreed about where they
should dig a well, for example, or whether they should build a new

school (and "until they agreed" implies that they will have produced many conflicting arguments before they did eventually agree), they have practiced democracy. No, the Western parliamentarians will want to know whether the talking was properly organized. They will want to know whether there was an organized group whose duty was to talk *for* the motion, and another organized group whose duty was to talk *against* it. They will also want to know whether, at the next debate, the same two groups will remain opposed to each other. In other words, they will be asking whether the opposition is organized and therefore automatic, or whether it is free and therefore spontaneous. Only if it is automatic will they concede that here is democracy! The way they generally put it is: "How can you have democracy with a one-party system?" It may surprise them to know, therefore, that some "heretics" like myself—who also claim to be democrats—are now beginning to ask: "How can you have democracy with a two-party system?"

I must confess that, not so long ago, I would have been content to answer the first of those questions. If I had posed the second it would have been in jest rather than in earnest. Recently, however, I have found myself questioning the democracy of the two-party system very seriously indeed.

Here in Tanganyika, for instance, we have adopted the Westminster type of representative democracy. With it, we took over the whole pattern of parliamentary and local government elections designed for a multiparty system. But it soon became clear to us that however ready we leaders might have been to accept the theory that an official opposition was essential to democratic government, our own people thought otherwise, for the idea did not make sense to them. As a result of the people's choice freely expressed at the polls, we found ourselves with a one-party system.

Now nobody who knew anything about Tanganyika could deny that, in spite of our having only one party, we were very democratic. But we were more democratic within the party than we were outside it. When, for instance, we met to elect our party leaders, nothing could have been more democratic. And our members' freedom of expression during our debates at the party's national executive meetings left nothing to be desired! But since we had adopted the method of election to Parliament and local government bodies which was designed for a contest between parties, we had to apply the party-unity rule. Once we had selected an official TANU candidate, we required all party members to support him. And if any other member disobeyed this rule and stood in opposition to our official candidate, he had to be punished. Invariably his punishment was expulsion from the party. As there is only one party in Tanganyika, the inevitable result of enforcing this rule was to make a contested election a very rare thing indeed. Most TANU candidates for Parliament and for local government councils are returned unopposed, which means, in effect, that they are elected by a party committee. Again, when it came to debates in Parliament we "naturally" (according to the book of rules of the two-party system) had to apply the party-unity rule. . . .

Because of the absence of any rival party, the membership of the TANU Parliamentary Party [TPP] is almost identical with that of the Parliament itself. Yet it is at private meetings of the TPP, and not in the Parliament, that we expect members to speak their minds freely. Here it is that they learn from their leaders what the "party line" is to be, and just how far they may go in criticizing any particular piece of legislation when this comes up for "debate" in Parliament. Fortunately, and I use the word deliberately, this has not so far prevented our members of Parliament (particularly those who are accustomed to the freedom of speech which is characteristic of the national executive) from expressing their own opinions in Parliament from time to time with a most "unparliamentary" independence of the party line! Nevertheless, whenever one of them does this, we leaders are rather disconcerted, and we generally feel obliged to rebuke him severely for his lapse from party discipline.

Now if we can encourage this freedom of expression at national executive meetings, and within the TPP, why do we discourage it in Parliament? There is, of course, a good theoretical reason. At the national-executive level we are deciding in broad terms what the party's policy shall be. This, naturally, requires a free discussion —to which anybody may contribute his suggestions, objections, countersuggestions, and so on. There obviously cannot be a "party line" to conform to at that stage, because the policy has not yet been agreed upon. And this is equally true under a one-party or a two-party system. But when we go into the Parliament we are no longer debating *what* the policy shall be, for by that time it has been settled—at least in outline. Theoretically, then, all that is still open to discussion in Parliament is detail—the question of exactly how, when, in what order of priority, and so on, the agreed policies shall be put into effect. And here we assume that the party leaders know best, and therefore the rest of us must support their decisions. But *why* should we assume this? Why should the question of timing and detail be left entirely to the leaders to decide? In a two-party Parliament there would be, of course, the need to avoid giving accidental support or encouragement to the rival party by any lack of unity between the leaders and their backbench supporters. Where there is only one party, the sole reason—apart from sheer habit—is that the leaders (i.e., the government) are said to have based their decisions on advice made available to them by experts. But this is really nonsense. For there is no valid reason why the relevant information could not also be placed before the people's representatives in the Parliament, so that such decisions were approved after a free and informed discussion had taken place in public. It is not particularly democratic to say, simply, that the details have been decided by the government "in the light of certain knowledge which is available to us but not to you people," and to leave it at that. Nor is it particularly democratic if the people's representatives are given this inside information privately. An intelligent public must know that decisions are only reached after argument. Why, then, should we try to fool them by keeping these arguments out of Parliament? In fact, where there is no opposition party, there is no reason why the debate in Parliament should not be as free as the debate in the national executive.

Given the two-party system, then, some limitation of freedom is essential—both at election time and in debate—in order to enforce party discipline and unity. And we have seen that these restrictions are not necessary where you have only one party. It seems at least open to doubt, therefore, that a system which forces political parties to limit the freedom of their members is a democratic system, and that one which can permit a party to leave its members their freedom is *un*democratic!

I realize that the political theorists are so attached to the pattern of democracy which depends on the existence of opposing parties, that they are likely to have been shocked by my expressing a doubt as to its being so very democratic after all. I am afraid they may be even more shocked by what I am now going to suggest: that where there is *one* party, and that party is identified with the *nation as a whole*, the foundations of democracy are firmer than they can ever be where you have two or more parties, each representing only a section of the community!

After all, we do have it on very reliable authority that a house divided against itself cannot stand! So it is surely up to the advocates of the two-party system to defend their own case more convincingly. It is not enough for them simply to insist that it *is* more democratic than a one-party system, and then be horrified when we presume to disagree with them!

Now my argument is that a two-party system can be justified only when the parties are divided over some fundamental issue; otherwise it merely encourages the growth of factionalism. Or, to put it another way, the only time when a political group can represent the interests of a section of the community, *without* being a faction, is when that group fights to remove a grievous wrong from society. But then the differences between this group and those responsible for the wrong it fights are fundamental; and there can therefore be no question of national unity until the differences have been removed by change. And "change" in that context is a euphemism, because any change in fundamentals is properly termed "revolution." What is more, the reason why the word "revolution" is generally associated with armed insurrection is that the existence of really fundamental differences within any society poses a "civil war" situation, and has often led to bloody revolution. Benjamin Disraeli, who was certainly no advocate of a one-party system, once referred to this situation as tantamount to "two nations" within a state. . . .

. . . In any country which is divided over fundamental issues you have the "civil war" situation we have been talking about. If, on the other hand, you have a two-party system where the differences between the parties are *not* fundamental, then you immediately reduce politics to the level of a football match. A football match may, of course, attract some very able players; it may also be entertaining; but it is still only a game, and only the most ardent fans (who are not usually the most intelligent) take the game very seriously. This, in fact, is not unlike what has happened in many of the so-called democratic countries today, where some of the most intelligent members of society have become disgusted by the hypocrisy of the party games called politics, and take no interest in them. They can see no party whose "line" they could support without reservation and are therefore left with no way of serving their country in the political field, even should they wish to, except, perhaps, by writing a book! For the politics of a country governed by the two-party system are not, and cannot be, *national* politics; they are the politics of *groups*, whose differences, more often than not, are of small concern to the majority of the people.

It is hard to avoid the conclusion that people who defend the two-party system are actually advocating "football politics"; that they really consider a spirit of purely artificial rivalry, like that which exists between a couple of soccer teams, is appropriate to the relationship between opposing political parties. . . .

Our critics should understand that, in Africa, we have to take our politics a little more seriously. And they should also remember the historical difference between parties in Africa and those in Europe or America. The European and American parties came into being as the result of existing social and economic divisions —the second party being formed to challenge the monopoly of political power by some aristocratic or capitalist group. Our own parties had a very different origin. They were not formed to challenge any ruling group of our own people; they were formed to challenge the *foreigners* who ruled over us. They were not, therefore, political "parties"—i.e., factions—but nationalist movements. And from the outset they represented the interests and aspirations of the whole nation. . . .

Now that the colonialists have gone, there is no remaining division between rulers and ruled; no monopoly of political power by any sectional group which could give rise to conflicting parties. There can, therefore, be only one reason for the formation of such parties in a country like ours—the desire to imitate the political structure of a totally dissimilar society. What is more, the desire to imitate where conditions are not suitable for imitation can easily lead us into trouble. To try and import the idea of a parliamentary opposition into Africa may very likely lead to violence— because the opposition parties will tend to be regarded as traitors by the majority of our people—or, at best, it will lead to the trivial maneuverings of opposing groups whose time is spent in the inflation of artificial differences into some semblance of reality "for the sake of preserving democracy"! The latter alternative, I repeat, is an oversophisticated pastime which we in Africa cannot afford to indulge in; our time is too short and there is too much serious work to be done. . . .

The parties of our friends in the older parliamentary democracies outside Africa are sectional groups. So, too, are those within Africa which seek to imitate them. Nowadays such parties do not restrict their membership to those who can claim noble birth, or to the wealthy; but there are some which restrict it, instead, to those who belong to an equally exclusive aristocracy of the intellect! And in certain such modern "aristocracies," instead of the blueness of blood which was once the qualification for membership of the ruling class, we now find that it is by the "redness" of his thought that a man is judged worthy of entry into the ranks of the elite. . . . And in all such parties—whether the factional parties of a two-party democracy, or the vanguard aristocracies of an ideological dictatorship—it is the leaders themselves who "elect" each other. The elections, if any, in which the people are permitted to take part, are not for the purpose of choosing their own representatives; they are merely for the purpose of deciding from which sectional group the "people's representatives" shall be selected for them! . . .

. . . Our friends, the Communists, have made their policies a creed, and are finding that dogmatism and freedom of discussion do not easily go together. They are as much afraid of the "other party" as any government in a two-party democracy. In their case the "other party" is only a phantom, but a phantom can be even more frightening than a living rival! And their fear of this phantom has blinded them to the truth that, in a one-party system, party membership must be open to everybody and freedom of expression allowed to every individual. No party which limits its membership to a clique can ever free itself from the fear of overthrow by those it has excluded. It must be constantly on the watch for signs of opposition, and must smother "dangerous" ideas before they have time to spread.

But a national movement which is open to all—which is identified with the whole nation—has nothing to fear from the discontent of any excluded section of society, for there is then no such section. Those forming the government will, of course, be replaced from time to time; but this is what elections are for. The leadership of our movement is constantly changing; there is no reason why the leadership of the nation should not also be constantly changing. This would have nothing to do with the overthrowing of a party government by a rival party. And, since such a national movement leaves no room for the growth of discontented elements excluded from its membership, it has nothing to fear from criticism and the free expression of ideas. On the contrary, both the movement itself and the nation have everything to gain from a constant injection of new ideas from within the nation and from outside. It would be both wrong, and certainly unnecessary, to feel we must wait until the leaders are dead before we begin to criticize them!

Any member of the Movement (which, in this context, means any patriotic citizen since it is a National Movement we are talking about) would be free to stand as a candidate if he so wished. * And in each constituency the voters themselves would be able to make their choice freely from among these candidates; they would no longer be obliged to consider the party label rather than the individual. Of such elections it could truly be said that they were for the purpose of letting the people choose their own representatives. If that is not democracy, I do not know the meaning of the word!

* Under the system adopted for the elections of September, 1965, the TANU District Conferences chose two candidates in each constituency from among those who had received twenty-five signatures on nominating papers. The entire list of nominees was then forwarded to the National Executive Committee, which could (and occasionally did) substitute other nominees for the candidates endorsed by the District Conference. In 6 out of 107 constituencies, a single candidate was unopposed.—ED.

PART IV

LATIN AMERICA — An Overview

2L

The Latin American experience is different from that of Asia, Africa, or the Middle East, yet the area faces many of the same problems of modernization and development. Although Latin America has been politically independent since the early nineteenth century, government has until recently been the monopoly of a small, European-oriented upper class, which wielded economic, political, and often military and ecclesiastical power. Ideological conflicts among the Latin American elite reflected the ideologies of Europe—with the positivism and anticlericalism of the European radicals, as well as the conservatism of the European landowning feudal classes.

In this century, radical and reformist ideologies have begun to involve the masses in political life. In some cases, European doctrines have been altered to fit the Latin American scene. (Christian Democratic, socialist, and Communist theories are represented in the selections by Eduardo Frei, José Figueres, and the later speeches of Fidel Castro.) In other cases, new formulations or combinations have been developed to deal with the special situation in Latin America (as, for example, the theories of Haya de la Torre and Betancourt). Even when the political leader has no systematic and integrated political theory, he is still aware of the necessity to respond to the pressing problems of Latin America— the concentration of economic power in the hands of a few wealthy landowners, the lack of industrial development, and the preponderance of foreign (particularly American) influences in Latin American economic life.*

* It should be noted that there are considerable variations among the Latin American countries in the extent of industrialization and the seriousness of

Latin American leaders share the reforming zeal and anti-imperialist sentiments of those of Asia, Africa, and the Middle East. Until recently, however, there has been little awareness of a community of interest with other underdeveloped nations—partly because of cultural and linguistic barriers, partly because of the absence of the political links that the French and British colonial empires provided to bring the African and Asian nationalists into contact with one another. The Cuban revolution has considerably altered this situation. Certainly at its outset, and even today, the politically conscious elements in Asia, Africa, and the Middle East consider it a nationalistic, anticolonial revolution similar to their own. Speeches at the Tricontinental Solidarity Conference in Havana in January, 1966, revealed this attitude.

In addition to a desire for social reform and opposition to imperialism, other goals of modernizing nationalism are present in Latin American political thought. Economic development through planning and government action, industrialization at a rapid rate, and the expansion of literacy and educational opportunity are all objectives of the Latin American leaders. Although a multiparty system flourishes in such countries as Chile and Uruguay, there is also a desire for strong government and an end to party strife. The single party has not been defended with the vigor with which the Africans defend it, but in the case of Mexico, an effective and democratic dominant party system has been in control for a number of years. Latin American nationalism has not led to a significant revival of interest in traditional culture, but Haya de la Torre of Peru has spoken of "Indo-America" as a distinctive cultural entity, and Eduardo Frei of Chile has called upon Latin America to make its distinctive contribution to world civilization. That a loosening of political and economic ties with the United States also appeals to many Latin Americans is evident in the support for programs of Latin American political and economic integration.

Counterbalancing the neutralist and anti-American tendencies are programs of political cooperation (through the Organization of American States), of military alliance (through the 1947 Treaty of Rio de Janeiro), and of economic assistance (through the Alliance for Progress, initiated in 1961). In addition, there is

---

the economic and social problems. Thus Walt W. Rostow, in The Stages of Economic Growth, classes Argentina and Mexico as already in the "take-off" stage of economic development.

the vigorously anti-Communist attitude of many groups in Latin America—including the Catholic Church. It may thus be possible to attain the social and economic objectives of modernization without destroying the inter-American system, but the task will be among the most difficult ones confronted by United States policymakers in the years to come.

22. Fidel Castro

Fidel Castro was born in 1926, on a sugar farm owned by his father. He received his primary and secondary education in Catholic schools. At the University of Havana, where he studied law and was active in student politics, he was elected president of the student government. Castro joined an unsuccessful expeditionary force against General Trujillo of the Dominican Republic in 1947. A year later, he attended a student meeting in Bogotá, Colombia, and participated in the riots marking the meeting of the Organization of American States there. He received his law degree in 1950, and two years later sued unsuccessfully in the Constitutional Court of Havana for a decision that Batista's seizure of power had been unconstitutional. On July 26, 1953, after an attack on the Moncada barracks in Santiago de Cuba, he was captured, tried (his defense was later published as History Will Absolve Me), and sentenced to fifteen years in prison on the Isle of Pines. Released in 1955 under an amnesty law, he went to Mexico, where he formed the 26th of July Movement. In November, 1956, he returned to Cuba and began the resistance movement in the hills of Sierra Maestre that was finally to come to power on January 1, 1959. History Will Absolve Me promised a return to the 1940 constitution, an agrarian reform, and the nationalization of the telephone and electricity "trusts." After coming to power, Castro did not hold elections (although this was implied by his promise to restore the 1940 constitution and by his references to the "popularly elected" government that would follow). In May, 1959, however, at the Economic Council of the Organization of American States in Buenos Aires, he spoke of elections as a check against oppression, and asked the United States to set up a $30 billion aid program for Latin America in the next ten years. At this time, he also repeatedly denied that he or his revolution was Communist. A year later, he *asserted that because of "the intimate union and identification of the government with the people," elections were not necessary (see Castro's speech on "A Real Democracy").* In late 1959 and 1960, with the defection of many of the original revolutionaries on the grounds of increasing Communist control of Cuba, it became apparent that the Popular Socialist Party (PSP)—as the Cuban Communist Party was known—was becoming dominant in the group around Castro. This development was reinforced by Castro's increasingly close military and economic ties with the Soviet bloc, links that were strengthened after the United States cut off the Cuban sugar quota in mid-1960. Finally, in December, 1961, Castro announced his allegiance to Marxism-Leninism (although he did not say, as press reports first had it, that he had always been a Marxist-Leninist), and described the newly established Revolutionary Integrated Organizations as a preparatory step to the creation of an elite party, the United Revolutionary Socialist Party, under collective leadership along Leninist lines (now known as the Communist Party of Cuba). Since 1963, he has put forth the Cuban Revolution as a model for armed revolt throughout Latin America, and, since early 1967, he has attacked various Latin American Communist parties for their lack of support for Castroite guerrilla movements.

HISTORY WILL ABSOLVE ME*

In the brief of this case there must be recorded the five revolutionary laws that would have been proclaimed immediately after the capture of the Moncada barracks and would have been broadcast to the nation by radio. It is possible that Colonel Chaviano may deliberately have destroyed these documents, but even if he has done so, I conserve them in my memory.

The First Revolutionary Law would have returned power to the people and proclaimed the Constitution of 1940 the supreme law of the land, until such time as the people should decide to modify or change it. And, in order to effect its implementation and punish those who had violated it—there being no organization for holding elections to accomplish this—the revolutionary movement,

* Excerpts from Fidel Castro's defense statement at his trial (see biographical sketch) in 1953, later published as *History Will Absolve Me* (New York: Lyle Stuart, 1961); reprinted by permission.

as the momentous incarnation of this sovereignty, the only source of legitimate power, would have assumed all the faculties inherent to it except that of modifying the Constitution itself. In other words, it would have assumed the legislative, executive, and judicial powers.

This approach could not be more crystal-clear or more free of vacillation and sterile charlatanry. A government acclaimed by the mass of rebel people would be vested with every power, everything necessary in order to proceed with the effective implementation of the popular will and true justice. From that moment, the judicial power, which since March 10 has placed itself *against* the Constitution and *outside* the Constitution, would cease to exist, and we would proceed to its immediate and total reform before it would again assume the power granted to it by the Supreme Law of the Republic. Without our first taking those measures, a return to legality—by putting the custody of the courts back into the hands that have crippled the system so dishonorably—would constitute a fraud, a deceit, and one more betrayal.

The Second Revolutionary Law would have granted property (not mortgageable and not transferable) to all planters, subplanters, lessees, partners, and squatters who hold parcels of five or less *caballerias** of land, and the state would indemnify the former owners on the basis of the rental they would have received for these parcels over a period of ten years.

The Third Revolutionary Law would have granted workers and employees the right to share 30 per cent of the profits of all the large industrial, mercantile, and mining enterprises, including the sugar mills. The strictly agricultural enterprises would be exempt, in consideration of other agrarian laws which would have been implemented.

The Fourth Revolutionary Law would have granted all planters the right to share 50 per cent of the sugar production and a minimum quota of 40,000 *arrobas*† for all small planters who had been established for three or more years.

The Fifth Revolutionary Law would have ordered the confiscation of all holdings and ill-gotten gains of those who had committed frauds during previous regimes, as well as the holdings and ill-gotten gains of all their legatees and heirs. To implement this,

* A *caballeria* is a tract of land equivalent to about 33.3 acres.—ED.
† An *arroba* is equivalent to 25 pounds.—ED.

special courts with full powers would gain access to all records of all corporations registered or operating in this country, in order to investigate concealed funds of illegal origin, and to request that foreign governments extradite persons and attach their holdings. Half of the property recovered would be used to subsidize retirement funds for workers, and the other half would be used for hospitals, asylums, and charitable organizations.

Furthermore, it was to be declared that the Cuban policy in the Americas would be one of close solidarity with the democratic people of this continent, and that those politically persecuted by bloody tyrants oppressing our sister nations would find generous asylum, brotherhood, and bread in the land of Martí—not the persecution, hunger, and treason that they find today. Cuba should be the bulwark of liberty and not a shameful link in the chain of despotism.

These laws would have been proclaimed immediately, as soon as the upheaval was ended and prior to a detailed and far-reaching study. They would have been followed by another series of laws and fundamental measures, such as agrarian reform, integral reform of education, nationalization of the utilities trust and the telephone trust, refunds to the people of the illegal excessive rates this company has charged, and payment to the treasury of all taxes brazenly evaded in the past.

All these laws and others would be inspired in the exact fulfillment of two essential articles of our Constitution. One of these orders the outlawing of feudal estates by indicating the maximum area of land any person or entity can possess for each type of agricultural enterprise, by adopting measures which would tend to return the land to the Cubans. The other categorically orders the state to use all means at its disposal to provide employment for all those who lack it and to ensure a decent livelihood for each manual laborer or intellectual.

None of these articles may be called unconstitutional. The first popularly elected government would have to respect these laws, not only because of moral obligation to the nation, but because when people achieve something they have yearned for throughout generations, no force in the world is capable of taking it away again.

The problems concerning land, industrialization, housing, unemployment, education, and the health of the people—these are the six problems we would take immediate steps to resolve, along with the restoration of public liberties and political democracy....

It is not by statesmen such as Carlos Saladrigas*—whose statesmanship consists of preserving the *status quo* and mouthing phrases like the "absolute freedom of enterprise," "guarantees to investment capital," and "the law of supply and demand"—that we will solve these problems. Those ministers can chat gaily in a mansion on Fifth Avenue† until there remains not even the dust of the bones of those whose problems required immediate solution. In this present-day world, social problems are not solved by spontaneous generation.

A revolutionary government with the backing of the people and the respect of the nation, after purging the various institutions of all venal and corrupt officials, would proceed immediately to industrialize the country, mobilizing all inactive capital (currently estimated at about $500 million) through the National Bank and the Agricultural, Industrial, and Development Bank and submitting this mammoth task to experts and men of absolute competence, completely removed from all political machinations, for study, direction, planning, and realization.

After establishing the 100,000 small farmers as owners on land they had previously rented, a revolutionary government would proceed immediately to settle the land problem. First, as the Constitution orders, we would establish the maximum amount of land to be held by each type of agricultural enterprise and would acquire the excess acres by expropriation: recovery of the lands stolen from the state, improvement of swampland, planting of large nurseries, and reserving of zones for reforestation. Secondly, we would distribute the remaining land among peasant families (with priority given to the larger ones) and would promote agricultural cooperatives *for the common use of expensive equipment,*‡ with a single technical, professional direction of farming and cattle raising. Finally, we would provide resources, equipment, protection, and useful guidance to the peasants.

---

* Batista's presidential candidate in 1944 elections, Saladrigas was defeated. He became an influential member of Batista's government after 1952.—ED.

† Located in the Miramar residential district in Havana.—ED.

‡ Italicized words omitted in the translation from which this excerpt is taken.—ED.

A revolutionary government would solve the housing problem by cutting all rents in half, by providing tax exemptions on homes inhabited by the owners, by tripling taxes on rented homes, by tearing down hovels and replacing them with modern multiple-dwelling buildings, and by financing housing all over the island on a scale heretofore unheard of, with the criterion that, just as each rural family should possess its own tract of land, each city family should own its home or apartment. There is plenty of building material and more than enough manpower to make a decent home for every Cuban. But if we continue to wait for the miracle of the golden calf, a thousand years will have gone by and the problem will still be the same. On the other hand, today there are greater possibilities than ever of bringing electricity to the remotest corner of the island. The use of nuclear energy in this field is now a reality and will greatly reduce the cost of producing electricity.

With these three projects and reforms, the problem of unemployment would automatically disappear, and the work to improve public health and to fight against disease would be made much less difficult.

Finally, a revolutionary government would undertake the integral reform of the educational system, bringing it in line with the foregoing projects, with the idea of educating those generations who will have the privilege of living in a happy land. Do not forget the words of the Apostle:* "A serious error is being made in Latin America: Where the inhabitants depend almost exclusively on the products of the soil for their livelihood, the educational stress is on urban rather than farm life." "The happiest people are the ones whose children are well educated and instructed in philosophy; whose sentiments are directed into noble channels." "A well-educated people will always be strong and free."

The spirit of education lies, however, in the teacher himself, and in Cuba the teaching profession is miserably underpaid. Despite this, no one is more dedicated than the Cuban teacher. Who among us has not learned his ABC's in the little public schoolhouse? It is time we stopped paying pittances to these young men and women who are entrusted with the sacred task of teaching the young. No teacher should earn less than $200, no secondary pro-

* "The Apostle" refers to Jose Martí.—Ed.

fessor should get less than $350, if they are to devote themselves exclusively to their high calling without suffering want. Moreover, all rural teachers should have free use of the various systems of transportation, and, at least every five years, all teachers should enjoy a sabbatical leave of six months with pay so they may attend special refresher courses at home and abroad to keep abreast of the latest developments in their field. In this way, the curriculum and the teaching system may be constantly improved.

Where will the money be found for all this? When there is an end to rife embezzlement of government funds, when public officials stop taking graft from the large companies that owe taxes to the state, when the enormous resources of the country are brought into full use, when we no longer buy tanks, bombers, and guns for this country (which has no frontiers to defend, and where these instruments of war, now being purchased, are used against the people), when there is more interest in educating the people than in killing them—then there will be more than enough money.

Cuba could easily provide for a population three times as great as it now has, so there is no excuse for the abject poverty of a single one of its present inhabitants. The markets should be overflowing with produce, pantries should be full, all hands should be working. This is not an inconceivable thought. What is inconceivable is that anyone should go to bed hungry, that children should die for lack of medical attention; what is inconceivable is that 30 per cent of our farm people cannot write their names and that 99 per cent of them know nothing of Cuba's history. What is inconceivable is that the majority of our rural people are now living in worse circumstances than the Indians Columbus discovered living in the fairest land that human eyes had ever seen.

To those who would call me a dreamer, I quote the words of Martí: "A true man does not seek the path where advantage lies, but rather, the path where duty lies, and this is the only practical man, whose dream of today will be the law of tomorrow, because he who has looked back on the upheavals of history and has seen civilizations going up in flames, crying out in bloody struggle, throughout the centuries, knows that the future well-being of man, without exception, lies on the side of duty."

THE ACCUSATION OF COMMUNISM*

I do not know whether the calumny against the Revolution—that it is Communist and infiltrated by Communism—is due solely to the fact that we do not persecute the Communists and do not shoot them. I do not know how the ideas of the Revolution can be defined in such a way that there will be no more intrigues or lies than there are at present, and that the infamous attacks against our Revolution will finally cease. Is it perhaps because we have a firm conviction of the freedom of mankind and the rights of man, and of equity and human equality, that we cannot conceive that anyone would desire to have rights that he keeps from others? Is it because we have pledged to discuss our ideas in conditions of equality with all others? Is it because we have pledged to carry out our ideals, not by force, but by reason and justice? On the contrary, if the theory is accepted that someone has a right to suppress others' rights, the easiest thing for the Revolution would be to suppress the right of everyone except those who are members of the revolutionary government to speak. But that would not be democratic, nor is it our philosophy, for clearly the right to think and speak belongs to all equally. Is it because we think this way, because this is our political philosophy, that the fear of Communists is being aroused, in order to incite division in the country and bring together the enemies in other countries against us? Can our Revolution be accused of being Communist? Can the ideals of our Revolution be confused? Have we not spoken with sufficient clarity on the doctrine of the 26th of July Movement? Are our purposes not clearly defined? Then why are these fears and fantasies pursued? Are they not trying to create obstacles for the path of our Revolution? If our ideas are very clear, if the majority of the people are behind those ideas, and we are all at the command of that movement and that Revolution, do the people not trust us? Can someone perhaps maintain that we have ever lied to the people? Can anyone think that we have lacked courage to

---

* Excerpts from a speech delivered by Castro in the Plaza Civica, Havana, on May 8, 1959; translated by the editor from the text in *Guia del Pensamiento Político Económico de Fidel* (Havana: Diario Libre, 1959).

speak to the people? Can anyone think that we lack the necessary sincerity to speak what we think to the people? Can anyone perhaps think that we are hypocrites or cowards? Then why do we say that our Revolution is not Communist? Why, when we prove that our ideals are different from Communist doctrine, that the Revolution is not Communist or capitalist, that it is a revolution of its own . . . that it has its own ideology—entirely its own—which has a Cuban basis and is entirely Cuban, entirely Latin American, why then, do they start to accuse our Revolution of being something it is not? It is necessary to explain for once that if our ideas were Communist, we would say so here, and if our ideas were capitalist, we would say so here. We do not give anyone the right to decide for our conscience what we are and what we have a right to be. . . .

PLAN FOR THE ADVANCEMENT
OF LATIN AMERICA*

Democracy and Dictatorship

How is it possible for democracy to be preserved under these conditions? We have declared the democratic ideal to be the ideal of the peoples of this hemisphere. We have declared that the democratic ideal is the ideal that can best satisfy the dreams of the peoples of this continent. Nevertheless, the economic and social conditions of Latin America make it impossible for our countries to attain their ideal of democracy. Be it a dictatorship of the Left or a dictatorship of the Right, a dictatorship is a dictatorship, and those in power completely deny the principles toward which the peoples of Latin America aspire. . . . The Pan-American ideal is true democracy with absolute respect for the dignity of man, a true democracy in which all the liberties prevail, a true democracy in a regime of social justice. The peoples of Latin America want neither bread without liberty nor liberty without bread. . . .

* Excerpts from a speech delivered by Castro in Buenos Aires, on May 21, 1959, at the Sixth Plenary Economic Council of the Organization of American States, reprinted from *Plan for the Advancement of Latin America* (Havana, 1959).

We have said that underdevelopment is an insidious enemy of constitutional governments—governments that find themselves so strangled by conditions of poverty that they are pushed into the grip of armed minorities. We made this statement precisely because we have known two kinds of governments. We have been subjected to strong-arm governments that suppress all liberties—freedom of press, of assembly, of association, of election—and use fire and sword to maintain the so-called peace and order about which they brag so much. Under these strong-arm governments, resentment grows, poverty worsens, suffering increases.

Thus, as soon as the people can overcome the restrictions imposed upon them, they put constitutional governments into effect. Full of dreams, and with their hopes high, they begin to exercise the rights that the new regime guarantees them. They begin trying to satisfy all their needs as quickly as possible. Then, since the tremendous problem is precisely that there are not enough resources to satisfy their needs, since the resources available do not reach far enough, all kinds of conflicts arise. These conflicts are forthwith called disorder or anarchy by the enemies of democracy —by those who are waiting for the opportunity to seize power again by force.

Democratic governments cannot solve these problems which are becoming more and more acute—with theories, or arguments, or reasoning. The theory is advanced that if investments are to be attracted, there must be complete peace and order. The theory is advanced that in order to attract investments, there should be no strikes. In other words, these are the requisites often cited for the economic development of a country. But what is never explained is just how such conditions can be achieved by the use of democratic procedures and without placing further restrictions on the people, without further depriving the people. What democratic government can stay in office after placing restrictions on the people, after depriving the people further in order to comply with the conditions demanded as a requisite for capital investment—sacrificing thereby its popular support at the very time that armed minorities are waiting for the democratic government's vulnerable moment in order to seize power? . . .

No system of government is more corrupt than a dictatorship. It is true that some constitutional governments are also corrupt, but the constitutional governments must be careful because they have to submit to elections; and if there is true democracy, if the citizens really vote, the governments can lose these elections. Furthermore, in a democracy, public protest serves as a check on corruption. In a democracy, freedom of expression serves as a check. In a democracy, the electoral process serves as a check, and this electoral process is repeated every few years. . . .

Sources of Development Capital

There are three ways to obtain capital—by saving, by obtaining financing of our own, or by private investments. I understand that until now, the economists have discovered no other way. Saving would be a solution, if we could freely sell all we produce. If the United States and Canada should remove all the protective tariffs that affect our basic products, if they should remove the subsidies on those articles, then we could sell to them everything that we produce and thereby obtain the gold and dollar reserves necessary for our industrialization. If Cuba, for example, could sell 8 million tons of sugar, we would be able to obtain the capital needed for our industrial development. But such changes would imply a change in the economic structure of the United States, and I am not going to be utopian because our experience has taught us the difficulties that, as a result of certain well-established interests, are always to be encountered when an attempt is made to eliminate some of those restrictions. . . .

The second way to obtain capital is by private investment. This is the formula that has been proposed lately as a solution, but it is no solution. On other occasions, when the possibilities for our economic development have been studied, it has been insinuated and more or less implied that private investment could provide the capital for industrialization, but that certain previous conditions were required for private investments. To begin with a "climate": What is meant by a "climate"? In the midst of 700,000 unemployed, can there be a "climate"? . . . A "climate" cannot be achieved in the midst of conflicts that stem from hunger, poverty, and unsatisfied need. . . . Private capital would go to those countries with the best conditions, those countries which are in the best economic situation and in which for that very reason the social conflicts are less. Private capital would not go to the countries in which the greatest social conflicts appear. Then large areas of the continent would remain neglected and abandoned to their own fate. Private investment would not solve the problem in these areas.

Furthermore, there are investments that do not interest private capital—for example, hydroelectric plants, which require $200 million or $300 million as initial investment. Private capital prefers to exploit petroleum resources. That is a sure investment. Private capital is not interested in certain kinds of investment that do not produce big profits. These investments have to be financed by loans rather than by private investments.

We are not opposed to private investment. But in our industrialization program, the private investments we should encourage are those that can be made by private sources of capital within our respective countries. Funds should be made available to them by government credit institutions, mobilizing resources provided through international credit institutions. We believe in the usefulness, the experience, and the enthusiasm of private investors. But we should hope for the private investments to be made by firms within our respective countries. Does this mean that we will exclude international investors? No. Companies with international investments will have the same guarantees and the same rights as the national firms. . . .

The third type of investment, the one that is made through public finance, remains. Why not agree that under the present conditions the best way to cooperate in a program of economic development is through a program of public financing? . . . The financial consultants of the Cuban delegation estimate that a ten-year loan of $30 billion is needed to carry out the economic development of Latin America. . . . I declare that what we need we can obtain only from the United States and through public financing. We understand, furthermore, that this is the easiest way for the United States to help Latin America; experience in recent years shows us that any other procedure—such as that of eliminating trade tariffs —would be politically more difficult. Furthermore, the large-scale loan is the foreign-aid program that the United States has used in Europe and the Near East. Why ignore in Latin America the program that was considered best for other places and would benefit both Latin America and the United States? . . . The important thing is that we should be convinced that the solutions I have discussed are the true solutions and that the assistance that Latin America needs should be made available in the amount needed really to solve the problem of underdevelopment—not to solve it halfway, but to solve it completely, so that we can build a lasting foundation for a democratic family of nations in this hemisphere.

A REAL DEMOCRACY*

You who produce things, you who work, who sacrifice yourselves, who have been missing the pleasant things of life, you always were, are now, and will be tomorrow, members of the majority of the people.

And yet, you did not run things; you were the majority, and others used to run things for you. You were managed, you were governed by others who not only did what you were supposed to do, but as a rule did it to the detriment of your interests. They ruled in your place and against you.

They invented a democracy for you, a strange, peculiar democracy in which you, who represented the majority, had nothing whatever to say about anything; in which you, peasant, and you, workman, you fellows who produce most of what is worth anything and who, combining efforts with the white-collar workers, produce all our wealth, all our income—you, who produced everything, did not even have the chance to learn how to read or write, often not even to sign your name.

They invented a very peculiar democracy for you who were the majority and yet were practically nonexistent as a political element of our society. They spoke to you about rights and privileges of the citizen, and all those rights and privileges only meant that your child had to starve to death before the closed eyes of an indolent government, that your other child had to go through life without learning his ABC's, that you yourself had to sell your hard work for whatever they condescended to pay for it—if you were lucky enough to find someone who would buy it.

They spoke to you about rights that never existed as far as you were concerned. Your children were not sure of even the right to a country school, or the right to medical attention, or

* Excerpts from Castro's May Day, 1960, speech; reprinted, by permission, from *Monthly Review*, XII, No. 5 (September, 1960).

the right to a piece of bread; and you yourself were not sure of even the right to work!

They invented a democracy in which you, who represented the majority, did not mean anything. And thus, despite your tremendous strength, regardless of your colossal might, in spite of your sacrifice and your endless toil for others as a mere cog in our national life, you, who were the majority all the time, neither governed anything nor could even manage your own affairs!

A democracy is that form of government in which the majority runs things, where the majority means something, and the interests of that majority are protected; a democracy is that in which a man is assured of all his rights, not only the right to think freely, but also the right to know how to think, the right to know how to write what he thinks, the right to know how to read what others think and say. Also the right to eat, to work, to become educated, and to mean something within your society. That is why this is real democracy, the democracy brought to you by the Cuban Revolution, by our Revolution.

A real democracy is one in which you, peasant, get the land we have been recovering for you, after wresting it from foreign hands! A true democracy is one in which you, sugar-cane plantation worker, receive nearly 3 million acres of planted land so that you will no longer have to live as an outcast! A true democracy is one in which you, workman, are assured of your right to work, and know that nobody can kick you out into the gutter to starve to death! A real democracy is that in which you, poor student, have just the same opportunity to get a university degree, if you are talented enough, as the son of any rich man. A true democracy is one in which you who are the son of a laborer, or of a poor peasant, or of any poor family have a schoolteacher and a decent school to educate you. A real democracy is one in which you, old man, will not live in want when you no longer can earn enough for your own support! A true democracy is one in which Cuban Negroes have the right to work and do not have to be afraid of seeing anybody take it away from them because of stupid racial prejudices! A bona fide democracy is one in which you, woman, are recognized as an equal of all other citizens, and even have the right to take up arms to defend your country, next to your man! A pure democracy is one in which the government transforms fortresses into schools and is trying to build a house for every family, so that every Cuban father will have a roof for his children!

A real democracy is one in which whoever falls sick has a physician to treat him. A true democracy is one that does not go around recruiting peasants to convert them into soldiers (who, after being thoroughly corrupted, are converted into enemies of the workman and of their own peasant brothers), but changes that peasant soldier, not into a protector of the privileged, of the heartless landlords, but into a defender of his brothers, the peasants and the workers of his country. A real democracy is this, your democracy, which does not divide the people and does not play brothers against brothers; whose government discovers the strength of the people and combines its various elements, makes the people stronger by uniting them, hands a gun to the peasant, to the workman, to the student, and the women, and the Negroes —hands a gun to the poor man and to whoever is willing to fight for a just cause.

A real democracy is this, our and your democracy, in which not only the majority's rights prevail, but loaded weapons are handed to that majority! That, my friends, can be done only by a really democratic government, ruled and managed by the majority. This is the sort of thing that could never be done in any of those phony democracies.

I would like to know what would happen if a loaded rifle were delivered to each of those Negroes of the South in the United States, where so many of them have been lynched, abused, humiliated, and robbed for centuries!

What an oligarchy of despoilers or a military caste of plunderers and tyrants can never do, what no minority government will ever dare to do is to hand a gun to each worker and to each student, to each young man and each poor citizen—to each one of those who make up the majority of the people!

Of course, that does not mean that the rights of the others should not be considered. The rights of the other people are worth considering in the same measure as the interests of the majority, to the same extent that the rights of the majority are considered. However, the truth is that the rights and interests of the majority are the ones that should prevail over the rights and interests of the minority, and not vice versa.

And that real democracy, that pure, bona fide democracy, that true and honest democracy, is the kind of democracy we have in this country now, the kind of democracy we have had since January 1, 1959.

That democracy has asserted itself directly in the intimate union and identification of the government with the people, in this direct dealing, in this determination to do things and strive for the good of the great majority, in the interest of the great majority of the country. That direct type of democracy has been exercised here more purely, a thousand times more purely, than that false democracy, that phony democracy that resorts to sly methods, predicated on corruption and fraud, to distort and falsify the true will of the peoples.

And this democracy of ours has operated in that direct way because we are going through a revolutionary process. Tomorrow it will be as the people say, as the people decide, as may be demanded by the needs of the people, by the aspirations, hopes, and desires of the people. Today we have here a direct interdependence between the people and the government. Someday, when this revolutionary process will have advanced far enough, when the people freely decide (and the revolutionary government will immediately interpret and obey the will of the people) that we should adopt new policies and procedures; once the most important tasks have been completed and the most fundamental goals of the Revolution (among which is, in the first place today, the defense of our Revolution and of the country) have been reached, then the people and the government will adopt the procedure considered most fitting to the circumstances and characteristics of a revolution already consolidated and victorious in every way—a procedure chosen by you and us, the people and the government!

Nobody holds a public office for sport or personal gain; we are only fulfilling our duty, all of us; we are all willing and ready to sacrifice everything, to work until sheer exhaustion overcomes us; we are all intent on reaching a single goal, a single purpose, and that purpose is to serve our cause and to carry it to final victory! . . .

I AM A MARXIST-LENINIST*

The Revolution and Socialism

This was the method the Revolution had to follow, the method of anti-imperialist struggle and of socialism—that is, the nationalization of all the large industries and businesses, the nationalization and social ownership of the basic means of production, and the planned development of our whole economy at the pace permitted by our resources and by the aid we have been receiving from outside. This is something else very favorable to our Revolution: the fact that we can count on aid and solidarity, which enable us to carry our Revolution forward without the enormous sacrifices that other countries are required to make.

We have had to carry out an anti-imperialist and socialist revolution. The anti-imperialist and socialist revolution had to be a single revolution because there is only one revolution. This is the great dialectic truth of humanity: imperialism, and, opposed to imperialism—socialism. The result of this opposition is the triumph of socialism, the supremacy of the epoch of socialism, the overcoming of the stage of capitalism and imperialism, the establishment of the era of socialism and, after that, the era of Communism.

If there are still any anti-Communists here, they need not be afraid. We will not have Communism in less than thirty years. This is the way it is with Marxism. One cannot simply leap over a historical stage. Perhaps the historical stage that some underdeveloped countries can omit today is the construction of capitalism —that is, they can begin the development of the economy of the country by way of planning and socialism. What cannot be skipped is socialism. The Soviet Union itself, after forty years, is beginning to construct Communism and hopes to have advanced considerably in this direction at the end of twenty years.

Thus we are in a stage of construction of socialism. What is this socialism we should apply? Is it utopian socialism? Clearly, we must apply scientific socialism. On this subject I had to begin by saying with complete frankness that we believe in Marxism,

* Excerpts from a speech delivered by Castro on December 1, 1961; translated by the editor from the text printed in *Revolución*, December 2, 1961.

that we believe it is the most correct, most scientific theory, the only true theory, the only true revolutionary theory. I say this here with complete satisfaction and confidence. I am a Marxist-Leninist, and I will be a Marxist-Leninist until the last day of my life.

Past Attitude toward Communists

And how am I a Marxist-Leninist? Am I one halfway? We revolutionaries do not know how to be anything halfway. We can only be something 100 per cent. And we will devote our energy entirely to this. Besides, it is a great satisfaction to have been an illiterate at eighteen years of age and to be a revolutionary, which I feel I am, at thirty and a "little." The "little" I believe is thirty and six. At eighteen, I had learned something, but there was much that I did not know. And we say this with all frankness to the people, with loyalty and clarity, as we have always spoken to the people—I have always spoken with complete frankness.

Did I have prejudices? I believe it is good to speak of this. Did I have prejudices with regard to Communists? Yes. Was I at times influenced by the propaganda of imperialism and by the reaction against the Communists? Yes. What did I believe regarding the Communists? Did I believe they were thieves? No, never. I always considered the Communists both in the university and elsewhere to be honorable people, honest and all that. But this has no special merit, because nearly everybody recognizes this. Did I have the idea that they were sectarian? Yes. Why did I have these opinions about the Communists? I am absolutely convinced that the ideas I had concerning the Communists (not with regard to Marxism, but with regard to the Communist Party) were like the ideas of many people, the product of propaganda and prejudices inculcated practically since childhood, almost since school days—in the universities, in the movies, and everywhere. Do I consider they could be wrong? Yes, I feel that they could be wrong. Marx, Engels, and Lenin are themselves the first to admit that they could be wrong, that they could make mistakes, because they did not consider themselves infallible.

What was my opinion of the militants of the Communist Party? Was it the opinion they really merited? If for a long time they were ignored, attacked, excluded, left out because they were considered a kind of plague, we should also recognize that it took great courage to be a Communist. Not today—no, we are going to see to it that it is rewarded from now on, of course!

It took courage to be a Communist at that time. Felix Torres has told me how they took him out of the prison of Santa Clara and made him go to Yaguajay on foot—on foot to Yaguajay! And this was the way it was, an infinity of sacrifices and efforts. The merit in being Communists when they were persecuted, when all doors were closed to them, when all presses, newspapers, and opportunities were shut off—we should recognize that merit. Much more, of course, than to be one today. Today, conditions are different. On that point, I have said that we must make efforts that the socialists and Marxists are real Marxists in the complete meaning of the word, that they are prepared for all contingencies.

But I wanted to say that I had prejudices against the [Popular] Socialist Party, prejudices that originated in the electoral campaigns. I confess it with the complete honesty with which I should confess all things. I am not going to ask anything from the Socialists. I say this when we are completely united and are all comrades, all socialists.

At certain moments at the beginning of the Revolution, we had some friction which arose out of differing conceptions on some points, but, fundamentally, because we were not talking to one another. I ought to say that there are people here who were victims of the intrigues of the first days, when, each time something happened, it was said that a group of Communists was creating a problem and instigating a riot. I must say myself that at one time I thought it was the Communists that were creating a riot in one place where a group of people had taken action with clubs against a citizen. . . . Afterward, I discovered that it was not Communists who had created the riot, but divisionist elements. . . .

This is the way it was at the first stage—the conflict between two things, in reality between prejudices, between a series of things. If a Communist was working on anything, his Communism had to be clandestine. But immediately there were the UPI, AP, and all the American newspapers crying out "ten, twelve, fifteen Communists." It was curious in those days that they called all the comrades Communists, and there were a number of comrades who were not members of the Communist Party but members of the 26th of July Movement. They called them that already, and published their Communist antecedents to all the world. They began a campaign that had, in many areas, a response influenced by the propaganda of anti-Communism and imperialism. Fortunately for all our efforts, these stages have passed.

I think that one of the bad aspects of those first days was the lack of greater interchange among the various organizations. Each of us was going somewhat on his own. It was the same revolutionary struggle which should have been more and more in contact, in discussion, and in interchange, to promote more and more unification.

I should mention one of the things in our terrible experience. Someday, when historians write about this stage and want to describe some characteristic of this revolution, they may say that we were establishing a socialist revolution without socialists. At that time, there was so much anti-Communist prejudice that when a Communist functionary was assigned to the smallest matter, a wave of protest arose, followed by numerous intrigues on the subject. At that time, our methods were socialist—a collective farm, a cooperative, a nationalized industry—those were all socialist institutions. We had good comrades for those jobs—wonderful comrades of the revolutionary movement of the 26th of July—but they did not succeed. If those men did not succeed, how were we going to succeed?

One of the most difficult things, then, was to carry out a socialist revolution without socialists. Later, when the process of unification of the revolutionary forces and the revolutionary organizations had begun, when anti-Communism was being defeated and destroyed, a stage came in which it was easier for a number of the members of the Socialist Party to carry out numerous functions without so much intrigue and divisionism.

The Integrated Revolutionary Organizations (ORI)

What was the meaning of this union? What was the significance of this moment in which the unification of all the revolutionary organizations took place? It meant—among other things—hundreds, thousands of cadres, of trained people, of people who had passed through sacrifices, through hard and difficult tests, and had a political education. On this point, I remember that some people came to me and said, "When are we going to carry out the program of the 26th?" And I said, "What program of the 26th are we going to carry out? Why not a Marxist-Leninist program?" And, "Why are we going to carry out two Marxist-Leninist programs?" This is reality. Anything else is a figment of the imagination.

Therefore, it meant the addition of thousands of trained leaders, who were indispensable, fundamental, and necessary for the creation of socialism. It signified the addition of all the cadres of the Revolutionary Directorate. They did not have the number of experienced leaders that the Socialist Party had, because there were people who said that no, they would rather do this or they would rather do that. You have to be a complete ignoramus with regard to the facts of revolution to think that a revolutionary can choose to do this or that. What we know about all revolutions is that work is divided today among all, and it is so great that it cannot be carried out; that many comrades, if they are in the army, would prefer to go to a military academy; if they are civil servants, they would prefer to go for something like a vacation to a school of revolutionary instruction. That is, the revolutionary considers it a rest—compared to the work which he must do—to be a pupil in the school.

The revolution today can count on all the cadres of all the revolutionary organizations. The important addition of the [Popular] Socialist Party has brought the cadres of the old militants educated in socialism by the Socialist Party. The addition of the Directorate has brought young people. The 26th of July Movement could not bring older, politically educated people, but has brought many young persons who were enthusiasts and revolutionists by vocation. It has also added all the experience acquired in the seizure of power. That is, we all have brought something, one way or another, and we represent the basic forces.

These forces were asked to unite in one single organization, and they have, therefore, joined together in the ORI. It was not easy. It took a long time, and at the end they joined together into the Integrated Revolutionary Organizations (ORI).

The manifestations of sectarianism have been disappearing in the same way that exclusiveness is going to disappear, in the same way that the practice of excluding people because they are Socialists is going to disappear, naturally, and so will sectarianism and these manifestations.* Certain manifestations of extremism are also going to disappear. Often extremism is a type of disease

---

* On March 26, 1962, Castro criticized a number of leaders of the Popular Socialist (Communist) Party for their "sectarianism" and attempt to dominate the ORI. Other groups in the ORI include the Union of Pioneers, the Cuban Women's Federation, the Young Rebels (later changed to Young Communists), and the Committees for the Defense of the Revolution.—ED.

that should not be confused, of course, with revolutionary firmness. Extremism is also a manifestation of a petty-bourgeois spirit in the revolutionary movement, and we must struggle against extremism just as much as against sectarianism.

There are many things that our people have had time to learn. They have had time to get rid of widespread prejudices picturing socialism as something terrible, inhuman, and hard—as a type of slavery—which is precisely the description that imperialism tries to impute to socialism. . . .

The Party of the Vanguard

We have all contributed to this unity, and we feel satisfied that we have contributed to it. We are all of us struggling to organize and create a strong, disciplined, and firm political organization of the vanguard of the working class and of the Cuban Revolution. How are we trying to do this? In the same way that the traditional parties do it—by inviting everyone, by opening up one's gates wide, so that all can come into the party? No.

What did the bourgeois parties, when in power, do? They opened their gates wide and invited everyone. Whatever party came to power immediately had a million members—all of a sudden. When we were naïve and did not know anything about politics, we accepted what the newspapers said—"As proof of what the Soviet Union is, the Communist Party does not have more than 5 million members in a population of 200 million"—as evidence, by capitalism and imperialism, that a minority ruled! In this way, they tried to make us see a Marxist revolutionary party from the standpoint of a bourgeois party. With a bourgeois party, the more people, the more boasting. The bourgeois party does not have ideology: It is a gang of politicians, a group of individuals who stick together and defend class interests. When more people belong, then there are more jobs and more boasting. They are not in the least concerned with the thinking of the members of the party. Hence, they try to conceal very carefully the fact that a Marxist revolutionary party is a party of the vanguard, a party that gives direction, and an elite party—that if the Soviet Union attempted to enlist Party members, there would be tens of millions of them. They conceal the fact that . . . a revolutionary party is an elite party, which directs and works fundamentally through mass organizations, through trade unions, through the youth, through women's federations, through committees for defense (an invention of the Cuban Revolution and a phenomenal mass organization), the peasant associations, the cooperatives (the collective farms are already in the trade unions). That is, the party gives direction and orientation through all the mass organizations.

Thus, the standard which the political organization of the Cuban Revolution should have is, in the first place, that of selection and quality. It will not be a quantitative organization; it will be a qualitative organization. . . .

And since, besides, we are conscious of the great enthusiasm of the masses, and of their revolutionary spirit, a party that is developing and becoming articulate in these conditions has all favorable conditions to select the best elements and the most positive and valuable people from the masses, and, to make them members of this organization. It is fundamental that these be precisely the best people, the best of the mass organizations—those who attain the honorable function of being members of the United Party of the Socialist Revolution (PURS).

The more that this is the case, the more every worker, peasant, intellectual, and citizen will realize that it means that every citizen can be a member of the United Party of the Socialist Revolution apart from whether he is a worker or not. That is, the gates are open for every true revolutionary who builds the revolution and is disposed to carry out his assignments and accept the program of the United Party of the Socialist Revolution fully and with complete conviction. . . .

Thus, I think that the ideal system, the most perfect encountered by man for governing a country (a system that does not aspire to be eternal but simply transitory, as are the stages which the history of a country is destined to realize) is a system of government with a revolutionary, democratically organized party under collective leadership. This means that this party ought to exercise the functions of leadership.

This is the best system if democratic standards function, if the standards of collective leadership function. If democratic standards do not function, if the standards of collective leadership do not function, then the system can be very bad, like any other system. But if the fundamental principles of internal democracy maintain a collective leadership, this is without any doubt the most perfect method of government, especially for a country in a stage of revolutionary transition.

What does this mean? In the first place, if this party is not a party that amasses membership but a party that selects them, the best citizens of the country will enter this party, on the basis of their conditions and merits. They will enter into revolutionary cells. There will be a long-term process of learning, direct experience, and the fulfillment of duty.

Little by little, because of his merit, a citizen can go on assuming responsibilities that continually grow greater. This citizen can arrive at membership of the regional directorate, of the central directorate, of the national directorate. He can hold these positions according to his merit. This is not the case of the king who passes on his power to his idiot son. It is not the case of a military leader who happens to be successful, because there can be men who are excellent war-makers and, as war-makers, acquire fame and prestige and, as rulers, are perfectly stupid. This is not a question of demagogues, or of clowns, or of theatrical personalities. In a party where the standards of discipline, principle, selection, internal democracy, and collective leadership predominate, a stupid person cannot advance—an idiot cannot become head of state. The lucky adventurer cannot do so. This school will be a school in which men are proving themselves, where they are learning and where they are acquiring proficiency. . . .

So what can the party of this revolutionary people do? This party will be the great instrument of merit, the instrument of revolutionary calling and revolutionary intelligence. This party should be above individuals, because it is the party that is going to include not the value of one intelligence, but the value of tens of thousands, of hundreds of thousands of intelligences; not the value of one hero, but the value of the heroism of all; not the value of one spirit of sacrifice, but the value of the spirit of hundreds of thousands of citizens and the spirit of combat, of love of the revolution. This is what the United Party of the Cuban Socialist Revolution must be.

THE ROAD TO REVOLUTION
IN LATIN AMERICA*

. . . This date is important—not as something concerning the past, but as something concerning the future. Here in our country there was a powerful professional army at the service of the exploiters; there were numerous bourgeois parties that dragged a section of the masses along wrong roads; and there was a whole system of press, radio, and television at the service of the vested interests. Even more, when Batista seized power, the country had a financial situation such as no other country in Latin America enjoys today because in the vaults of the National Bank of Cuba were more than $500 million in foreign exchange. This is not the situation in Guatemala. This is not the situation in Ecuador. This is not the situation in Peru. This is not the situation in Argentina. This is not the situation in Colombia. This is not the situation in Venezuela. This is not the situation in Nicaragua, in Honduras, and other countries of Central America.

And in spite of this, under these difficult conditions for the Revolution—as always happens in history when the efforts and the ideas of a few, if the effort is well directed and the ideas are correct, become little by little converted into the effort and the ideas of the masses—in those difficult conditions our people found a way out.

The Moncada Barracks did not fall. Unforeseen factors caused the failure of the attempt to seize the fortress—imponderable factors. That could have been a hard blow for us, to our convictions and our faith that this was the right road. It could have strengthened particularly the position of those who said it was not possible to fight against Batista's army. It could have strengthened particularly the position of the machine politicians and their arguments in favor of election deals in which the people never get anything. Nevertheless, our faith remained firm, unshakeable, that

* Excerpts from a speech delivered by Castro on July 26, 1963; translated and published by Pioneer Publishers (New York, 1963), and reprinted by permission.

this was the road, and we resumed work—now with more experience, with greater carefulness, in advancing the struggle.

But when we landed from the "Granma"—eighty-two men— we were still betrayed by our inexperience, by our immaturity as fighters, and once again a stiff reverse hit our forces. This expeditionary force—organized and prepared at great effort and sacrifices —was virtually dispersed and annihilated.

That could have been a tremendous blow to our faith and our conviction that this was the road. Nevertheless, our faith and our conviction remained unshakeable. We believed that this was the road and finally history and facts, reality and life, proved that it was the road!

And those who were surrounded in the cane fields that day, so few that they could be counted on the fingers of one hand, and who have lived through these ten years of revolution and of struggle and who today stand before a whole people like this—a great people like this, which is both the creator and the product of the Revolution—how can we not feel in the depth of our souls the conviction and the faith that for peoples there is always a road— that for oppressed peoples there is always a solution?

But this road does not open by itself; this road must be opened up; this road must be opened by the revolutionary fighters. There is a means of opening up the road and that is to say, "We must open the road!" And there is a means of never opening the road and that is to say, "We don't want to open the road!"

In many Latin American countries the prerevolutionary conditions are incomparably better than those which existed in our country. There are countries in Latin America, plundered and made destitute by the monopolies and the oligarchies, where hungry and desperate masses await an opening to erupt into history.

And it is the duty of revolutionaries to make this opening. The duty of the revolutionary is not only to study theory. The duty of revolutionaries does not consist of gorging on theoretical knowledge, forgetting the practical realities of the revolution. The duty of revolutionaries is not only to learn, to know, and to feel convinced of a conception of life, history, and revolutionary society, but also the conception of a road, of a tactic, of a strategy that leads to the victory of those ideas.

That is the duty of revolutionaries—not to wait for the "Greek calends" to see if the roads open by themselves, or if by some miracle the exploiting regimes disappear.

And the duty of the revolutionaries, above all at this moment, is to know how to perceive and catch the changes in the correlation of forces which have taken place in the world, and to understand that this change facilitates the struggle of the peoples. The duty of revolutionaries, of the Latin American revolutionaries, is not to wait for a change in the correlation of forces to produce the miracle of social revolutions in Latin America, but to make full use of everything that favors the revolutionary movement in this changed correlation of forces and to make revolutions! This is something only too clear and obvious.

And the blame if certain conditions are squandered, if the opportunity is not seized, if circumstances are not properly utilized, will not fall on anyone—no other party or revolutionary state, nor on us—the blame will fall on the revolutionaries in each country, on whom it lies to make a revolution.

To us this is an obvious fact; it is a very evident fact for Latin America and we are quite clear about this.

If we had not made the revolution, would somebody have made it for us? We made the revolution and then we found support in favorable circumstances—support and advantage in the extraordinary change in the correlation of forces; the support of the Soviet Union and of the entire socialist camp.

We know, from experience and conviction, that every people that does what the Cuban people did will have the firm support of the Soviet Union and of the entire socialist camp. And where the revolutionaries do not know how to fulfill their duty, they alone will be held responsible before their people; they alone will bear the guilt before history—because it lies with them to decide and to act. What we can do is to reaffirm this conviction, reaffirm this absolute faith that the Cuban Revolution opened the perspectives for the struggle in many countries of this continent, and that the Cuban Revolution opened a road, provided an experience and an example which, if fully understood, will be very useful to other Latin American peoples.

What is the situation of Latin America? That of a continent in crisis, a continent where revolution is inevitable.

When we use the general term "Latin America" in speaking about revolution, we do not mean that conditions are exactly the same in all countries. There are some countries where a certain political stability exists, greater political stability than in others, an economic situation which differs from others. We refer to those countries where the oligarchies have imposed an iron power on the exploited masses, and where all roads ahead are closed to the people.

But, in general terms, Latin America's situation is that of a continent where the population grows at a faster rate than its wealth, and where poverty, consequently, is continually increasing; a continent producing raw materials and agricultural products the price of which is dropping lower and lower in the market while the price of imported articles is constantly rising; a continent where the nations each year export more and receive less in exchange for what they export; a continent where the masses are daily acquiring greater revolutionary awareness and where political crises follow each other with amazing rapidity.

You have had the opportunity of reading the news about what has been happening in Argentina, in Peru, in Ecuador, Colombia, Guatemala, Paraguay, Nicaragua, and other countries. The Alliance for Progress is in crisis, and in crisis for a series of reasons. The imperialists try to blackmail the oligarchies and the oligarchies try to blackmail the imperialists.

The imperialists tell them, "If you don't carry out some reforms, Communism will spread." And the oligarchies say to the imperialists, "If you don't give us some money, Communism will spread."

And, of course, the oligarchies are not capable of carrying out reforms and the imperialists don't have any money to squander. The oligarchs are incapable of making reforms and the imperialists are incapable of conceiving of any kind of aid that is not aid for their own interests, aid for their own companies, their monopolies. And, consequently, it is absolutely impossible for this offspring of imperialism and the oligarchies to bring the slightest benefit to the people. . . .

What do the imperialists say? That they won't re-establish diplomatic relations with a "Soviet satellite in the Caribbean." The only country in America—the only one—where there is no foreign-owned property, the only country in America which is the owner of all its wealth, its mines, its oil, its land, its factories—which does not have to give a centavo in tribute to the Yankee monopolies; the only country in America that can say, "These riches are ours; we're going to develop them now; we're going to use them the way that best fits our interests"—that's Cuba. And they say it's a satellite. This people who own their small island, its lands, its mountains, its coasts, its buildings, its factories, its schools; who are putting all these riches at the service of the future, of the growing generations, of youth who constitute the hundreds of thousands of technicians that will make our country advance toward horizons perhaps unforeseeable today!

Clearly, in the same way that this is a "captive people"—according to these gentlemen—"the captive people of Cuba," this is the "satellite" country of the Americas: the only country that is in a position to benefit completely from its wealth.

And what has it received from the Soviet Union? Aid so extraordinary that possibly what they have provided us with in a year is more than imperialism has provided to all the oligarchies put together. And the Soviet Union, the Soviet people, have made sacrifices to help us and have given extraordinary aid in building factories. Are they the property of the Soviet Union? No, they are Cuban. They have sent fifteen modern fishing ships, which have enabled us to supply fish for our population, and they are training the crews in order to deliver these ships to us. They have delivered planes to maintain our communications and established a direct line in spite of all the obstacles placed by imperialism, thanks to which we maintain secure our communication with the world. In Mariel they are building a thermoelectric plant of 500,000 kilowatts. For whom? For Electric Bond and Share? No! For the people of Cuba! In Renté they are building a thermoelectric plant of 200,000 kilowatts. For whom? For the Electric Company to rob the people? No! For the people of Cuba; for our needs, for our industries! They are going to solve the problem of mechanizing cane cutting in our country, hard work, at which hundreds of thousands of workers have to make enormous sacrifices every year. This will make possible enormous harvests in the future. Because in the future—we say it so the whole world will know—we are going to produce great quantities of sugar. And we propose in the year 1970 to produce 8 million tons of sugar, because our country has the conditions for sugar—plans which we could not even dream of without mechanizing cane cutting.* And the Soviet Union is solving this problem for us, making efforts, making sacrifices.

And this is what Mr. Kennedy [President John F. Kennedy] calls a "satellite." In order not to be a "satellite" we would have

* In 1963, Cuba produced 3.8 million tons of sugar, compared to the 1961 high (before collectivization) of 6.7 million tons.—ED.

to be exploited. All the sugar mills here would have to belong to the imperialist Yankees; all the mines, the electricity, the public services—as in many countries of Latin America—and these are "free countries!" But these "free countries" can't get even "four cats" together in a meeting generally. Let them ask Betancourt to call a meeting . . . and see how many turn out. These are the "free countries." They are not captives. No!

What do they mean when they say they cannot coexist with a satellite? We can live without coexisting with them, of course, in the first place, since we do not exist because of them; we exist in spite of them—which is not the same thing. But they can't coexist with us? What do they want? That we make ideological concessions? We will not make an atom of ideological concession to the imperialists. And if they want to discuss, if they want to negotiate, they have to discuss and negotiate with the Marxist-Leninist Cuban Revolution. And without the slightest alteration in our position of fraternal, warm, indestructible friendship with the Soviet Union and the socialist camp!

Concessions of an ideological order we will not make. In the ideological sphere we will not make a single concession. We are a firm people, a revolutionary people, a people with only one policy, and a loyal people that knows how to maintain friendship without a shadow of opportunism in our policy. . . .

We said, "We are ready to discuss." Yes, we are ready to discuss indemnity formulas, as we have done with the Canadians, the relations with whom we can point to as a model of relations between a socialist country and a capitalist country, and they are good, because they don't interfere in our internal affairs. When the nationalization laws went into effect, we indemnified the Canadian interests, and we have always resolved any differences in a friendly way.

Likewise, speaking to the British ambassador, we told him we were ready to discuss indemnity matters, to discuss some sort of economic agreement which would include indemnification for the interests that were nationalized. And in a similar way we have talked with the Swiss. In other words, we have applied this policy.

We are ready to discuss. They don't want to? The worse for them, we won't discuss! They don't want to establish relations with us? We are very sorry; we will wait; We will even wait until there is a socialist government in the United States. We are perfectly able to wait! . . .

THE COMMUNIST PARTY OF CUBA*

Starting from the conception of the Party as the representative of the laboring masses, organized and operated with the constant participation of the workers, we conclude that the Party, as the most legitimate representative of the workers of the country, can and has the right to elect local government officials. And at the same time, the Party can and should, if necessary, remove from office any officeholder, even the head of the local government, if he does not carry out his responsibilities.

As to the title which we were going to give the officeholders, we discussed some earlier titles and finally decided almost unanimously that they should be called president—president of the local government, president of the regional government, and president of the provincial government. We did not work out the manner in which they should be elected. Later, when the comrades were preparing the report, they decided that they should be elected at a meeting of all the Party members. . . .

Since it is not possible for all the representatives of the [Party] cells to participate in a provincial or national election, all the cells will meet together up to the regional level, where they will elect representatives to a provincial assembly, which will then elect representatives to a National Congress. What does this mean? That the cell will be the base of the Party, the cell members will go to the municipality and to the region and there in the region the representatives of all the cells will elect representatives of the Party for the province and the nation. This is a very direct method, a more efficient method, and a method that will certainly work better. The other way, in an assembly of five or six thousand, it is difficult to have any discussion of an election. In practice certain formulas and proposals are simply presented without any possibility of analyzing and considering the reasons for a decision or in favor of one person or another. . . .

I think we can go to any part of the world and convince anyone that our system is a thousand times more revolutionary, a thousand times more democratic, than all those systems by which the bour-

* Excerpts from speeches by Fidel Castro at the first meeting of the Central Committee of the Communist Party of Cuba, September 30–October 2, 1965; translated by the editor from *Granma*, October 10, 1965.

geoisie try to sell their worthless representative democracy, their bourgeois democracy in which they have elections every four years but the masses have no participation in [solving] social and economic problems. The so-called representatives of the masses who are the representatives of a specific class are a thousand miles from the masses. They do not represent anyone, certainly not those who elect them.

When the time comes to defend the institutions of our Revolution, we can discuss them in any university or intellectual center in the world and prove that we have a very superior governmental system, a much more democratic governmental system, a government henceforth by one class, that of the workers. When all the citizens are workers, then it is a government of the whole people. To achieve this we must keep this objective before us and struggle unceasingly to establish this society—the Communist society. . . .

When the forces of the revolution began to unite, the name we used was the Integrated Revolutionary Organizations (ORI). Because there were errors in the way in which this was done, problems of sectarianism arose and consequently it was necessary to make a thorough criticism of that vice which had developed. Instead of the name which had been used thus far, we conceived the idea of using a new and, we may say, more advanced name. First, there was the Integrated Revolutionary Organizations, then came the name, the United Party of the Cuban Socialist Revolution. There is no doubt that this name is a valued one, one which has been used throughout the process of formation of the Party. But still it is not a name which can be used for all time. . . .

We are fighting for a higher type of society, the Communist society. This name has been calumniated by the exploiters in the capitalist society, and even before capitalism—in the period of slavery, in the period of feudalism, and even in the period of the bourgeois revolutions—it has been a name which the exploiters, those who live by the sweat and labor of other men and other peoples, have tried to blot out.

When we say a Communist society, we are speaking of a higher type of society, a thousand times more just and perfect than that rotten bourgeois imperialist society which discriminates against men and sacrifices them, which condemns women to prostitution and children to misery, which shows no mercy and has no ideal but the worship of riches and money.

We are fighting for a new higher type of society which no nation today has achieved and I think that we can compete in this effort to try to be among the first to achieve these more advanced forms of human society. If we pursue this objective, we should raise up the ideals of the Revolution for men to see, expressed in the name of the Party so that the members of our Party may always keep in mind what those objectives are and how we must try to achieve them—objectives which I am sure our people will achieve among the first in the world.

And therefore to adopt a name which implies both the absolute unity of all the people and at the same time expresses the final goals of our Revolution, we have suggested the name of the Communist Party of Cuba. . . .

23. *Victor Raúl Haya de la Torre*

Victor Raúl Haya de la Torre was born in Trujillo, Peru, in 1895, and educated both in that country and in England. He began political activity as a student and, after leading a protest movement against the government, was jailed and expelled from the country. While in exile in Mexico, in 1924, he formed the Alianza Popular Revolucionaria Americana (usually referred to as the APRA, or Aprista Party). Its program called for the involvement of the Indian in political life, Latin American unity, and opposition to foreign imperialism. In 1931, he returned to Peru from exile to run for the Presidency. He probably won the election, but the government imprisoned him and killed many of his followers. He was released in 1933, but went underground to avoid being arrested again. In 1945, he came out of hiding, and his party, supporting the election of a Conservative President, won a considerable electoral victory. In 1948, however, dictatorship returned to Peru, and Haya de la Torre took refuge in the Colombian Embassy, where he remained until 1954, when he was given a guarantee of safe conduct to leave the country. After the overthrow of the dictatorship in 1957, he returned to Peru.

Now once again active in national politics, Haya de la Torre was a Presidential candidate in June, 1962. The military annulled this election, and he ran again unsuccessfully a year later.

His political writings are characterized by an effort to develop a distinctively Latin American (he would say Indo-American) political formula which does not imitate European or American models. He is anti-Communist and anti-imperialist, but believes that an alliance of the workers, the peasants, and the middle classes can control and utilize foreign investment (for "imperialism is the first stage of capitalism in underdeveloped countries"), establish rural cooperatives, and develop the countries of Latin America under a "directed" economy which also allows private enterprise and initiative. The works from which the following selections are taken were published two decades apart. In his more recent writing, as is evident here, Haya de la Torre has somewhat softened the dogmatism of his original theory, particularly with regard to nationalization and relations with the United States.

INDO-AMERICA*

In my opinion, the term "Spanish America" corresponds to the colonial epoch, the term "Latin America" corresponds to the republican period, and the term "Pan-America" is an expression of Yankee imperialism. "Indo-America" is the expression of the new revolutionary conception of America which, having passed through the period of Spanish and Anglo-Saxon conquests, will create a definite political, economic, and social organization on the national base of its workers, who represent the tradition, and the race of the exploited indigenous masses who, throughout the economy of [Central and South] America (the unity of which is indestructible) have formed the basis of our productivity and the core of our collective life from the time of the period before Columbus.

It is true that the terms are used at the same time. Some say Pan-America, others Spanish America, some Latin America, and others Indo-America. But this coexistence has a social and economic significance. Up to the present day in [Latin] America, there has also been both a coexistence and an opposition between the various periods of historic evolution that followed after one an-

* Excerpts from Victor Raúl Haya de la Torre, ¿A Dónde Vá Indoamérica? (Santiago de Chile: Biblioteca América, 1936); translated by the editor, by permission.

other in other continents. In [Central and South] America, we have, living together and at the same time in opposition, within the frontiers of our continent or even within the frontiers of each country, all forms of social organization and every level of economic development—savagery, barbarism, and civilization, communal primitive agriculture, feudalism, manufacturing, industrialism, and imperialism. Indians who have never known the use of a wheel as a means of locomotion see swift airplanes in the skies above their mountains. The young gentleman of Buenos Aires who plays golf and visits London has as compatriot and fellow citizen the half-naked Indian in the Chaco. The same thing is true in Peru and Mexico and Colombia and Central America.

This lack of definition, this contradiction, this historic juxtaposition, if the terms are appropriate, describes in great part the dialectic of our educational development. [Latin] America has been and is a land that has experienced invasions—as Europe once did. From the immigrations and transmigrations of the period before Columbus . . . from Asia, from Indo-America, from Oceania, from the North to the South and back, America has been the site of invasions and countless conquests. Three centuries of Spanish domination represent a long period in our history. It seems to us almost an eternity because it was so recent, but it is less in time than the eight centuries of Arab domination over Spain, for example. The Arabs gave Spain a great civilization and formed a southern racial mixture. They left behind 10 per cent of the word-roots in the language, according to the philologists. The Arabs would have the right to demand, as thanks from the Spaniards, that they call Spain Ibero-Arabia or something similar. But the Arab invasion was just that—an invasion—and historically it created a movement of independence in which many Hispano-Arabs fought to free themselves from the tutelage of their racial ancestors. The religious factor in this struggle corresponds to the period and is less clear than in the struggle of the natives [of Latin America] against Spain. Yet, in both conquests and "reconquests," we can see economic causes which are the basis of all great historic phenomena.

In [Central and South] America, after suffering the inroads of feudalism and mercantilism along with the conquest and Spanish colonization, we now have been suffering the invasion of industrialism or capitalism. . . . It may be that this new invasion will be less extensive in this period, when everything proceeds at a faster pace, but it *is* an invasion with its own particular characteristics, its own particular politics, and with formidable social effects. The question for the future is whether we will undergo further invasions. Underneath these conquering influences from outside, there persists one economic fact—the conqueror always seeks wealth. And the Indian or his descendants, in the great majority, work to create this wealth. It has been calculated by experts that there are more than 75 million Indians in [Latin] America. This means approximately 75 per cent of our total population.* Those Indians, with their own traditions, their own languages, their own suffering and aspirations, with their own great problem, constitute in their immense majority a work force, "productivity," the hand that creates the riches. This is the way it has been from the social point of view until now and, relatively speaking, always in [Latin] America. . . .

We in the vanguard, the Apristas, the anti-imperialists of [Latin] America, who are inclined to interpret history economically, have adopted the term Indo-America as a fundamental expression. The invasions of the Anglo-Saxon, Spanish, and Negro races have come to us, are coming to us, and will come to us; they have contributed and continue to contribute to the context of a new [Latin] America. Yet there survives underneath all these the force of the labor of the Indian. If in Cuba he has been wiped out and in Argentina and Costa Rica absorbed, the Indian continues to be the ethnic, social, and economic basis of [Latin] America. This is true both for those who live in the framework of modern civilization and for those who in great number are still grouped in primitive tribal organizations. Many other races are mixed with the Indian race, but this America of ours will find its identity and its course before those 75 million natives have disappeared. Every immigration, every conquest has partially modified the Indo-American race, but the ethnic basis of our people is still definitely native.

Those who live in this period struggle against the Yankee capitalist imperialism just as those who lived 100 years ago struggled against feudal Spanish, French, and Portuguese imperialism. Yankee domination, if it lasts, will also leave its profound traces on us, just as the Spanish domination did. The "Latin American" period, which historically replaced the "Spanish American" period,

* The present population of Latin America is more than 200 million—double Haya de la Torre's 1936 estimate.—Ed.

can be succeeded also by a "Pan-American" stage. We are working against this, especially as regards its imperialist implications. After these three stages, which result from ethnic, political, economic, and spiritual invasions, will come the Indo-America which is to be established and defined. The new revolution in Latin America will be a revolution with an Indian base and orientation, with the native conscience and subconscious expressed in an economic and social renaissance. The Mexican revolution is a symptom of this great movement. The countries where the Indian does not predominate in Latin America cannot withdraw from his influence. . . .

Imperialism in Action

The first stage of industrial capitalism in Central America, as in the majority of our countries, begins with imperialism, which is "the last stage of capitalism" in the typical industrial countries. Capitalism arrives then in these agrarian countries at the height of its expansion, voracious, and developed, without any of the bourgeois virtues that emerged during the historic evolution of European societies in the period of transition from feudalism to industrialism. In Central America, as in most of the Latin American countries, capitalism arrives already imperialist, violent, and piratical, not to construct but only to exploit and withdraw all, leaving almost nothing behind. Vice, corruption, false views of life and of progress are raised up in consequence, and only sorrow and disillusionment are left, a grave danger for those people—their most complicated and serious political, economic, and social problem. . . .

The Struggle of the Two Imperialisms

There are two imperialisms struggling for Latin America, that of Europe and that of North America. But European imperialism is continually losing its influence, while North American imperialism is increasing. Business . . . is one of the aspects and manifestations of imperialism. The commercial struggle between Europe and the United States for Latin American markets is one of the most important consequences of the imperialist struggle between the United States and Europe, a struggle that has other manifestations in the battle for special concessions—linked to the tendencies for political domination of our countries of which

Pan-Americanism is an instrument—and to the subjection of the economic life of our countries to the investors. . . .

The Reform of Cordoba

After 1918, from one end to the other of the Latin American continent there arose a new awareness among the youth. From the old University of Cordoba there was the first outcry: "Until now, the universities have been a perennial haven of mediocrities, a source of profit for the ignorant, a secure shelter for the weak, and, what is still worse, a place where all forms of tyranny and stupidity find a source of inspiration. The universities have succeeded in being the faithful reflection of those decadent societies which present a sad spectacle of senile immobility. For this reason, knowledge passes silently by those mute and closed dwellings, or enters mutilated and grotesque into the service of bureaucracy. If in the name of order we are asked to follow along deceitful and docile, we proclaim aloud the sacred right of revolution. Henceforth, the only hope is the heroic destiny of the youth. Sacrifice is our greatest stimulus, the spiritual redemption of the youth of Latin America our only recompense, for we know that our ills are the ills of the entire continent." And the "sacred right of revolution" was exercised in Cordoba, in Buenos Aires, in La Plata, in Lima, in Montevideo, in Santiago de Chile, in Havana, in Bogotá, and in Mexico. The students of the old universities revolted against the past. In that tumultuous and lyrical movement against the old educational systems, there streamed a new spirit of youth which sought to free itself from everything that closed off the past from the future. Henceforth, there was only one [Latin] America. In its broad and fertile lands, a struggle has arisen that will be final. On the one side, the spirit of the past—reactionary and diminishing; on the other side, the revolutionary impulse of youth, which sees its destiny looming up before it. From 1918 to 1925, the conscience of the youth developed and became more precisely defined. At that time, it aimed at the renovation of the educational system and a spiritual confederation of Latin America. Today it seeks a more profound transformation. It struggles for the renovation of the social systems. It aspires to a political confederation of our twenty republics which are divided by artificial nationalism and menaced in common by the conquering imperialism of the United States and the North.

The spirit of [Latin] American youth continually advances to the future. Misunderstood by the old generations of our bourgeois classes, by our bureaucracies, by our oligarchies, it has in them a near and implacable enemy. Young blood, blood of the new liberators of America, has watered our soil. Graves for our new victims have been dug in our land each time that our youth has proclaimed "the sacred right of revolution." But our struggle has hardly begun. Our enemies are powerful and inexorable. They consist in the alliance of Latin American feudalism, the sad remnant of the conquering brutality of Spain, and powerful Yankee imperialism—animating spirit of our new bourgeois class, exalter of our provincialisms, inciter of our tyrannies, creator of our governments, and accomplice in our degenerate internal struggles. . . .

The Aprista Thesis

For the fulfillment of *Aprista* doctrine, a party has been created which, like the work it hopes to accomplish, is Latin American in character. The base of this party is in the producers, in alliance with the middle classes, also involved in the struggle against imperialism. The party attempts to form an "anti-imperialist consciousness" in the working classes—a consciousness that they are the ones who produce for imperialism, and they alone are those who can place conditions upon it and constitute a force of liberation—without hoping that the proletarians of Europe and the United States will destroy the capitalist system, the origin of imperialism. The alliance with the middle classes reinforces the action of the working classes, especially those which are specifically laborers—new in their role as controlling forces in the state, just as the (economic) system in Latin America which determines their existence as a class is new.

Aprismo already has opened the doors to the future because, following the economic independence of Latin America—an independence that will have to be based on equality in the exchange of raw materials and finished products and the investment of capital according to the principle of progressive nationalization of the sources of production under the control of the state—it will bring about the industrialization of our countries. As a result, a working class will be formed, and favorable conditions will be created for the rapid total direction of the economy and the abolition of the capitalist system. While this revolutionary process is being carried out, *Aprismo* will utilize the anti-imperialist forces of today, not excluding the middle classes, which are threatened with extinction by imperialism. It will seek to defend them through the anti-imperialist state which, by nationalization and progressive socialization of the sources of production, will be definitely oriented in the direction of state capitalism, preventing the middle classes from tending toward large private capitalism, which would mean a return to imperialism.

Aprismo thus presents a complete doctrine and a realistic method of realistic action—that is, an integral economic, social, and political program to secure the economic independence of Latin America.

THIRTY YEARS OF *APRISMO**

The Land of Reflection

Aprismo can demonstrate a particular origin that distinguishes it from the other movements and doctrines of the same type in Indo-America—not only because of its characteristic Bolivarian militancy (it is in Bolivar's glorious name that only the APRA demands the unification of the continent), but also because of the special quality of the numerous movements that preceded it. One can trace their beginning from the active youth movement that between 1918 and 1923 established and propagated the University Reform in all of our republics. From this movement, the founders of APRA have drawn two active inspirational ideals to be translated into moral slogans: to liberate our generation from the "mental colonialism" of Europe, and to unite the intellectual and manual workers to attain together the ambitious goal of a democratic civilization—to establish a confederation of all of our peoples and to attain for them economic justice, without impairment of their liberty. . . . Without these guidelines, it would have been unthinkable, unexpected, and perhaps heretical to conceive or attempt a judgment from *here* and not from *Europe* of our particular historical reality and our special sociological problems.

*Excerpts from Victor Raúl Haya de la Torre, *Treinta Años de Aprismo* (Mexico City: Fonda de Cultura Económica, 1956); translated by the editor, by permission.

This continent was still the "land of reflection," alluded to by Hegel. In its soil were the buds, offshoots, and seedlings—accidental in all cases—of all the ideas, philosophic sects, literary novelties, and partisan tendencies that could be of use to the Old World. And thus, just as we had countless spokesmen of the utilitarianism of Bentham and Mill, of Saint-Simonianism and of Comte's positivism, of materialism with all its varieties, and of idealism of various kinds, and as there was no lack of monarchists, Jacobins, anarchists, and others, all with their respective heterodoxies and oppositions, by the same process—to pass over a century and move to the world conflagration of the first great war and beyond—Marxism was developed and the Bolshevik echo of Marxism resounded and then there sprang up the totalitarians, the racists, and the perennial growth of jingoism. But one or the other, those for, and those against, always in imitation—inasmuch as it was obligatory not to go beyond the European models, and not to be separated from their pre-established patterns of thought. . . .

Aprismo *and Communism*

The total separation between *Aprismo* and Communism is obviously fundamental. They start out from divergent historical conceptions. For Communism, the pronouncements of Marx, conceived in one area and one given period (Europe in the nineteenth century), are unimpeachable truths of universal validity. For *Aprismo*, the Marxist conception is an important historical antecedent, but not unchangeable. It is limited and relative to the particular conditions of space and time that make it dialectically opposed to a reality that is different from that of Europe. Marx himself declares in the prologue of *Capital* that the basis of his observation was England—the England of the industrial capitalism of the middle of the nineteenth century—and that from the examination of the English reality, he deduced his "theoretical ideas" as "physics observes the physical phenomenon wherever it occurs." The "classic soil" of the capitalist system is England—that is, the country which, being in the forefront of industrial development at that time, was the prototype of all the others. From here, in a generalization of universal scope, the founder of scientific socialism goes on to say in the same prologue: "The country that is the most industrially developed alone shows the way of the less developed, the image of their own future."

That is the English model. And this was an unfulfilled *European* prediction of world economic development. In the "mirror" (as some translators have figuratively translated the idea of Marx's word "image"), there was hardly the reflection of the future of many countries, and none was reflected as an exact replica. The evolution of capitalism has taken unexpected directions in the last hundred years, and some non-European areas have prospered economically without in any way resembling the special English model. . . .

Then, distinct from the Communist transplantation to Indo-America of the "party of only one class" and of the European employer, *Aprismo* has put forward arguments that thus far have not been answered: among others, that of the lack of comparability of the proletarian class of the large capitalist countries in a state of advanced industrialization which *produce machinery*, to the producing class of the colonial and semicolonial countries whose infant industrialism, working with raw or half-finished materials, *does not produce machinery*—a fundamental distinction to which I shall return shortly; also the various types of class-consciousness which cannot be confused, that of the long-standing and highly trained proletariats at a high level of civilization, and that of those with a brief history and a much slower and lagging development. *Aprismo* emphasizes the different character—so often referred to by the *Aprista* thesis—of the urban and rural middle classes of Europe and those of Indo-America and the necessity of incorporating our middle classes in the single popular front of *Aprismo*. For these classes are the first ones affected by imperialistic expansion, and from this source have come excellent leaders and vigorous civic movements in defense of the economic emancipation of our peoples. . . .

Between the Communist anti-imperialism in the service of the Soviet empire, and *Aprista* anti-imperialism in defense of our countries, there is the firm separation between two economic and social scenes which cannot be compared—that of the Old World and that of the New World. They should not be confused, despite the way in which the imperialists and their agents and helpers have thoughtlessly claimed to involve us against our will with domestic Communism, which is clearly obedient to foreign ideologies and direction and which attacks us unscrupulously and ceaselessly. . . .

Latin America and the French Revolution

For the discontented colonials of Portuguese and Spanish America, the French Revolution was a great example. Despite the fact that the social and political content of the French movement corresponded to an economic and social stage much more advanced than that which historically was the case among the Indo-American peoples, we adopted the slogans, the precepts, and the formulas of Paris as an infallible recipe that could give us also "liberty, equality, and fraternity." While in France this signified the collapse of feudalism, in Indo-America it represented the affirmation and independence of the feudal colonial power. There the landowning aristocracy was crushed, while here the landholding native aristocrats liberated themselves by revolution from the empire of the mother country and captured the state as an instrument of their class domination.

In these circumstances, the same antifeudal ideology of the French bourgeoisie was used in a revolution of the feudal landowning Spanish- or Portuguese-American class against the economic and political yoke that the Spanish (and Portuguese) crown imposed on it. And from this paradox alone, the result was that, paradoxically, the revolutions of emancipation of Indo-America resulted in political regimes that were democratic in name and corresponded to a later economic and social stage of bourgeois capitalism, but in contradiction to the feudal organization of the dominant system of production in our lands—since independence did not destroy the large plantation but confirmed it. The ideas of the French liberals and radicals lost their subversive effect once the Indo-American republics were established. The slaves were not liberated at once, in spite of the democratic creed. Despite the initial cry of emancipation, the slavery of the Indian continued. Isolation, dear to the landowner, the single class that triumphed from the revolution of independence, brought about the division and subdivision of the ancient viceroyalties of Spain into many republics. All this took place because the economic basis on which society rested was feudal. . . .

Imperialism, the First Stage of Capitalism

Aprista theory recognizes that imperialism, the first stage of capitalism in our countries, brings with it industrialization, although this is unilaterally imposed, and it represents a period of evolution of the economy and of civilization superior to that of colonial feudalism. Modern imperialism, especially North American imperialism, which is so advanced and refined in its methods, only offers advantages and progress at its outset, and produces in our country a progressive movement of the working masses who pass from semislavery and servitude or from the elementary forms of free labor to its specifically proletarian type.

It should be said that as "the *first* stage of capitalism," imperialism brings about the emergence in our countries of the industrial proletarian class, although, for this particular type of industrialism, which is not metalworking, manufacturing, or heavy production, this proletariat is very far from displaying the same characteristics, and having the same experience and same class-consciousness as the long-standing and highly trained proletariats of the imperialist countries of developed industrialism. Our industrial working classes in a semicolonial industry of raw materials have a different character.

Thus, imperialism as an economic phenomenon, as the first stage of capitalism in Indo-America—as a stage of ineluctable, progressive industrialization—is both dangerous and necessary. With it, we run the risk of subjection, but without it, there would be inevitable stagnation and retrogression.

Given the preceding propositions, we can conclude that the way for the Indo-American peoples to defy imperialism is to defend themselves from inundation, but without making the water disappear. With this advanced figurative comparison, we mark one of the fundamental *Aprista* declarations, different from those which serve as pretexts for the Communist theses on the phenomenon of imperialism. These tend to direct revolutionary action to stop up the very sources and foundations of the whole system of capitalist production, one of whose huge and widespread effects is imperialism. My book in 1928 has already explained with all exactness that industrial capitalism, which is imported into Indo-America with the imperialist stage, is incipient, young, and colonial or semicolonial in type; that it cannot be compared, as to both its origin and its method of production to the industrial capitalism of the regions of the world in which this economic system has developed. Consequently, this imperialist capitalism has created an industrial proletarian class that is also distinct from the old and organically established industrial proletarian class of Europe. Using their own Marxist teachings as a weapon of argument against the

Communist generalizations—according to which the capitalist system can be eliminated only by the revolutionary activity of the industrial proletariats of countries that are highly developed, where class-consciousness and organizational strength have made possible that transformation—my book concludes "that the radical abolition of the capitalist system cannot be accomplished except where capitalism has arrived at the climax of its development, namely in the large countries, which are in the vanguard of world industry. It does not then have to be in the colonial or semicolonial countries—which, recently, are experiencing the first capitalist stage or stages—that capitalism can be destroyed."*

On the other hand, the economic capacity of the United States does not permit us to assume that an impending collapse of its power is so near that it would signify our unexpected emancipation. Still, supposing the defeat of the United States in a military conflict with another imperialist power, would this bring liberty to Indo-America or reduce it to submission under a new master? . . .

The Mexican Revolution

This is the first instructive lesson of the agrarian revolution in Mexico upon which APRA draws. This movement and the University Reform are the two particular Latin American developments of this century that are precursors of *Aprismo*. From the latter comes the current of reform leading to our emancipation from mental colonialism through a new interpretation of Indo-American life; and from the former come numerous lessons in iron and steel given by a social revolution that is not socialist, but agrarian, antifeudal, and anti-imperialist.

In my book of 1928, I reiterated these concepts, which I had already published earlier, from 1924 on: The Mexican revolution is the first social movement of our century. It antedates the Russian Revolution and, obviously, that of China, although the imperialist element of the United States press calls it retroactively Bolshevik or Communist, in the same way in which subsequently until today every democratic social movement of the Left in Indo-America has been labeled. But it is not only an agrarian and antifeudal revolution, as it referred to itself in its adopted title, but something more. It is an anti-imperialist revolution and a heroic prelude of revolution. This double character of the Mexican revo-

* *El Anti-imperialismo y el APRA* (Mexico City, 1928), p. 22.

lution is, as I understand it, indivisible, and this explains many of the frustrations of that particular movement.

Aprismo recognized, then, in the Mexican revolution its particular social, nonsocialist character, although many Latin Americans repeated the European terminology in pompously calling it socialist, and I noted that, as far as that was concerned, "it is not indispensable to be Communist in order to be a revolutionary." But I noted as the principal cause of its "limitations and errors" the isolation of that cruel and heroic popular revolution, and with that assertion I confirmed one of the basic conclusions of our doctrine. No country of Indo-America can liquidate feudalism or emancipate itself economically from imperialism by itself. Both these tasks of general liberation go beyond our nationalist insularity and demand joint action by the countries of Indo-America. Feudalism and imperialism are economic and social systems that are continent-wide and exceed, in their organic field of activity and interdependence of interests, the frontiers of our twenty divided countries. . . .

Aprismo has maintained its premises: Capitalism, or the industrialization of Indo-America, begins in the form of imperialism. Our countries cannot destroy the capitalist system, whose roots and focal points are very far from us. The capitalist system, because of its economic capacity, does not allow us to assume its imminent downfall. Communism, with its dictatorship of the proletariat and its soviets, is unthinkable in Indo-America, whose socioeconomic reality is not Russian. Both Communism and fascism are specifically European phenomena. Our resistance to imperialism is in no form a doctrine of chauvinism against the people of the United States, because imperialism is an economic problem. Our anti-imperialist resistance supposes as the "first step" the political and economic unification of Latin America, and this union will bring us to the end of feudalism by progressive nationalization and cooperativist organization of agricultural production and of other types of wealth and the creation of a new type of state—the anti-imperialist and democratic state of the four powers: legislative, executive, judicial, and economic—based on economic and functional democracy. . . .

The Aprista State

The state proposed by APRA should be, first of all, a state of economic defense that is in opposition to the capitalist system, which generates imperialism—a distinct and special system that results in the abolition of the old oppressive regime. But the new state cannot be capitalist or bourgeois along the lines of France, England, or the United States (countries where capitalism has its origin and its base), nor can it be a feudal state. It is described as the "anti-imperialist state" because it should organize a new economic system, scientifically planned under the form of state capitalism—different from that attempted in Europe during the war, although aimed at directing the national economy and progressively bringing the production and circulation of wealth under state control. In my book of 1928, written more than four years before the election of Franklin D. Roosevelt as President of the United States, I could not use the North American New Deal as an example of that state control of the economy, but there was a clear reference to it as "cases of partial state control of the economy," as in Argentina with petroleum and in Uruguay with the reforms (so little studied in the other countries of Indo-America) introduced by the Colorado Party and its famous statesman Jose Batlle Ordónez. The new state, which would not be based on one class, but would be democratic and representative, involving the three major classes of our country—the peasant, the worker, and the middle class—would efficiently channel and coordinate the effort of the three classes represented in it, and would be the cornerstone of Indo-American unity and the effective emancipation of our peoples. . . .

Nationalization

The "progressive nationalization of wealth" can mean ownership, shared ownership, or control and supervision by the state (according to the situation) of certain sources of wealth—in particular, those which, since they are possessed by foreign businesses, end up in the hands of the governments of those nations of which the owners of the enterprises are citizens. *Aprista* nationalization is inclined to state control through development corporations, in accord with the mechanism of the democratic state of the four powers, and to the stimulation of agricultural and industrial cooperatives, but with respect and guarantees for private property, as in Mexico.

The program does not claim that nationalization without anything more is enough, since we place much emphasis on the scientific magnitude of the problem and the immediate necessity of studying it profoundly in order not to incur the very grave responsibility for having adopted under pressure a nominal and artificial nationalization that would lead to the failure of the business and the loss of the reform itself. In addition—and this ought to be clarified without equivocation—it is necessary to leave a wide field for private initiative, both national and foreign, in its constructive action to promote the ending of feudalism, and the industrialization which is indispensable for the progress of our people. There is a simultaneous, twofold task, to activate and to accelerate the evolution of the backward regions of our economy.

What, then, are those backward regions of the Indo-American economy that need to be activated and transformed in a new type of progress? I have said it already: They are fundamentally our feudal and semipatriarchal systems of primitive production; the reality and the spirit of the *latifundio*, which is still predominant in Indo-America. They are the feudal system that gives us the class of great semibarbarous lords of the lands and mines, slave-holders, masters of the country, and holders of power. They are the allies of imperialism who day by day become its agents and its subordinates. . . .

Relations with the United States

And this essential postulate (essential because on it *Aprismo* bases all its program of the relations between imperialist capital and our countries which require it) is expressed also in the concrete and repeated sentence which is the key to our conception of the problem of imperialism as an economic phenomenon: "The United States is as necessary for us as we are for her." On the basis of this premise, whose reiteration is always timely, the idea and program of the *Apristas* becomes more attainable.

But today, when the doctrine of the Good Neighbor Policy has begun to bear fruit with the detachment of political imperialism from economic imperialism, when North American capitalist investment in Indo-America has lost the unconditional protection of Washington, it is more feasible to demonstrate that imperialism, as the first and necessary stage of capitalism in the underdeveloped countries, has a constructive economic function and fulfills a historic mission of progress with respect to the systems of production which preceded it. Still more, it has also been possible for it to become evident that imperialism, freed from the patronage of the Department of State, could and can meet with the states of Indo-America in conditions of relative equality, and thus negotiate with them, and that this negotiation would bring mutual benefits, because it is based on a principle specifically established beforehand—that foreign capital which seeks areas of investment in our country is driven by an economic necessity as pressing as that which requires us to receive it. By such a reciprocity of interest, it is possible for our states to control investment by a planned and coordinated economy and through appropriate legislation, which guarantees just security to foreign capital. All this depends on us and not on the United States. . . .

Intervention

What is important is to begin by distinguishing good and licit intervention from bad and illicit intervention. . . . Collective intervention can be justified when it is a matter of defending the very existence of a democratic regime based on popular sovereignty —without which the state lacks the institutions of national sovereignty since the government cannot show the real mandate of the people when it has usurped it. It is this case of flagrant usurpation, the most frequent and demoralizing type of attack against democracy in our continent, which should bring about a collective intervention which is fully permissible. Nevertheless, the restrictive propositions of the Inter-American Treaty of Reciprocal Assistance of 1947, of the Charter of the Organization of American States, and of the Pact of Bogotá of 1948 refer exclusively to "external aggression," whether by force or not, of one state against another which can endanger the peace of America from within our hemisphere or outside it, and this is where the weakness of the so-called Inter-American system is evident, the principal objective of which is "to maintain the peace and security of the continent" and not to protect the integrity and security of the democratic order based on pure respect for human and civil rights. For, if indeed it is announced in the Charter of the Organization of American States that "the solidarity of the American states and the high purposes with which it is pursued require the political organization of these states on the basis of the effective exercise of representative democracy," and if they proclaim "the fundamental rights of the human person" and point out what this means for well-being, for work and culture, without any distinctions of any kind, all this is only so much poetry, as beautiful as it is elusive, in the majority of our republics. No democratic principles can be valid and lasting when the fulfillment and implementation of those precepts is confined to governments whose democratic values can be trampled underfoot by any general seizing power and supplanting popular sovereignty with the bayonet.

24. José Figueres

José Figueres, former President of Costa Rica, was born in 1906. He was educated at the Universities of Costa Rica and Mexico and at the Massachusetts Institute of Technology. He lived as a coffee planter in Costa Rica until political events drove him into exile in Mexico in 1942. In 1948, he led a revolution against a corrupt government which had refused to accede to the victory of an opposition candidate. In 1948–49, he served as chief of the revolutionary junta which ruled the country while a democratic constitution was being framed. In 1953, he was elected President, serving until 1958. He has been active in hemispheric affairs, and in 1963–64 was a Visiting Professor of Economics at Harvard University.

Figueres identifies himself and his party with the ideology of social democracy. Like the other populist parties of Latin America (e.g., Acción Democrática in Venezuela, APRA in Peru), his Partido de Liberación Nacional (PLN) has been described as socialist; as the selection below indicates, however, Figueres favors a mixed economy combining features of both socialism and capitalism. Figueres is perhaps more ready than other populista leaders in Latin America to view the post–New Deal American economy as a model of this kind of mixture, although he goes further than the Americans in supporting the creation of independent national authorities in such fields as electricity, housing, and land reform.

In the second selection, Figueres analyzes Latin American eco-

nomic problems and political ideologies in relation to the Alliance for Progress. Christian Democracy is significantly absent from his list of Latin American ideologies, perhaps because its political and economic programs are very similar to those attributed by Figueres to social democracy. However, Christian Democracy differs from populismo in that it is much more directly influenced by the political and economic thinking of European Catholic thinkers and the papal social encyclicals.

SOCIALISM AND CAPITALISM*

In this epoch of Cold War with Soviet Russia, it is fashionable in the United States, among uninformed people, to connect the word "socialism" with undemocratic political doctrines.

On the other hand, in England, the Scandinavian countries, and other places, socialist parties take an active part in present-day politics, enjoying the prestige of being considered democratic.

On its part, the term "capitalism" has a bad reputation in Latin America, where it is frequently considered a synonym for "colonialism" or "imperialism," and in Europe, where it is frequently the equivalent of a "reactionary" attitude, of exploitation of workers.

In this letter, which I address to the common citizen of Costa Rica, I intend to use these words in their original meaning, as terms for two different *economic* systems, which should not be tied to the various *political* systems. . . .

Socialism, as an economic doctrine, has nothing to do with political "totalitarianism," that is to say, with despotism. And the theoretical capitalistic system, of absolute freedom of enterprise, should not be connected with colonial exploitation of one people by another. . . .

As you know, socialism is an economic system inspired by the ideal that "all things belong to all." Of course, it does not refer to things for *personal* use, such as clothing, housing, toothbrushes, but solely to productive properties, such as real estate, factories, buildings, railroads, etc. Socialism recommends that all the means

* From *Cartas a un Ciudadano* (San José: Imprenta Nacional, 1956); translated by the editor and Ignatius Di Cola.

of production belong to the entire nation, and that the state administer them. . . .

For many centuries many well-intentioned thinkers have held that if the system of private property is replaced by public ownership of the means of production, social injustice and misery will cease.

Socialism, basically a noble and generous idea, has much in common with the Christian spirit—that there should be no rich or poor, that we should hold everything in common as brothers in an ideal family. The Mexican Revolution, which was the precursor of all the great revolutions of the twentieth century, put forward one of the best expressions of socialism of all time: "No one has a right to excess when there are those who lack the necessities."

The ideal society will come about, says classical socialism, simply by changing the property system. In our time, socialists who have kept up with the advances in the study of economics are aware that their predecessors overemphasized the role of the property system in producing abundance and prosperity for all. There are other factors, such as productivity, that is, the returns to labor and capital, which were not studied earlier. Nevertheless the old polemic is now taking on a dramatic character. Today a vigorous world movement, Communism, is at its height. It tries to change the property system by force and violence, sacrificing the great human achievements of liberty, respect for personal dignity, morality, and the other spiritual values of our civilization. . . .

Capitalism, in the usual meaning of the word, is an economic system of private ownership of land, industry, and other means of production, which permits everyone to produce what he likes, without any planning or aid, to buy and sell as he wishes, to pay the lowest wages that he can, and to obtain the most advantageous prices which the market will bear, without any sense of responsibility toward his fellow creatures.

Against this economic irresponsibility, the results of which are low production in general and an unjust accumulation for a few, there appeared the idea of socialism, proposing a society diametrically opposed to capitalism.

In practice, neither of the two systems has prevailed in any nation in absolute form, least of all today. The nations that call themselves socialistic have had to leave in private hands at least petty trade, which is difficult to administer through a central organization, and a great part of the land, because the habit of prop-

erty is deeply ingrained among all the peasants of the world. On
the other hand, the great so-called capitalistic nations, and principally the United States, have organized their industry and commerce more in the form of business firms, the capital of which
belongs to the public which buys "stocks," or partial titles to property. . . .

The number of stockholders is increasing, so that property is
more diffused. At present the firms themselves facilitate the purchase of stocks by their workers. This is a new form of socialization,
stimulated precisely by the people who most fear the word "socialism."

There also exist, in those nations, many thousands of small and
medium-size businesses, and private farms, and there is a determination to maintain them. However, the state imposes upon them
numerous regulations: minimum wages, maximum work day, fixed
prices, compulsory insurance, an income tax, etc. The state determines the rates, the scope of operation, the schedules, etc., for
transportation and other public service enterprises. With all of this
"interference," those businesses are at the service of the community more than at the service of their owners. There is no such
thing as "capitalism."

What has happened is that while people in the newspapers were
discussing such words and phrases as "directed economy" and "free
enterprise," "inviolable property" and "social necessity," developments have taken, almost independently, the only possible path—
a combination of the two systems, capitalist and socialist, which
endeavors to combine the advantages of both and to minimize the
disadvantages of each. To this synthesis of the two historical trends
the name *mixed economy* is now given. . . .

The Movement of National Liberation has openly decided for a
mixed economy combining private property with state regulation,
individual business with public institutions, because it considers
this convenient for the country, because this is the system which
prevails in the democratic world, and because the majority of our
citizens prefer it although not all of them are able to express their
desires with precision. . . .

In order to orient a large number of enterprises, businesses, and
individual efforts of all types, without intervening in their administration or restricting freedom, the state in a mixed economy
makes use of the system of stimuli and correctives. . . .

When the modern state intervenes judiciously as a stabilizer in a mixed economy, it forestalls disruptive tendencies, applies remedies in time and with moderation and skill, and avoids much loss and suffering. . . .

With more or less accuracy (since historic periods are not set off by a precise line of demarcation), the system of stimuli and correctives has been indelibly associated with the Roosevelt revolution in the United States. Likewise one can say that the Great Depression was the deathblow to the outdated economic system which we call "liberal," or, in a more exaggerated fashion, "capitalist." At the same time it produced the painful birth of a reformist ideology which has led the United States to a prosperity which could never have been foreseen.

From 1933 to today, the technique of orienting private enterprise through the organs of the state has been perfected very well in North America. Not only were further depressions avoided after World War II and Korea, but for the first time in history the economy has continued to grow. The figures for the end of 1955 are spectacular.

At this moment in the history of the world, the mixed economy, in common cause with the whole civilization of the West, is undergoing its greatest test. The Communist prophets announced half a century ago that the great fluctuations in the capitalist system (depressions) would destroy the whole democratic system. God willing, it is not too early to reply that democracy, by adopting state economic planning which respects freedom and stimulates initiative, has put an end to depressions.

And now what must be done next? Probably an international New Deal. The less developed countries have a right to benefit from the economic knowledge of today. The United States in its pivotal role in the world economy cannot afford the luxury of repeating the mistakes which almost destroyed its domestic economy and its democratic way of life. . . .

The mixed economy, with all its ingenious mechanisms of controls and compensations, does not fully satisfy the socialist mentality, which prefers a simpler formula, such as the fusion of all activities in a single great enterprise, the state. The mixed system gives the impression of being too complicated, insecure, and not very scientific.

Neither does this combination satisfy "liberal" or capitalist thought, which considers it artificial or not very "natural."

Nonetheless, if one takes a good look at it, the system of stimulations cannot be more scientific, nor more natural. What could be more proper than to observe *the natural inclinations*, the tendencies of events, and to place them at the service of man, by means of his intelligence? . . .

Every economic system, every political movement, every social order, has to be judged, in the final analysis, for its spiritual effect upon the men who adopt it; that is to say, for the *human type* which it tends to form, or at least to encourage.

The socialist ideal (which has never been fulfilled, except within small groups) tends to make men less egoistic, more generous, more responsible before society. How? Through an educational process: by making men see that they work in order to serve others, and not merely in order to carry on their own business; by convincing them that the productive effort of each person, his daily contribution to the great economic task, is in reality a *social function*.

In theory, in a completely "free" economy of pure individual initiative, where anyone can form whatever business he wants, or is empowered to form without the state's help or restraint, man must feel like the hunter who goes out to shoot the deer in uninhabited land, shooting big or small, male or female, all that he encounters during every season.

What we are saying is that a totally capitalistic society (which has never existed) would tend to produce a human type who is oblivious of his fellow man, selfish, greedy for goods or self-gratification, without any sense of social responsibility.

It is necessary to note, however, that the possession of goods, and the exercise of property, in a certain way enhances man and makes him more responsible, at least before himself and his family. Accordingly, the capitalist system can also take note of its beneficial effect on the spiritual order. The favorable effects of capitalism emerge plentifully in a mixed economy (such as Costa Rica's, for example), which not only respects property, but also encourages the development of many small farmers. . . .

All businesses and agricultural, industrial, or commercial enterprises, big or small, although they enjoy a large degree of autonomy which their "private" character gives them in accordance with the right of property, nonetheless are subject to a series of laws, controls, inducements, and corrective measures which confer upon them, in reality, a social function. . . .

If the principle that *economic activity is a social function* is adopted, . . . the laws of the nation, the government's orientation, and the public's education can all be directed toward the attainment of a more just and generous society, which will better be able to fulfill the aspirations of those who compose it.

POLITICAL AND ECONOMIC FORCES IN THE HEMISPHERE*

. . . What chance is there of the Alliance's [the Alliance for Progress] realizing its objectives?

To answer this question calls for an analysis of the political forces at work in Latin America. The political situation there is not analogous to that of the United States. Here, granted that many shades and factions exist within the spectrum of the two political parties, it may generally be said that the public mind is either of a conservative bent, anxious to keep things pretty much as they are, or of a liberal bent, desiring to push forward.

In Latin America the ideological picture cannot be thus dichotomized. There are at least three distinct forces at work. There is, of course, the conservative mind, and it is a brand of extreme conservatism with which most North Americans are not familiar. It is a mind which wants no reform, fears all change, and wants to freeze the social reality as presently structured. It has, in fact, managed to immobilize it for a long time.

Opposed to this conservative mind, we have not one but two distinct forces. One is, broadly speaking, the world Communist movement. This certainly is a very important movement of our time. It is active in Latin America and it does attract many followers. The other force is that of social democratic reform. It rallies the support of those who, during 175 years of independence, have been deeply influenced by the ideals of democratic government, although they have generally been defeated in their efforts to realize them. This movement seeks to achieve social justice within the framework of Western-style democratic society. It wishes to make government an instrument of social justice. Its aim is to

* Selections from "Unity and Solidarity in the Hemisphere," in William Manger (ed.), *The Two Americas* (New York: P. J. Kenedy, 1965); by permission of Georgetown University.

create a democratic welfare state, such as the United States and every other successful Western democracy today, whether some people like to admit it or not.

Which of these three forces is likely to prevail? There is little room for doubt. The kind of conservatism familiar to Latin America has lived its time. It is a thing of the past. Its day is done. The future in Latin America lies either with the triumph of the Communist world revolution or with the achievement of some form of the democratic welfare state.

What should be done if we are to achieve social development along democratic lines? I shall not here discuss what is at the moment being done, or go into the question of what are the immediate possibilities of realizing desired objectives. Instead, let me simply call attention to the special magnitude of our problem.

It is not simply a matter of raising wages, although indeed in some areas of the Latin American economy wages must be raised and raised now. It is not simply a question of land reform in the sense of a redistribution of land ownership, although this too needs to be done.

The special nature of our problem is that these, and other similar or related objectives of social justice, are indeed imperative; but no less imperative is the need for capital formation. To concentrate social effort either upon the systematized formation of capital or upon the widest possible distribution of the national income is one thing. It is quite another thing, and incomparably more difficult, to attempt both at the same time.

European countries and the United States were able to build up capital and lay the foundation of their highly productive societies at a time when social pressures were much less than they are everywhere today. They were able, without much fear of provoking social revolution, to ignore the protests of the poor while they laid the foundations of their prosperity. They were permitted first to achieve the capital formation prerequisite to industrialization and then to turn their attention to the demands of social justice.

In Latin America we do not enjoy the luxury of alternatives. We are obliged to tackle both problems simultaneously. We have to concern ourselves with capital formation at the same time that we concern ourselves with the equitable distribution of national income. This calls for a great deal of wisdom on the part of government and a great deal of understanding on the part of the public and a great deal of effort by everybody. These are objectives not easily accomplished, nor soon. These are goals easier to recommend than achieve.

Another important objective for which we must strive in Latin America is the creation of a common market. Our countries are too small to support, each one severally, a structure of modern industry. A great effort has to be made to integrate our economies, to break down the barriers to commerce, and to foster interregional trade.

Headway is being made. In Central America a common market area is being developed with relative speed. Progress, although slow, is being made toward a free trade zone, including almost all the countries south of Mexico.

These measures are important; but here again we must not overestimate what they can do. By themselves they will not bring about a high production of goods and services and usher in the millennium in Latin America. Mexico and Brazil serve to remind us of this. Each of these two countries, in terms of population and area, is a far larger common market than anything being created in Central America. Yet the per capita income of both is lower than that of some of the Central American countries. This proves that a common market alone, without proper communications, transportation, and many other factors, will not create an economic miracle.

Another aspect of our problem is that Latin American countries must maintain extensive commercial relations with the industrialized world. They need to import many goods and services. Imports have to be paid for, and payment is becoming more and more difficult for Latin America as time goes on.

It is an elementary truth of economics that imports must be paid for by exports. The products which most Latin American countries can export are largely determined by the tropical latitudes in which they lie. These are the traditional products such as coffee, bananas, cocoa, and the like. Perhaps some of our countries will imitate the Japanese and begin to produce interesting gadgets with marketable value abroad; but the time is far off when we shall see them shipping Cadillacs to Detroit.

Now the entire trade relationship between countries which must rely upon selling the kind of products peculiar to Latin America and those which produce industrial goods is out of joint. The advance of technology is in fact forcing it more and more out of kilter and steadily widening the gap between the industrial and the nonindustrial societies. . . .

Will we ever have the mechanisms needed to stop the deepening of this gulf between the industrialized and the nonindustrialized world? Will we ever be able politically to subsidize exports from the industrial nations to the nonindustrial nations? Or to subsidize imports from the poor countries into the rich countries? Will we be able to establish the preferential treatment which, together with certain necessary measures of internal reform, will accelerate the development of the poorer countries? Will the politics of the advanced countries or the politics of the retarded countries, where the problems confront us on every side, prevent us from adopting these bold measures so badly needed in our time? Or will the world continue to be divided between developed and underdeveloped countries facing each other across an ever widening gap? These are difficult questions.

Perhaps nothing will be done and the world will move on to a new catastrophe, either war or another great depression. I do not know which is worse in terms of human suffering. My impression at the moment is that we are justly worried about war, but perhaps not sufficiently worried about the possibility of a world depression.

In some respects the world may be back in the 1920's, heading toward 1929. The markets of the world are not being developed enough to keep abreast of the growth of productivity in industrial countries. There are other serious symptoms, like the problem of balance of payments in the United States, which cause concern. . . .

We need a revolution. I hope it will be a revolution from the top, a revolution of enlightened people who think in terms of such conceptions as the Alliance for Progress, Point Four, the Marshall Plan. We have reached the point where mechanisms must be found to redistribute fairly the world income. This calls for a great conception. I do not know what that conception will be. I do not have the solutions to offer. I do not have the institutions in mind. I do know that they must be found. . . .

. . . As I examine Latin America, country by country, I see a very hard decade ahead. As a consequence of the economic situation, I anticipate setbacks for democracy. We have allowed the situation to deteriorate far too much. It will take a long time to remedy this.

What alternatives to democracy are there? There is dictatorship of the old-fashioned type and dictatorship of the new type, led by young officers, known as Nasserism. Can they bring about the successful transformation of our societies? I am not asking whether they can successfully maintain themselves in power. Almost anybody, given the proper means, can do this. I am asking whether either type of dictatorship, and both have their advocates, can accomplish a rapid development of Latin America in the direction of social justice and in an atmosphere benign to human values. Definitely not.

The military of Latin America may supply the power. Somebody else will have to supply the ideas. In some cases they will turn to the oligarchy for ideas. They have traditionally done so. They are still doing so. This would mean stagnation. In other cases, they will have recourse for ideas—as some are actually doing now although they would be the last to admit it—to the Communist intellectuals. For the Communists do have a plan and they do offer a solution, however ruthless the former and however destructive of spiritual values the latter may be. In this event the future would lie with the Communists.

Can the Communists solve the problems of the next decade, or the next two decades, more successfully than our weak democracies have been able to do? Some people think they can. Many intellectuals, especially in our Latin American universities, maintain that if we would adopt the Communist plan and employ Communist methods, supported by all the authority of a totalitarian state, we could rapidly develop the resources of our countries. I question this on several counts.

First, to carry out their plan, the Communists would have to antagonize the whole managerial class. They would, in fact, have to sacrifice or eliminate the whole owning or managerial class. They would have to improvise a new generation of managers and technicians. They would also inevitably eliminate a great part of the middle class. This would automatically result in a terrific reduction of the national income. This might have only a temporary effect, but meanwhile the people would be starving.

With all of our wants, we do have, relatively speaking, a great deal of administrative machinery, business talent, and enterprise in our Latin American economies. We are doing our best, within our democratic systems, to make use of them, to make use of whatever is valuable. We are not trying to destroy these assets. This is one of the great advantages democracy has over Communism in meeting our problems. Because Communism would be forced, by its very goals and methods, to destroy these assets, it would undoubtedly have to seek outside financial support far more than we do. It would even need to look abroad for food merely to survive.

Can any of the Communist powers supply this kind of aid in the amount needed? I think this is out of the question. From all appearances, supplying Cuba is enough of a burden for the Russian economy. Could they undertake to supply the needs of a single Latin American country the size of Brazil? I doubt it. I sometimes think that, if they could, they would have taken on the task before this.

Again, in assessing the chances of Communist success in developing Latin America, one must take into account the opposition of the United States. This opposition, whether one considers it good or bad, would make it too much of a risk.

What can be done today in the Western Hemisphere, or in the world for that matter, without some kind of coordination with the United States? And what can be done against the will of the United States in an area in which it feels, rightly or wrongly, that its own security is menaced?

Can democracy do the job of development? Can we meet this challenge democratically? No matter what our difficulties are, no matter what the shortcomings of the Alliance for Progress are, this is the system attuned to our way of thinking, the system which we have in our veins. This is the political conception which we share with the United States as common heirs of European culture. . . .

There is something supreme which has brought mankind so far along the path of development, that seems to move us more and more toward world integration under a broad political philosophy of democracy and a wide-embracing ethical system—Christianity or something similar, I hope. Looking back into the centuries and into the millennia and forward into the future, I cannot believe that mankind faces only two alternatives, either universal Communism or universal destruction that would make the earth as barren as the moon. No, I think the earth will go on and that it will be fertile and that people, better than many of us, will continue to enjoy its blessings.

The difficulties facing us are immense. We have to keep faith. We have to keep working, with faith in man, faith in mankind, faith in divine destiny. This alone can keep us going. This alone offers hope for the future.

25. Raúl Prebisch

Raúl Prebisch was born in Tucumán, Argentina, in 1901. He was a member of the faculty of economics at the University of Buenos Aires from 1925 until 1948. Beginning in 1925, he was also a member of the Argentine civil service, filling a variety of administrative and advisory posts. In 1935 he was put in charge of organizing the Central Bank of Argentina and he served as its Director General until he was dismissed by Juan Perón in 1943. Political difficulties with Perón caused him to leave Argentina in 1948 to work for the United Nations Economic Commission for Latin America (ECLA). In 1950, he became the Executive Secretary of ECLA, a position he held until 1962, when he was appointed Director General of the Latin American Institute for Economic and Social Planning. In 1963, he was appointed Secretary General of the United Nations Conference on Trade and Development; when the Conference established a permanent organization at Geneva, Prebisch became its Secretary General.

Although Prebisch is not a political leader, his economic writings have taken on an ideological quality and become a rallying point for those Latin Americans (and, since 1964, Africans and Asians) who demand greater concessions from the developed countries. Prebisch blames Latin America's economic difficulties on both domestic and international factors. Domestically, there is a lack of capital, excessive concentration of power in the hands of the wealthy, an inefficient system of land tenure, and inadequate domestic markets. Internationally, the terms of trade between the developed countries at the "center" and the underdeveloped countries at the "periphery" are increasingly disadvantageous to the latter, because over the long run material and agricultural prices tend to decline while those of manufactured goods remain stable or increase. The Prebisch solution is agrarian and tax reform, planning, and economic integration domestically, combined with international commodity price agreements and preferences for goods *from underdeveloped countries. The Prebisch program has now been adopted by the UNCTAD organization and is frequently referred to in writings and speeches by Latin American leaders. (See, for example, the selections by Eduardo Frei and José Figueres.)*

TOWARD A DYNAMIC DEVELOPMENT POLICY FOR LATIN AMERICA*

Structural Reforms to Clear the Way for Development

The ills besetting the Latin American economy are not determined by circumstantial or transient factors. They are an expression of the critical state of affairs in our time and of the incapacity of the economic system—owing to structural defects that it has been beyond our ability or our power to remedy—to achieve and maintain a rate of development consonant with the growth of the population and with its demands for a speedy improvement in its standards.

The increase in the population is certainly phenomenal. At the beginning of the century, there were 63 million inhabitants in Latin America, and the annual rate of demographic growth was 1.8 per cent. Now we number 220 million, and we are multiplying at an annual rate of 2.9 per cent which shows signs of rising even higher.

On the basis of conjectural data, it may be estimated that about half the existing population has a tiny average personal income of $120 a year. And this vast social aggregate accounts for only about one-fifth of total personal consumption in Latin America, showing the highest coefficients of undernourishment, poor clothing, and worse housing, as well as of disease and illiteracy; and, at the same time, the highest rates of reproduction.

It is here that the development effort must be primarily concentrated. The notion, which dies hard, that development takes place spontaneously, without a rational and deliberate effort to achieve it, has proved to be an illusion, both in Latin America and in the

* Excerpts from a report presented at the meeting of the United Nations Economic Commission for Latin America, Mar del Plata, Argentina, May, 1963.

other peripheral regions of the world. For a century now our economies have been linked to the international economy, and 50 per cent of the population is still stagnating in pre-capitalist conditions which are incompatible with its growing economic and social aspirations.

Even so, average per capita income in Latin America is appreciably higher than in other peripheral regions, and thus affords an advantageous starting point for the realization of what is no longer a utopian dream: the eradication of poverty and its inherent evils, by virtue of the tremendous potential of contemporary technology and the possibility of assimilating it much more quickly than was the case with the capitalistic evolution of the more advanced countries. However, this rapid penetration of technique demands and brings with it radical changes: changes both in the pattern of production and in the structure of the economy which could not be effectively brought about without a basic reform of the social structure.

The social structure prevalent in Latin America constitutes a serious obstacle to technical progress and, consequently, to economic and social development. The principal manifestations of this fact are three in number:

1. The structure in question considerably hampers social mobility, that is, the emergence and rise of the dynamic elements in society, men of drive and initiative, capable of taking risks and responsibilities both in technical and economic matters and in the other aspects of community life.

2. The social structure is largely characterized by a situation of privilege in the distribution of wealth and therefore of income; privilege weakens or destroys the incentive to economic activity, to the detriment of the efficient utilization of human resources, land, and machinery.

3. This state of privilege in regard to distribution is not reflected in a rapid rate of net capital formation, but in extravagant patterns of consumption in the upper strata of society, in contrast with the unsatisfactory living conditions of the broad masses of the population.

In these days of zeal for planning there is a great deal of talk about the supreme importance of the role of private enterprise in Latin America and the need to keep it intact. But what is meant by this, in the last analysis? Is it suggested that the present system, under which the energies of individual initiative are cramped by social stratification and privilege, should be kept intact? Or is the way to be cleared for this initiative by the structural reforms referred to, so that the system may acquire the full dynamic force it lacks at present?

Capital Formation and Income Distribution

The test of a system's dynamic strength lies in its ability to accelerate the rate of development and progressively improve the distribution of income. If the annual rate of growth of average per capita income could be raised from the very low figure of 1 per cent registered of late to a minimum of 3 per cent in Latin America as a whole, a rational redistribution policy would enable the personal income of the underprivileged half of the population to be doubled in seventeen years, and the lot of the middle-income groups also to be improved, although at a less rapid rate.

This is where the first step must be taken toward reform of the social structure, since such a rate of growth is not feasible without substantial restriction of the consumption of the higher-income brackets.

The social contrast is striking indeed. While 50 per cent of the population accounts for approximately two-tenths of total personal consumption, at the other end of the scale of distribution 5 per cent of the inhabitants of the region enjoy nearly three-tenths of that total, according to the conjectural estimates referred to above. A policy of austerity mainly affecting this latter social group, and supplemented by the contribution of international resources, would permit an increase in net capital formation and the attainment of the above-mentioned growth target for per capita income, while at the same time redistribution policy would see to it that the income increment thus obtained was passed on to the lower strata of the social aggregate.

Here is essentially what redistribution policy means. It is not a matter of taking income away from the upper minority and simply and solely distributing it among the broad masses of the population, for with per capita personal income in Latin America as a whole barely amounting to $370, the benefits of such a redistribution would not stretch very far. But if, on the other hand, restrictions on the consumption of the privileged groups were reflected in a steady increase in net capital formation, the standard of living of the bulk of the population would rise progressively faster.

Technology has made this dynamic concept of redistribution viable, for the first time in history, for without the immense potential it places at the disposal of developing countries, the effects of the redistribution operation would be very limited in their scope. Thus, the problems of capital formation and income distribution assume very different forms from those they took during the capitalistic evolution of the more advanced countries.

At that time it was capital formation that came first, and the gradual redistribution of income followed. Now, on the other hand, both these requirements present themselves—as they are bound to do—simultaneously, under the increasing political and trade-union pressure exerted by the lower income groups.

The only available means of meeting them is by directly combating one of the anomalies that most affect the development of Latin America, namely, the marked failure of capital formation to reach the levels demanded by contemporary technology, as against the extravagant pattern of consumption of the high-income groups.

Among these upper strata (5 per cent of the population), which account for about three-tenths of Latin America's total consumption, average consumption per household is fifteen times greater than that of the lower strata (50 per cent of the population). If this ratio were reduced 11:1, by the restriction of consumption in favor of increased investment, the annual rate of growth of per capita income could rise from 1 per cent to 3 per cent. And if compression of consumption brought the ratio down to 9:1, the rate of growth might reach 4 per cent or even more, according to the political feasibility of this operation and the capacity of each country to put it into effect.

International Cooperation and the Structure of Trade

This capacity might be seriously handicapped by the external bottleneck in development, which, in conjunction with the limitations of domestic production of capital goods, would mean that not all the additional saving obtained could be invested in such goods. Hence the vital need for international resources, until the structural reforms advocated here enable full advantage to be taken of the increase in savings.

The contribution to be made by international resources is thus of a temporary nature. It would cease to be necessary once the reforms referred to had borne the full crop of results to be expected of them. This is not solely a Latin American concern, since it is also essential to work for the elimination of the external bottleneck by remodeling the existing structure of international trade.

The countries in which industrialization advances most rapidly tend to be affected more and more by the bottleneck in question. Their difficulties do not originate solely in the social structure, but also in the type of trade structure which characterized the epoch of externally geared development that preceded the world depression of the 1930's. Here again, as in other aspects of our development problems, a whole series of out-of-date ideas survives. It is true that the peripheral industrialization of the regions has at last been accepted as an indispensable requisite for economic development. But what is still perpetuated is the anachronistic trade pattern inherent in the peculiar concept of the international division of labor which was prevalent up to a short time ago—the trading of primary commodities against manufactured goods. This is the framework within which the industrialization of our countries has been taking place. And the obstacle to economic development that it represents is now beginning to loom larger at every turn, for whereas the upward trend of demand for the manufactured goods we import is very sharp, primary exports are expanding relatively slowly, largely for reasons over which the Latin American countries have no control. Thus there is a latent tendency toward disequilibrium which is aggravated as economic development gains speed.

This is a new phenomenon not experienced by the more advanced countries in the past. Hence it is that its significance is only now beginning to be understood and recognition accorded to the vital need to encourage the industrial exports of the peripheral countries, especially those which have completed the first stage of the industrialization process.

This encouragement of industrial exports, in addition to exports of primary commodities, cannot be achieved within the narrow bounds of the existing markets. It is essential to alter the geographical structure of trade, as well as its composition by products.

Latin America's exports are of course affected by the universal slowness of the growth of demand for primary commodities, in contrast with the buoyancy of demand for manufactured goods as per capita income rises. But this circumstance is combined with other factors of considerable importance. In the first place, the moderate rate of economic development of the United States, together with its import restrictions, has exerted an adverse influence on Latin America's export trade. And, secondly, the protection and discrimination practiced by the European Common Market prevent us from taking full advantage of the steady expansion of demand for primary commodities in the vast economic area it represents.

Without prejudice to measures aimed at eliminating or reducing these barriers to trade, it is a matter of urgent necessity to explore with the utmost diligence the possibilities for trade with other regions of the world, especially those—the socialist economies, for example—which show a high rate of development.

While it is true that basically the solution of such problems depends upon the great industrial countries and the degree to which their trade policy favors liberalization, it is no less certain that the Latin American countries too must put forth a tremendous effort in the same direction. In this sense, the formation of a common market is an undertaking that brooks no delay. Its importance has been realized by the Central American countries, whose determination to establish such a market has been bold and resolute. The problem of the Latin American Free Trade Association is more difficult, for the very reason that the development of industrialization in watertight compartments has created vested interests and prejudices which oppose reciprocal trade without taking account of the serious effects of such an attitude on economic development. This is not a merely technical matter, it is a question of important policy decisions which must follow up the Montevideo Treaty.* The technical groundwork for these decisions is basically complete; all that remains to be done is to study and select the best ways of putting them into practice.

The Closed Type of Development in Latin America

The external bottleneck in development is not due solely to the slow upward trend of exports of primary commodities as against the rapid expansion of industrial imports from the great centers, or to the low level of inter-Latin American trade; it has also largely been determined, in recent years, by the deterioration of the terms of trade and its serious effects on the purchasing power of exports.†

* The treaty signed in February, 1960, by seven Latin American countries, establishing the Latin American Free Trade Association.—ED.

† For Prebisch's argument on the terms of trade, see the next selection.—ED.

The action of all these factors in combination reduced the per capita value of Latin America's exports from $58 in 1930 to $39 in 1960 (at 1950 prices).

The recent decline in the terms of trade is yet another indication of the peripheral countries' congenital incapacity to retain the whole of the benefits accruing from their technical progress. It is not much of a consolation to reflect that when, in the future, the Latin American countries reach more advanced stages of development and their industrialization process is complete, this state of affairs will one day be ended. This is hardly consoling, since it will all take a long time, and in the meanwhile the deterioration of the terms of trade is aggravating the external bottleneck and exerting a marked depressive influence on domestic capacity for capital formation, to the detriment of development itself.

From a different angle, the other notion that still survives in some circles, to the effect that the external bottleneck and the disequilibria in international accounts in which it is reflected are mere matters of monetary operation, has had deplorable consequences, since its practical application—besides adversely affecting economic development—has diverted attention from the basic solutions which this structural phenomenon demands.

This is a point of considerable importance for Latin America, for unless such solutions are resolutely sought, our countries will be swept by the force of circumstances toward an increasingly closed type of development, and a steady contraction of their share of trade with the rest of the world, which will add further difficulties to those inherent in this process. In default of sufficient international cooperation in overcoming these difficulties, both in the field of trade and in that of financing, all kinds of authoritarian measures might supervene, with grave consequences for the progressive development of democracy in Latin America.

Internal Bottlenecks

The intensification of development is not simply a question of increasing net capital formation. While this is necessary it is by no means sufficient, since development may be hampered by a variety of factors. Those of an external kind have already been mentioned, but there are also internal bottlenecks that circumscribe or hamper the expansive force of net capital formation.

Furthermore, there is usually a wide margin for the immediate growth of production in our countries because of idle capacity in a number of branches. But the factors in question either rule out this possibility or bring inflationary pressures of a nonmonetary kind in their train if a policy directed toward the full utilization of idle capacity is put into force.

There is no doubt that the most stubborn bottleneck in the whole of Latin America's development process is generally to be found in agricultural production. Several factors are jointly responsible for this: the system of land tenure, which makes it difficult for modern techniques to be assimilated; inadequate state aid in the work of adapting and diffusing these techniques; and the unsatisfactory investment situation. However thoroughly these problems are coped with, unless farmers are given proper incentives, efforts to accelerate development are liable to find their most formidable stumbling block in the agricultural sector, as has been the case in various countries with differing economic systems.

The incentives may be of different kinds, but the most important is that agriculture should reap the benefits of the technical progress it makes, as regards both external aspects and the interplay of internal economic forces. This is the only way in which the wide gap between average income in rural and in urban areas can be gradually narrowed. The fact is that the impoverished sectors of the population are largely to be found in rural areas.

With a little thought, it will be seen that the externally geared growth of earlier periods, based on the characteristic foreign enclaves which did not spread technical progress to the internal economy, broke up the original pre-capitalistic integration of the countryside with the towns. And industrialization tends to accentuate rather than reduce the breach by aggravating the social and economic dichotomy. Steps must now be taken to remedy this.

The widening of the gap was due not only to the structural features of the rural sector, but also to the fact that internal development has not been dynamic enough to raise the farmer's income. What is more, it is the farmer who is usually called upon to bear a considerable part of the cost of import substitution, excessive protection, and unfair marketing practices, as well as social security and other state services from which the rural worker reaps virtually no benefit because he can exert no trade union pressure and has no political contacts. In fact, he continues to play Lazarus to the Dives of urban politics.

No exhaustive examination has yet been made of all the repercussions of these factors on the drift from the countryside to the bigger Latin American towns, which is a disquieting and striking sign of economic and social disequilibrium. There is no doubt that in-migration is bound to take place; nor is there any doubt that the increased technical progress of the rural areas will tend to give it greater momentum. But is it necessary for the displaced population to congregate in the big towns? Why should they not stay in the rural milieu, living in small and medium-sized communities and employed in industries and services that would satisfy some of the requirements of that milieu itself? Why have the bigger towns in Latin America grown, at the expense of the medium and small towns, to an extraordinary extent that is quite disproportionate to the trend of developments in more advanced countries?

These questions cannot be answered satisfactorily except on the basis of careful research. Perhaps the weakness of rural demand or, to put it another way, the concentration of demand in the big towns as a result of the structural and adventitious factors mentioned above may have played an important part in this phenomenon. And, as in the case of other social phenomena, there have been no countervailing reactions but a self-perpetuating spiral, since the agglomeration of people in big towns concentrates demand there even more, and leads to further population congestion. It may therefore be concluded that the geographical redistribution of income is also of great social importance.

Why Should Development Forces Be Deliberately Controlled?

One dominant idea runs through the whole of this paper: Latin America must quicken its rate of economic development and redistribute income in favor of the broad masses of the population. The attainment of this objective cannot be postponed indefinitely, nor are there grounds for expecting that economic development will take place first and be followed in the natural course of events by social development. Both must be achieved in measured stages. This will need the exercise of rational and deliberate action on the forces of development which cannot take place through the spontaneous interplay of these forces, as happened in the evolution of capitalism in the advanced countries.

The notion that this type of evolution might be reproduced in our countries has proved very disturbing. In the advanced countries economic development has been essentially a spontaneous phenomenon, unlike social development which has largely been shaped by deliberate policy measures. And the need for this type of action, the need to plan, is obviously becoming accepted there as well.

There is one overriding premise to all this: today, when man is acquiring a power hitherto undreamed of over the forces of nature, he is not resigned to remaining at the mercy of the spontaneous play of economic forces with their manifest incapacity to maintain or achieve a satisfactory rate of growth, while at the same time reducing cyclical fluctuations, and to bring about equitable income distribution.

The fact that it is impossible for history to repeat itself in this matter makes the reasons for finding new paths highly cogent. The assimilation of an already highly developed technique in a fairly short space of time is very different from the gradual development of such a technique since serious incongruities or disparities appear which have to be dealt with by state action.

Firstly, during the evolution of capitalism, technology was gradually incorporated into the productive process as the necessary capital accumulated. The countries in process of development, on the other hand, have to assimilate a technology that is ready-made. And if they have to climb progressively toward the higher stage already reached by the more advanced countries, their per capita income will have to increase at a swifter pace than the traditional tempo there.

Then, too, this technology and the continual innovations it entails call for substantial capital per head that the advanced countries can easily build up on the strength of their high per capita income. The developing countries, on the other hand, faced with the same highly capital-intensive technology, have an average per capita income that is barely comparable to that of the former countries nearly a century ago. Hence there is no way out but for the state deliberately to reduce the consumption of the higher income groups in the community, whereas there was no necessity for this when capitalism was evolving as a result of the spontaneous and almost automatic saving on the part of those same groups.

These two incongruities bring in their train another, already mentioned. Whereas in the advanced countries net capital formation came first and the redistribution of income later, in our countries the two problems have now to be solved simultaneously, particularly with the ever present temptation of the Soviet method of economic development.

To add to this, there is the rapidity with which techniques for the prevention and cure of disease are spread, and the ensuing sharp fall in the mortality rate, a phenomenon that took place very slowly during the evolutionary stage of the more advanced countries and was accompanied by an equally gradual fall in the birth rate. The increase in income there fostered changes in the psychological attitude to family formation which are not yet in evidence among the broad masses of the Latin American population with their meager resources. This explains the disparity between the exceptionally high rate of population growth in Latin America and the relatively moderate rate prevailing in the course of capitalistic evolution.

The high rate of demographic growth entails a more intensive effort toward net capital formation and enhances the incongruity between the persistent abundance of labor in our countries and the technology we must assimilate, as evolved in the big industrial centers under the spur of an ever increasing labor shortage.

Lastly, mention must be made of the other incongruity or disparity of import and export demand, which was likewise no problem in the past. Thus the big centers, as they grew, did not show that trend toward the formation of external bottlenecks which is characteristic of the Latin American countries.

The task of coping with these incongruities and promoting development entails three forms of state action. First and foremost, changes in the social structure so as to remove the obstacles to development; this consists essentially in making full use of the savings potential, encouraging the intensive utilization of land and capital, and freeing the huge potential of individual initiative now going to waste, thus giving the system its full dynamic force.

These changes in the social structure pave the way for other changes in the production pattern and structure of the economy which are inherent in the spread and absorption of contemporary technology. Lastly, state action is indispensable as a means of progressively remedying the marked disparities in income distribution by virtue of the increase in income accompanying the changes. . . .

. . . It would be a tragedy if in order to free man from want we had to sacrifice other values and subject him to the demands of an arbitrary power. The very idea is fundamentally incompatible with the genius of the Latin American peoples, with their innate urge to free themselves from want in order to liberate the human personality and give full rein, by means of economic development, to democracy and human rights, especially as regards the under-privileged half of the population of Latin America, and to ensure that both there and in all strata of society, social mobility will allow the best elements to move upwards, for the good of economic development and of democracy. The goal must be a social order free from privilege, and not only economic privilege, but also the baneful privilege by which some men usurp dominion over the ideas of the rest, over the creative forces of the spirit, and over the deepest feelings of the heart.

PRIMARY COMMODITY EXPORTS AND THE DETERIORATION IN THE TERMS OF TRADE*

As has been pointed out, the trend toward external imbalance in the developing countries is mainly a manifestation of the disparity between the rate of growth of their primary exports and that of their imports of industrial goods. While primary exports, with certain exceptions, develop fairly slowly, demand for industrial imports tends to accelerate. This is a spontaneous feature of economic development.

The slow growth of primary exports is an inevitable result of technological progress in the industrial centers. On the one hand, there are direct consequences, since technological progress leads to the increasing substitution of synthetics for natural products; and it is also reflected in one way or another in the smaller raw material content of finished goods. On the other hand, there are indirect consequences, since only a small part of the increased per capita income generated by technological progress goes into the demand for foodstuffs and other staple consumer goods, as compared to the demand for industrial goods and services which tends to rise rapidly. It is significant for example, that, in absolute terms, total consumption of wheat in the United States has remained almost constant since the beginning of the century, in spite of the rise in both population and per capita income.

* Excerpts from *Proceedings of the United Nations Conference on Trade and Development* (Geneva, March 23–June 16, 1964), Vol. II (Report by the Secretary General) (New York: United Nations, 1964).

To all these developments must be added the remarkable effects of the propagation of modern agricultural techniques in the advanced countries.

One of the characteristics of technological progress is that it has not permeated all productive activities or all countries evenly, a fact which largely explains the structural differences and consequent contrasts and disparities in the development process. Until fairly recent times, technological progress was confined to industrial production and had not spread to agriculture to any great extent, except for mechanization. Finally, however, the technological revolution reached this lagging sector, first in the United States and then in Europe. Modern farming techniques made rapid headway and in fact agriculture is becoming industrialized; thus, new dynamic elements are being introduced into the economic complex, at both the internal and the international levels. The old pattern of trade, under which less developed countries were the suppliers of agricultural exports, is undergoing a change which may become permanent and thus help to develop new forms of the international division of labor.

It so happens, however, that the enormous increase in output that has ensued in some major industrial countries has further weakened the export trade in a number of agricultural products from the temperate zones and also in some tropical or semi-tropical products. And here a very significant fact emerges which is not the inevitable result of technological progress but of political attitudes toward this progress, attitudes that are certainly capable of being changed. In spite of the huge increases in productivity, domestic prices in the industrial countries concerned usually stay higher—and often much higher—than those on the international market. In this way, or through the payment of subsidies to farmers, the adverse effects of technological progress on prices are countered. But this policy also provides an additional incentive to expand production, and the expansion is often carried out on marginal holdings and at excessive costs. In order to guarantee a domestic consumer market for the increased output, imports from other producing countries are restricted or eliminated by various devices. . . . If this encouragement results in exportable surpluses, such surpluses are exported by means of subsidies or other incentives which tend to depress world prices, while other producing countries are unable to follow suit because of the very weakness of their economies. . . .

The easing or elimination of protectionism in the industrial centers could have a far-reaching effect on the prices of the goods benefiting thereby. But it would be idle to believe that this can have any decisive effect on the downward trend of the terms of trade for primary commodities in relation to industrial products, which has again prevailed in the past decade. The factors operating in this direction have deeper roots in the peripheral countries than in the industrial centers. The former suffer from a congenital weakness that makes it extremely difficult, if not impossible, for the deterioration to be checked by a decision on their part and on their part alone. . . .

. . . It should be remembered that, although there are differences from country to country, about 60 per cent, on the average, of the economically active population of the developing countries is still engaged in agriculture and other branches of primary production, working generally at a low rate of productivity, and that to this figure must be added that part of the economically active population engaged in artisan activities and personal services at very low scales of remuneration. All these sectors of the population exert constant pressure on the real level of wages in the developing countries and make it extremely difficult for this level to rise in direct proportion to productivity as the latter improves with technological progress. The increase in income generated by higher productivity in the agricultural sector thus tends to shift to other parts of the domestic market or abroad, as the case may be, provided that the shortage of available land does not absorb the increase in income by raising the rent for the benefit of landowners and provided that the play of market forces is left undisturbed.

In the industrial countries, on the other hand, the relative shortage of labor and strong trade-union organization allow wages not only to rise as productivity increases but even, as often happens, to outstrip the increase.

Thus there is a fundamental disparity in these trends. It is a consequence of the structural differences between industrial centers and peripheral countries and it explains the tendency of the terms of trade to worsen. The protection enjoyed by the primary commodities of the industrial centers obviously encourages this tendency because it accentuates the disparity between demand for primary commodities in the centers and demand for imports of manufactures in the periphery. . . .

With an effort of the imagination it is possible to visualize a situation of dynamic equilibrium in the distant future in which the trend in question disappears as a result of the world-wide process of industrialization. If the advanced centers themselves have not yet succeeded in reaching that stage, the countries on the periphery of the world economy can hardly be expected to do so within a short space of time. The readjustment will come about in the end when the structural change is completed, but the period of transition will be very long. In the meantime, it is precisely through this period of transition that the present and successive generations are destined to live, and it is those generations which will have to bring about the change. The change will also require capital formation on a vast scale, to say nothing of time. In the developed economies, capital formation, intrinsically very strong, is facilitated by the very increase in productivity which accompanies technological progress, whereas in the developing countries, owing to the transfer abroad of income caused by the deterioration in the terms of trade, the capacity for capital formation, intrinsically very feeble, will be further diminished. . . .

. . . Ought we to face up to this phenomenon with a great sense of foresight?

There are various ways in which this can be done: by means of commodity agreements, which not only improve prices but also facilitate access to the markets of the industrial countries, or by compensatory financing. These are in fact convergent measures, the nature of which will be analysed in the appropriate part of this report. Suffice it to say here that there are difficulties but that they can be solved. However, for the technical discussion to be profitable, it must be preceded by a political decision of the first importance, namely, a decision to transfer, in one way or another, to the countries exporting primary commodities the extra income accruing to the industrial countries as a result of the deterioration in the terms of trade.

From a pragmatic point of view this means recognizing that countries experiencing a deterioration in the terms of trade have a *prima facie* claim upon additional international resources—resources over and above those which they would have received in the normal course of events. . . .

26. Eduardo Frei

Eduardo Frei, the President of Chile, was born in Santiago in 1911. He took a law degree at the Catholic University of Chile, where he was active in national and international student organizations. After finishing his studies, Frei went to edit a newspaper in Iquique (in the provinces), where he wrote his first book, Chile Desconocido (The Unknown Chile). In 1938, he was one of the group of young Catholic leaders who withdrew from the Conservative Party to form the National Falange, which stood for a reformist policy very different from that of its counterpart in Spain. Frei was President of the Falangist Party three times, and, in 1949, was elected to the Chilean Senate. In 1957, the Falangist Party changed its name to the Christian Democratic Party of Chile, and a year later nominated Frei as its candidate for the presidency. He was unsuccessful in that election, but in 1964, he was elected President with the largest plurality in Chilean history.

In the first selection below, written before he became President, Frei attacks the evils of Communism and capitalism, and develops the Christian Democratic conception of a "middle way" which consists of the involvement of the worker in management and ownership, the promotion of intermediate groupings between the individual and the state, and government action to limit the power of large economic concentrations. Subsequent selections show how the Christian Democratic ideology has been translated into practice in a series of reform bills which propose the creation of community and occupational organizations on all levels of Chilean society, the redistribution and restructuring of Chilean land tenure, and the "Chileanization" of the U.S.-owned copper industry.

CHRISTIAN DEMOCRACY
IN THEORY AND PRACTICE*

Capitalism and Communism

If we compare the proposals of *Quadragesimo Anno* with the realities of the present, we can observe that they are still perfectly valid. The world of economics is still oscillating between the extremes of liberalism and collectivism, capitalism and Communism, free enterprise and statism. In the face of these, the encyclical proposed a system of moral ideas that can produce a different formula. The task that was presented to Christians was precisely to construct this formula. Can we say that they have constructed it?

If we continue our observation, we can assert that the formulas presented at the two extremes are simple, effective, and, from their point of view, efficient. Are we able to offer a formula that is characterized by equal efficiency and clarity? This is the problem. . . .

There is something that we should understand. Capitalism as a system dehumanizes the economy, although, in its first stage, it meant an enormous expansion of economic development and the creation of wealth. Yet there is no doubt that it tended to concentrate economic power in a few hands, to allow the great monopolistic powers to control the market so that, by a fierce dialectical process within its own structure, it led to the disappearance of economic freedom. In the productive process, it separated labor from management and, more than that, from the concept of property and the exercise of that right.

With regard to [the evils of] capitalism, we note that there are two well-defined plans of action: the reformist and the revolutionary. The revolutionary aims at the destruction of the regime in a sudden, violent, and total manner. In fact [in revolutionary regimes], private capitalism has been replaced by that of the state, the property holder who controls capital by the bureaucrat who controls the power of the state, the business manager delegated

---

* Excerpts from *Pensamiento y Acción* (Santiago de Chile; Editorial del Pacifico, 1958); translated by the editor, by permission.

by the stockholding property owner, by the managerial bureaucrat delegated by the government which administers the state, and the more and more concentrated powerful monopoly capitalists by the powerful supermonopoly of the state.

Basically, we could say of the two systems that Communism is a continuation of capitalism, drawing the latent tendencies in its structure to their logical conclusions. The two differ not in technique, but in purpose. Technically, there is no difference if the administrative group is made up of private stockholders or of bureaucrats representing state ownership. The difference is that the first is directed by various groups that exercise control for their own interests, and the second is directed by those who administer the state for the purpose of collective goals. This could be a greater justification of the second system, but if we analyze what has happened more profoundly, we will see that this advantageous result is more apparent than real.

On the theoretical level, this seems very clear, but at the practical level, it does not occur with the simplicity that the scheme appears to offer. When capitalism is a monopoly under the sole control of the state, there results as a consequence a concentration of power in the bureaucracy that is as merciless or more merciless in its operation than the private businessman. According to the classic example of the textbooks of sociology, a worker, representing labor, alone and isolated, appeared before the employer burdened by a triple inferiority—psychological, economic, and legal. But the condition of the worker who confronts the bureaucrat-employer suffers from the same inferiority and adds a fourth—political inferiority. The private employer wielded the weight of his economic power, while the state employer wields the weight of his economic and political power, since he also has behind him the purposes of the state. Hence, for the worker, his real juridical condition has not changed, only the name of his employer. . . .

But Christians refuse to accept the alternatives of capitalism or Communism, because they know how closely the two are linked in their basic development. It is curious that some have appropriated the idea of capital as if capital and capitalism were synonymous, although there is also a statist and Communist capitalism. Similarly, there are those who think that private initiative and personal liberty are synonymous with individualistic liberalism. The goals of liberty and initiative can only be conceived and realized in a new system of values. If they could be attained in the past century, in a limited class and social type, present historical conditions demand that they be indicated in a different social situation and with a different purpose and meaning. Freedom today depends on a decent standard of living, and initiative cannot be a matter of appetite and interest, but must be integrated into the collective common good.

It is a fact that capitalism and philosophic and social liberalism have not succeeded in giving expression to the desires of the common man. They have brought the world to an increasing proletarianization, which is the reverse of what is affirmed by some superficial arguments concerning the distribution of small property or corporation stocks. In economics, secondary facts are of no importance, and the terms are essentially relative. It is a question of power. Today someone who has a piece of land exercises his property right, but economic power resides in high finance, in the cartels, and in the concentrated holdings of the large corporations.

In this, everything is subject to change. A century ago, the one who dominated the textile industry controlled industrial power. Twenty years ago, a nation with a heavy steel industry led in economic and political domination. Today power resides in nuclear energy, and in time the possession of a steel industry will be no more important than the production of textile fabrics.

Production has become technically complex. It requires an immense effort of scientific creativity. It means the domination of vast markets, variable and delicate in their reactions, which are aimed at satisfying human necessities, but which do this by periodically destroying the man who produces the goods in order to serve the same man when he tries to satisfy himself as consumer. There is the latent danger of a machine system that is so fearful, moving at such a continually increasing velocity (it is enough to look at the production figures in the European countries which, seven years after being devastated by war, surpassed all the prewar levels, without citing the American figures, which can only be expressed in billions) that it can only be managed by concentrated and absolute power, because the uncontrolled expression of its demands cannot be resisted by a normal democratic state. On the other hand, to leave this machine system uncontrolled in a fundamentally weak state which does not have the active specific mission of defense of the common good would be even more fatal and impossible. The system of counterbalances of which Donoso Cortés spoke a century ago would be operative here: no internal control on man; propaganda that arouses an unlimited appetite for goods; economies that are incapable of satisfying the desire for these goods, arousing the multitude to desperation when it considers its misery. What is the only state which is able to discipline and contain this?

Thus it is that capitalism leads inevitably finally to Communism. Thus it is naïve to find the remedy in a system of partial improvement—a house and a salary. The problem of the economic system is much more profound and concerns the whole structure, the motivations, the fundamental conceptions of the economy and its purpose, and of man as a moral being.

A Third Alternative

But here there arises a new problem with regard to this productive mechanism whose technique dominates the world and whose moving force appears to subjugate it. The extremes present formulas that fasten on us like claws. Do we possess a way, a method, that offers something other than aspirations, intentions, or principles? . . .

We are going to outline our position not only to those who accept Christian thought, but also to the groups called humanistic socialists, who have had practical experience with the program of Marxist socialism, but who also recognize the essential principles that have been maintained by Catholic philosophy on the sociological plane. The great task of Christians consists in being able to explain this method, which can be perceived only uncertainly and inexactly. Its principal elements have, as a matter of fact, been demonstrated to be valid.

The action of the state cannot be an absorbing and paralyzing intervention, but must respect intermediate organisms—the family, the city, the region, the trade union, the business enterprise. It must exert an effective authority for orientation, planning, and leadership. It ought to be strong enough to prevent the creation beyond its regulatory authority of economic powers which can oppress and control the market for products and for work. It cannot be the impotent witness of what goes on in the market, because it would mean the end of liberty if each citizen were left to act according to his interest and his influence.

For this purpose, it is necessary to have higher controls, to create new conditions and to coordinate but not to constrain them. It is necessary to have planning, because this represents the common good of the whole nation and because all isolated efforts represent only a part of the interest of the whole. We know today that the income of a nation is distributed among labor, capitalization, and profit. The state should know which part can be used for consumption and which should be utilized for capital, which proportion can go to the public sector and which to the private sector. It can and ought to maintain a monetary flow according to the volume of economic activity. No one today can believe that this must be subjected to a freedom that would be a fiction, destroying itself by the very mechanism of economic factors.

But this action for the common good can better develop and perhaps can only be developed when it is not thought that a progressive statism is being established when colossal bureaucratic powers are created, which, by their very ineffective existence, consume the resources they are administering so that the mechanism created by man destroys man rather than serving him.

We think, for example, that the government of the United States, when it created the Paley Mission to study raw-material resources, reserves, and conditions in the world, fulfills its task of watching over the destiny of the nation better than when an improvising government of ours thinks that it has made progress by its improvisation in creating new supervisory groups. . . . The same thing happened in Italy, where the government faced the problem of housing by establishing construction areas and factories for prefabricated materials, substituting for direct construction a national effort with the cooperation and initiative of all citizens. Thus the state served man better than by creating institutions which, whether for financial or technical reasons, have demonstrated themselves incapable of resolving this difficult problem. But this is hardly a mention of a fundamental theme whose concrete application must be worked out and defined. Nevertheless, there remains the fundamental question—namely, that of the economic structure itself, the functioning of the productive unit, and the harmonization of the factors that compose it. On this subject, it has been difficult to make progress. Some try communitarian forms, which are attractive without as yet having any experimental validity. The experiences of codetermination are thus far varied, but one cannot say that they are conclusive.

Today a new era is opening up. The business enterprise is composed of the investor who provides the capital, the manager, and the worker. If we could imagine a vast process of universal extension of property through the organized acquisition of shares by the worker, not in the limited context of the old worker-stockholder, but a planned and large-scale access of labor to capital, we could imagine a social organization in which man would participate in the economic process in two ways—as worker, by his salary, and as owner of capital, through profit. This process ought not to be thought of solely as limited to the enterprise in which the worker is employed, but applied to any enterprise, since the important thing would be to give the worker property and, more than that, to involve him in the process of capitalization, which is the foundation of the economic process, the condition of stability for the worker himself, and the sole form that offers the possibility of raising his standard of living.

This would require action that would make it easy for organized savings to go into investment, something that could not occur without a more equitable distribution, the present goal of the worker movement and of the employees. This type of investigation requires an effort of creative imagination, but it is an especially difficult problem that must be resolved, like all those which aim at transforming structures and institutions in which very diverse factors enter, which cannot be foreseen. Their difficulty cannot be appreciated except at the time when they are carried out, and no effort of logic is capable of anticipating it. It is for this purpose that I make these observations, to arouse others to the study of those possibilities which are open to reflection and action. . . .

The foundations of a humanistic economy should be the result of an encounter between our philosophy and the scientific experience that emerges from the economy—the vivid comprehension of the reality in which we live and the will for presence by the Christian as a constructive element in the society to which he belongs. . . .

THE ROLE OF POPULAR
ORGANIZATIONS IN THE STATE*

At the present time, no nation can progress satisfactorily if its economy does not expand rapidly in conditions of monetary stability and a just distribution of income. Still less can it do so if a minority controls power and the majority is excluded from its exercise. Electoral power is not enough to satisfy the needs of the people. Electoral power is only a part of political power, and this in turn a part of power in general, which also includes economic and cultural power. If a nation is to be really democratic, the people should have access to all these forms of power and participate in their exercise. Furthermore, we believe that once the people are aware that they have electoral power, it is indispensable that they have access, through appropriate channels, to the other forms of power. Otherwise a tendency toward state control and the perversion of the role political parties should play in a democracy will inevitably develop. Whoever is opposed to state control and at the same time refuses to give the people access to other forms of power is involved in a tragic contradiction.

The road to power is through organization. The present crisis consists in the fact that the majority of our population is unorganized, even in the trade unions. As is well known, only 10 per cent of the wage-earners in Chile belong to trade unions. Participation in power through organizations necessarily involves the delegation of power to representatives who act in the name of others. The exercise of power by those representatives is legitimized by their capacity to interpret the aspirations of those whom they represent and to lead them to the goals which they wish to achieve. Legitimacy is assured by means of a system of elections and of mechanisms which provide sufficient information to prevent the representatives from deceiving the electorate. Where a system of elections and the mechanisms mentioned above do not function, there is a crisis of representation.

In too many organizations, real political machines have been

* Excerpt from *Primer Mensaje del Presidente de la República de Chile al Congreso Nacional* (May 21, 1965), published by the Presidential Department of Publications, Santiago, Chile; translated by the editor.

constructed which make it impossible to judge the representatives and apply sanctions where necessary. The persistence of these abuses is one of the most formidable obstacles to the operation of integral democracy, and my government proposes to make every effort in its power to eliminate them. . . .

A very important symptom of our crisis situation is the failure from generation to generation to develop an image of what we wish to be as a nation and as a member of the community of nations—an image which is indispensable to mobilize the latent vigor of the people. The attempts which have been made have been feeble and ineffectual, since we have not oriented our efforts to see what we are and what we can become. As social thinkers, up to the present, we have been great imitators of the history and ideas of other peoples. . . .

[In the coming year] the entire nation will be covered with a network of community organizations, such as neighborhood committees, centers for mothers and children, and economic and occupational organizations, such as trade unions, cooperatives, and organizations of artisans. All of these organizations will be associated at the regional and national levels to form a National Council of Community Organizations and of occupational groups which will be able to sit down and negotiate with the government, or with any other interest group, in conditions of equality. The people will finally be participating in power. . . .

We will see a very different picture in the economic organization of our society. The unions will be strong. Cooperative enterprises will prosper everywhere and will constitute one of the most powerful tools to combat monopoly and to develop our economic and social life in a healthy way. . . .

This program means the construction of an authentic economic, social, and human democracy with a profound popular content. It is not a movement toward statism or against private property and individual initiative. We do not share in the ideological folklore which holds that there are intrinsic virtues or defects in the state or in the system of private property. The important thing is to organize the state, private property, and business so that they serve the common good and not that of one group, class, or party which controls power.

This is the idea which inspires popular development: to give value to each man, to the family, to the municipality, to the group, to the cooperative, to the business enterprise, and to the region.

The state is the expression of an organized society, not of a society in which certain centers of power predominate and control the life of the nation at the expense of a populace which remains anonymous.

This program and this movement are likewise rooted in the conviction that we live in a pluralistic society in which we should respect fully the exercise of freedom of expression and of religious and political liberty. For this reason we are opposed to the system of the single party. As democrats we believe in free and periodic elections and in the possibility and the right of minorities one day to become majorities if that is the will of the people. . . .

AGRARIAN REFORM IN CHILE*

Agrarian reform involves a profound change in the structure of land tenure and in the social order. It means the full involvement of the peasantry in the life of the nation. In the agrarian reform which we are going to undertake we will not take away the right to property but complete it; we will not despoil individual persons but redistribute the national patrimony. We intend to carry out that task with a profound sense of justice and liberty, creating thousands of new property holders, strengthening the [role of] the small and intermediate property holders already in existence, and encouraging those who are farming their lands efficiently today.

In the near future I will send an Agrarian Reform Bill to the National Congress.† The agrarian reform which we will propose has two primary objectives. Economically, it will be aimed at a rapid increase in production and productivity and the equitable division of the profits derived from agricultural production; socially, it will seek to produce a sense of self-respect and a higher level of education in the peasant so as to produce a favorable attitude toward progress and the improvement of his way of life.

The bill proposes the expropriation (1) of uncultivated lands

* Excerpt from *Primer Mensaje del Presidente de la República de Chile al Congreso Nacional* (May 21, 1965), published by the Presidential Department of Publications, Santiago, Chile; translated by the editor.

† An amended version of the Agrarian Reform Bill was approved by the Chilean Congress in early 1967.—ED.

and of those which are notoriously underexploited compared to the normal level of production in the area, (2) of farms which have been abandoned or which keep a large part of their productive land out of proper use for agricultural or grazing purposes, and (3) of lands which have benefited from extensive development or investment by the state.

Farms which are of excessive size will be affected only to the extent that they exceed the limits laid down by the law, which will vary in different parts of the country according to the quality of the land. Even those farms, if they are being systematically cultivated and developed economically and if they create systems for the participation of the [agricultural] workers, will not be affected by the bill. For those farms which are expropriated, the bill proposes that all investments and improvements made after November 4, 1964, be paid for in cash at their current commercial value. Hence there is no reason to restrict investment because a farm may be subject to expropriation. Payment for expropriated land will be partly in cash and partly in short-term bonds, the form of which will be designed to provide the largest measure of support and guarantees.

In order for this bill to be fully effective it will be necessary to amend the Political Constitution of the State in the section on the right of property, its social function, and the community interest.

In the course of the agrarian reform it is essential to encourage the general development of the whole peasant population of the country, including both those who receive property and those who do not. . . . The basic effort of the state will consist of the following: (a) aid to small and medium property holders and landless peasants to organize into Peasant and Cooperative Committees, which together with the agrarian syndicate will comprise the basic forms of organization for the rural population, and (b) the provision of technical assistance, credit, and housing to these small peasant organizations.

The peasant as producer must emerge from a subsistence economy to supply the national market. The organization of the market is an essential condition for the success of the development of agriculture. In the case of small producers the way to do this on the local level is through peasant cooperatives. On the regional and national level we are establishing cooperatives for consumers, credit, marketing, the provision of seed, and other services.

Basic education is one of the central points of the government agrarian policy. The provision of elementary schools available to all the children in the countryside is an accomplishment already achieved in the few months during which my government has held office. We are also encouraging the development of vocational and specialized education so that the young people in the country may become technically qualified; that the natural leaders and peasant talent can be directed toward agricultural development and participation in social change; and that those who emigrate to the city may find effective and well-paid opportunities for productive work.

The peasant problem is not only economic and educational but also social, cultural, and political. It will be necessary therefore to eliminate the legal obstacles to the creation of community-based economic and specialized organizations. . . .

. . . The present legislation has meant in practice that agricultural unions do not exist in this country. After so many years there are no more than twenty such unions in Chile, with fewer than 2,000 members altogether, although the number of workers and wage-earners capable of receiving the benefits of a union organization is possibly on the order of 200,000 persons or more. To correct this situation, I sent to the Congress on February 9 of this year a bill to establish various principles on the right of union organization. This bill seeks to modify in a fundamental way the present legislation on the subject of unionization so that the workers can organize freely and in accord with the agreements which our country has signed with international organizations.

I am perfectly aware that to propose agrarian reform in a country involves risks. The organization of agriculture is not an economic problem. It is a way of life, involving traditions, political power, even family relations. To change that structure always implies painful adjustments for many. For this reason agrarian reform will always arouse resistance, dissatisfaction, and opposition. Many will combat it in good faith without knowing its advantages. Others, passionately defending their positions and often their egoism, will use every manner of means from rumor to outright attack, from paralyzing labor to firing workers, to create a climate of lack of confidence which will make this task, however long it lasts, still more difficult.

In the majority of the countries of the world, especially in the underdeveloped areas, agrarian reform has taken place in the midst of revolution and violence. This we wish to avoid for our country at all cost. But the government is convinced that agrarian reform is necessary both from a technical point of view, in order to increase productivity, and from a social and human point of view, because it is necessary to open up new possibilities to large sectors of the Chilean people. It is also fundamental from a political point of view because it is the only way to create genuine democratic stability in our national life.

A NEW POLICY FOR CHILEAN COPPER*

Before assuming the presidency I pointed out clearly and precisely the objectives I would pursue if elected. I wish to recall them, for they are embodied in the text of my program and of my statements and speeches:

First, a substantial increase in copper production, in order to attain a production of 1 million tons within this period.

Second, refinement within the country of the total production of copper, meeting the technical and trade conditions of the world market, which always maintains a quota of nonrefined copper.

Third, a definite increase of consumption within the country on the part of the producing companies, and, therefore, a definite increase in their complete participation in the development of the national economy.

Fourth, a decisive intervention of the state, as representative of the interests of the national community, in the guidance and implementation of Chilean copper trade, which includes, as we have stated on a number of opportunities, the trade of copper with all countries in the world, with no other limitation than the interest of the nation.

I have clearly stated that Chilean copper, as a supply destined to fulfill universal human needs, expresses the solidarity of our people with all men on earth and with all countries. Consequently, our copper mining is not an industry that intends, in any case whatsoever, to obtain advantages without in turn giving a true service to those who are called upon to consume its product.

For this reason, my government has sought from the outset,

* Excerpts from a Presidential address, December 21, 1964; translated and published by Editorial del Pacifico and reprinted by permission.

after the election of September 4, the ways and means to meet with those who can really play an effective role in the development of our copper industry, and who show their willingness to enter into a relationship based on dignity and full respect of Chile's sovereignty and superior interest. . . .

The most general purpose of these negotiations has been that of profoundly changing the basis and form of relationships between the country—its economy and its public opinion—and foreign investments, especially those devoted to the exploitation of its natural wealth.

Chile can no longer accept the traditional trend: that these investments, searching for excessive safeguards, become true islands within the national activity. Therefore, it has been a condition of our objectives in production, refining, and in other matters, to seek a way to give concrete forms to the association of the interests of these investments with those of the Chilean national community.

During the course of the negotiations we have found in the enterprises a determined will for cooperation with this government in the broadest fulfillment of this purpose.

Thus we have reached agreement on the formation of important mining partnerships, in which the foreign investor contributes a part of the capital and his technical experience, and the Chilean state intervenes as a partner also contributing the capacity and experience of our community, through its specialized agencies.

Negotiations in this aspect were initiated with Cerro Corporation, a North American firm which until the present day has exploited deposits of great importance in Peru, and which is interested in the exploitation of the Rio Blanco deposits in the province of Aconcagua, through the Andean Mining Company. The state offered specific contributions, through which it receives a 25 per cent share in the capital stock and an equivalent share in the administration of the firm, that is, in the production and marketing of its products. The Andean Mining Company was, therefore, the first step in this transformation of the copper policy of the country.

Subsequently, in negotiations with companies of the Anaconda Group, the same possibility was put forth, and it was agreed to organize a new mining enterprise in charge of exploiting the deposit called Exótica, next to the Chuquicamata mine, and containing 153,000,000 tons of copper ore with a possible productive capacity of 100,000 metric tons a year. In this company, as in the Andean Mining Company, the Chilean state will own 25 per cent of the capital stock and the equivalent share in its administration.

Moreover, in the case of companies of the Anaconda Group, an agreement was reached that all its present unexploited mining properties, some of which offer great prospects, will be given over for thorough and prompt study to a new exploration company in which the Chilean state will own 49 per cent of the stock.

When these studies recommend the exploitation of new deposits, mining companies will be formed in which the Chilean state will have one-third of the stock and an equivalent share in its administration.

In short, a large new mine will be opened, with a yearly production of 100,000 metric tons, in which the Chilean state will be a partner. Moreover, any new mine which this group may have in Chile will be given over to a new joint exploration company to be operated with participation of the Chilean state.

Finally, no doubt the most important result obtained is that concerning the Braden Copper Company, the present owner of the El Teniente mine, with whom the following agreement was reached and which I ask my fellow citizens to weigh in all its significance.

The Braden Copper Company will become a Chilean corporation under the name of Sociedad Minera El Teniente, Sociedad Anónima.

In this new company, the Chilean state, through its present Department of Copper, which in the future will be called Corporación del Cobre de Chile [Copper Corporation of Chile], will acquire 51 per cent of the stock, and the Kennecott Copper Corporation of the United States, owner of Braden, will retain the remaining 49 per cent.

The purchasing price of the government shares will be U.S. $80 million, which will not be withdrawn from Chile but fully invested in increasing production, and its amortization will be made in a twenty-year period, at the minimum interest rate.

The new El Teniente company will moreover have to seek new financial contributions in the amount of U.S. $120 million to complete the investment, with support of the Chilean state and of Kennecott.

In other words, the Chilean state acquires control of one of the largest mines in the world and one of the two most important in the Chilean territory.

This policy of partnership is a true challenge to the Chilean community, for it commits the economic effort of the country, and also the national conscience regarding the destiny of its leading industry, so that whatever the industry will mean in the future life of the country will be placed in our hands—a responsibility which we must fully assume, for we are thereby fulfilling one of the great aspirations of the Chilean people. The opportunity is thus laid open to show to ourselves and to the world that our country is capable of managing one of the most important copper industries in the world. . . .

It is also an obvious condition of the entire agreement with the enterprises, especially in the larger copper-mining activity, to establish a close association between activities of the state, its institutions and those of the enterprises, and the copper-workers' organizations. In this sense, the Confederation of Copper Workers may rest assured that it can count on maximum guarantees for the fulfillment of responsibilities which my government deems essential.

This Confederation, in whose organization and patriotic spirit I feel confident, will have an extraordinary responsibility in the conduct of the social policy to be developed in the large copper industry, and especially with regard to the final solution of all problems affecting living conditions in the large mining camps, so that the copper workers will represent all the Chilean people in their association with the Chilean state and with the enterprises in the progress of this industry. . . .

I have always asserted that it was in the mining industry that the country could obtain, in dramatic fashion, the resources required to adjust its balance of payments and the necessary capital for its economic development.

But, of course, the country cannot be content with this alone, nor can it live only on what is produced by copper. These developments imply another serious obligation for Chile, and that is to take advantage of the opportunity and of the time it grants us to diversify the economy. We will lose this opportunity if we are not capable, in the next years, of giving a decisive impulse to our agriculture and of hastening development in our industrial sector.

These agreements, which entail enormous investments, also imply an act of confidence on the part of the largest foreign investors in the institutional stability of the country and in the capability of the Chilean people. Therefore, these agreements will tell investors throughout the world, and will do so better than any other declaration, about the solid prospects to be found in Chile; they are also an imperative call to Chilean entrepreneurs to have equal, or I would say greater, enthusiasm to undertake new enterprises that will give work to our people and increase our wealth.

If all respond in this way, I am certain that the country will be taking definite steps to place itself, in revolutionary fashion, among the most advanced people on earth, and we shall open to our youth the broad horizon of a truly sovereign country offering the bold new possibilities characteristic of modern communities.

27. Jaime Castillo

Jaime Castillo is the chairman of the Christian Democratic Party of Chile. He is also the principal ideologist of Latin American Christian Democracy by virtue of the large number of books and articles he has written on the subject. The selection below is taken from a speech delivered at a seminar organized by the Institute of Political Studies, a Christian Democratic research group of which Castillo is the director. In the article, Castillo tries to define the goal of communitarianism, the term now being used by Latin American Christian Democrats to describe their alternative to the extremes of both individualism and collectivism, represented by the United States and the Soviet Union. In common with most writers on Catholic social thought, Castillo analyzes the property right in terms of the ethical requirements of the natural law, but he also finds it necessary to defend the notion of natural law itself from the increasing criticism which has been leveled at it by Catholic writers since the Second Vatican Council. The refusal of Castillo to give specific details on the structure of communitarian society reflects the bitter dispute within the Christian Democratic Party over whether communitarianism is to remain only an ideal vision of a future society or become the basis for an immediate and radical restructuring of property relationships in industry, agriculture, and society.

PROPERTY AND THE COMMUNITARIAN SOCIETY*

Individualism—Its Essential Insight and Historical Development

Individualism developed as the assertion of the rights of the individual against a tyrannical society, not against a just society, for that would make no sense. The virtue of individualism, then, was that it defended certain rights which had been ignored. It asserted the existential reality of the individual against those who would deny the value of the individual, [and] it demonstrated that the individual had a role in history, or, rather, that society could not be explained by reducing it to social factors. . . .

In our view, this position is open to criticism when we see its ideological implications and when its essential intuition is distorted as it is applied to reality.

On the first point, individualism is based on an illegitimate abstraction because it sets the individual and society in opposition to one another. We believe, and in this we agree with Marx, that society is not an abstraction which exists above the individual. The individual is a social being. Individuals do not exist in the way that individualism conceives of them. Only the social individual exists. Hence the individual and society are not opposed to one another; they harmonize with one another and require each other.

On the second point, that of historical reality, individualism in the modern age produced a capitalism which is based on an individualistic concept of property and a nonsocial view of man. It also developed the system of government known as liberal democracy, which was a necessary prerequisite for an economic order which is now socially and morally passé, and for a society which rejected the idea of community and impeded its development. Thus, this democracy became a regime which destroyed the possibility of true human community life and lost its original meaning.

Individualism holds an erroneous conception of human rights—

* Excerpt from *Propiedad y Sociedad Comunitaria*, presented at the International Seminar on Property, organized by the Instituto de Estudios Políticos, Santiago, Chile, in February, 1966; translated by the editor.

they are considered as rights of man against society, in circumstances which require that they be oriented toward the community. Marx said this in criticizing the human rights which were proclaimed by the French Revolution. Liberty is not the right to oppose or remove oneself from the life of a community but is a condition of its progress. To understand differently is to encourage disassociation from society, which is basically nothing but monstrous egoism.

Collectivism—Its Essential Insight and Historical Development

Applying the same scheme, the essential insight of collectivism seems to us to be a reassertion of the rights of society against an individualistic system which had been carried to its logical conclusion. Historically it was a reaction, but at the same time a fundamental value was involved—the reassertion of the fact that the individual cannot realize himself except in the community. . . . The social sphere has a value, as is demonstrated by social science, and it cannot be ignored in the explanation of the process of history. . . .

In its historical development, collectivism takes on the character of a kind of absolutism. In the field of economics, a collectivist economy implies the forcible suppression of all forms of private property. In politics, it has meant a totalitarian system in which dictatorship appears to be essential. In this way, the possibility of a rich, organic, natural life of human association is prevented, for, when the individual is suppressed, what is essentially human also disappears.

Communitarianism as a Synthesis

As we have seen, a false opposition of the individual and the group presents the problem in a unilateral form and leads to individualism or collectivism. As we understand it, communitarianism results from the realization that by applying proper categories of analysis we can succeed in harmonizing the two extremes. In this way, communitarianism is the assertion of the individual *and* the community. It prevents us from falling into the error of conceptual alienation by virtue of which, as Marx says, we create fetishes which hypnotize and capture us under the spell of unilateral views of reality.

The synthesis is based on conceptions of the person and the community which basically point to the same thing. The person is a social individual. This is the only reality because man always exists in society and is a social being. This means that reality has two aspects, the person and the community, both of them inseparable. Consequently, when we think about the problem we must take account of the two aspects. Hence we reject the definition of society which individualism offers us because it makes it appear that society is composed of atomized individuals, unrelated to one another. This is to falsify reality, not to describe society.

These ideas can be expressed with some precision in two formulas. One is that of Maritain,* "the community of free men." This sums up our ideological goal—a community, or rather a spiritual community, of many individuals, of free men in a community with the highest degree of freedom. The second formula is that of Toniolo,† "a community of communities." Here one can see what the political and social organization of the communitarian society would be. There would be a multiplicity of organizations which implies a greater possibility of realizing freedom than if the society were simply reduced to a single social segment. . . .

Individualism put into action fails because the egoistic instinct which inspires it leads to injustice and abuse. Collectivism also fails due to a spiritual inadequacy which fatally leads it to reproduce the situation which it claims to avoid. Communitarianism on the other hand, for the reasons pointed out, opens the way to an infinity of approximations of truly human forms of community life. . . .

Property and Natural Law

. . . In response to those who claim that private property is a matter of natural law, we hold that that system is not required by natural law but only conforms to it when at a given time it is the best method to regulate and permit the most efficient use of all the goods of the earth. . . .

What is a matter of natural law is what we call the right of common use, that the enjoyment of goods is a demand of human

---

* Jacques Maritain, a French Catholic philosopher whose political works are a major source of Christian Democratic ideology.—ED.

† Giuseppe Toniolo (1845–1918), an Italian social thinker whose writings influenced the founders of the Italian Christian Democratic Party.—ED.

nature because man should satisfy his needs with the goods which have been placed at his disposal.

Nevertheless, there are those who, without denying that the right of common use is essential and permanent and that systems of appropriation are mutable, would deny the existence of natural law itself. In my opinion to deny the theory of natural law is as absurd as claiming to deny the theory of being. It is an impossible claim. And if we deny the existence of the natural law we will of necessity develop the same solution under a different name. Ultimately it seems to me that discussion on this matter is a dispute over terms rather than over concepts.

What is meant by natural law has to be conceived, it seems to me, as that minimum of rational terminology which is necessary to explain an obvious fact—that there exists in human nature a certain need to use and dispose of things in a way which accords with the ethical and social character of every human act. The formula, natural law, therefore expresses something very minimal and perhaps excessively vague—that man proceeds in accordance with the integrity of his being. To concretize a theoretical system to reflect this exigency is inevitable from the point of view of logic, but it runs the risk of seeming to set down in precise terms what is a complex of visions. These then become for some a substitute for reality, abstractions in the bad sense of the word. The polemics of those who in their turn develop another set of abstractions or ideological fetishes exaggerate the problem and prevent simple and authentic reflection. . . .

The Communitarian Society

First, in a communitarian society there will be the full realization of community in the sense which we explained above. There will be a plenitude of human life in common. It will be a fraternal society [in which] the highest human values will prevail. This is the same as saying that the full human life of each man will be realized in its plenitude.

Second, the communitarian society will give preference to social values over those of the individual. On this point I must also refer to something which we have debated elsewhere—the opposition of communitarianism and socialism. I have said it already—I think that both terms point to the same thing. At least their relation is very intimate. Nevertheless, I personally think that the term communitarianism is an expression which is more vivid, more vigorous, and more expressive of our thinking. In addition, the term socialism implies certain doctrinal principles which are questionable as far as we are concerned and which are also linked to the experiences of totalitarian collectivism. Therefore, I prefer to use the term communitarianism. In any case the idea is the same, but to use the term communitarian socialism is to involve oneself in an unnecessary redundancy and at the same time to create certain doubts on our part.*

The communitarian society will possess a structure which is in accordance with what has been said above. Its decisive characteristic will be a communitarian type of property holding (by communities of workers, cooperatives, and other social forms), but it will allow for personal property when it has a social function as well as for the retention of some property by the national community. The dichotomy between capital and labor will be superseded by communitarian relationships, that is, by uniting labor and capital in the hands of the workers themselves. This will take place gradually and in different ways which it would be useless to try to describe in detail at this time.

Third, the driving motivation of the communitarian society will be the interest of all its members in its establishment, a solidarity derived from a common effort to reach a goal which benefits everyone. On this point we can recall the "organic solidarity" which Durkheim† describes as characterizing developed societies. In addition, the stimulus of material interest will also be present, combined not with an individualist spirit of monetary gain (for that will tend to disappear as repugnant to the ideal of community) but with a spiritual interest in the construction of a fraternal society. These two interests, intimately linked to one another, are human, living, vital, real interests and this will tend to assure that they will be satisfied. . . .

---

* This is a reference to the increasing use of the term communitarian socialism by the left wing and the youth organization of the Chilean Christian Democratic Party in order to indicate their opposition to the continued existence of "capitalist" property relationships in Chile.—ED.

† Emile Durkheim (1858–1917), a French sociologist.—ED.

28. CLASC

CLASC is the shorthand abbreviation for the Latin American Confederation of Christian Trade Unionists (Confederación Latinoamericana de Sindicalistas Cristianos). Founded in Santiago on December 8, 1954, it is affiliated with the International Federation of Christian Trade Unions, and comprises worker and peasant organizations of Catholic inspiration in Latin America. Generally sympathetic to Christian Democracy, it takes a much stronger position of opposition to the United States than do most Christian Democratic politicians. However, the desire for Latin American economic and political unity expressed in the Charter adopted at the CLASC meeting in Rio de Janeiro in early 1964 is a common sentiment among Latin American leaders and a central doctrine of Christian Democracy in Latin America.

THE CHARTER OF RIO DE JANEIRO*

Revolution and Unity

One of the fundamental requirements of the revolutionary process among our peoples is Latin American unity in the cultural, social, economic, and political fields. We represent twenty-two isolated republics and several territories still under colonial domination which have been atomized and impotent, incapable of taking action for the supranational unification which would allow us to unite our disparate fragmentary countries into one large Latin American fatherland. The real solution for our problems, the effective base for the integral development of our resources, the

* Translated by the editor from *Carta de Rio de Janeiro*, published by the Servicio de Prensa Obrera Campesino Internacional, Caracas, 1964.

effective force for the transformation of our structures, can only take the form of a policy of supranational integration. Latin American unity is the sole way to satisfy the individual needs of our countries and the collective hopes of our peoples.

Integration or Death

International relations are being rapidly transformed in the contemporary world. The policy of imperialistic blocs is being left behind. Nations are joining together in definite regional organizations, such as the Organization of African Unity or the Common Market, the basis for a supranational political integration of the countries of Europe. In this new relationship of world forces, Latin America must resolve its destiny in a simple and dramatic choice, whether to remain disunited as in the past and lose its identity in the disintegration and misery of impotence or to unite in a new economic, social, and political unit, retaining in that integration its personality and historic destiny, and able to play a decisive and preponderant role among the peoples of the Third World in the face of the powers which direct world politics.

Pan-Americanism Does Not Represent the Interests of Latin America

Many factors have been and are opposed to the realization of the unification of Latin America, but the most constant factor in our history has been and continues to be the predominant presence of the United States, which has interfered and continues to interfere in all developments in Latin America.

Numerous military and political pacts tie us to the United States. Innumerable economic, commercial, cultural and other links give rise to a colonialist interdependence. Pan-Americanism, inspired by the Monroe Doctrine of "America for the Americans," has been the institutional instrument which has enabled the United States to maintain the domination of its interests over Latin America, concealed behind the humanitarian objectives of consolidating democracy, overcoming misery, and developing our countries. Pan-Americanism is a failure. It has served neither to strengthen democracy, nor to overcome misery, nor to promote the rapid development of our peoples as a whole. Pan-Americanism has been solely a unilateral policy of the United States to safeguard its interests, its security, and to maintain a facile façade behind which to infiltrate and impose a character and destiny on Latin America which have nothing to do with Latin American interests.

Pan-Americanism has directed the whole system of relations between Latin America and the United States in all areas, including that of the trade unions. The functioning, dynamic, and *raison d'être* of the Inter-American Regional Organization of Labor (ORIT)* is simply a projection of that policy of the domination of American interests in the field of Latin American trade unionism, seeking to mold, influence, and monopolize the labor organizations in our countries to serve a policy and a system which has been the permanent cause of our disunited state and humiliating dependence which must be overcome once and for all. The ORIT is already condemned to disappear because it does not correspond to the historic development of Latin America.

Latin American Nationalism—Basis of Unity

Two worlds face one another: the Latin American world and that of North America. Pan-Americanism is the enemy of Latin Americanism—the new feeling and perspectives which must serve as the basis for unification. In condemning Pan-Americanism we are condemning a system, a policy, and an institution which do not correspond to Latin American interests. We are not attacking the American people in any way, for we know the profound values of a nation which could produce the figure of John F. Kennedy, who put the youth of America behind the New Frontier and tried to give loyal support to the Latin American revolution.

But we declare that the destiny of Latin America is in the hands of Latin Americans and that Latin America ought to be for Latin Americans. The first alliance which should be established is an alliance among Latin Americans. And solutions should not come from the outside but everything should depend on the efforts, the responsibility, and the power created by Latin Americans themselves. The Latin American nation toward which we are energetically moving should be a world of Latin Americans united and freed from all external dependence and humiliating oppression.

---

* ORIT is the regional organization for North and South America of the International Confederation of Free Trade Unions. It is nonsectarian and includes the AFL-CIO in its membership.—Ed.

To Build Latin American Institutions

For Latin American unification to be built along definite historical lines we must establish Latin American instruments, organisms,
and institutions. It is necessary to terminate all our agreements
with Pan-American institutions and organisms and create a new
type of relation between the countries of Latin America through
and within institutions which are typically Latin American.

Our relations with the United States in all areas, and especially
in the area of trade unionism, cannot continue in the framework
of Pan-Americanism, for it is a structure which is unequal, contrary to our historical development, and hostile to the unification
of Latin America and the realization of the social revolution for
which all of the people of Latin America hope. Future relations
must be within a new context—a united Latin America facing
North America and the world. Latin American workers wish to
participate actively in the unification of Latin America and in the
struggle to overcome all the factors which oppose the unity of the
people of Latin America. The organized workers should be the
ferment and the vanguard of Latin American unity since they are
also the ferment and the vanguard of the Latin American revolution. With this in mind, the Seventh Council of Latin American
Workers, convened by the Latin American Confederation of
Christian Trade Unionists (CLASC) in order to accelerate the
process of Latin American unity and facilitate the participation
of the workers in this process decides:

1. To struggle for the creation of an Organization of Latin
American States as the necessary instrument for the economic,
social, and political development of the countries of Latin America,
and to give concrete form to Latin American unity.

2. To struggle for the constitution of an Economic and Social
Council of Latin America as an organism for the planning and
coordination of the entire process of economic and social integration in Latin America with genuine supranational authority and
effective and decisive participation by the organized workers and
mass popular organizations.

3. To support the establishment of a Latin American Parliament
to facilitate the political coordination of the whole process of Latin
American unification.

4. To favor and support the creation of Latin American au-

thorities in the field of petroleum, atomic energy, and communication, such as a Latin American Petroleum Authority, Suratom, and a Latin American Airlines and Merchant Marine—with effective participation in management by the workers.

5. To struggle that the process of Latin American unification may serve as the basis of a fundamental change in our economic, social, political, and cultural institutions—opening access to power, wealth, and culture to the masses of the people.

6. To help, support, and participate in all official and private movements which promote the unification and integration of Latin America.

7. To promote the creation of a Latin American Trade Union Front which will serve as the basis for the functioning of a Latin American trade-union force at the loyal service of the unification of the Latin American Revolution.

29. Celso Furtado

Celso Furtado is a Brazilian economist living in exile since the 1964 military revolution. Born in 1920 in northeastern Brazil, he was educated at the Universities of Brazil, Paris, and Cambridge. His first major post was as head of the Development Division of the United Nations Economic Commission for Latin America, where he was influenced by the ideas of Raúl Prebisch. From 1958 to 1961 he was a director of the Brazilian National Development Bank. His 1959 report on the problems of the development of the depressed Northeast of Brazil led to the creation of the Superintendency for the Development of the Northeast (SUDENE), of which he was appointed head. He held this post until 1964, when he was removed by the new military government and stripped of all political rights for a period of ten years. (For three months in 1963, he was also President Goulart's Minister of Planning.)

Although Furtado describes himself as a "man of the left," and was so regarded by the military, the following selection indi-

cates that he is critical of Communist methods and is humanist rather than Marxist in orientation. His opposition to the influence of foreign capital, his demands for basic structural changes, and his critical attitude toward private enterprise mark him as one out of sympathy with the economically conservative policies of the present Brazilian regime.

REFLECTIONS ON THE BRAZILIAN PREREVOLUTION*

. . . Many people both in Brazil and abroad have asked me why Marxism has permeated Brazilian youth so deeply. The reason is simple: Marxism, in any of its varieties, affords a diagnosis of the social reality and a guide to action. We must approach this subject with absolute frankness if we are to maintain an effective dialogue with the idealistic and active youth of our time. What does their Marxism consist of?

It may be summed up by describing a few of their attitudes. They maintain: (1) that the present social order is based to a great extent on the exploitation of man by man, which favors the well-being of a class sheltering many a parasite and idler and leaves the great majority in poverty; (2) that the social reality is *historical* and thus in permanent change; therefore the present order must be superseded by another; and (3) that it is possible to identify the strategic factors which affect the social process; this in turn opens the way to a conscious policy of social reconstruction.

If we go deep into the core of this philosophy, we shall find on the one hand the wish to liberate man from all chains that socially enslave him, allowing him to fulfill his potentialities, and on the other hand an optimistic attitude concerning the capacity of human communities for self-determination. In the last analysis, what we find is a higher stage of humanism, for while it places man in the center of its concerns, it recognizes that full individual development can be attained only through a rational guidance of social relations.

* From Irving Louis Horowitz, *Revolution in Brazil: Politics and Society in a Developing Nation* (New York: E. P. Dutton, 1964), pp. 65–73; translated from an article that appeared in *Revista Brasileira de Ciências Sociais* in March, 1962; reprinted by permission.

Whatever name we choose to give this conception, it is impossible to object to it openly, for it is inspired by the most profound longings of modern man. It has its roots in the humanism of the Renaissance, which taught man that he could affect his own destiny; and its inherent optimism emanates from the Industrial Revolution, which gave man the power to affect his own environment.

In our dialogue with the new generation we must reach agreement as to what is really fundamental. We should relegate to the background all things that are merely instrumental or subordinate to the ends pursued. For example, it would not be possible to ascribe more than an instrumental character to the private ownership of means of production—in short, to private enterprise. We are all agreed that private enterprise is merely a decentralized form of organizing production which must be ruled by social criteria. Whenever there is a conflict between the social aims of production and its organization as a private concern, measures have to be taken to preserve the social interest. On the other hand, as a greater abundance in the supply of goods is reached, that is to say, in the higher stages of development, the actual organization of production becomes less important while the control of political power increases in importance. It is the latter, finally, that dictates the patterns of distribution and utilization of social income, in the form of either public or private consumption.

We may well ask, therefore, what are the fundamental aims on which we can unite? Should these aims be considered as ends in themselves and related to our own conception of life? It is of the highest importance, I believe, that we define these objectives clearly. Otherwise we shall not distinguish means from ends and will risk treating what others consider merely means as though they were ends. We have the right to take a stand as to the ultimate ends we are trying to attain without reference to the issue of Russian or American pre-eminence on the world stage. To subordinate the future of our culture to the tactical conveniences of either of the two great centers of military power would mean to give up the struggle before it is joined. We must consider the Russian-American stalemate as a given fact of the present day. By doing this we admit that it is not in our power to change the balance of forces to any significant degree. Our very helplessness regarding the world conflict gives us a wider margin of liberty to establish our own aims. And, as often happens, greater freedom gives rise to greater awareness of responsibility.

It is against this background that we must establish irrevocable aims of political action. I believe that they can be described as humanism and optimism concerning the material development of society. Or, to use more current terms, liberty and economic development.

I have used the word humanism because liberty can also be understood in terms of nineteenth-century individualism, which often saw the individual as opposed to society. There is not the slightest doubt that aspirations of our present-day youth center about authentic humanism. What makes them angry is the inhuman aspect of our development—the growing contrast between wasteful wealth and abject poverty. They see peasants living in the country but unable to grow enough food and suffering hunger almost every day of the year. They see state capitals where 10 per cent of the population are listed in hospital registries as suffering from tuberculosis. And we know that all this can be remedied, indeed has already disappeared from a large portion of the world. We can see then that what worries youth is man and his degradation, and the consciousness that we are also responsible for it.

Once we have defined our aims, the question is how to pull ourselves together to achieve them. How can we prevent the struggle for intermediate or secondary objectives from making us forget our authentic ends? It is an extremely difficult problem, especially as the historical experience of recent decades has suggested that the underdeveloped countries must make a choice between individual liberty and rapid material development. This false dilemma is posed both by the champions of liberty and by the promoters of mass welfare.

It is now clear that the rapid material development of the Soviet Union, until recently an underdeveloped country, was achieved partly by the use of inhuman methods. The requisitioning of agricultural surpluses in order to finance industrial development was accomplished by the use of armed force, through compulsory collectivization and the violent suppression of all resistance. In order to justify these drastic methods, the "theory" was put forward that the peasant was fundamentally an individualist and that the only way to overcome such "individualism" was by enforced collectivization. This is the theory of salvation through punishment. To achieve administrative efficiency an enormous price was paid in human lives. But even if we put aside the painful Soviet experience, account must be taken of the evidence that the rapid economic development of the Communist countries has been achieved under forms of sociopolitical organization in which individual liberty was restricted beyond the limits which we would consider tolerable.

It must be recognized, however, that the masses in the underdeveloped countries have not generally put the same high valuation on individual liberty that we do. Since they have not had access to the better things of life, they obviously cannot grasp the full meaning of the supposed dilemma between liberty and quick development. Also, if we were to assert that rapid economic development of socialist countries was achieved only at the price of restricting civil liberties, we must then accept the corollary that the liberty enjoyed by the minority in our society is paid for by a delay in general economic development, hence it is at the expense of the welfare of the great majority.

Even less effective with the peasant is the argument that the development of the socialist countries is being obtained at an enormous human cost, including forms of semi-slave labor. The fact is that the underdeveloped peoples are quite prepared to pay a price, even a very heavy one, for their development. They know by hard experience the extremely high price they pay for remaining underdeveloped. How many millions of lives are sacrificed every year in a country like Brazil by underdevelopment? How many millions of lives are lost through hunger and physical exhaustion? How many millions of human beings live without access to primary education, or any opportunity of sharing in secondary and higher education? Very few of us have sufficient awareness of these deeply inhuman characteristics of underdevelopment. When we do become fully aware, we understand why the masses are prepared for any sacrifice in order to overcome it. If the price of liberty for the few had to be the poverty of the many, we can be quite certain that the probability of preserving freedom would be practically nil.

Insistence on false alternatives nevertheless goes on, elaborated in different forms by opposing champions. The self-appointed defenders of liberty argue that the structural changes in the social order necessary for the rapid acceleration of economic development have always been associated with the suppression of fundamental human liberties. Those who take the opposite side argue from the historical fact that the only effective method for introducing the social changes necessary for rapid development has been a revolution of the Marxist-Leninist type, which by its own nature requires the setting up of a rigid dictatorship. So both sides acknowledge that social change is the effective instrument for accelerating material development in underdeveloped countries.

The discussion of this very important point has been bedeviled by a great confusion of ideas, either unconscious or deliberate. We should not forget that the method of Marxism-Leninism was created and perfected in the struggle for the overthrow of an entirely rigid sociopolitical structure—that of Czarism. The historical experience of the last decades has shown that such a revolutionary technique applied against other rigid structures—Nationalist China, Japanese-occupied China, and Batista's Cuba are obvious examples—can be highly effective where accompanied by a Spartan discipline in the rank and file and the daring of an Alexander in the leadership.

The same does not apply, however, to "open" societies. The example of Western Europe seems conclusive: huge party machines guided by Marxism-Leninism found themselves bewildered by an ever changing sociopolitical reality. This was because Marxism-Leninism sees in the state—which it defines as "a special repressive force"—the dictatorship of a class, the bourgeoisie. From the moment the state ceases to be the mere dictatorship of a class to become a composite system, though under the aegis of a certain class, the unity of revolutionary action is weakened by an inability any longer to define the party's aims. The need to discriminate between good and bad policies of the state requires a capacity for adaptation that a monolithic revolutionary party cannot have.

We cannot, then, ignore the historical fact that the Marxist-Leninist techniques have been proved ineffective in dealing with open societies. Nor can we escape the following conclusions: (1) that dictatorships were not created by the acceleration of development but preceded it; (2) that the acceleration took place only in structures which were previously rigid (dictatorships); and (3) that the techniques which have so far been used for the rapid transformation of social structures have been effective only in rigid societies (dictatorships).

So the fundamental problem we face is to develop techniques which will make rapid social transformations possible, while retaining the pattern of an open society.

Before turning to specifically Brazilian questions, I will indulge in one more observation on revolutionary methods: since Marxism-Leninism is based on the substitution of the dictatorship of one class for that of another class, it would be politically retrogressive to apply it to societies which have attained more complex social forms—that is, modern open societies. It would mean, in the last resort, a sacrifice of the very objectives previously described as essential. While it is true that economic development means a fuller life for man, it is no less true that the pattern of social and political organization is the warp that sustains the woof of a fuller and richer life. Although it is probable that in the future material abundance will coexist with forms of sociopolitical organization which permit the full realization of authentic human values, that does not necessarily occur at the present historical stage. To have attained higher forms of social and political organization is at least as great an achievement as that of high standards of material development.

Historical experience has demonstrated that whenever a revolution of the Marxist-Leninist type has been imposed on a complex social structure—as in the case of certain European countries—socialism as a form of humanism becomes perverted. As there is no possibility of converting an open society into a dictatorship without creating a climate of frustration, there is a deterioration of social values. Since the dictatorial regime does not permit the individual to play his proper part in society, a series of social myths is put forward in order to replace genuine human values. Thus, material development can take place at the same time that the dictatorship is consolidating itself upon principles which are the antithesis of humanistic revolutionary ideals.

Let us now face up to the Brazilian problem. The fact is that our society is an "open" one to the industrial workers, but not to the peasants. It is therefore not hard to explain why the peasant is much more susceptible to revolutionary techniques of the Marxist-Leninist type than is the industrial working class, although from the orthodox Marxist point of view the latter should be the vanguard of the revolutionary movement. But our political system allows the urban workers to organize themselves in order to press their claims, within the rules of the democratic game, whereas the situation of the peasants is altogether different. Since they have no rights, they cannot have legal claims. If they organize themselves, the inference is that they do so for subversive purposes.

The necessary conclusion we must draw is that Brazilian society is rigid at least in that large sector composed of agricultural laborers. As regards this sector, we have to accept the fact that the Marxist-Leninist revolutionary techniques are effective.

We come now to a conclusion of great importance in Brazil. To the extent that we live in an open society, the attainment of higher social aims tends to assume the form of gradualism. To the extent that we live in a rigid society, those objectives will tend to be attained by cataclysmic disruption. Thus there is a duality within the Brazilian revolutionary process.

What is the likelihood of an effective Brazilian revolution through Marxist-Leninist methods? I believe there are two ways in which this might occur. As suggested above, the first one is connected with the land problem. We must not forget that over half of the Brazilian population gets its living from the land. If this sector maintains its present rigidity, every peasant movement will tend rapidly to adopt revolutionary techniques of the Marxist-Leninist type. Thus we have an important segment of the population with a Marxist-Leninist bias which, given certain conditions, might be able to take the lead in the Brazilian revolutionary process. The practical results would be the predominance of the least developed sector of our society. The real objectives of our development, as previously defined in terms of humanism, would thus be partially frustrated at the very start.

The second way in which a revolution of the Marxist-Leninist type might be carried out would be as a result of social and political retrogression. We have observed that a revolution of this type is hardly likely in an open society, unless it is imposed from without, as happened in some countries of Central Europe. Nevertheless, the possibility of "putting the clock back" must not be excluded. The imposition of a right-wing dictatorship, making the whole political structure rigid, would create favorable conditions for an effective revolution of the Marxist-Leninist type. But even in this case, the agrarian sector would be likely to predominate. In the absence of conditions resulting from political retrogression, the only possibility of a Marxist-Leninist revolution lies in the persistence of an archaic agrarian structure.

In order to achieve a high rate of economic development, in accordance with truly social criteria, we shall have to bring about some important changes in our basic structures. Because we have not been prepared for such changes, anxiety has grown from day to day. We have come to live in what may properly be termed a prerevolutionary period, in which drastic change is a political necessity. Thus techniques of social transformation and revolutionary methods are in the forefront of present-day political concern. If we are to avoid dictatorial regimes, whether of a social class or ideological group or rigid party machine, we must: (a) prevent all forms of retrogression in our social and political systems; and (b) create conditions for fast and effective change in the country's archaic agrarian structure.

These general directives must be elaborated into specific lines of action. Political retrogression will not come haphazardly, but as a reflection of panic among some privileged groups confronted with growing social pressure. Where structures are rigid, preventing gradual adaptations, these pressures may create cataclysmic situations, leading to emergency solutions or preventive coups. Thus, the first task is to give more flexibility to the existing structures. We have to tread boldly the path of constitutional change which will permit agrarian reform and a radical change of government administration of the fiscal system and the banking structure. We have to subordinate state action to a clear definition of the aims of economic and social development. The Congress has the right to draw up directives, but local politicians must be deprived of the power to allocate public monies. We have to give the government effective means to punish those who embezzle public funds, to control extravagant consumption, and to dignify the function of civil servants. We must have legal statutes to subordinate the action of foreign capital to the aims of economic development and to the requirements of political independence. The recent law affecting the remittance of profits constitutes a clear indication that, even in a legislature where conservative views prevail, there is an awareness of a need for such discipline. Passed at a moment of serious political tension, the law contains ambiguities and, therefore, ought to be improved. It is taken for granted that the cooperation of foreign capital is indispensable for the development of any underdeveloped country; but in the absence of regulation, conflicts of economic interest may become conflicts of a political nature, harmful to international cooperation. Also, the government must have thorough knowledge of the sources of all investment in means of mass communications. And above all we must have a plan for economic and social development compatible with our own possibilities and in conformity with the aspirations of the people.

What must we do to translate into action all these objectives? I believe that the most immediate task is to organize public opinion so that it can express itself. It is up to the students, workers, entrepreneurs, intellectuals, and perhaps even the peasants, through their incipient organizations, to start a frank debate about what they expect from their government. The more complex problems must be given systematic study by groups of specialists, and their conclusions must be publicly debated. Brazil is mature enough to start thinking about its own destiny. From general debates and from expressions of public opinion must emerge programs that will serve as a basis for the renewal of popular representation.

I am convinced that the youth have to be capable once more of containing the direction of this great mobilization of national public opinion on behalf of the authentic cause of the development of our country.

30. Roberto Campos

Roberto Campos was Minister of Planning and Economic Coordination of Brazil under President Humberto Castelo Branco (1964–67). He was born in 1917 and educated in Brazil and the United States. Following graduate work in economics, he joined the Brazilian foreign service and worked with various economic agencies of the United Nations. From 1952 to 1959 he was an officer and later president of the Brazilian National Bank for Economic Development; from 1961 to 1964 he served as Brazil's ambassador to the United States.

Campos is one of the most articulate defenders of a neo-capitalist or orthodox approach to economic development for Latin America, which emphasizes the importance of the private sector and the market system but uses government fiscal and monetary policy to encourage economic growth. His experience with the administrations of Presidents Kubitschek and Goulart and his own economic training and attitudes have convinced him that inflation, government subsidies, and politically motivated economic policies are disastrous for the economy. As one of the most influential members of the Castelo Branco government which came to power after the military coup of April, 1964, he was responsible for a return to *a realistic price and tax system, a government austerity program against inflation, and the encouragement of foreign investment and assistance. The first of the following selections defends his economic policies; the second explains the government's role in supplementing, correcting, regulating, and stimulating a market economy. Campos's views on the government role in economic development are sometimes described as a "monetarist," in opposition to the "structuralist" views of Raúl Prebisch.**

ECONOMIC POLICY AND
POLITICAL MYTHS†

. . . A second fallacy is *the confusion of the means and the end.* The intervention of the state in certain sectors of the economy is certainly a means to attain specific economic objectives. It should not be an end in itself. How many of us are aware of this subtle difference?

A third fallacy is that of *false options.* It is imagined, for example, that when the government eliminates subsidies on fuel and opts for more realistic prices for transportation and electricity, it does so out of a kind of masochistic tendency, taking pleasure in its disregard for the suffering of the people, the people whom the demagogues claim to love but whom they know so well how to deceive. . . . Nothing could be more incorrect. The real options were and are between financing the necessary investments in roads and electricity through correct prices and realistic exchange rates as the basis for the taxation of fuel—and, on the other hand, either ceasing to invest or doing so at the price of printing more paper money. Ceasing to invest means economic stagnation, rationing, and ultimately the perpetuation of poverty. Printing more money

---

* For a discussion of the structuralist-monetarist controversy, see Albert O. Hirschman (ed.), *Latin American Issues: Essays and Comments* (New York: The Twentieth Century Fund, 1961).

† Excerpts from *Política Econômica e Mitos Políticos* (Rio de Janeiro, 1965); translated by the editor.

means an acceleration of inflation with the greater sacrifices being made by the poor, when the illusory goal of maintaining some prices stable forces an increase in all the others. That would be so futile and ignorant an effort that it reminds me of the ancient Chinese proverb, "It is useless to go to bed early in order to save money on light, if the result is twins." . . .

Let us turn for a moment to consider what the government is trying to do, attempting to evaluate its successes and failures and assessing its future. The government does not fear self-criticism, nor objective analysis, since it believes, as Galbraith has said, that "Without public criticism, governments appear much better and are really much worse."

Perhaps the best way to achieve an effective assessment would be to indicate what the government proposes to do rather than accuse it of not doing what it never intended to do. The government has proposed the following objectives. First, the gradual containment of inflation. The objective for 1964 will be only to alter the nature of the inflation, transforming it from a cumulative to a corrective process terminating the tendency to hyper-inflation which reached crisis proportions in the first four months of 1964 and was leading us to an annual inflation rate of 150 per cent.

For 1965 the government proposes to complete the process of correction of the distortions of the economy in the first three months of the year and to concentrate its efforts on limiting the inflationary process, reducing it to tolerable levels in the second half of the year. Finally, it has planned a return to a near-equilibrium in 1966. I say "near-equilibrium" because complete stability would be reached in Brazil only with the nation contemplating its navel in a state of Buddhist impassivity.

This is what the government proposes. Only this. I do not promise miracles. . . . We hope that the inflation rate in 1964 will not exceed that of the previous year, despite the strong inflation in the first four months before the revolution and the vast and painful corrections which were necessary in the exchange system, in the cost of public services, and in the subsidized prices which acted as a kind of morphine for the consumer, in some cases discouraging the producer, and in others undermining our capacity to invest.

More important, much more important, than the rate of inflation, in my view, is its nature. No one in good faith will deny that the prices which have gone up the most are exactly those which should have gone up in order to correct the artificial patterns of the past which were leading us into the blind alley of rationing and stagnation which we were already confronting face to face. What good is it to keep the price of electricity cheap when in a short time it leads to rationing because of a lack of investment? What good is it to maintain artificial prices for gasoline so as to keep transport cheap if we lessen our capacity to build and pave highways, the only realistic way to reduce transportation costs? . . .

[In 1965] external aid will begin to flow in on a more substantial scale since in 1964 Brazil has tried to help herself, making the necessary sacrifices to appear before the financial world not as an irresponsible beggar, but as an austere partner ready to sacrifice and aware of its responsibilities.

On the matter of reforms, the government plans to initiate a process of institutional modernization. It would be difficult to deny it credit for having confronted problems which are both controversial and fundamental: agrarian reform, fiscal reform, housing reform, and reform of the banking system.

President Castelo Branco declared recently that 1965 would be the year of modernization of our obsolete and inflexible administrative system joining with it a determined effort to democratize the business firm, so that we can finally enter into the era of democratic capitalism. . . .

. . . To initiate industrial recovery we must have a fundamental change in the attitude of our businessmen. They must abandon the psychology of low volume and high prices; they must abandon their propensity for excessive indebtedness through recourse to officially subsidized credit. They must abandon their morbid aversion to competition. . . .

The problem is less one of scarcity than of discipline—less a failure of natural resources than of character and human capital. In summary, we should have a passion for development but also sufficient rationality to organize it. We must purify our own qualities rather than engage in the infantile sport of transferring to others—the monopolies, the United States, the angels, or the devil—the blame for our poverty. We should apply ourselves to correct our defects rather than cultivating our prejudices for, as the poet says, the fault is not in the stars but in ourselves. No one will resolve the problems which we ourselves leave unresolved because of incompetence or cowardice.

A long and bitter road separates us from our goal, a dangerous and difficult period separates us from the day when we will have a just and prosperous society where everyone will have the right to enjoy riches because we have succeeded in eliminating poverty. But to attain that goal and to see that day, it is clear that the government must proceed with the resolution of those who will brave the storm and the patience of those who do not seek to be loved.

I do not know of better words to describe the triple challenge which we have before us—of stabilization, reform, and development—than those of President Kennedy, the young suffering hero who was taken from the world on an afternoon without meaning, in a crime without meaning, for a motive without meaning:

"We will not reach," he said, "We will not reach that goal today or tomorrow. Perhaps we will not reach it until the end of our life. But seeking it is the greatest adventure of this age. We may be impatient at times with the weight of our obligations, the complexity of decision, the agony of choice. But for us there is no comfort or security in evasion, no solution in abdication, and no release in irresponsibility."

THE MEANING OF PLANNING IN A DEMOCRATIC ECONOMY*

Planning and the Price System

The action of the government in democratic political systems should be directed at establishing the conditions which will assure the most efficient possible functioning of the free enterprise economy, or rather of the price system. In this context, economic planning consists in the systematic and coherent definition by the government of measures which will tend to create an order in which what are conventionally called the "forces of the market" will operate in a manner compatible with the desired distribution of income and the pragmatic goal of the maximization of the rate of economic development.

Action by the public authorities which will lead the economic system to better achieve the objectives chosen by the community,

* Excerpts from *Programa de Acão Econômica do Govêrno, 1964–1966* (2d ed.; Rio de Janeiro and Brasília: Ministry of Planning and Economic Coordination, 1965); translated by the editor.

notably in underdeveloped countries, is generally based on accepted principles, such as the following: (a) the free play of the forces of the market does not necessarily guarantee the formation of a desirable volume of savings; (b) the price system does not always promote the adequate formation of external economies (investment in education, roads, etc.), due to the disproportion between their respective profitability and their corresponding social productivity; (c) the free play of market forces does not necessarily lead to a satisfactory distribution of national income among persons and regions; (d) the efficiency of the price system can be appreciably distorted by spontaneous or institutional imperfections of the market.

These principles do not argue for the elimination of the regulatory role of the price system. The action of the government complements, but does not necessarily replace, the mechanisms of the market. The idea of planning as such is not incompatible with the predominance of free enterprise in the economic system. The most traditionally capitalist nations resort to at least an embryonic planning when they program their public investment and adopt economic legislation. Conversely, no real economy can completely abandon the forces of the market. Even in the most orthodox socialist countries one does not encounter full-scale planning, since at least some economic decisions, particularly those involving consumption, escape the control of the government. The real world is thus composed of mixtures of planning and market systems. The proportions of the mixture vary according to the economic systems but the one is never wholly substituted for the other.

The Essential Content of the Plan

The complex of governmental decisions concerning economic policy are an essential part of a plan. In an economy in which free enterprise predominates, the content of the plan is restricted to the sphere of decision by the public authorities. In the particular case of Brazil, a development plan should include: the programming of the investments which will be carried out by the Federal Government, directly or through the autonomous corporations and mixed companies and their respective sources of funds; an indication of the private investments to be aided by the Federal Government; the fiscal estimate and financial program of the union; the program of operations of the monetary authorities; and, finally, the instruments of indirect action by the government on the private sector represented by economic legislation in general and including tax, credit, and exchange policies.

The decisions on economic policy contained in a plan should not consist of disconnected and uncoordinated provisions but should form a complex of the necessary measures to attain certain pre-established general objectives. Thus the efficiency of the plan is measured by the extent to which the measures contained in it assure the realization of those objectives, a relationship which is more difficult to define when there is a greater degree of predominance of free enterprise—and therefore of decentralization of economic decisions—and the statistical basis on which the plan is developed is more precarious. In the Brazilian case the inadequacy of statistical information does not permit the elaboration of a pretentiously specific plan, for this would be a waste of effort due to the lack of relationship between the norms of action and the quantitative objectives.

The program which follows is not presented as a pretentious global plan for development but only a program of coordinated action by the government in the economic field. The general figures used are merely in the nature of estimates. The result is thus the formulation of a strategy of development and a program of action for the next two years, a period in which we will establish the bases for a more organic and long-range plan.

Selected Bibliography

For background and further reading related to the themes treated in this book, the following works are recommended:

Introduction

ALMOND, GABRIEL, and JAMES S. COLEMAN. *The Politics of the Developing Areas.* Princeton, N.J.: Princeton University Press, 1960.

ANDERSON, CHARLES W., FRED VON DER MEHDEN, and CRAWFORD YOUNG. *Issues of Political Development.* Englewood Cliffs, N.J.: Prentice-Hall, 1967.

APTER, DAVID (ed.). *Ideology and Discontent.* New York: The Free Press, 1964.

BAYLEY, DAVID H. *Public Liberties in the New States.* Chicago: Rand-McNally, 1964.

BLACK, CYRIL E. *The Dynamics of Modernization.* New York: Harper & Row, 1966.

EMERSON, RUPERT. *From Empire to Nation.* Boston: Beacon Press, 1962.

JANOWITZ, MORRIS. *The Military in the Political Development of New Nations.* Chicago: University of Chicago Press, 1964.

JOHNSON, JOHN J. (ed.). *The Role of the Military in Underdeveloped Countries.* Princeton, N.J.: Princeton University Press, 1962.

KAUTSKY, JOHN H. (ed.). *Political Change in Underdeveloped Countries.* New York: John Wiley, 1962.

McCORD, WILLIAM. *The Springtime of Freedom.* London and New York: Oxford University Press, 1965.

MILLIKAN, MAX F., and DONALD L. M. BLACKMER (eds.). *The Emerging Nations.* Boston: Little, Brown, 1961.

ORGANSKI, A. F. K. *The Stages of Political Development.* New York: Alfred A. Knopf, 1965.

PENNOCK, J. ROLAND (ed.). *Self-Government in Modernizing Nations.* Englewood Cliffs, N.J.: Prentice-Hall, 1964.

PYE, LUCIAN W. *Aspects of Political Development.* Boston: Little, Brown, 1966.

426 SELECTED BIBLIOGRAPHY

SETON-WATSON, HUGH. *Neither War nor Peace.* New York: Frederick A. Praeger, 1962.
VON DER MEHDEN, FRED. *The Politics of the Developing Nations.* Englewood Cliffs, N.J.: Prentice-Hall, 1964.
WEINER, MYRON. *Modernization.* New York: Basic Books, 1966.

Part I: Asia

BRECHER, MICHAEL. *Nehru: A Political Biography.* London and New York: Oxford University Press, 1959.
JACK, HOMER A. (ed.). *The Gandhi Reader.* Bloomington, Ind.: Indiana University Press, 1956.
KAHIN, GEORGE McT. (ed.). *Major Governments of Asia.* 2d ed. Ithaca, N.Y.: Cornell University Press, 1963.
MINTZ, JEANNE. *Mohammed, Marx, and Marhaen: The Roots of Indonesian Socialism.* New York: Frederick A. Praeger, 1965.
PYE, LUCIAN. *Politics, Personality, and Nation-Building.* New Haven, Conn.: Yale University Press, 1962.
SCHRAM, STUART. *The Political Thought of Mao Tse-tung.* New York: Frederick A. Praeger, 1963.
SMITH, DONALD E. *India as a Secular State.* Princeton, N.J.: Princeton University Press, 1963.

Part II: The Islamic World

BINDER, LEONARD. *The Ideological Revolution in the Middle East.* New York: John Wiley, 1964.
CREMEANS, CHARLES D. *The Arabs and the World.* New York: Frederick A. Praeger, 1963.
HALPERN, MANFRED. *The Politics of Social Change in the Middle East and North Africa.* Princeton, N.J.: Princeton University Press, 1963; paperback edition, 1965.
LERNER, DANIEL. *The Passing of Traditional Society: Modernizing the Middle East.* Glencoe, Ill.: The Free Press, 1958.
MANSFIELD, PETER. *Nasser's Egypt.* Baltimore, Md.: Penguin Books, 1965.
MOORE, CLEMENT H. *Tunisia Since Independence: The Dynamics of One-Party Government.* Berkeley, Calif.: University of California Press, 1965.
RIVLIN, BENJAMIN, and JOSEPH S. SZYLIOWICZ (eds.). *The Contemporary Middle East.* New York: Random House, 1965.
SHIRABI, HISHAM. *Nationalism and Revolution in the Arab World.* Princeton, N.J.: D. Van Nostrand, 1966.

VATIKIOTIS, P. J. *The Egyptian Army in Politics.* Bloomington, Ind.: Indiana University Press, 1961.

Part III: Africa

ABRAHAM, WILLIE. *The Mind of Africa.* London: Weidenfeld & Nicolson, 1962; Chicago: University of Chicago Press, 1963.

AUSTIN, DENNIS. *Politics in Ghana, 1946–60.* London and New York: Oxford University Press, 1964.

CARTER, GWENDOLEN M. (ed.). *African One-Party States.* Ithaca, N.Y.: Cornell University Press, 1964.

COLEMAN, JAMES S., and CARL ROSBERG, JR. (eds.). *Political Parties and National Integration in Tropical Africa.* Berkeley, Calif: University of California Press, 1964.

FRIEDLAND, WILLIAM H., and CARL ROSBERG, JR. (eds.). *African Socialism.* Stanford, Calif.: Stanford University Press, 1964.

HODGKIN, THOMAS. *African Political Parties.* Baltimore, Md.: Penguin Books, 1961.

LEGUM, COLIN. *Pan-Africanism, A Short Political Guide.* Rev. ed. New York: Frederick A. Praeger, 1965.

LEWIS, W. ARTHUR. *Politics in West Africa.* London and New York: Oxford University Press, 1965.

MORGENTHAU, RUTH SCHACHTER. *Political Parties in French-Speaking West Africa.* London and New York: Oxford University Press, 1964.

NKRUMAH, KWAME. *Africa Must Unite.* New York: Frederick A. Praeger, 1963.

SENGHOR, LÉOPOLD SÉDAR. *On African Socialism.* New York: Frederick A. Praeger, 1964.

SNYDER, FRANK G. *One-Party Government in Mali.* New Haven, Conn.: Yale University Press, 1965.

THIAM, DOUDOU. *The Foreign Policy of African States.* London: Phoenix House; New York: Frederick A. Praeger, 1965.

ZOLBERG, ARISTIDE. *Creating Political Order: The Party-States of West Africa.* Chicago: Rand-McNally, 1966.

Part IV: Latin America

ADAMS, RICHARD, et al. *Social Change in Latin America Today.* New York: Random House Vintage Books, 1960.

BLANKSTEN, GEORGE. "Political Groups in Latin America," *American Political Science Review,* LIII, No. 1 (March, 1959), 106–27; reprinted in John H. Kautsky. *Political Change in Underdeveloped Countries.* New York: John Wiley, 1962, pp. 140–66.

DAVIS, HAROLD E. *Latin American Social Thought Since Independence.* Washington, D.C.: University Press, 1961.

DRAPER, THEODORE. *Castro's Revolution: Myths and Realities.* New York: Frederick A. Praeger, 1962.

———. *Castroism in Theory and Practice.* New York: Frederick A. Praeger, 1965.

HALPERIN, ERNST. *Nationalism and Communism in Chile.* Cambridge, Mass.: M.I.T. Press, 1965.

HIRSCHMAN, ALBERT O. (ed.). *Latin American Issues: Essays and Comments.* New York: The Twentieth Century Fund, 1961.

LAUTERBACH, ALBERT. *Enterprise in Latin America: Business Attitudes in a Developing Economy.* Ithaca, N.Y.: Cornell University Press, 1966.

MARTZ, JOHN. *Acción Democrática.* Princeton, N.J.: Princeton University Press, 1965.

NEEDLER, MARTIN C. (ed.). *Political Systems of Latin America.* Princeton, N.J.: D. Van Nostrand, 1964.

POWELSON, JOHN P. *Latin America: Today's Economic and Social Revolution.* New York: McGraw-Hill, 1964.

TOMASEK, ROBERT D. (ed.). *Latin American Politics.* New York: Doubleday, 1966.